Praise for *The Lawyer Bubble*

"The legal profession is facing some fundamental changes, and Harper deserves credit for sounding the alarm. . . . Harper's big-picture argument is undoubtedly correct, and it is a real cause for concern." —*Time*

"Withering critique. . . . [Harper's] passion and varied experience make *The Lawyer Bubble* an engaging, persuasive read. His analysis is as complex as his most critical point is simple: Would-be lawyers must ask themselves why they want to be lawyers, what they expect to gain and at what cost." —*Pittsburgh Post-Gazette*

"Harper has written a heartfelt, stats-laden indictment of what has happened to his beloved profession." —*Louisville Courier-Journal*

"[Harper has] a complete mastery of his subject matter, both from an economic and legal perspective. . . . Not only is Harper a gifted lawyer able to marshal facts, but he is an especially deft writer, and he tells his story as only a gifted author can. . . . Harper does not simply criticize the current state of affairs; he offers solutions, if only we are wise enough either to embrace them, modify them, or come up with additional curatives. . . . *The Lawyer Bubble* is a wake-up call for those of us who love our profession, and it is a book that all lawyers should read." —*Circuit Rider*

"The solutions [Harper] proposes are eye-catching."
—*Chicago Daily Law Bulletin*

"*The Lawyer Bubble* is a most worthwhile read, both for people already in the legal profession and those thinking about entering it. The book is a clear-eyed, sometimes harsh, but always fair-minded indictment of our deeply troubled profession. . . . [Harper] does a fine job of synthesizing recent developments, analyzing their root causes, and providing sensible solutions."
—David Lat, Above the Law

"In addition to actual solutions, along with a comprehensive analysis of the problems, Harper provides a masterpiece of fine writing."
—Law and More

"The perfect book for a terrible time. If every big law partner, law professor, and law school dean read this book and followed its prescriptions, we just might get our profession back on track. . . . Harper's analysis is spot-on." —Lawyerist.com

"This is an important and timely book. It's two books, really. The first is a powerful recitation of how we got into this 'unfortunate place,' which may be more of a revelation to civilians than to lawyers who have paid attention to their alma mater's struggles or their firm's business plans. The second may not be so easy for lawyers to shrug off. It's a call to remedy the problems [Harper] so vividly describes. His answers aren't neat or in many cases likely. But he's identified the root problem—and he's looking at you!" —*American Lawyer*

"This exposé is by a lawyer who has worked in the trenches. . . . Startling and depressing. . . . Readable, well-researched, and scholarly." —*Library Journal*

"*The Lawyer Bubble* is a cogent critique of the legal profession by Steven J. Harper, who speaks with authority. . . . With the thoroughness of a skilled trial lawyer, Harper marshals impressive statistics and other materials to make his case." —*Shelf Awareness*

"Harper is a seasoned insider unafraid to say what many other lawyers in his position might. . . . [W]ritten with keen insight and scathing accusations . . . Harper brings his analytical and persuasive abilities to bear in a highly entertaining and riveting narrative. . . . *The Lawyer Bubble* is recommended reading for anyone working in a law-related field. And for law school students—especially prospective ones—it really should be required reading."
—*New York Journal of Books*

"Harper, an attorney and law school professor, investigates the causes of what he sees as a rapid decline in the sustainability of and professionalism in the legal profession while providing novel solutions. . . .

Anyone looking into a career in law would be well-advised to read this thoroughly eye-opening warning." —*Booklist*, starred review

"[Harper] is perfectly positioned to reflect on alarming developments that have brought the legal profession to a most unfortunate place. . . . Essential reading for anyone contemplating a legal career." —*Kirkus Reviews*

"[Harper] burns his bridges in this scathing indictment of law schools and big law firms. . . . His insights and admonitions are consistently on point." —*Publishers Weekly*

"*The Lawyer Bubble* is an important book, carefully researched, cogently argued, and compellingly written. It demonstrates how two honorable callings—legal education and the practice of law—have become, far too often, unscrupulous rackets."
—Scott Turow, author of *Presumed Innocent* and other novels

"Imagine that the elite lawyers of big law and the legal academy were put on trial for their alleged negligence and failed stewardship. Imagine further that the state had at its disposal one of the nation's most tenacious trial lawyers to doggedly build a complete factual record and then argue the case. The result would be *The Lawyer Bubble*. If I were counsel to the elite lawyers of big law and the legal academy, I would advise my clients to settle the case."
—William D. Henderson, director of the Center on the Global Legal Profession and professor at the Indiana University Maurer School of Law

"If they're smart, lawyers, would-be lawyers, and corporate clients will consider carefully what Harper has to say."
—Paul Barrett, author of *Glock: The Rise of America's Gun* and *Law of the Jungle*

"Every sentient lawyer realizes that the legal profession is in crisis, but nobody explains the extent of the problem as well as Steven Harper. Fortunately, he also proposes some solutions—so there is still room for hope. This is an essential book."
—Steven Lubet, author of *Fugitive Justice* and *Lawyers' Poker*

"This is a fine and important book, thoughtful and beautifully written. It makes the case—in a responsible and sober tone—that we are producing far too many lawyers for far too small a segment of American society. It is a must-read for leaders of law firms, law schools, and the bar, as the legal profession continues its wrenching transition from a profession into just another business."
—Daniel S. Bowling III, senior lecturing fellow, Duke Law School

"With wit and insight, *The Lawyer Bubble* offers a compelling portrait of the growing crisis in legal education and the practice of law. This book is essential reading for anyone concerned about the profession or contemplating a legal career."
—Deborah L. Rhode, professor of law and director of the Center on the Legal Profession, Stanford University

"Steven Harper's *The Lawyer Bubble* is an expression of tough love for the law, law firms, and the people who work in them. The clear message is take control of your destiny and your firm to avoid the serious jeopardy that confronts far too many firms today. Whether you are a partner, associate, or law student, you should read this compassionate and forceful work."
—Edwin B. Reeser, former managing partner, author, and consultant on law practice management

"In this superb book, Steven Harper documents, ties together, and suggests remedies for the deceit that motivates expanding law school enrollment in the face of a shrinking job market, the gaming of law school rankings, and the pernicious effect of greed on the leadership of many of our nation's leading law firms. The lessons he draws are symptomatic, and go well beyond the documented particulars."
—Robert Helman, partner and former chairman (1984–98), Mayer Brown LLP, and lecturer, University of Chicago Law School

The
LAWYER
BUBBLE

The

LAWYER BUBBLE

A PROFESSION IN CRISIS

STEVEN J. HARPER

BASIC BOOKS

A Member of the Perseus Books Group
New York

Published by Basic Books,
A Member of the Perseus Books Group
First paperback edition published in 2016 by Basic Books

Books published by Basic Books are available at special discounts for bulk
purchases in the United States by corporations, institutions, and other
organizations. For more information, please contact the Special Markets
Department at the Perseus Books Group, 2300 Chestnut Street, Suite 200,
Philadelphia, PA 19103, or call (800) 810-4145, ext. 5000, or e-mail
special.markets@perseusbooks.com.

Designed by Pauline Brown
Typeset in 11.5 point Adobe Caslon Pro

Library of Congress Cataloging-in-Publication Data

Harper, Steven J., 1954–
   The lawyer bubble : a profession in crisis / Steven J. Harper.
      p.   cm.
   Includes bibliographical references and index.
   ISBN 978-0-465-05877-8 (hardcover)—ISBN 978-0-465-05874-7 (e-book)
1. Practice of law—United States—Popular works. 2. Lawyers—Job satisfaction—
United States—Popular works. 3. Law firms—United States—Popular works.
4. Law—Vocational guidance—United States—Popular works. I. Title.

KF300.H3687 2013
331.7'613400973—dc23

                                                        2012048153
ISBN 978-0-465-06559-2 (paperback)
ISBN 978-0-465-09763-0 (paperback e-book)

For my wife, our children,
and our grandchildren

CONTENTS

INTRODUCTION

W HEN I APPLIED TO LAW SCHOOL in 1975, the nation was recovering from a severe and prolonged recession. Even so, I always assumed that I'd be able to make a comfortable living with a legal degree, although I didn't think that practicing law would make me rich. Three and a half years later, I became a new associate at one of the nation's largest law firms, Kirkland & Ellis. It had about 150 attorneys in two offices, Chicago and Washington, D.C. My annual salary was $25,000, which is $100,000 in 2012 dollars. There were rumors that some partners in large firms earned as much as ten or fifteen times that amount; by any measure, that was and is a lot of money.

The unlikely prospect of amassing great wealth wasn't what attracted me to the law. Rather, I saw it as a prestigious profession whose practitioners enjoyed personally satisfying careers in which they provided others with counsel, advice, judgment, and a unique set of skills. Mentors at my first and only law firm taught me to focus on a single result: high-quality work for clients. If I accomplished that goal, everything else would take care of itself.

Today, the business of law focuses law school deans and practitioners in big law firms on something else: maximizing immediate profits for their institutions. That has muddied the profession's mission and, even worse, set it on a course to become yet another object lesson in the perils of short-term thinking. Like the dot-com, real estate, and financial bubbles that preceded it, the lawyer bubble won't end well, either. But now is the time to consider its causes, stop its growth, and take steps that might soften the impact when it bursts.

The Lawyer Bubble is about much more than lawyers. It's about a mentality that has accompanied the corporatization of America's most important institutions, including the legal profession—a dramatic transformation that is still unfolding. Behind the change is a drive to boost current-year performance and profits at the expense of more enduring values for which there are no quantifiable measures. But omitting critical costs from the decision-making calculus doesn't make them any less important or their damaging consequences any less profound.

This book focuses on lawyers because I know them best. For more than thirty years, I've been a successful and generally satisfied one. I led what anyone would call a charmed life in the law. I grew up watching lawyers on television trying cases. As a real attorney, that's what I did, too. Neither of my parents attended college, but they assumed that any child who entered the legal profession would gain society's respect in ways they'd never achieved. For me, that turned out to be true as well. Then as now, most people assumed that the legal profession offered financial security and a way to climb out of the lower or middle class. Career satisfaction, upward mobility, social status, financial security—who could ask for more?

It was always a naive view, but today's rewards are far less certain. From start to finish, the profession now faces a largely self-inflicted crisis. Unfortunate trends began twenty-five years ago, accelerated as the new millennium approached, and continue to this day. The Great Recession worsened them.

As I've noted, this phenomenon isn't unique to the law. In fact, it afflicts many professions that people traditionally regarded as callings rather than just another job. Doctors find themselves at the mercy of nonmedical bean counters establishing incentive structures that determine how they treat their patients. Journalists become news marketers because corporate media owners see more profit in entertainment than in maintaining large news bureaus filled with investigative reporters. As professors sit through budget meetings while pondering their institutions' incentives toward writing grant proposals and away from educating students, they wonder what qualifies their colleges or universities as "not-for-profit." Pick almost any once proud profession—the great transformation is killing them all.

The legal profession has become a victim of these trends, resulting in a massive oversupply of lawyers, growing career dissatisfaction among practicing attorneys generally, and the increasing fragility of the prevailing big-law-firm business model in particular. At a moment when psychologists, sociologists, and even national leaders are beginning to recognize the importance of well-being and morale to health, worker productivity, and society as a whole, lawyers suffer from disproportionately high rates of depression, alcoholism, and substance abuse. Recent surveys report that six out of ten attorneys who have been practicing for ten years or more say they advise young people to avoid law school. As new attorneys scramble for spots in the nation's premier firms, some of those venerable legal establishments are failing and many others have more problems than they realize or are willing to admit.

This book focuses on two important segments of the legal profession: law schools, because they're points of entry for every would-be lawyer, and big law firms, because their combination of power, prestige, and wealth gives them a special role. Although attorneys working in law firms of more than 160 lawyers account for only 15 percent of practicing attorneys today, their influence is far greater than their numbers. For example, almost all law schools lure prospective students into their JD programs with promotional materials that cite six-figure starting salaries for new graduates, even though only some large law firms pay that kind of money and most schools have little chance of placing any of their graduates in those jobs. Another indicator of big firms' importance is the media attention they generate. The *New York Times,* the *Wall Street Journal, Bloomberg News,* Thomson Reuters, and many other news outlets employ reporters whose principal assignment is to cover large law firms and their partners. Sometimes those stories even make the front page.

THE LAWYER BUBBLE began to form when vital institutions—law schools and the American Bar Association (ABA)—abdicated their responsibilities in favor of misguided metrics and insularity. Law school deans are supposed to be the profession's gatekeepers, but far too many have ceded independent judgment in an effort to satisfy the mindless criteria underlying law school rankings, especially *U.S. News & World Report*'s annual list. Those rankings didn't exist until 1987; now they rule the law school world for both students and administrators. Flawed methodology infects each category—quality assessment, selectivity, placement, and resources. But with the acquiescence of the ABA, deans inflate their schools' rankings with incomplete and misleading information and encourage prospective students to pursue dreams that, for most of them, are impossible, all in the name of increasing applications, enrollments, and tuition revenues.

Vulnerable young people become convinced that anyone can succeed as a lawyer. Because much of their undergraduate audience consists of liberal arts majors who can't decide what to do next, law schools appear to be an attractive default option. Add a universal human affliction—confirmation bias—and the fit becomes too perfect: law schools tell prospective students what they want to hear, and sure enough, they hear it. The *U.S. News* rankings then tell them which schools to attend. Easy money for student loans fuels the entire system.

Meanwhile, the proliferation and growth of law schools offer a stark contrast to the shrinking job market. The number of JDs awarded annually grew from thirty-eight thousand in 2001 to more than forty-four thousand in 2011, but legal employment opportunities have trended in the opposite direction: nine months after graduation, only about half of the class of 2011 had secured long-term full-time work requiring a legal degree. Staggering educational debt burdens thousands of young attorneys who have no hope of getting the legal jobs that inspired them to incur those loans in the first place. Many of those lucky enough to find work in big law firms, traditionally the most envied segment of the profession, soon find themselves trapped in a hell of attorney dissatisfaction because the people running those firms now view their primary mission as perfecting a relatively new business model that prioritizes specially adapted metrics.

The big-law-firm analog to the *U.S. News* law school rankings had arrived a few years earlier when the *American Lawyer,* a publication that Yale Law School graduate Steven Brill founded, put out its first-ever list of the nation's fifty largest law firms, the Am Law 50. Even more important, it disclosed average equity partner earnings for each. Beginning with the magazine's inaugural issue in 1979, Brill had already begun reporting on the big money that some lawyers made. But the 1985 listing of the top firms—now referred to as "big law"—was a watershed event. A delicate subject that had been off-limits in polite company became a new, highly public basis for competition among lawyers, who are a fiercely competitive bunch. It hasn't brought out the best in us.

Of course, lawyers are only one example of our cultural obsession with rankings. The search for supposedly objective certainty through the illusory comfort of a numerical answer makes any list of the supposed "best" or "top" of just about anything attractive. From high school football teams to liberal arts colleges to hospitals and more, any ranking takes on a life of its own. It guides consumer behavior and creates incentives for those who run the ranked institutions. But an emphasis on near-term results—namely, the organization's immediately upcoming ranking—sacrifices enduring values.

The special role of the legal profession in our society made the impact of rankings particularly insidious. Big law became big business as a kind of arms race to the top of the new *Am Law* charts began. With the help of a new cottage industry—law firm management consultants—the prevailing business model for large law firms accelerated toward a handful of indicators that measure immediate results: billable hours, client billings, and associate-to-partner leverage ratios. Lost along the way to record equity partner profits were large elements of what once made the law a profession. To paraphrase the *American Lawyer*'s editor in chief, Aric Press, writing twenty-five years after the Am Law 50 first appeared, when the bonds of partnership are no stronger than last year's IRS Form K-1 income statement, the essential attributes of partnership become casualties.

The principal victims of this phenomenon have been those lawyers who become trapped in the culture of short-termism. That culture is especially rampant among the prestigious big firms, where, as a group, attorneys are the unhappiest. As growth itself became another key element of the strategy, increasing numbers of lawyers at larger and larger firms have become dissatisfied with their careers. As attention moved to current-year profits, the new model also led individual partners to jettison long-standing traditions of lifetime loyalty to a single firm in exchange for the promise of more money elsewhere—now. Among the two hundred largest firms in 2000, there were two thousand lateral partner moves; in 2011 there were almost twenty-five hundred (out of a total of approximately forty-five thousand equity and non-equity partners). Particularly among senior partners with large client billings, lateral movement among firms has become widespread; recruiting "stars" has become a central business strategy for many law firm leaders.

As a consequence, interpersonal and institutional allegiances have become frayed, dangerous destabilization has followed, and some long-established firms have even disappeared.

All of this has persisted because the pyramid model—with equity partners at the top and a far greater number of salaried employees (including most lawyers) filling the bottom and middle—has worked well financially for a few. In fact, things got better for them as they made entry into their select group of fellow firm owners more difficult. As law firms and their profits grew, limits on the number of equity partners brought many partners great wealth. But it also destroyed institutional cohesion. While rainmakers offered their books of business to the highest bidder and reaped enormous benefits, overall attorney satisfaction plummeted to record low levels.

FOR ME, all of this came together in 2008 when I started teaching an undergraduate course at Northwestern about the good, the bad, and the ugly of what it means to be a lawyer. From the first day of the first class, I saw students who had great expectations for their potential law careers but little awareness of the likely reality, even for graduates of a prestigious college who were headed for top law schools. I know now that my students were not alone in displaying this gap between expectations and reality; from talking to young lawyers, I realize that it contributes significantly to the personal crisis that many new attorneys experience when they leave law school and try to get a job.

You might think that the American Bar Association, the profession's leading organization, would step in to help address the growing crisis. After all, it has a central role in accrediting law schools. Moreover, the ABA's stated mission includes promoting its members' professional growth and quality of life. But the organization has become a victim of regulatory capture by those it is supposed to oversee.

The picture isn't pretty: students with false expectations, deans with an overwhelming incentive to tell students what they want to hear, and few people with any reason to offer an effective counternarrative. It's not surprising that there have been so many more law students than jobs, and so many unhappy lawyers.

If you follow the legal profession, you may have heard recent rumblings of change. Legal observers have heralded what appeared to be a trend: the number of applicants to law schools has declined in the past two years. From 2010 to 2011 it dropped by almost 10 percent, "the steepest decline in at least ten years." Likewise, the Law School Admission Council reported that Law School Admission Test (LSAT) administrations for June 2011 had declined by more than 18 percent from a year previously—the highest percentage decline in twenty-four years. For the class entering in the fall of 2012, the number of law school applicants dropped another 14 percent, to sixty-eight thousand.

The popular explanation for these phenomena was that information about the profession's darker side, including the Great Recession's exacerbation of the attorney glut, was finally reaching prospective law students. Marginal candidates and those choosing law school by default must be opting out, some asserted. Viewed in that light, the numbers seemed to prove that the law school market was capable of self-correction.

Perhaps that analysis will turn out to be correct. But time may reveal that such views combined the effects of obfuscation with the triumph of hope over reality. The reported drop in law school applicants was a positive development, but the absolute number—sixty-eight thousand a year when the total number of new full-time jobs requiring a legal degree is twenty-five thousand a year and falling—remained absurdly high. In fact, the reduction in the number of LSAT takers in summer 2011 merely brought it back to 2008 levels. The onset of the Great Recession had driven more students to consider law school as a place to wait out reverberations from the economic collapse. The number of June 2009 and 2010 tests had surged to almost thirty-three thousand. To put that in historical perspective, the June 1987 testing session drew just under nineteen thousand students.

The bottom line is that when—as in 2012—almost seventy thousand students apply for fifty thousand first-year law student openings *each year*, but only half of those who are admitted will find full-time jobs requiring a legal degree, the market hasn't self-corrected. For full-time long-term jobs requiring bar passage, only a dozen schools reported employment rates exceeding 80 percent nine months after graduation. Considering the investment in money, time, and brainpower that law school requires (not to mention the promises that law schools make to prospective students), the present outcome is not acceptable and the foreseeable future offers little hope for meaningful improvement.

Sure, scandals occasionally bring the profession's darker side to the fore: a law school gets caught cheating on LSAT scores that it submits to the ABA and *U.S. News & World Report;* a newspaper article describes an unemployed attorney hobbled with six-figure debt and no prospects of ever repaying it; someone exposes a law firm that exaggerated revenue and profits numbers to help its *Am Law* ranking; a respected law firm spirals to a spectacular death; a seemingly successful attorney in a big firm commits suicide. Such episodes get headlines for a while, but the underlying culture that produces them survives and thrives.

The pages that follow expose the evolution of that culture. From law schools to the pinnacle of the profession at America's most prestigious law firms, unrestrained self-interest—let's call it greed—has taken key legal institutions to an unfortunate place. As leaders of the bar, especially law school deans and many managing partners of the nation's biggest law firms, focus on the near future, disastrous long-term consequences are becoming apparent. But there is hope. Those who attribute the current state of the legal profession to market forces beyond anyone's control are wrong. Human decisions created this mess; better human decisions can clean it up.

PART I
LAW SCHOOLS

CHAPTER 1

TRACKING
THE BUBBLE

*In the spring of 1974—purely speculatively, I told
myself—I took the Law School Admissions Test.*
—Scott Turow, *One L: The Turbulent
True Story of a First Year at Harvard Law School*

UNLIKE SCOTT TUROW, I always wanted to be a lawyer. Once I entered law school in 1976, it never occurred to me that using my JD to earn a living would be a significant challenge, or that my student loans from college and law school—roughly $50,000 in 2012 dollars— would be anything other than a minor inconvenience. I'd heard stories about unemployed lawyers driving taxicabs, but they were irrelevant to the life I'd planned. In that respect, I was similar to most of today's prelaw students, who are convinced that bad things happen only to someone else. The difference is that the current prospects for law graduates are far worse than my contemporaries' and mine ever were. Over the past two decades, the situation has deteriorated as student enrollments have grown to outpace the number of available new legal jobs by almost two to one. Deans who are determined to fill their classrooms have exploited prospective students who depend on federal student loan money to pay tuition. The result has been an unsustainable bubble.

Law school applicants continue to overwhelm the number of places available for them, ignoring data that on their face should propel most aspiring attorneys away from a legal career. As noted in the introduction, only about half of today's graduates can expect to find a full-time position requiring a legal degree. Meanwhile, law schools have grown in number and size to accommodate demand without regard to whether there will be jobs for their graduates. The first part of the equation— student demand—is the product of media images projecting the glamour of attorneys' lives, the perception that a legal degree ensures financial security, and law school's status as the traditional default option for students with no idea what to do with their lives. The second part of the equation—the increase in law school supply—was made possible by a revolutionary change in the method of legal education more than a century ago. It gave educators an easy way to transform law schools into profit centers for their universities. Decades later, student loans would provide the funding.

Today there's a lawyer for every 265 Americans—more than twice the per capita number in 1970—but for future attorneys, there won't be enough legal jobs for more than half of them. In 2008, the US Department of Labor's Bureau of Labor Statistics (BLS) estimated that for the ten-year period ending in 2018, the economy would produce an additional 98,500 legal jobs. In 2012, after the Great Recession decimated the market for attorneys, the BLS revised that estimate downward, to 73,600 openings from 2010 through 2020. Another prediction considered attrition in combination with the number of anticipated new attorneys on a state-by-state basis and concluded that through 2015 the number of new attorneys passing the bar exam would be more than twice the expected number of openings. Whichever of these statistics turns out to be closest, there's little doubt that law graduates are already feeling the crunch. Fewer than half of 2011 graduates found jobs in private practice. Nine months after graduation, only 55 percent held full-time, long-term positions requiring a legal degree.

Along with their degrees and dubious job prospects, 85 percent of 2010 graduates from ABA-accredited law schools carried debt, and the average debt load was almost $100,000. Average law school debt for the graduating class of 2011 broke six figures, and that number has been growing in tandem with unemployment rates for new graduates. Even if a career in law turns out to be the right path, the financial burden can be staggering. If the law ends up being the wrong path, then debt becomes the rock that Sisyphus had to push uphill for the rest of his life.

FOR MOST LAWYERS, the idea of pursuing a legal career comes early in life. One-third of respondents to a survey of recent applicants said that they had wanted to attend law school since childhood and, while still in high school, made the decision to apply after college. Another third made the decision as undergraduates, in either their freshman or sophomore year. One reason for this phenomenon is the media: popular images make a legal career look attractive to young people long before they get to college. Any middle school student who reads *To Kill a Mockingbird* (1960) or *Inherit the Wind* (1955) takes in an image of the admirable lawyer-statesman. Recent portrayals include the CBS hit series *The Good Wife*, which continues a legacy of noble lawyers in television dating back to *Perry Mason* and proceeding through *The Defenders, L.A. Law, Law & Order*, and others. Every week, an episode of *The Good Wife* focuses on junior associate Alicia Florrick, a single mom who was raising two teenagers by herself until her philandering husband, a former state's attorney, got out of jail near the end of the first season. Regularly she finds herself in tense courtroom scenes cross-examining key witnesses in high-stakes trials. While making a lot of money, she finds clever ways to unearth critical facts, reveal truth, and vindicate clients. Then she goes home every evening in time for dinner with her kids.

There are negative images out there, too, most notably in the work of John Grisham. For example, no pre-law student should want to emulate the crooked attorneys in *The Firm*, his 1991 best seller about lawyers who operate their enterprise as a front for the mob. But they also should be wary of identifying with the novel's protagonist, Mitch McDeere. He follows the very track to which most of them aspire: he graduates from a top law school and joins a high-paying law firm to earn big money. However, he gets swept away by the billable-hour culture, which deprives him of sleep and a home life, and his marriage deteriorates. These pressures, which nearly destroy him, are wholly apart from the underlying criminality that his firm's partners pursue.

Yet most pre-law students ignore the persistent warnings. Somehow those negative images can't compete with the positive ones. Psychologist Daniel Kahneman, who won a Nobel Prize in economics, may have a partial explanation. Kahneman researches and writes about a universal human characteristic: clinging to preconceived notions, even as contrary information and unambiguous data undermine them. The phenomenon is a variant of confirmation bias, the tendency to credit information that comports with established beliefs and jettison anything that doesn't.

In the context of the legal profession, most prelaw students think they'll be the exceptions—the traps that ensnare people like Mitch McDeere won't get them.

ANOTHER REASON that people become lawyers is to make money. But if prospective lawyers allow themselves to be dazzled by headlines about the wealthiest attorneys, such as the partner who recently left one big firm to join another where he'd earn a reported $5 million a year, they're making a mistake. Nine months after graduation, members of the law school class of 2009 fortunate enough to have *any* full-time job had a median salary of $72,000, comparable in buying power to the $50,000 median salary for new lawyers in 1990. That may not sound bad, but even that number is misleadingly high, as it masks a skewed income distribution. Each year 10 to 15 percent of graduates get jobs in big law firms, where the starting salary can be as high as $160,000. But those firms constitute only a tiny slice of the profession, and it's shrinking. Furthermore, the median salary has been falling. For all *law firms,* the median starting salary for the class of 2011 was $85,000; for all *lawyers* who graduated that year, it was $60,000 (a 17 percent drop compared to the $72,000 median starting salary for the class of 2009). Even those numbers overstate new graduates' financial reality for another reason: they're based solely on salary information for the 65 percent of graduates reported to be working full-time in a position lasting at least a year.

For most employed lawyers, the money gets better. The median annual income of all practicing lawyers in 2010 was $112,000—double that of all US households. The nagging problem is that the seemingly decent (but shrinking) payoff usually isn't sufficient to justify the enormous investment in time and money. Professor Herwig Schlunk of Vanderbilt University Law School calculates that for the vast majority of graduates, getting a legal degree will never yield a return equal to the financial cost of becoming a lawyer.

SOME PEOPLE GO to law school because it's the last resort of the liberal arts major who doesn't know what to do next. In that respect, the decision to enroll has long resulted from a process of elimination that proceeds something like this: being a member of a profession is the ultimate achievement, but medical school requires science-oriented interests and talents that don't fit most students in the humanities; postgraduate degrees in history, philosophy, English, and the social sciences are for future professors; business school is for those whose principal ambition is to make lots of money. That leaves law school, which offers students a three-year reprieve from the world while they pursue a noble course that presumably creates even more options. Sometimes that plan works out okay; for too many others, it leads to a place where dreams go to die.

Proof that law school is a default solution for the undecided lies everywhere, even in newspapers' sports pages. In the fall of 2011, twenty-six-year-old infielder Josh Satin made his major league debut for the New York Mets. An article about him included this line: "After graduating as a political science major from Cal, Satin was selected by the Mets in the sixth round of the 2008 draft. And like any number of 20-somethings with a liberal arts degree and nebulous career prospects, he kept law school applications at the ready."

ON THE SUPPLY SIDE of the lawyer bubble, some of the necessary conditions for its creation date to a nineteenth-century innovation in legal education—the case method. Credit for that development goes to former Harvard Law School dean Christopher Columbus Langdell. Prior to 1890, no other law school used the case method of instruction that he pioneered; today it's pervasive.

Langdell didn't set out to create what became an essential basis for the current mass production model of legal education. Rather, he was simply pursuing his penchant for thoroughness. He viewed the law as a science and believed that its ultimate truths could be discovered through the study of primary specimens, namely, the decisions of appellate court judges. Law students could divine general principles that, once mastered, would enable a graduate to practice anywhere. As Langdell saw it, differences in state law were inconsequential to the overall jurisprudential picture.

The large body of common law itself created a challenge for Langdell's approach. No student could read every reported decision going back to Blackstone's *Commentaries on the Laws of England,* an eighteenth-century treatise that first summarized the English common law as part of a unified system. For his Harvard contracts course, Langdell instead collected a selection of reported cases (there were more than two thousand at the time) from which an entire classroom of students could induce general legal principles.

The Langdell case method was a radical departure. Previously, prospective attorneys had learned the law from secondary sources as rules to memorize and skills to hone before engaging in one-on-one apprenticeships. For example, after a year of study consisting of the traditional lecture and drilling at the University of Michigan in the 1870s, Clarence Darrow received on-the-job legal training while working for an attorney in rural Ohio. He then proved his competence to a few lawyers before whom he literally sat to be examined for the bar. Darrow passed. A system that required students to learn specific legal rules and then receive training with practicing attorneys constrained the number of new lawyers admitted to the bar each year.

Langdell changed that model with what he regarded as a noble aim. Practical aspects—simply learning the rules—weren't the key. Instead, a true lawyer's most important work was to understand the governing principles so as to "be able to apply them with consistent facility and certainty to the ever-tangled skein of human affairs." One by-product of the approach was that large groups of students could receive simultaneous legal training from a handful of instructors. The system became an early building block in the current business model of legal education.

Langdell's new teaching protocol didn't create the current lawyer bubble, but it provided an essential foundation that facilitated the mass production of attorneys. From 1890 to 1916, the number of law schools doubled from 61 to 139, but the schools themselves became larger, so the number of law students increased fivefold—from 4,500 to almost 23,000. As recently as 1963, there were still only 135 law schools, but total JD enrollment had doubled to 47,000 students.

During the next decade, baby boomers made their way into higher education as the Vietnam War popularized three-year law school deferments from the draft. Enrollment doubled again to 100,000 by 1972, but there were still fewer than 150 law schools. As the last of the boomers made their way through law school, enrollment leveled off, hovering around 127,000 through the 1990s. On a per capita basis, the United States had 1.58 lawyers per 1,000 citizens in 1960; by 1980, the number had grown to 2.38 lawyers per 1,000. But that was only the beginning.

In the 1990s, *U.S. News & World Report*'s law school rankings began to gain in popularity and became a key element in the competition for new students. Meanwhile, as applications to first-year classes rose generally, universities increasingly saw law schools as profit centers worth expanding. Recently the Maryland Department of Legislative Services concluded that the University of Baltimore School of Law sent 31 percent of its 2010 revenue back into the general university budget. For private schools the data are difficult to uncover, but the University of Baltimore report corroborates a widely held view that universities in general impose a "tax" amounting to between 20 and 25 percent of their law schools' gross revenues.

Law school enrollments climbed even as tuition rose faster than at undergraduate colleges. In 2003, there were more than ninety-eight thousand applicants to the first-year class that enrolled about forty-eight thousand students nationwide. Average annual tuition for private law schools was $26,000. By 2010, it had increased to more than $37,000. Even as law school applications declined sharply after 2010, private law school tuition went up annually by 4 percent—more than twice the rate of inflation—to an average of $40,585 per year in 2012. Public law schools have followed an even steeper curve: for in-state residents, average tuition doubled from $11,860 in 2003 to $23,590. In 2012 alone, it went up by more than 6 percent.

When *U.S. News* published its first rankings in 1987, total law school enrollment in the 175 ABA-accredited institutions had remained around 120,000 for a decade. Since then, twenty-five more law schools have come on line and enrollments have steadily risen to more than 145,000. By 2010, there were more than 1.2 million lawyers in the United States—almost 4 for every 1,000 citizens. In the United Kingdom, the comparable number is about 2.5 per 1,000; in Germany, it's slightly more than 1.5.

LAW SCHOOL DEANS defended the growth and proliferation of law schools after 2000 as a market reaction to student demand. After all, an excess of applicants over available spots sent an unambiguous signal: consumers wanted more openings in law schools. Anyone running a business would respond as most deans did: raise tuition, increase profits, and add capacity. Wrapping themselves in the rhetoric of free markets and individual choice, even deans at some of the best law schools avoided important disclosures, including meaningful employment and salary data for their recent graduates. After all, better information about the limited opportunities actually available to new attorneys might reduce student demand.

Of course, some of the widespread career dissatisfaction among attorneys is the fault of college students making shortsighted and unsound judgments about their future. But bad information shares the blame for what turned out to be a poor career choice for many of them. Law schools operating on the outer perimeter of candor to fill their classrooms worsened the problem. But without free-flowing student loan money for which law school deans never have to account, the entire system would look much different.

The law school business model permitted (and still permits) a perverse market response—increasing tuition in the face of declining demand for lawyers—for two reasons: student demand for law school still exceeds supply, and students have little difficulty borrowing whatever they need to cover the cost of a degree. For decades, lenders faced no risk of default because the federal government guaranteed the loans. Then in 2008, out of concern that the credit market freeze would leave insufficient financing for student loans, the government essentially took over most such lending directly. Two years later, it completed the transition from insuring all loans to issuing the vast majority of them. Meanwhile, revisions to the bankruptcy laws essentially bar students from ever discharging public or private educational debt. In its totality, the current regime insulates law schools from the problem of graduates who can't find jobs needed to repay their student loans, while giving schools no incentive to control tuition costs. Of the various parties involved—students, government, private lenders, and law schools— only the students and, to a growing extent under new income-based repayment programs discussed in Chapter 3, the federal treasury bear any significant risk that such borrowing might turn out to have been imprudent.

The combination of irresponsible lending and inadequate law school accountability has been deadly for many attorneys and the profession. It's a story of good intentions gone awry.

The origins of the government student loan program generally date to 1958, when Congress followed the recommendation of economist

Milton Friedman in creating a system of direct federal loans for higher education. When it expanded the program in 1965, existing federal budget accounting rules required booking direct student loans as total losses in the year made, regardless of whether they would be repaid in full with interest. But the rules also provided that a loan guarantee didn't count as a federal budget cost item—not a penny. At the urging of economists, Congress finally revised the budget rules in 1990, but the most important feature remained: federal guarantees of all private and public student loans.

For lenders, such guarantees mean no risk of nonrepayment because the government picks up the tab for any shortfall. For students, they mean the growth of another industry that will chase them forever: debt collectors. When someone defaults on a student loan, the government turns it over to private collection agencies. In 2011, the US Department of Education paid more than $1.4 billion to such companies. Summarizing that industry's attitude, a business consultant described his thoughts in 2011 as he watched Occupy protesters at New York University wearing T-shirts with the amounts of their student debt scribbled across the front: "I couldn't believe the accumulated wealth they represent—for our industry. It was lip-smacking." His article included a picture of some students in their T-shirts, including one with "the fine sum of $90,000" and another with "a really attractive $120,000." Another consultant suggested that student loans might be the accounts receivable industry's "new oil well." Something is terribly amiss in a society where policies and incentive structures make debt collection a growth business.

In addition to government guarantees, private lenders gained another layer of protection against losses from their student loan portfolios. As noted previously, today such debt almost always survives a young lawyer's bankruptcy filing. The cumulative impact of these policies is becoming clearer. As one recent graduate observed, a federally guaranteed student loan may be "the closest thing to debtor prison that there is on this earth."

It wasn't always so. In the early 1970s, the federal student loan program was still relatively new and the US Department of Health, Education, and Welfare sought to avoid any negative public image that might tarnish the young system. The agency proposed making government student loans nondischargeable in bankruptcy unless a borrower had been in default for at least five years or could prove "undue hardship." Enacted in 1976, the undue-hardship requirement placed student loans in the same category as child support, alimony, court restitution orders, criminal fines, and certain taxes. No data supported the suggestion of a student loan default problem, but anecdotal media reports of isolated abuse carried the day.

The concern was moral hazard—the fear that graduates on the verge of lucrative careers would avoid responsibility for the federal educational loans that had made those careers possible. But as the legislative history makes clear, the basis for such concerns was "more myth and media hype than reality." A lead editorial in the July 25, 2012, edition of the *Wall Street Journal* reveals the enduring power of that myth thirty-five years later: "After a surge in former students declaring bankruptcy to avoid repaying their loans, Congress acted to protect lenders beginning in 1977." That's simply not true. Although a House of Representatives report and analysis from the General Accounting Office had confirmed that abuse was "virtually non-existent," the provision found its way into the Bankruptcy Reform Act of 1978.

In 1990, Congress extended the requisite five-year default period, requiring a seven-year wait as a precondition to relief from educational debt. In 1997, the Bankruptcy Reform Commission found no evidence to support claims of earlier systematic abuse. Even so, in 1998 Congress amended the statute to provide that no amount of time would render federal educational debt dischargeable in bankruptcy. In 2005, Congress extended nondischargeabilty to private lenders as well, although, as Senator Dick Durbin asked in 2012, "How in the world did that provision get into the law? It was a mystery amendment. We can't find out who offered it." A fruitful place to begin the search might be with lobbyists for the banking industry.

Apart from the unwillingness of any legislator to claim responsibility for the now orphaned provision, there was little factual justification for it or the earlier revisions that eliminated bankruptcy relief from federal loans in the first place. Nonfederal loans accounted for only 7 percent of all student borrowing in the 2010–2011 academic year. Repeated legislative inquiry yielded no empirical evidence to validate stated fears about systemic abuse for either private or government loans. But now that the limitations are in place, some have theorized that returning even to pre-2005 rules could lead to a parade of horribles, including higher interest rates for all students, reduced affordability, and tighter credit requirements throughout the system.

Two recent examples of the undue-hardship requirement illustrate the daunting task facing a debtor who seeks relief from educational debt today. In May 2012, a sixty-three-year-old Maryland woman had more than $330,000 in school loans dating back to her enrollment at the University of Baltimore School of Law in 1992. She didn't graduate. Later, she received a master's degree from Towson University and a PhD from an unaccredited online school. The judge decided that the debtor's Asperger's syndrome qualified her for relief from student loan debt. Expecting that she could "ever break the grip of autism and meaningfully channel her energies toward tasks that are not in some way either dictated, or circumscribed, by the demands of her disorder would be to dream the impossible dream." Even the debtor's attorney expressed surprise that his client had succeeded in discharging her debt under the demanding undue-hardship standard.

In July 2012, a sixty-four-year-old woman who had worked on an assembly line earning $11 an hour until she received a layoff notice obtained discharge of loans she had first taken on in 1981, when she was thirty-three and enrolled in Canisius College. After pursuing a five-year partial repayment plan under Chapter 13 of the Bankruptcy Code, she'd whittled only $2,400 from her loan balance and still owed more than $56,000, most of which was accrued interest on her original $17,000 loan. The court concluded that the debtor was "at the end of her 'rope' at age sixty-four, facing job loss and no prospects other than Social Security," and ordered her loans discharged.

Such cases in which students get relief from burdensome student loan debt are unusual. In fact, the applicable legal standard for discharge isn't even consistent across the federal circuits. Some appellate courts require judges to predict the future and conclude, as a prerequisite to discharge, that a debtor will *never* be able to repay the loans—that is, the "certainty of hopelessness." One attorney described how he jokes about the absurdity of the standard: "What I say to the judge is that as long as we've got a lottery, there is no certainty of hopelessness. They smile, and then they rule against you."

More attorneys are finding themselves in plights similar to that of the thirty-four-year-old lawyer with more than $200,000 in school loans and a job that would never pay enough to retire them: "It's a noose around my neck that I see no way out of." It takes little imagination to foresee the domino effects as she and similarly situated others become unable to fund their children's higher education. The accumulating social costs over generations could haunt America for a long time.

AS A CONSEQUENCE of these dynamics, some not-so-funny things happen to many of those who choose law school for the wrong reasons—or for no particularly good reason. The promise of a secure future at a well-paying job is often illusory. The persistent problem of lawyer oversupply rose to crisis level, and the market for new talent has remained weak. Compounding the difficulties with which they began law school, newly minted, less-than-passionate, and deeply indebted lawyers are now having trouble finding the secure, well-paying, and exciting work they thought would be waiting for them when they graduated. For most of the nation's forty-four thousand annual graduates today, those positions were never there at all.

Because students rely on rankings to choose a school, such listings are now a critical element in the prevailing law school business model. *U.S. News & World Report* publishes what everyone regards as the gold standard. As a consequence, deans use its methodological criteria to run their institutions. Single-minded self-interest in selling a law school education—and the failure of colleges and law schools to offer a competing perspective that challenges students' assumptions about most lawyers' actual lives—has disserved many graduates and damaged the profession. But try telling that to deans who pander to the annual *U.S. News* rankings.

CHAPTER 2

THE ROLE OF THE ABA AND *U.S. NEWS* RANKINGS

*A ranking system that exemplifies the shortcomings of all
"by the numbers" schemes is the one produced annually by*
U.S. News & World Report. . . . *The "weights" attached to the
variables are arbitrary and reflect only the view of the magazine's
editors*. . . . *As the deans of schools that range across the spectrum of
several rating systems, we strongly urge you to minimize the
influence of rankings on your own judgment.*
—Excerpt from a 1997 open letter to all prospective law students signed by
more than 160 deans of the country's 179 accredited law schools

*I feel strongly that rankings are an important form of
consumer information*. . . . *My position, which is not
universally shared among my peers, has always been that*
U.S. News *rankings offer invaluable comparative data
to anyone trying to make an informed choice.*
—David E. Van Zandt, at that time dean of the
Northwestern University School of Law, who refused to sign the 1997 letter

THE METHODOLOGY underlying the annual *U.S. News & World Report* rankings now dictates how most students choose a law school and how most deans run them. In a recent survey, 86 percent of pre-law students taking Kaplan Education's test preparation courses said that a school's ranking was either very important or somewhat important in choosing where to apply. As a result, the profession's gatekeepers allow the superficial appeal of a few key metrics to displace their independent judgment. Those metrics are fatally flawed; prospective lawyers, law students, and the profession itself suffer the consequences.

It's easy to forget that the whole rankings system is relatively new. Somehow, prospective students and law schools managed to find each other long before *U.S. News* entered the scene. Well into the 1980s, pre-law students understood the general pecking order based principally on the difficulty of gaining admittance to each school. There were widely accepted groupings (e.g., Harvard, Yale, and Stanford have been the top three for a long time), but the precise order within any group depended on individual preferences and didn't seem particularly important. All of that gave way to a numbered list in 1987, when *U.S. News & World Report* first published its top twenty. By 2012, the magazine was ranking 195 ABA-accredited law schools, although it didn't publish numerical standings below number 145.

Outwardly, deans expressed disdain for the rankings. In 1997, virtually every law school dean—with the most notable exception being Northwestern's dean at the time, David Van Zandt—endorsed a statement condemning the *U.S. News* law school evaluations as counterproductive to reasoned thought and informed individual choice. Van Zandt dissented, ignoring the unfortunate fact that bad information can be worse than no information at all. His outlier position made him a self-styled maverick among law school deans. Even more important, it reflected an approach to running law schools that relied on measurement-driven criteria that make no sense and distort decisions.

In that respect, Van Zandt's greatest sin may have been candor. Most deans still say publicly that they despise the *U.S. News* lists, but their conduct says something else. Rankings of all kinds permeate law school websites. Whether the impact is on students' decision making or on deans' behavior, the *U.S. News* listing remains the mother of all misguided metrics.

As reliance on the *U.S. News* ranking system intensified, the perverse behavioral impact of its methodological criteria became more apparent. The *U.S. News* rankings consist of four components—quality assessment, selectivity, placement, and resources—each of which is subject to manipulation. Individually, deans focus on rankings as a way to sell their schools and thereby enhance short-term profits. Collectively, the result is a contest that increases student demand. Phillip J. Closius, then dean of the University of Baltimore School of Law, describes the phenomenon: "Millions of dollars [are] riding on students' decisions about where to go to law school, and that creates real institutional pressures."

Whatever else it may do, the frenzy over rankings has combined with most law schools' profit-maximizing business models to inflate the lawyer bubble. That the focus on the *U.S. News* list disserves students, law schools, and the profession becomes evident when analyzing the individual ranking components, almost all of which have produced scandals at some law schools. The one component that hasn't, quality assessment, should be considered a scandal in and of itself, both for the amount of weight it receives and for the total lack of rigor behind it.

QUALITY ASSESSMENT is the biggest contributor to a school's ranking, accounting for 40 percent of the total score. The category itself is a misnomer because it doesn't reflect quality at all. Rather, using statistically suspect samples of academics and practicing attorneys, it's a superficial and unreliable assessment of a school's reputation.

Twenty-five percent of every law school's total *U.S. News* score comes from responses to a survey that the magazine sends each year to four individuals at every ABA-accredited law school: the dean, the dean of academic affairs, the chair of faculty appointments, and the most recently tenured faculty member. They receive a list of the country's accredited law schools, along with a request to rate each—all 195 in 2012—on a scale from 1 to 5. The survey doesn't ask those responding if they've ever set foot on the campuses, met any of the faculty, or have any familiarity with the schools they're reviewing. Respondents have a "don't know" option, but *U.S. News* doesn't disclose how many people use it for particular schools on the list. After all, such meaningful information would undermine *U.S. News*'s reported response rate, which was 66 percent for the rankings published in 2011 and 63 percent for 2012.

The rest of the quality assessment component—accounting for 15 percent of the total *U.S. News* score—comes from a similar 1-to-5 survey that goes to unnamed "legal professionals, including the hiring partners of law firms, state attorneys general and selected federal and state judges." The response rate is abysmal—14 percent for the 2011 rankings and 12 percent for 2012, for example. Here again, the extent to which respondents replied with "don't know" isn't disclosed. Likewise, whether someone returning the survey actually knows anything about any law school that he or she rates is irrelevant. As a matter of statistical theory, the entire sampling process that produces the quality assessment component suffers from numerous deficiencies.

Former New York University School of Law dean (and later NYU president) John Sexton suggested that if the recipients of the survey "were asked about Princeton Law School, it would appear in the top twenty. But it doesn't exist." Retired Michigan supreme court justice Thomas E. Brennan, who founded the Thomas M. Cooley Law School in 1972, proved Sexton right. Prior to 2000, Brennan sent a law school survey to one hundred of his fellow lawyers. His list included Harvard, Yale, and the University of Michigan, along with lesser-known schools, such as John Marshall and Thomas M. Cooley. "As I recall, they ranked Penn State's law school right about in the middle of the pack," Brennan said later. "Maybe fifth among the ten schools listed." At the time, Penn State didn't have a law school.

Penn State did acquire one when it merged with the Dickinson School of Law in 2000. True to Brennan's earlier survey, Dickinson has ranked consistently in the middle of the *U.S. News* listings. In 2012, the school's middle-of-the-pack quality assessment rating of 3.2 (out of 5) contributed to an overall score that placed it in a three-way tie for seventy-sixth. In fact, the school's dean, Philip McConnaughay, complained that Dickinson's quality assessment score seemed to be stuck: "The law school's reputation score among law deans and professors has remained flat for several years, not yet reflecting the tremendous improvements to faculty stature, student academic credentials and diversity, and facilities the law school has enjoyed since establishing its principal campus in University Park."

An apt analogy to the *U.S. News* quality assessment component would be evaluations by car owners who aren't required to disclose whether they've ever seen or driven the automobiles they're reviewing. Under the current system, "quality assessment" is more about how effectively schools are able to brand and market themselves than about how effectively they turn out capable, employable lawyers.

SELECTIVITY COUNTS for 25 percent of a school's score. Its subparts are undergraduate grade point average (GPA), LSAT scores, and the law school's rejection rate for first-year applicants. *U.S. News* knows about rejection rate manipulation: "The Association of American Law Schools has reported that some schools increase rejection rates—and boost selectivity scores—by encouraging students with no chance of admission to apply."

With respect to the LSAT component, many schools encourage applicants to take the test multiple times because the rules allow them to report only the highest score to *U.S. News*. That's good news for the testing companies: the average number of times that students took the LSAT increased from just under 1.5 in 2002 to almost 2.0 in 2011. Another beneficiary of the increased emphasis on LSATs has been test preparation services. They're not unique to law schools, but they are relatively new in this arena and they improve students' test scores. As schools have increased their reliance on LSAT results, those who can't afford test preparation courses are at a worsening disadvantage in the law school application process.

Other efforts to bolster selectivity scores are far more egregious, such as schools that knowingly submit false GPA and LSAT data. A recent example of that behavior led to a scandal at the University of Illinois College of Law. The resulting investigation provides an inside view into the pernicious power of the *U.S. News* rankings over law school culture. The university's outside lawyers blamed a rogue, but they also observed that leaders of the institution created the environment in which he operated. The title of a major section of the investigators' findings speaks for itself: "Institutional Emphasis on USNWR [*U.S. News & World Report*] Ranking." In that respect, the scandal in Illinois symbolizes a larger phenomenon: administrators' willingness to allow rankings considerations to run their schools for them.

The supposed rogue was Paul Pless, who graduated from the university's College of Law in 2003. His alma mater hired him as assistant director for admissions and financial aid at a salary of $38,500. (For years, putting unemployed new graduates on the payroll, often temporarily, has bolstered schools' *U.S. News* rankings; this tactic artificially inflates their graduates' employment rates.) Pless stayed on and was promoted. By December 2004, he was earning $72,000 yearly as an assistant dean.

Not until the College of Law's 2005 annual report did the school—not Pless—explicitly adopt two new goals driven by the *U.S. News* rankings: increase the incoming class's median LSAT from 163 to 165 and raise its GPA from 3.42 to 3.5. When the following year's class median LSAT came in at 166, the law school's dean, Heidi Hurd, sang Pless's praises to her boss, the interim provost: "Had we been able to report this increase last year, holding all else equal, we would have moved from 26th to 20th in the *U.S. News* rankings."

Hurd's observation was misleading, as the school had actually *dropped* in rank. That's because the admissions office hadn't held "all else equal" to get its LSAT boost. Rather, it had sacrificed the average GPA of admitted students. The median GPA had plummeted to 3.32 and the school's overall *U.S. News* ranking declined to twenty-seventh. In May 2006, a new strategic plan noted that the admissions emphasis on LSAT scores had left it "with a GPA profile worse than any other top-50 school." So the school announced a new and even more ambitious goal: raising the incoming class median LSAT and GPA to 168 and 3.7 by 2011.

Once again, Hurd sought a big pay raise for Pless because, she said, he was "in the hiring sights of every dean in America who wants to improve student rankings." Why that should have been true is puzzling. The bump in the incoming students' average LSAT score had occurred because the school had accepted those with lower average GPAs. As a result, its overall rank had fallen. Nevertheless, his salary jumped to $98,000.

Not long thereafter, a handful of discrepancies between actual and reported GPA and LSAT data for the incoming class of 2011 (those who enrolled in 2008) marked the beginning of a "sustained pattern . . . that increased in practice and scope through the class of 2014." In October and November 2008, administrators debated which of several different LSAT/GPA combinations would raise the school's overall *U.S. News* ranking. Apparently rankings have become a subject of scholarly legal inquiry—at least insofar as some law professors and school administrators seek insight into how best to manipulate them. While teaching at another school, University of Illinois professor Robert Lawless had developed a methodology for determining how changes in various *U.S. News* factors affected a school's rank. When he shared it with his fellow

College of Law faculty members, they dubbed it the "Lawless Calculator." In November 2008, Lawless reported to interim dean Ralph Brubaker and associate dean for academic affairs Bruce Smith that an LSAT/GPA combination of 165/3.8 would produce a higher ranking than 167/3.6.

In February 2009, Bruce Smith became dean. One of his first major decisions was to set the school's combined LSAT/GPA goal for the incoming class of 2012. Should the median LSAT/GPA target be 165/3.8 or 166/3.7? In later remarks to the College of Law's Board of Visitors, Smith described how he resolved the issue: "I told Paul [Pless] to push the envelope, think outside the box, take some risk, do things differently . . . [and s]trive for a 166/3.8 . . . a level never attained before at [the College of Law] and, frankly, thought to be unattainable at such a large class size."

In other words, rather than choose between maximizing LSAT scores and maximizing GPA, he told Pless to "take some risk" and increase both. Surely Smith wasn't suggesting that his admissions dean falsify data, but when the person at the top of any law school issues a directive, subordinates ignore it at their peril. The targets became increasingly ambitious and unrealistic, and the dean knew it as he set them.

The university's outside investigators absolved Smith of any wrongdoing associated with Pless's misconduct. But a footnote in their final November 2011 report observed that Smith's management style "is goal-oriented and intense, and occasionally intimidating, and that it is not inconceivable that certain employees subordinate to him would be uncomfortable bringing bad news to him."

For the two years following Smith's 2009 directive, Pless didn't: "I haven't let a Dean down yet, and I don't plan on starting with you Boss," he'd assured Smith in April 2009. The median LSAT score and GPA for the school's accepted students showed continuing improvement, and Pless's salary jumped to $130,000 on the strength of Smith's glowing review. Indeed, Pless's exploding compensation at a public university in tough economic straits—especially for financially strapped Illinois—itself reveals much about the power of rankings and the discretionary clout that a dean exercises in allocating a law school's resources.

On August 22, 2011, Pless touted the class of 2014's median LSAT score (168) and GPA (3.81). The actual numbers, however, were 163 and 3.7. Those discrepancies may seem insignificant, but they are enormous in the *U.S. News* world; evidently the Lawless Calculator proves it. So do the College of Law's subsequent rankings, which plummeted when the truth caught up to them. The University of Illinois College of Law dropped twelve spots, to number thirty-five. But for a tip to the university's ethics office on August 26, 2011, the wrongdoing might have remained undiscovered for years more. As a penalty to the institution over which it wielded accreditation power, the ABA issued a public censure, imposed a $250,000 fine, and required a compliance monitor to check the school's data submissions for the next two years.

Villanova Law School endured a similar scandal based on false data that it submitted from 2002 to 2010. In response, the ABA issued a public censure noting that the school's conduct had been "reprehensible and damaging to prospective law school applicants," required an independent compliance monitor to verify admissions data submitted for the next two years, and mandated that the ABA sanctions letter remain on the school's website, also for two years. The correct numbers dropped Villanova's ranking from 67th to 84th in 2012, and it continued falling, to 101st place, in the 2013 *U.S. News* rankings, published in March 2012.

Most law school deans are too smart to engage in or approve such intentional misconduct. Instead, these creative attorneys find ways to take advantage of *U.S. News*'s methodological loopholes. For example, during David Van Zandt's final years as dean, Northwestern University School of Law's solicitation of transfer students became a high-profile example of institutional behavior that catered to *U.S. News* ranking criteria.

When it comes to LSATs, the *U.S. News* rule is simple: the LSAT scores of students transferring from another law school don't count in the incoming school's ranking. Exploiting that rule is easy: a school can bring in second-year students from elsewhere who have low LSAT scores and they won't adversely affect that component of the receiving school's selectivity rating, even as they bring in significant additional tuition revenue.

On a small scale, it's appropriate to give transfer applicants a second chance at a better school when an opening arises. As prospective first-year students, they may have performed poorly on the LSAT or not achieved undergraduate GPAs that reflected their full potential. An exemplary first-year performance can redeem a multitude of earlier sins. When utilized in that limited manner, the selective enrollment of transfer students may even have the salutary effect of undermining *U.S. News*'s undue emphasis on numbers in initial admissions decisions.

The problem arises when law schools recruit transfer students aggressively and in large numbers as a part of a strategy to expand tuition revenues while minimizing the adverse impact on the school's *U.S. News* ranking. For example, during the 2006–2007 academic year, Northwestern sent "conditional acceptances" to first-year students at other schools—students whom Northwestern had previously rejected when they'd applied as entering first-year students. Eventually, forty-three students transferred to Northwestern and increased the 238-member class by almost 20 percent. Collectively, the new additions contributed almost $2 million in tuition revenues (forty-three students times $43,000 in tuition) for that year and a similar amount for the year that followed. It was a win-win because the new tuition money arrived without reducing the LSAT scores that Northwestern reported to *U.S. News*.

The school might have taken a minor hit in the faculty/student ratio component of its *U.S. News* ranking (3 percent of its total score), but it would have been trivial compared to the negative LSAT component (12.5 percent) that it successfully bypassed. However low they were, the new transferees' scores didn't matter to the school's standing on that all-important list. Northwestern accepted even more transfers the following year, fifty-nine, but with Van Zandt's departure as dean shortly thereafter, the number subsequently dropped back into the thirties.

Van Zandt wasn't alone in implementing an aggressive transfer student strategy. According to schools' individual ABA reports for 2012, Columbia Law School admitted forty-six transfer students, Georgetown University Law Center brought in seventy-one, NYU's law school added fifty-six, and UCLA supplemented its class with forty transfers. As Loyola University of Chicago School of Law dean David Yellen observed, "If the *U.S. News* incentive went away tomorrow, transfer acceptance would drop."

At the time, Van Zandt defended his approach in straightforward business school jargon: "Chrysler and General Motors don't agree not to poach each other's customers." Such poaching increases the second- and third-year student enrollment at the receiving schools, enhancing the bottom line immediately. Any school that increases class size makes more money for itself and its university.

But there are hidden costs. For example, the number of JDs that Northwestern awarded grew from 224 in 2005 to 288 in 2011. It's difficult to imagine how the transfer students contributing to this increase enhanced the educational experiences or employment opportunities of the original classes into which they landed. For schools that lost entering second-year students to Northwestern, Georgetown, NYU, UCLA, and elsewhere, maintaining the size of their classes—and resulting tuition revenues—leaves them with only one option: recruit replacements. If victimized deans also anticipate a similar loss of students who will transfer to other schools in future years, they'll admit more first-year students initially. As this process ripples through the *U.S. News* pecking order, the lawyer bubble grows.

The *U.S. News* rules additionally encourage deans to buy higher LSAT scores for their entering classes. Schools use merit scholarships to implement the strategy, luring high-achieving students who otherwise might not attend with the promise of a free or discounted ride. It can lead to unfortunate behavior and perverse outcomes.

In 2011, the *New York Times* profiled a Golden Gate University School of Law student who needed a 3.0 to keep her scholarship for the second year and beyond. By the end of her first year's classes, which were graded on a curve (as is the case at most law schools), she'd "curved out" at 2.967—no rounding up, apparently. Her Teamsters dad had driven a tractor before he was laid off, but she and her parents came up with $60,000 in tuition to complete her degree.

At first blush that result appears to be reasonable: a B average shouldn't be difficult to maintain. Is this just whining from what some online commenters to the article called "the gimme generation"? Only if the victims knew how they would be evaluated. Otherwise, the strategy of awarding LSAT scholarships in combination with grading on the law school's mandatory curve looks more like intergenerational exploitation of the young by the old. Although more than half of the first-year class at Golden Gate had merit scholarships in 2011, historically only the top third of students graduate with a 3.0 GPA or better, which is what the school requires of students seeking to retain their scholarships.

Underlying this admissions strategy is a basic flaw in the premise: high LSATs don't necessarily translate into good law school grades. In 2010, validity studies investigating the connection between LSAT scores and first-year grades at 189 law schools demonstrated a correlation coefficient range of 0.12 to 0.56, with a median of 0.36. (For context, 1.00 is a perfect positive correlation—that is, a high LSAT score would always correlate with high grades. A correlation coefficient of 0 implies no relationship at all between the two factors. A number between 0 and –1.0 suggests a negative relationship between the two factors under investigation.) For schools at the low end of the range (0.12), there is virtually no statistically significant relationship between LSATs and first-year grades. Even at the median of 0.36, the positive relationship is not particularly compelling; it's certainly not determinative. Of course, even strong correlation doesn't prove causation. Nevertheless, law school deans cling to performance on the LSAT as one of the single most important factors in admitting applicants and in awarding merit scholarship money.

The strategy of buying high LSAT scores inflicts collateral damage, too. Albany Law School dean Thomas F. Guernsey noted that such catering to the rankings has "strange and unintended consequences," such as reducing need-based financial aid by redirecting it to those who otherwise would go somewhere else. That is, some first-year students who didn't qualify for need-based financial aid got merit scholarships based on their LSATs. Without those scholarships, those students would have attended a higher-ranked school that offered them no money. Meanwhile, students at the lower-ranked school whose financial hardship warrants assistance suffer because the school's resources are finite. Once the money goes to those who don't need it, it's not available to those who do.

From 2005 to 2010, the number of law students receiving exclusively need-based scholarships declined by more than 3,000 (from 20,781 to 17,610) while the number receiving non-need-based scholarships increased by over 8,500 (from 31,265 to 39,845). Rising tuition costs pushed the aggregate dollar amounts up for both categories over that period. But non-need-based scholarship awards increased by $230 million (from $290 million to $520 million), dwarfing need-based scholarships, which went up by one-tenth of that amount—$23 million (from $120 million to $143 million). Such trends in allocating resources away from the most needy among the next generation of would-be lawyers have obvious societal implications.

PLACEMENT HAS GENERATED more public attention than other *U.S. News* factors, but it accounts for only 20 percent of a school's total score. The American Bar Association has contributed mightily to the abuses associated with this ranking component.

U.S. News gathers its employment data from the ABA's annual accreditation questionnaire, which measures employment at only two discrete moments in time: at graduation and at a date nine months later. As with all of the information that law schools provide, it's self-reported and never subject to independent audit or verification.

For purposes of the ABA survey, employment was an extraordinarily expansive concept until 2012. When schools reported graduates as employed, they made no distinction between working as an associate in a prestigious law firm and being a barista in a coffee shop. As the *New York Times* reported, such "Enron-type accounting" allowed a recent average of all law schools to reach 93 percent.

Just don't ask those supposedly employed graduates whether they needed a JD to do their jobs. In 2012, employment rates for the class of 2011 hit an eighteen-year low: nine months after graduation, only 66 percent were in jobs requiring bar membership, and some of those were part-time or limited-term positions. Only 55 percent of 2011 graduates had found full-time, long-term employment necessitating bar passage. Another study estimates that the true legal employment rate for graduates at an undisclosed top-fifty school is even lower— less than half.

In 2010, Georgetown—universally regarded as a top school even before *U.S. News* gave it a numerical rank—sent a message to alumni still seeking employment that it had created three new temporary positions in the admissions office. At $20 an hour, the jobs started on February 1 and lasted for six weeks. That timing would allow the school to count them as employed on the key *U.S. News* nine-month employment date, February 15. Georgetown wasn't the first or last school to offer unemployed graduates temporary work that would enhance its *U.S. News* placement score. Northwestern, Indiana University's Maurer School of Law, UCLA, and many others have done it, too.

Recently, ABA-mandated disclosure requirements began forcing law schools to reveal when they hire their own graduates or offer them temporary stipends to work for other employers who do not pay them. In April 2012, the ABA finally released initial data on that subject. Three schools—the City University of New York School of Law, the University of the Pacific McGeorge School of Law, and the University of San Francisco School of Law—hired more than 15 percent of their own 2010 graduates. Twenty percent of schools hired more than 6 percent of their graduates, including the University of Virginia's law school, Vanderbilt Law School, and Washington and Lee University School of Law, each of which hired 11 percent.

Not all law school hiring of graduates is bad. Some temporary programs benefit students and society. For example, CUNY's LaunchPad employs new graduates to represent indigent New Yorkers in housing court. In turn, that experience can lead to employment as a public interest attorney. Duke University School of Law achieved a 100 percent hiring rate for its graduates by paying employers to hire some of them. But Duke's program, too, has often been a bridge to permanent work in public interest law, legal services, or the government.

The definitive test of law schools' motives with respect to temporary hiring will come if *U.S. News* rankings guru Robert Morse ever makes good on his threat to stop counting graduates as employed when their alma maters pay them. Even if he does, prospective law students will still remain in the dark with respect to how much money graduates earn in law-school-funded positions.

RESOURCES CONTRIBUTE the final 15 percent toward a school's ranking. Its largest subcategory is school "expenses per student." Here again the *U.S. News* rule is simple: more is better. Although this component, too, is subject to manipulation, the larger problem is that it rewards law schools' expenditures without regard to the value they add to a student's education.

The potential for mischief exists because, as with LSAT scores and GPA, schools self-report the data. Prior to 2006, the University of

Illinois College of Law multiplied by a factor of eighty the actual amount it had spent on LexisNexis and Westlaw database subscriptions. Its per-student expenditure included the fair market value of the services rather than the deeply discounted amount that the school actually paid. Claiming to have the ABA's earlier approval, dean Heidi Hurd defended the higher amount as an attempt "to get at the relative discount value, as it were, which was deemed to be of genuine value to the students." Until the ABA told the school to stop the practice, the net dollar impact on the University of Illinois College of Law's resources component of its *U.S. News* score was $12,000 per student.

The overwhelming majority of law schools probably report honest expenditure numbers, but there's no way to verify them. The larger problem with the resources component of a school's ranking is the behavior that results from its obvious incentives. The more a school spends, the better its ranking, regardless of how it uses the money. The more it charges for tuition, the more it can spend—and the more students have to borrow.

Meanwhile, students have funded their law school educations with mounting personal debt that now averages six figures by the time they graduate. In 2011, 85 percent of graduates from ABA-accredited law schools carried debt, and their average debt load exceeded $100,000. At fifty schools, the 2011 average exceeded $120,000. Coupled with the absence of legal jobs for graduates, the rising cost of a law school education has fueled intergenerational tension as an older generation squeezes a younger one.

EVERYTHING THAT YOU'VE JUST READ is publicly available information, known to law school deans throughout the country. Considering the substantial flaws in the system, why should anyone pay attention to the *U.S. News* rankings? The answer is they just do, even though some academics candidly acknowledge the pernicious impact of the resulting distortions.

For example, University of Iowa College of Law dean emeritus N. William Hines bemoans the *U.S. News* rankings while explaining their pervasive power: "The answer may be hard for someone outside the academic realm to believe, but the *U.S. News* rankings cause problems simply because too many consumers of the rankings, some of whom should know better, take them far too seriously. These consumers include central university officials, boards of trustees, legislators, alumni leaders, potential donors, faculty candidates, upwardly mobile faculty, current and prospective students." Many hiring partners at large law firms could be added to that list.

As a remedy to limit the damage that rankings inflict, Hines suggests that *U.S. News* limit itself to the top twenty-five or fifty schools, as it does with its other rankings. But he doesn't expect that to occur anytime soon: "Until such a change is made, deans will continue to be fired or retained, faculty will accept or reject offers, law firms will hire or not hire graduates, and students will enroll or not enroll on the basis of unreliable, if not misleading, information published in the *U.S. News* rankings."

Even more to the point, Hines's suggestion of limiting the rankings to the top twenty-five or fifty schools still wouldn't ameliorate the cultural impact that *U.S. News* has on those schools. In fact, Iowa has been a top-thirty school on the *U.S. News* list since the rankings began. Hines and his successors at Iowa qualify under his definition of people who "should know better." But the persistent influence of *U.S. News* rankings is still evident on that campus.

For example, rather than challenge the notion that the rankings should count at all, the school's website identifies 1991 as a milestone year in its history because "over the next fifteen years Iowa's average [*U.S. News*] rank was twenty-first among all law schools and seventh among public schools." There's no mention of its annual drops after 2006—from twenty-second to twenty-fourth to twenty-seventh—or that the school became obsessed with halting that descent.

In a March 28, 2008, email, dean Carolyn Jones told students: "The *U.S. News and World Report* law school rankings for this spring show that our ranking is 27 (down from 24 last year). Some members of [the] law school community have expressed anxiety about that change." The dean then explained that the drop a year earlier had already swung the institution's leaders into action: "Please be assured that the law school administration has not been asleep at the switch on this issue. Indeed, we have been studying the *U.S. News* rankings at a very high level over the past year. Hundreds of hours of sophisticated thought by alumni, faculty and staff have gone into this project, informally dubbed the Apollo Project. We have been considering ways of bringing new resources to the law school that will enhance our rankings and—more importantly—substantively strengthen the institution." It's not surprising that the dean's final phrase—"substantively strengthen the institution"—appears almost as an afterthought at the end of a long paragraph devoted to hand-wringing over the school's drop in rank.

Whatever else came from the "hundreds of hours of sophisticated thought" by those at "a very high level" who pondered ways to improve the school's *U.S. News* ranking, the Apollo Project didn't launch the law school to a higher place: it was twenty-sixth in 2009 and 2010 and twenty-seventh in 2011. Perhaps it's a coincidence, but the University of Iowa College of Law got a new dean in 2011. In the rankings released in March 2012, the school dropped again—into a five-way tie for twenty-ninth.

It's unlikely that the quality of legal education at Iowa has declined as steadily as its rankings slide implies. Nevertheless, the school's effort to move back up the list at *U.S. News* continues unabated. As Iowa Law's class of 2012 approached graduation, they received a memo from the associate dean reminding them to clean out their lockers and mailboxes. It included this line: "When you obtain employment, update CSO [Career Services Office]. The College reports that information to the ABA and NALP [National Association for Law Placement]. Graduate employment rates affect school rankings which can affect the college's *U.S. News and World Report* ranking."

At the highest levels of academia, administrators obsess over the *U.S. News* rankings. They can't help themselves, even though they admit they know better. They say they understand the destructive impact of the resulting behavior on their students and their institutions, yet they soldier on, claiming that they have no choice: as long as everybody else panders to the magazine's flawed methodology, they must do the same. Collectively, they're contributing to an unsustainable lawyer bubble that will someday burst. When that happens, they'll have fewer opportunities to develop creative remedies.

THERE ARE OTHER rankings that are equally facile and flawed. For years, Northwestern's website bragged about its position on another list:

"For the past three out of four years, Northwestern Law has ranked first on *Princeton Review*'s list of law schools with the best career prospects."

Other schools' websites tout their *Princeton Review* ranking, too. How meaningful is it? Here's what its "Best Career Prospects" lists looked like in 2008, 2009, 2010, and 2011:

	2008	2009	2010	2011
1.	Northwestern	Michigan	Northwestern	Pennsylvania
2.	Michigan	Northwestern	Pennsylvania	Northwestern
3.	Chicago	Virginia	Michigan	NYU
4.	Harvard	Harvard	Chicago	Vanderbilt
5.	Boston College	Boston College	Stanford	Harvard
6.	Boston University	Stanford	Boston University	Chicago
7.	Vanderbilt	Chicago	Boston College	Virginia
8.	Pennsylvania	NYU	Harvard	Michigan
9.	Virginia	Pennsylvania	NYU	Boston College
10.	Notre Dame	Boston University	Georgetown	Boston University

In 2012, the list was:

1. Northwestern
2. Chicago
3. Columbia
4. Berkeley
5. Georgetown
6. Pennsylvania
7. Vanderbilt
8. George Washington University
9. Michigan
10. NYU

The 2013 list was:

1. Columbia
2. Chicago
3. Berkeley
4. Northwestern
5. NYU
6. Harvard
7. Pennsylvania
8. Michigan
9. Stanford
10. Virginia

Some questions are obvious:

- Why did so many schools skip around so much?
- Vanderbilt ahead of Harvard and Stanford in 2011 and 2012?
- Where's Yale?

The answers lie in the methodology behind the metric. *Princeton Review* compiled its "Best Career Prospects" list as follows: "Based on school reported data and student surveys. School data include: the average starting salaries of graduating students, the percent of students immediately employed upon graduation and the percent of these students who pass the bar exam the first time they take it. Student answers to survey questions on: how much the law program encourages practical experience; the opportunities for externships, internships and clerkships, and how prepared the students feel they will be to practice the law after graduating." In other words, in addition to the flawed placement data that the schools provided to the ABA and *U.S. News*, the publication relied on student *predictions* as to how they'd fare in the job market after graduation. Somehow Yale didn't make that best career prospects list, but its consolation prize was a different *Princeton Review* distinction: "Toughest to Get Into."

The publication continues to thrive and devotes significant resources to its undoubtedly profitable ranking efforts. During the academic years from 2007 through 2011, the *Princeton Review* surveyed eighteen thousand students attending 167 law schools. In addition to a dubious list of "Best Career Prospects" and "Toughest to Get Into," it created winners in other categories that included "Best Classroom Experience," "Most Competitive Students," "Most Conservative Students," "Most Liberal Students," "Most Diverse Faculty," and more.

The *Princeton Review* rankings appear to exist so that every school will have something to brag about on its website; they even extend this courtesy to schools that don't exist. In an October 12, 2010, press release, the company announced the winner in its "Best Law Professors" category: Brown University. Brown doesn't have a law school. *Princeton Review* quickly corrected the mistake, but the pointed symbolism remains.

Then there's the school that fared so poorly in the *U.S. News* rankings that it developed a ranking system of its own: Thomas M. Cooley Law School. Based on the number of enrolled students, it's the largest law school in the country.

Now-retired Michigan supreme court chief justice Thomas E. Brennan—the man who sent one hundred lawyers a survey of ten law schools and received responses that placed a nonexistent institution, Penn State's law school, in the middle of the pack—founded Cooley in 1972. In 1996, Brennan was dissatisfied with the subjectivity of *U.S. News* rankings methodology, which placed Cooley in its unranked lower tier. So he began publishing his own recompilation of the ABA's annual data from law school accreditation questionnaires. He took forty factors in the ABA survey and weighted all of them equally—2.5 percent each.

In Brennan's system the total number of volumes in the school library counts the same as students' overall average undergraduate GPA; the relative number of librarians is just as important as the relative number of full-time teaching faculty; the number of hours that a school's library is open each week is weighted equally with its job placement rate for recent graduates. Using that method, Cooley's size gave it a big edge over all other schools in most categories. In 2010, Cooley's overall ranking according to this system was number two—just behind Harvard but well ahead of Yale (number ten), Stanford (number thirty), and the University of Chicago (number forty-one). That's not bad for a school whose expansive ABA-defined employment rate for 2010 graduates was 78.8 percent—181st out of 193 accredited law schools on Brennan's list. (After newly mandated ABA disclosures first applicable to the class of

2011, Cooley reported a 38 percent nine-month employment rate for graduates in full-time long-term jobs requiring bar passage.)

Before concluding that the Cooley ranking system is sillier than what *U.S. News* publishes, it's worth pausing to ask whether the differences between them are in degree or in kind. Perhaps allocating rankings weight to a school library's seating capacity (as Cooley does) is no more or less informative than reporting results from a nonscientific reputational survey for which the response rate is under 15 percent (as *U.S. News* does).

As LAW SCHOOLS use creative approaches to exploit the *U.S. News* and other rankings methodologies, many students might assume that the profession's leading organization, the American Bar Association, is providing meaningful oversight. If a law school says that it leads a "Best Career Prospects" list, jobs must be plentiful for those graduates. If a law school reports postgraduation employment rates exceeding 90 percent and median six-figure starting salaries, there could be no better assurance of a return on a $100,000-plus investment in a legal education. If *U.S. News & World Report* rankings list one law school ahead of another, the one ranked higher must be better.

Of course, all prospective lawyers have a continuing responsibility to educate themselves so they can make informed decisions about their future careers. But if they think that the organized bar is assisting them in that effort, they're mistaken. Even the federal government can't seem to get anywhere in the quest for greater law school candor.

In May 2011, Senator Barbara Boxer wrote to the ABA's president, Stephen Zack, about press reports of misleading employment statistics incorporated into the *U.S. News* rankings. She asked him to provide the organization's plans to ensure "accurate and transparent information for prospective law students."

In June, *U.S. News*'s Robert Morse said,

> If more detailed information on types of legal jobs and full-time and part-time employment status was available from law schools for new J.D. graduates, *U.S. News* would collect it, publish it, and—where applicable—use these more detailed job type calcu-

lations in the law school ranking methodology. If the new ABA rules are implemented, *U.S. News* will use our own law school statistical surveys in fall 2011 to collect and eventually publish the entire new richer and more detailed set of employment and jobs data from each law school for 2010 J.D. graduates. When we gather this richer data set, we will be able to make a more exact determination of how our ranking methodology will change.

In other words, *U.S. News* used flimsy data for so long because those were the only data the law schools provided. A commenter on Morse's Web post argued for a disinterested third-party audit of all law school submissions to clean up this mess: "Bob Morse could wake up tomorrow morning and announce that his new methodology requires an independent audit. But he won't, because it's not in his interest. You see, Mr. Morse works for a private party and cannot compel law schools to submit data. No doubt that if Mr. Morse required independent audited data, many schools [that] rely on misinformation simply wouldn't participate. And that would leave the *U.S. News* law school 'rankings'—the *USNWR* swimsuit issue—incomplete. And an incomplete rankings issue isn't very marketable or likely to remain the gold standard."

In July 2011, the ABA announced that in early 2012 it would begin collecting better data on employment nine months after graduation. Two months later, the committee reported that it couldn't "come to a conclusion about what definitions there should be" on questions requiring disclosure of whether law graduates' jobs were part-time or required a law degree. As publicity brought added pressure, the ABA eventually announced new requirements that schools report whether graduates were employed in full- or part-time jobs and whether law schools themselves funded the jobs. But revealing whether those jobs required a law degree or bar passage would wait until the summer of 2012—even though the ABA described that timetable as "expediting the collection and reporting" process. That all schools could have provided this information sooner is proven by the few that did, including the University of Chicago.

Then in March 2012, the ABA's Council of the Section of Legal Education and Admission to the Bar rejected a recommendation of its special Standards Review Committee that would have required the reporting of school-specific salary information for graduates. A cynic might take a close look at the people rendering that decision. Law school representatives, especially deans and former deans, dominated the council's composition. Disclosing recent graduates' salary data wouldn't make any law school look better. It's likely that many of the schools with representatives on the ABA council would look much worse to prospective applicants.

The council's chair offered this spin: "There should be no doubt that the section is fully committed to clarity and accuracy of law school placement data. Current and prospective students will now have more timely access to detailed information that will help them make important decisions." Unless, of course, the information that students seek relates to the incomes they can reasonably expect to earn after paying more than $100,000 in tuition and incurring debt that they can't discharge in bankruptcy.

The ABA's official retreat offered this explanation: "The Council specifically declined to require the collection and publication of salary data because fewer than 45% of law graduates contacted by their law schools report their salaries. The Council felt strongly that the current collection of such data is unreliable and produces distorted information."

If a 45 percent response rate is so low that it produces unreliable data and distorted information—such that all responses should be disregarded—what does that say about the data *U.S. News* relied on to calculate almost one-seventh of every law school's 2013 ranking, that is, lawyers' and judges' "quality assessment"? As previously noted, the 2011 response rate for that *U.S. News* category was only 12 percent.

In June 2012, when law schools finally released the first wave of ABA-mandated data on full-time jobs requiring a legal degree, it became clear why so many schools had resisted such disclosures for so long. Overall, nine months after graduation, only 55 percent of the 2011 class had long-term jobs requiring bar passage. Only about 8 percent of 2011 graduates secured full-time, long-term jobs at large firms of more than 250 attorneys—and only some of those jobs paid the starting salaries of $160,000 a year advertised on many law school websites. Just twelve schools reported full-time, degree-required employment rates of 80 percent or higher. More than twenty schools—10 percent of all law schools—reported employment rates under 40 percent.

With those revelations, dissembling became the order of the day. Dean Drucilla S. Ramey of Golden Gate University said that her school's 22 percent employment rate under the new definition was somehow related to the fact that many of its students "do not characteristically go to work for the larger firms or clerkships which generally select and hire much earlier than other employers." More than nine months seems like a long time for a new lawyer to be searching for work.

Whittier Law School dean Penelope Bryan saw her school's employment rate of 85 percent for 2010 graduates plummet to the bottom of the new list, with only 17 percent of 2011 graduates in full-time long-term, degree-required jobs nine months after graduation: "We consider this a problem. We have redesigned completely our career development and we expect to see some improvement, but in the meantime we've had to live with this transition." Unfortunately, a new approach to career development won't create more legal jobs for the school's graduates.

Thomas Jefferson School of Law in San Diego reported that only 27 percent of its 2011 graduates had long-term, full-time jobs requiring bar passage. A year earlier, it had reported a 68 percent employment rate under the broader definition of "employed." Dean Rudy Hasl was unapologetic: "You can't measure the value of a law degree in terms of what your employment number was nine months after graduation." He went on to explain that many employers won't even interview a new graduate who hasn't passed the California bar.

That last observation raised another issue that didn't play particularly well for Hasl's school, either. Thomas Jefferson School of Law placed last—number twenty—in the percentage of first-time California bar exam takers from California ABA-approved schools who passed the July 2011 examination. Thirty-three percent passed. The pass rate for the eighty-nine Thomas Jefferson alumni who were repeating the test in July 2011 was even lower—13 percent. The school did better in the February 2012 administration: 59 percent of first-timers passed, and several other California law schools did worse than that.

The ABA president who succeeded Stephen Zack, William Robinson III, inadvertently revealed the intergenerational antagonisms at the heart of the organization's foot-dragging. In early 2012, Robinson announced that young lawyers themselves were responsible for their unemployed, debt-ridden plight: "It's inconceivable to me that someone with a college education, or a graduate-level education, would not know before deciding to go to law school that the economy has declined over the last several years and that the job market out there is not as opportune as it might have been five, six, seven, eight years ago."

Robinson's analysis was wrong. Recent graduates about whom he spoke had made the decision to attend law school in the mid-2000s, when the economy was still booming. At that point, the growing oversupply of attorneys was already well under way but receiving little attention. Even in early 2008, those who investigated law schools saw slick promotional materials that reinforced the pervasive media image of a glamorous legal career, claimed overall new graduate employment rates exceeding 90 percent, and suggested that median salaries were in the six figures. The truth was much different. What was really happening throughout the entire decade was the creation of a lawyer bubble, thanks in large part to ABA acquiescence to law school deception.

Some might have assumed that the ABA's accreditation role meant that it policed the profession. None had any reason to believe that schools would self-report misleading statistics to the ABA and the ubiquitous *U.S. News* rankings machine, or that no one would even attempt to verify the numbers. Most law schools didn't provide greater transparency because of what economists call the prisoner's dilemma: unless all of the schools act in concert, any one school's candor risks driving down its number of applications, a component of the selectivity score.

Students haven't been blind to the economy. But schools bragging about high employment rates didn't (and don't) deter prospective lawyers. Quite the contrary: the promise of a near-certain job with a good salary makes law school as a default solution for the undecided more appealing in tough economic times. Even the relatively few undergraduates paying close attention to big-firm layoffs in 2009 were hopeful. They thought that by the time they came out of law school, the market for attorneys would improve. So did many smart, informed people. Youthful optimism isn't a sin.

That leads to ABA president Robinson's most telling comment: "We're not talking about kids who are making these decisions." If he ever had twentysomething offspring, perhaps they avoided the growing law school bubble, but the current victims are somebody's kids.

AGAINST THIS BACKGROUND, it should come as no surprise that in 2011 disgruntled alumni began suing their law schools for the deceptive conduct that left many graduates deeply in debt without realistic prospects of a job to repay it. On May 26, 2011, a graduate of the Thomas Jefferson School of Law in San Diego filed a class action on behalf of herself and all similarly situated alumni. She alleged that after receiving her degree in 2009, she hadn't been able "to secure a full time job as an attorney that pays more than the non-legal jobs available to her." She claimed that the school's misleading statistics on employment and salary defrauded her into taking on more than $150,000 in law school loans.

In August 2011, unemployed alumni filed class action lawsuits against two more law schools—Thomas M. Cooley in Michigan and New York Law School (not to be confused with NYU's law school). The same lawyers representing plaintiffs in the Cooley and New York Law School suits filed complaints against a dozen more law schools in early 2012: Albany Law School, Brooklyn Law School, California Western School of Law, Chicago-Kent College of Law, DePaul University College of Law, Florida Coastal School of Law, Golden Gate University School of Law, Hofstra Law School, John Marshall School of Law, Southwestern Law School, University of San Francisco School of Law, and Widener University School of Law. The plaintiffs' claims against each school were similar: misleading employment statistics had caused them to incur massive debt for a law degree, but when they graduated, they couldn't find jobs requiring one. The plaintiffs' attorneys promised more lawsuits against additional schools at the rate of twenty to twenty-five every few months.

In March 2012, a New York state court judge dismissed the complaint against New York Law School. The court's core ruling in a thirty-five-page opinion was that the disgruntled alumni—"a sophisticated subset of education consumers"—should have known better. But the court acknowledged that the absence of a legal remedy should not become an excuse to avoid the large and growing lawyer bubble:

> There is no question that this dearth of [legal job] opportunity is an unprecedented situation in the modern history of the practice of law and it simply cannot be ignored. If lawsuits such as this

have done nothing else, they have served to focus the attention of *all* constituencies on this current problem facing the legal profession. . . . All must take a long, hard look at the current situation with the utmost seriousness of purpose. . . . [I]t is this court's fervent hope that all the heat generated around this issue over this last year will be replaced with a renewed sense of responsibility to prospective applicants and students, starting at the law school level, and extending to the entire legal industry as we strive to address the concerns that have risen to the surface in this changed, challenging career environment.

The judge's strong words were small consolation to any unemployed graduate who had incurred six-figure, nondischargeable debt for a legal degree and couldn't find a job with which to repay it.

On February 7, 2012, when a local television reporter asked dean David Yellen of the Loyola University Chicago School of Law what would happen if former students won their lawsuits seeking tuition refunds for several years' worth of still-unemployed graduates, he replied, "Those schools would probably go out of business." Deans have never considered that risk metric in a strategic or management plan.

IN DEFIANCE OF UNAMBIGUOUS DATA and disturbing trends, new law schools have continued to come on line: University of California at Irvine (2009), University of Massachusetts (2010), Belmont (Tennessee) University College of Law (2011), Indiana Tech Law School (2013), Louisiana College Pressler School of Law (2013), University of North Texas at Dallas College of Law (2014). Taxpayer dollars are getting some of them off the ground. Students who take out loans to pay tuition will keep all of them going.

In the current environment, using public funds to build additional law schools seems perverse. Perhaps supporters hope that state schools will be less expensive for students and/or drive more expensive private competitors out of business. On that theory, a reduced debt burden would also free students to follow less lucrative but more personally rewarding careers.

Such hopes require several leaps of faith. Although students graduating from public law schools have lower average debt than their private law school counterparts, both numbers for the class of 2011 were daunting: $75,700 (public) versus $125,000 (private). Moreover, it's not clear how much of the difference results from a divergence between tuition rates at public and private schools. Some state schools—the University of Michigan Law School, Boalt Hall at the University of California at Berkeley, the University of Virginia School of Law, and others—now charge as much for tuition as the most expensive private schools. At other public law schools, nonresidents pay tuition that likewise approaches that of their private counterparts. The long list of public institutions in this category includes the University of Texas at Austin, University of Minnesota, University of Washington, Arizona State University, Indiana University (Maurer School of Law), University of Iowa, University of Illinois, George Mason University, Ohio State University, and many others.

Likewise, history suggests that public schools aren't a panacea for the current problems. As an empirical proposition over the past twenty years, public law schools haven't displaced private ones; there's little reason to expect that situation to change over the next twenty. For example, Thomas M. Cooley Law School is private, has four campuses in Michigan, and charges full-time students more than $34,000 a year for tuition. Recently it opened a new campus in the Tampa Bay area of Florida, where more than a hundred students promptly enrolled—twice the number administrators expected—for September 2012.

The track record of state-funded law schools suggests that they have far to go before offering themselves as meaningful solutions to the lawyer bubble. In fact, commentator Matt Leichter takes an aggressively hostile stance toward public law schools, calling them obsolete because there are "more than enough private law schools throughout the country to meet the country's lawyer needs." He concludes: "We are slowly approaching the endgame for public law schools. Once state governments no longer consider training lawyers a public good, by cutting subsidies, public law schools mutate into vestigial state structures whose agendas are orthogonal to any public purpose, unless using their students' tuition for other university programs counts. They should either be privatized or closed."

Wholly apart from Leichter's extreme recommendation, the simple fact is that the number of unemployed new lawyers grows by tens of thousands every year. Encouraging even more students to incur crippling loans so they can fill new law schools as they're built isn't the answer. To the contrary, such behavior suggests a market incapable of self-correction, a profession inept at self-regulation, and a generation of so-called leaders who are willing to exploit their children and grandchildren.

CHAPTER 3

INADEQUATE
RESPONSES

I gather change is afoot at some law schools,
but it's going to be very slow.
—Scott B. Connolly, partner in the Philadelphia-based law firm
Drinker, Biddle & Reath, November 2011

WITH EVIDENCE of the growing lawyer bubble everywhere and the scope of its potential damage increasing daily, it's reasonable to ask whether any of the key players are responding appropriately to the crisis. The short answer is no. The American Bar Association's policies work with *U.S. News & World Report* rankings to deter educators otherwise inclined toward better policies, but those aren't the only obstacles to needed reform. Others include the academic tenure system, institutional inertia, the desires of students themselves, and federal legislation protecting the special interests that benefit from the bubble. Taken together, all of this constitutes a formidable barrier to necessary innovation. As a result, rather than pursue some of the more dramatic solutions to which this book will turn in Part III, most deans inclined toward any action at all find themselves hoping that the problems will go away, or at most tinkering at the edges.

Some of that tinkering is downright silly. In July 2010, Loyola Law School Los Angeles retroactively added 0.333 to every grade recorded in the last few years. At the time, at least ten other schools had "deliberately changed their grading systems to make them more lenient" since 2008. Schools across a wide range have used the tactic—including New York University, Georgetown, the University of Southern California, the University of California Hastings College of Law, Vanderbilt, and Golden Gate University. Evidently the goal was to make their students look more attractive to prospective employers.

Another, more substantive kind of tinkering consists of the popular drive to make law school curricula more relevant. Critics correctly observe that the standard course of study has changed very little over the last century. For a student's first two years, the emphasis is theoretical. Universally, first-year contracts courses dwell on the policies and principles behind offer, acceptance, consideration, breach, and damages. But students emerge from the experience unable to prepare a simple contract that a real client could use. Property law courses teach the intricacies of feudal estates in land, but not how to buy or sell a house. Civil procedure teaches the nuances of federal court jurisdiction, but not how to draft a simple complaint, much less file it with the court and serve it on a defendant. Criminal law classes focus on the elements of various crimes, but they offer little guidance in handling a client who calls after being arrested, and, while they explore the constitutional rights that underlie criminal trials, they don't prepare a lawyer to navigate through the world of plea bargaining, the mechanism that has resolved the overwhelming majority of criminal cases for decades.

The second year follows the same pattern: students taking corporation law don't learn how to prepare the documents needed to create a corporation or close a merger. The federal taxation class doesn't help anyone prepare a tax return or deal with an IRS audit. There are exceptions: elective courses on trial advocacy and the Federal Rules of Evidence have practical value, and some professors teaching estate planning require students to draft a simple will. But by and large, the first two years of law school focus on the intellectual aspects of legal thought, rather than the nuts and bolts of practice.

Learning to think like a lawyer is essential. But a greater nod to practicality, which is also needed, would fly in the face of what lawyers love: precedent. Just as Harvard's nineteenth-century dean Christopher Columbus Langdell put in place a system of legal education that lent itself to mass production of attorneys, he also bears some of the blame for the continuing emphasis of theory over practice. He moved Harvard's curriculum away from specific types of legal training toward more general principles of universal application, and other schools followed him.

His approach oriented legal education away from the set of skills that lawyers need to practice law.

Why Langdell's model has survived largely intact is an important question. Some critics blame tenure: academics with lifetime jobs can pursue parochial research interests. For too many, their specialized areas of study have little relationship to what happens in the real world. This argument implicates complicated questions relating to the merits of tenure and could consume another book. But the abbreviated version is that, on one hand, law school professors are supposed to prepare students to enter the legal profession—a place where lawyers grapple with client problems. On the other hand, they also have to survive in an academic world where "publish or perish" remains a central mantra. In addition, ABA accreditation standards reinforce traditional notions of a tenured faculty.

Tenure discussions have led to the controversy over legal scholarship. Like other academics, law professors seek to disseminate their ideas in specialized journals. The six hundred law-school-sponsored reviews in the United States exist primarily for that purpose and publish ten thousand articles a year, some of which contribute to the ongoing development of the law. Between 2001 and 2011, United States Supreme Court justices cited at least one law review article in nearly 40 percent of the Court's two thousand opinions. In 21 percent of cases, majority opinions cited such articles.

The problem is that 40 percent of all law review articles are never cited in any judicial opinion anywhere. Even ideologically diverse United States Supreme Court justices have agreed that too many law professors devote their time to meaningless discourse. In 2008, associate justice Stephen G. Breyer said, "There is evidence that law review articles have left terra firma to soar into outer space." In 2011, chief justice John G. Roberts Jr. observed, "Pick up a copy of any law review that you see, and the first article is likely to be, you know, the influence of Immanuel Kant on evidentiary approaches in 18th century Bulgaria, or something, which I'm sure was of great interest to the academic that wrote it, but isn't of much help to the bar." (As a third-year student during the academic year 1978–1979, Roberts was managing editor of the *Harvard Law Review*.)

Closely related to the dynamic of academic tenure is the absence of significant real-world experience on the resumes of most law school professors. Increasingly, schools are responding to the cry for practical training by employing adjuncts to supervise clinical work and teach practical courses, mostly for third-year law students. Subjects include trial practice, sports law, corporate reorganizations, and the like. Adjuncts provide another benefit: they're far less expensive than tenure-track professors, who typically consume about 80 percent of the faculty budget. But in the end, adjuncts are just that—adjuncts—and not central players in a law school's culture.

As a consequence, some tenured professors create daunting problems for deans trying to modernize law school curricula. For starters, most law professors have taken a similar path into academia. After graduating near the top of their law school classes, with the added credential of service on the school's law review, they went on to selective judicial clerkships. Some practiced for a year or two before returning to law schools as teachers. There are exceptions, but that's the traditional track to the classroom lectern. In fact, the trend toward interdisciplinary education in many law schools has resulted in recruiting professors who have both a JD and a PhD—that is, instructors who have spent even more time in the academic world and less time becoming familiar with the work that practicing lawyers actually perform.

Institutional inertia sets in when, understandably, faculty members without real-world experience resist demands from deans that they teach practical skills. At the time that these individuals chose to become law professors, practicing law wasn't a prerequisite. In fact, sometimes it was a disadvantage. One longtime lawyer and adjunct professor said that the stigma associated with actual experience "can be fatal, because the academy wants people who are not sullied by the practice of law. A lot of people who are good at big ideas, the people who teach at law school, think it is beneath them."

The career of United States Supreme Court associate justice Elena Kagan illustrates the problem. In 1995, she won tenure at the University of Chicago Law School. Four years later, she went to work as a senior adviser in the Clinton administration. When she left government in 1999, Kagan hoped to return to Chicago, but the invitation never came. The concern was that she hadn't produced a sufficient quantity of scholarly writing. Seizing an opportunity that the University of Chicago had missed, Harvard jumped into the breach and hired her. She rose to dean of that law school and then returned to government service as solicitor general of the United States in the Obama administration on her way to the nation's top court.

The University of Chicago's provost, Geoffrey Stone, had supported Kagan's reappointment there. He noted, "She was very disappointed. She'd gone from being adviser to the president to being basically unemployed—at least for the moment." Richard A. Epstein, a prominent libertarian and a longtime professor at the University of Chicago, offered his assessment: "Her papers were well-done, but they show exactly the same qualities of mind that prevent you from reaching the top ranks of academia." Devoted scholars, he continued, "take a small problem, make it smaller, break it into pieces, see if it will fit back together." A prolific writer and commentator since graduating from Yale Law School in 1968, Epstein's full-time work experience has been almost entirely academic.

To their credit, some deans have fought through institutional inertia, ABA accreditation criteria, and the constraints of the tenure system to make significant strides in providing students with more practical training. Many law schools now offer courses that help students develop skills such as interviewing clients, deposing witnesses, conducting court hearings, writing briefs, and negotiating with adversaries. The ability to handle such tasks competently will help them make a living if they hang out their own shingle.

For example, Stanford Law School has revamped its curriculum and expanded clinical opportunities. Washington and Lee University School of Law replaced lectures and seminars with "case-based simulations run by practicing lawyers." As dean, Elena Kagan turned Harvard's focus from the faculty to the students by dividing the class into smaller sections and updating the curriculum to consider globalization, teach alternative dispute resolution, and emphasize clinical programs. Indiana University Maurer School of Law teaches "project management" and "emotional intelligence." NYU offers courses in "negotiation" and "client counseling."

But there's a catch. As worthwhile as such initiatives may be, they should not offer false comfort to prospective lawyers who think that better job prospects will result. The sad truth is that the impact of such practical programs on the lawyer bubble is nil: none is making students more desirable to prospective employers. When asked whether current law school innovations will help new graduates get jobs, the recruiting committee chair of the large Washington, D.C.–based law firm Hogan Lovells said: "It could enhance the reputation of the law school . . . as places that will produce lawyers who have practical skills. As to the particular student when I'm interviewing them? It doesn't make much of a difference."

The same is true beyond the world of the big law firms: "There's no employer out there right now—not law firms, not the Department of Justice, not the ACLU—that [is] seeking out these graduates," Indiana University Maurer School of Law professor William Henderson observed. "These programs haven't affected hiring patterns. It's still all sorted out with credentials. It's based on the brand of the law school."

More emphasis on practical education may be valuable, but it's no solution to the lawyer bubble.

THE INCREASING COST of getting a law degree combined with law graduates' diminishing job prospects is forcing deans to demonstrate the value of the educational experience. In addition to complaints about outdated curricula, particular attention has turned to law school's third year, traditionally thought of as a waste of time. Many schools have expanded clinical programs in that year. But one radical innovation—compressing the time for legal study—is actually counterproductive.

For all of its faults, the first year of Socratic-method instruction in mandatory subjects trains students to think like lawyers. That is, students enhance their analytical skills, learn to distinguish relevant facts from irrelevant ones, develop the ability to construct and express a tight legal argument, and become familiar with the entirely new language of the law. Most first-year students find themselves tackling the experience in self-formed study groups, which often become petri dishes for paranoia.

The second year is more relaxed. The environment, teaching method, and language are no longer new. Professors who relied on intimidation and fear as teaching tools in dealing with first-year students adopt more positive forms of student engagement. The study groups that were a universal part of the first-year experience disappear, freeing up the time previously devoted to them. Students who studied for sixty hours a week during the first year find themselves getting by with forty in year two.

By year three, most students' principal aim is simply to get out of law school and get on with life. Class attendance drops; participation among those who show up is not particularly enthusiastic. In that context, clinical programs with the opportunity to work with real clients become a godsend.

Why does the third year of law school exist? Because almost all states require graduation from ABA-accredited schools, and related curriculum standards mandate course work consuming three traditional academic years. By the third year, the entire course of study is elective: students can take whatever they want. But law schools also make big money on the third year—one-third of all tuition revenues—so deans have no incentive to lobby for its elimination. Even so, the pressure from students to do something that shortens the duration of law school so as to reduce its cost has continued to build.

For example, in its 2008 long-range strategic plan, Northwestern's law school noted, "Almost everyone who participated in our focus groups [consisting of alumni, faculty, government attorneys, and leaders of big law firms] agreed that the third year of J.D. programs could be restructured to provide more value, and a significant number of participants believed that the third year could be eliminated entirely." Those views led Northwestern to become the first top law school offering an accelerated JD, joining a handful of less prominent schools with programs that move students through law school in two calendar years. That may sound like an improvement, but for participating students, it seems destined to make the overall law school experience worse while increasing the size of the lawyer bubble.

Once enrolled, Northwestern's accelerated students cram three years of academic work into two, starting with a Web-based course even before they arrive on campus and beginning full-time study in May. They continue into the fall and spring with the typically rigorous first-year academic schedule—*plus* an extra course throughout—as they compete with traditional second-year students in interviews for summer jobs. While contemplating the wisdom of such a regimen, ask any attorney what the rigorous first year of law school would have been like if another class had been added to the ordeal. For anyone on a two-year accelerated path, an already precious commodity—time during the first year to integrate experiences while contemplating one's place in a diverse and challenging profession—disappears.

As for other beneficial aspects of a balanced and holistic legal education, Northwestern assures accelerated students that they will have "the opportunity to participate in all extracurricular and co-curricular activities, including journals." But when the writing competition for the school's most prestigious publication, *Northwestern Law Review*, rolls around after fall semester grades during the already overburdened first year, it probably doesn't look appealing to them. Perhaps Northwestern has devised a way for accelerated students to reach editorial positions; at other schools, they're reserved exclusively for third-year students. Such law review positions are also gateways to judicial clerkships and academic careers.

In exchange for an experience that seems far worse than the traditional three-year program, Northwestern's accelerated JD candidates don't even save on their tuition. They pay the same as the three-year people because Northwestern prices the degree, not the time spent getting it. Two-year program participants receive a single financial benefit: they enter the workforce sooner, if they can get jobs.

In his keynote address to a *Southwestern Law Review* symposium (Southwestern was the first American law school to establish an accelerated JD program), David Van Zandt gave various reasons for pushing the two-year program. One was to "tap a different population of students to expand our pool of potential applicants." In particular, he hoped to "reach those who were planning on going to MBA programs."

In fact, as Northwestern rolled out its new program, demand for new associates in big firms was declining dramatically. In 2011, Northwestern sent 149 new graduates to the 250 largest law firms, down from 172 in 2007. But the school's total number of JD degrees awarded went from 265 to 288. Northwestern's strategic Plan 2008 envisioned adding another sixty accelerated JDs someday. In October 2015, Van Zandt's successor as dean suspended the accelerated JD program indefinitely.

LURKING BEHIND law schools' current efforts to innovate is the specter of too few jobs for their graduates. The way schools now deal with job placement reflects their attempts to spread the pain of the lawyer bubble's deleterious effects, rather than to shrink the bubble itself. Throughout the evolution of the placement process over the past three decades, one constant has remained: the top law schools focus on putting their graduates in large firms. This phenomenon reflects the desires of both the schools and their students.

The law schools' incentives are straightforward. Placing lots of graduates in high-paying jobs makes a school more attractive to prospective applicants. Moreover, in addition to being important consumers of what law schools produce, namely, new attorneys, many big firms and their wealthy partners have become important financial benefactors to the schools. Big law firms have endowed faculty chairs and donated enough money to get their names on classrooms, lounges, and living areas. In short, such firms are a customer and donor constituency that law schools ignore at their economic peril. Finally, compared to finding other jobs for their students, placement in big firms is easy. As a group, large law firms still hire more entry-level lawyers from top law schools than any other single category of legal employer. Compared to the time and effort required to help individual students pursue other career interests, schools find it relatively easy to set up on-campus interviews, where the big firms' recruiting begins. From there, the law firms control the process to its conclusion.

The student side of the equation is more complicated. According to a recent survey, almost 40 percent of pre-law students hope to land a job at a large law firm. About 15 percent of them actually will. Even for students who begin law school with wide-eyed idealism that would take them on a different path, external forces quickly conspire against them. In the first year, they encounter second-year students actively seeking employment as summer interns in big firms, especially if they attend a top law school, and peer pressure combines with competitive instincts to push most students in the same direction. Well-meaning parents and others provide subtle and, at times, not-so-subtle reinforcement. After all, one goal in attending law school is to become a member of the legal profession and make a decent living. Big firms have a large edge when it comes to the decent living component.

By the time second-year interviews roll around, some students have started to focus more intently on the troublesome six-figure debt that they're incurring for their legal degrees. Covering the monthly payments that will start soon after they graduate requires a well-paying job. Even those who might prefer a type of legal career outside the big firms must think practically about how they will support themselves.

Regardless of students' ultimate goals, anyone seeking a job in a big law firm follows a process that has become more challenging in recent years. Such firms have always confined their recruiting to the top law schools, but in earlier days the hiring process was relatively simple. After students submitted their resumes, the school's placement office would set up interview schedules whereby firm representatives would see interested candidates, typically spending an entire day or two conducting twenty- or thirty-minute sessions with each of them. After these on-campus interviews, the law firm notified students selected for additional screening in the firm's offices. Within a few days after those follow-up interviews, students would hear from the firm that it was either offering a summer position or declining to do so. Those receiving offers took as much time as they wanted to make a decision. They were also free to interview with as many firms as they desired.

With the growing shortage of jobs, law schools have rationed student opportunities. Typically, schools now limit the number of firms that a student can select for initial on-campus interviews. At some schools, students submit resumes and list their desired interviews. Law firms then use those resumes to select their preferred candidates. The intersection of the student and law firm preferences produces interview schedules for both.

A relatively new company, JD Match, has created an algorithm designed to match students and law firms in accordance with their respective preferences. In that system, firms list the number of slots they have available and rank the students they'd most like to hire, in order of preference. Students rank the firms for which they'd most like to work, in their order of preference. On "match day" during the traditional law student recruiting seasons, the results are revealed.

But the most profound impact on law student placement comes from another outside organization, the National Association for Law Placement (NALP). Created in 1971 by a small group of law schools and firms, NALP's original aim was "to promote the exchange of information and cooperation between law schools and employers." It has since morphed into a governing body that regulates the entire job placement process for all schools and big law firms. Unfortunately, although NALP's board consists of representatives from law schools and large firms, its rules have evolved to benefit the firms at students' expense. For

example, NALP's 2010 guideline relating to student job searches gives
students limited time to consider job offers, but it doesn't require uni-
form dates for firms to make them. In practice, this forces students to
accept a job even before they know all of their options.

Today's law students confront immutable deadlines, but law firms
can make rolling offers at their pleasure and revoke them at will. Even
an accepted offer can turn out to be bogus when the employer later
withdraws or defers it. During the Great Recession, that happened to
many graduates in the class of 2009, and they had no recourse.

YET TUITION MONEY continues to flow into law schools as students
accumulate burgeoning educational debt. Recent federal efforts to deal
with that problem have been insufficient to slow the growth of the
lawyer bubble. In fact, Indiana University Maurer School of Law professor William Henderson is concerned that one innovation—
income-based repayment (IBR) plans for students with direct loans
from the government—could make some aspects of the situation worse.
He argues that the current student loan financing system is not only encouraging the production of too many lawyers but also setting the stage
for potentially massive increases in future federal debt.

IBR plans allow graduates to repay direct federal loans in proportion
to their income for twenty years, at which time any outstanding balance
is forgiven. Graduates who adhere to that schedule of reduced payments
for the entire period never repay their loans in full. As the lawyer bubble
grows, well-paying jobs become scarce, and incomes for new attorneys
fall, the federal government could find itself holding debt worth far less
than its face value when originally issued. Although the debt forgiveness
option has allowed federal lending to dominate the direct loan market in
recent years, there's evidence that private lenders are trying to make a
comeback. The nondischargeability rule continues to give them special
protection against the risk of losses.

Henderson notes another problem with the program. For attorneys
who never get a job that justifies their law degrees economically, IBR
may be an improvement over previous alternatives, but requiring up to
15 percent of monthly income in student loan repayments operates as a
severe tax on their current resources. Twenty years is a long time to

labor in a job that leaves insufficient funds to save for retirement or for the expense of sending offspring to college.

Likewise, loan forgiveness is available for attorneys who work full-time in public service positions, but such programs typically require a ten-year commitment (except for a few law schools that supplement the federal plan with funds that give pro rata relief for those who fail to complete the ten-year minimum). Although the federal government could be left holding the bag after twenty years of IBR or ten years of public service, graduates themselves will bear the burden of reduced incomes throughout those periods.

In the end, the entire system produces predictable results. Private lenders have limited risk and little accountability. They have no reason to ask tough questions that might help prospective lawyers consider more carefully the wisdom of an expensive legal career before they apply to law school. In its role as a lender, the federal government has no process by which to begin such a conversation with a prospective law student. Law schools have little incentive to control tuition costs (and the *U.S. News* rankings encourage deans in the opposite direction). Meanwhile, student loan money for law school flows, and the lawyer bubble grows.

SOME DEANS DESERVE CREDIT for trying to grapple with the problems that the lawyer bubble continues to create. But notwithstanding the praiseworthy efforts on the part of a few, including deans who recently have announced plans to reduce entering class size, a key difficulty remains: a failure of vision. As deans focus on their law schools' bottom-line financial performance over the short term, the long-run future of their students becomes someone else's problem. Beginning almost immediately after they graduate from law school, too many new attorneys experience a profound failure of expectations. Whether it's discovering their limited prospects of finding a law job or realizing that a previously imagined life in a coveted firm position is more Gordon Gekko than Atticus Finch, many succumb to the psychological distress and career dissatisfaction all too common among lawyers. It's a special problem for big law firms, which are supposed to be the profession's beacons. Most of them are making things worse.

PART II
BIG LAW FIRMS

CHAPTER 4

ATTORNEY DISSATISFACTION

*Only four out of ten lawyers who have been practicing ten years
or more would recommend a legal career to a young person.*
—"The Pulse of the Profession,"
ABA Journal, October 1, 2007

FOR THE MOST PART, I enjoyed law school. That doesn't mean it was easy or without stress. In 1986, Professor G. Andrew Benjamin found that the proportion of students experiencing symptoms of depression increased from 4 percent for entering students to 40 percent by the third year. Professors Lawrence Krieger and Ken Sheldon blame the structure of legal education and students' emphasis on external rewards, such as grades and class rank. Yet somehow, a recent and wide-ranging survey reported that more than 80 percent of today's students are satisfied with their legal education. If so many students find their law school experiences satisfying, then the much higher levels of reported attorney dissatisfaction with their careers must develop after graduation. In turn, career dissatisfaction certainly exacerbates psychological distress. For the profession and for society generally, it's important to understand why so many lawyers find themselves in unfulfilling careers.

The search for happiness isn't new, but recent trends raise important questions. In particular, modern science reaffirms the value of a satisfied workforce generally and, as with just about everything else, today's researchers have developed methods of quantifying the dollar impact. Harvard Business School professor Teresa Amabile and fellow researcher Steven Kramer have found that "negative inner work lives" resulted in "a profound impact on workers' creativity, productivity, commitment and collegiality." Gallup-Healthways estimates that America's disengagement crisis—that is, workers' apathy toward their organizations and detachment from their jobs—costs $300 billion annually in lost profitability. Well-being also affects a person's health and, therefore, a society's medical care costs. At a time of straining government budgets, increasing debt, and enduring deficits, the current focus on career satisfaction is especially appropriate.

Lawyers provide fertile ground for examining the relationship between a person's job and the enjoyment it provides. Attorney job dissatisfaction is ubiquitous, especially in big law firms, where, ironically, financial rewards are the greatest. One important reason is that in most large firms, the gap between a new law school graduate's expectations and the reality of life as a young associate is especially sizable. Even worse, the continuing evolution of the prevailing business model for big law firms is making that gap even larger. Obsession with immediate results is exacerbating problems for the long run.

It's important to note at the outset that the profession isn't homogeneous or monolithic; some types of attorneys have better odds of a satisfying career than others. For example, a 2007 ABA survey looked at reported rates of attorney satisfaction based on type of practice:

Type of Practice	Percent Satisfied
Public sector	68
Medium-sized firms (21 to 100 lawyers)	58
Small firms (2 to 20 lawyers)	57
Solo practitioners	53
In-house lawyers	49
Large firms (101+ lawyers)	44

These results confirmed what many lawyers knew: there are more satisfied attorneys in the public sector than anywhere else. An important reason is that they have opportunities to perform work that feels meaningful. What they do often makes an immediate difference in people's lives. Compared to lawyers at large firms, public sector attorneys also function with greater autonomy, although both settings require coping with organizational hierarchies. Public sector lawyers are also more likely to perform the kinds of tasks that they expected to do when they decided to apply to law school.

An example is Francis Wolfe Jr., who returned to law school after a thirty-year career as a successful commodities trader at the Chicago Board of Trade. Upon graduating from Loyola University Chicago School of Law in 1998, he went to work as a public defender at age sixty-eight. When he retired eight years later, he described his respect for those who toiled in an underappreciated field: "From the time I was in law school until now, I stand in awe of these people [public defenders]. You have the most extraordinarily talented people laboring for these poor people. . . . I was talking to a person in lockup, and he said to me, 'Sir, I've been to the joint seven times, and you're the first person who's ever talked to me like a human being.'"

Attorneys in big firms seem to be the biggest losers in the career satisfaction contest. But a word of caution is appropriate for the ABA's survey category of "large law firm"—which many other surveys likewise report as having the greatest percentage of dissatisfied attorneys. The definition lumps together those with a single office of 101 lawyers and global behemoths with thousands of attorneys in locations around the world. The National Association for Law Placement subdivides large firms into three subgroups: 101 to 250 attorneys, 251 to 500, and 501 or more. NALP reports separate rates and ranges of hiring and departures for each. The differences across the various categories are significant. As later chapters discuss, the lawyer dissatisfaction problem has worsened as big firms have become bigger.

The prevailing model of the big law firm bears much of the blame for increasing dissatisfaction among attorneys in such institutions. Too often, the model deprives lawyers of autonomy, creates an environment that rewards selfish behavior, and does little to promote collegiality. As for their daily tasks, most big-firm attorneys spend the vast majority of their time on small slices of large cases or transactions. Those matters can be financially lucrative and professionally rewarding for the firm's senior partners, but junior attorneys often feel little connection to an overall mission.

A comprehensive longitudinal study, published as *After the JD*, has been monitoring a sample of 4,500 lawyers who first became members of the bar in 2000. The resulting data on career dissatisfaction corroborates the ABA survey finding that attorneys in big firms are among the most dissatisfied. In fact, lawyers from elite schools working in prestigious large firms are the least satisfied with their decision to become lawyers. Just two years after graduation, almost 60 percent of those new big-firm lawyers from top-ten schools said they expected to leave their jobs within the next two years. Maybe that's because, as discussed later, they expected to lose their jobs anyway; the prevailing big-firm model survives on staggering associate turnover rates—another contributor to attorney dissatisfaction. Only one-fourth said they were extremely satisfied with the decision to become a lawyer.

Interestingly, graduates from lower-ranked law schools reported higher satisfaction in all practice settings. Perhaps the more satisfied young lawyers from those schools had lower expectations about their careers. Maybe some saw their own sacrifices as the price of professional status that would secure them and their progeny a place in a higher socioeconomic class. Additional research might yield answers.

Still, it's important to remember that, despite the stereotypes, there are satisfied attorneys everywhere. A solo practitioner, Scott Forschein, describes a common thread that runs through many of them. Forschein finds professional rewards in the Brooklyn South traffic court: "I make a difference. For me, the stakes are just right. No one's going to jail for life, or making millions of dollars." A recent Valentine's Day issue of the *ABA Journal* quoted lawyers of every type who offered similar explanations of how they'd found professional satisfaction by helping people deal with their legal problems:

> I love being a lawyer because when I stand up before a jury and thank my clients for the privilege of representing them (and I usually feel pretty emotional whenever I say that, with chills) I realize I am being trusted to present them, what they feel, what they believe. And I take that very seriously.

> I get to think through problems every day for people I really like.

> I love being a lawyer because I can make a difference in someone's life.

America is a society based on law and justice. I love the fact that I have a role in making this ideal a reality, however small.

I was a practicing civil attorney for 57 years. I loved my profession because it gave me an opportunity to be of service. I always asked myself one question: What can I do to help the client? What advice can I provide that will be of some benefit? If you provide real and meaningful legal services, you will be properly compensated. I enjoyed every day and pursued my work with passion.

Aside from the sense that they're helping others, several common themes run through the ranks of satisfied attorneys; many aren't unique to lawyers. As already noted, personal autonomy and the fulfillment that comes with making meaningful contributions are important. Another theme is that those who understand in advance both the advantages and the downside of their contemplated careers are more likely to find a workday reality that matches their expectations than those who don't. Finally, the law is a career in which understanding one's own personality and predilections can help to produce a satisfying career. Those who know themselves well are more likely to find a job that suits them.

THE QUESTION BECOMES whether something special about lawyers or the profession accounts for the statistic to which any discussion of unhappy lawyers invariably returns: 20 percent of all attorneys will suffer from clinical depression at some point in their careers—three and a half times the rate for the rest of the workforce. This oft-repeated statistic comes from a 1990 Johns Hopkins University study. Although some aspects of the study's methodology and conclusions are suspect, subsequent research has confirmed that lawyers generally suffer from high rates of career dissatisfaction, alcoholism, and substance abuse—more indicia of a distressed profession.

The Johns Hopkins researchers didn't set out to find depressed lawyers; they merely used data that others had already collected as part of a larger study of mental health issues. The five-site survey estimated the prevalence and incidence of several categories of psychopathology, including major depressive disorder. Mental health professionals had followed a sophisticated scientific protocol in collecting data from more than eighteen thousand people working in 105 different occupations. The respondents were clerks, salespeople, waiters, secretaries, hairdressers, police officers, teachers, truck drivers, senior executives, carpenters, doctors, mechanics, and many others, including lawyers. A trained cadre of lay interviewers used the American Psychiatric Association's latest standards in mimicking a typical counseling session aimed at diagnosing mental disorders.

Years after the data were collected, a Johns Hopkins research team analyzed them, focusing on a single diagnostic category: major depressive disorder. To qualify for inclusion, a person had to satisfy the following diagnostic criteria: a period of two or more weeks of sadness, accompanied by symptoms in four or more of the following eight groups: appetite, sleep, fatigue, slowing of bodily movements or of thought, feeling worthless or sinful, loss of pleasure in something usually enjoyed, difficulty concentrating, and suicidal thoughts, desires, or attempts.

The statistical validity of the Johns Hopkins study is questionable. Most notably, the sample size of only fifty-two lawyers is small and the confidence interval of 1.374 to 9.286, which sets the range within which the stated result could actually fall, is large. (The large confidence interval implies that the true depression rate for lawyers could be anywhere from 37 percent above the rate found for the overall workforce [1.374 compared to 1.0] to more than nine times greater [9.286 compared to 1.0].) Even so, subsequent surveys seem to confirm a central point: as a group, lawyers are in psychological distress. The 2007 ABA survey mentioned above found that just over half of all responding attorneys were satisfied with their careers. Another recent ABA survey estimated that rates of alcoholism and substance abuse among lawyers are double the national average.

THERE ARE SOME DISSENTING VOICES to the perception of attorney despair, but either they're not persuasive or they ultimately corroborate the view that a significant portion of the profession is unhappy. For example, Northwestern University researchers surveyed Chicago lawyers in 1995 and found more satisfied attorneys than the conventional wisdom had suggested. But as the authors note, their methodology had an important caveat: they used face-to-face interviews, during which attorneys self-reported their job satisfaction—or admitted their dissatisfaction—to a stranger. Their answers may have been "biased toward the positive side of the scale by the respondents' desire to present themselves as successful persons. They may be reluctant to admit, to others or to themselves, that they made poor choices." Additionally, the profession has continued to undergo dramatic change since 1995, and the prevailing trends have made life more difficult for most attorneys.

Likewise, in twenty-eight national and regional surveys of lawyers from 1984 to 2008, the number of respondents who felt positive about their work ranged from 67 percent to 80 percent—with one outlier. A 1989 study reported a stunning 91 percent satisfaction rate from a survey of 770 attorneys who were children of lawyers. That study is outdated, but there may be a simple explanation for its unusual finding: children who grew up watching their parents practicing law probably entered the profession with a better idea of what was ahead of them. Reducing the gap between expectations and reality is bound to produce a greater number of satisfied attorneys.

NO SURVEY OR STUDY can or would suggest that all attorneys are miserable. The problem is that in a country with more than 1 million lawyers, 750,000 of whom are practicing, even the lowest dissatisfaction estimates still produce 150,000 to 200,000 unhappy attorneys. Even more disturbing would be the responses from those who never participate in such surveys because they can't get jobs that require a law degree or their feelings about their legal careers drove them out of the profession. (Of course, some nonpracticing lawyers have used their law degrees to pursue other rewarding careers.) Equally telling is the attitude of a large cohort of satisfied lawyers—those with over ten years' experience. Fewer than half responding to the 2007 ABA survey said that they would recommend law school to a young person.

Nor is there much consolation in the thought that workers in other jobs might be just as unhappy as lawyers are. According to a report published by the University of Chicago's National Opinion Research Center in April 2007, lawyers occupied the second-highest rank in occupational prestige. But they experienced job satisfaction rates languishing far behind many others, including clergy (87 percent satisfied), firefighters (80 percent), physical therapists (78 percent), authors (74 percent), teachers (69 percent), education administrators (68 percent), painters (67 percent), and psychologists (67 percent). Attorneys do, however, maintain a comfortable job satisfaction margin over butchers (32 percent satisfied), waiters (27 percent), bartenders (26 percent), and roofers (25 percent).

IT'S POSSIBLE THAT SOME COMPONENT of widespread dissatisfaction within the legal profession relates to the type of individual drawn to law school. Proponents of this "lawyer personality" theory argue that those with a particular set of traits gravitate toward the law. The posited characteristics include a marked drive to achieve, a preference for impersonal and strictly logical approaches to problem solving, a "masculine" orientation favoring dominance, aggression, and competitiveness, and an emphasis on rights and obligations over emotions and interpersonal relations. The argument is that the experience of law school and, thereafter, an attorney's work reinforce such characteristics to the detriment of such individuals' emotional health. Under this theory, the traits and predispositions common to lawyers have guided them into careers that actually exacerbate their misery.

The implications of the lawyer personality theory are that most unhappy attorneys are simply getting the life they have chosen and that anyone seeking to remedy the plight of unhappy lawyers labors in vain, as fundamental character traits predetermined their sorry outcomes. Because no one can change his or her basic self, the only hope would be to save those who actually lack the lawyer personality in the first place but somehow wandered into the profession. To make life more bearable for these outliers, supporters of this theory would tinker at the margins of the legal system. This has led to the "comprehensive law movement"—an emphasis on collaborative, healing, and humane forms of law practice. Insofar as such a program moves the system away from its adversarial underpinnings, courtroom lawyers need not apply, it seems.

The personality theory may be a useful tool for self-analysis, but one difficulty with the hypothesis is its breadth. In addition to the different satisfaction outcomes for the various practice settings outlined in the 2007 ABA survey, the legal profession includes many different types of people and practice specialties. Some lawyers belong in a courtroom; others do better if they remain in the back room. Some interact well with clients and fellow attorneys; others work best if they never leave their offices. Most attorneys who give advice about complex tax issues would be miserable as litigators—and no one would want to see them argue a case to a jury. Transactional lawyers who structure big deals have little desire to write wills. Some attorneys thrive on combat; others prefer to find amicable solutions to controversies. Most public interest lawyers would refuse to represent the parties opposing the causes they pursue. A single "lawyer personality" can't fit all of these attorneys.

OTHER THEORIES SEEK to explain attorneys as a unique group and their distress as understandable. One law firm management consulting company commissioned a study of lawyers' personality traits to help law firms identify characteristics that produced successful attorneys, that is, "associates most likely to fit in well and, consequently, enjoy and stay in their jobs longer." The study concluded that such lawyers "tend to deal with others in a direct, matter-of-fact way," have a tendency "to push or shy away from others when under pressure," and are "most attracted to environments that emphasize quality and are less commercially focused than professionals in other industries."

Psychologist Martin E. P. Seligman devotes several pages of his best-selling book, *Authentic Happiness,* to a discussion of lawyers. Seligman found three causes of what he called the demoralization among attorneys.

First, they're pessimists in the sense that they believe negative events are global, pervasive, and enduring. Most lawyers might respond that they're just being realistic, which is a positive trait in a profession that values prudence. Those who lack it initially will learn it in law school but, as Seligman notes, "a trait that makes you good at your profession does not always make you a happy human being."

Seligman's second cause for attorney unhappiness is what he calls "low decision latitude in high-stress situations." Especially if they work in big law firms, young attorneys in particular have little autonomy but confront great demands—meet targets for billable hours, cater to partners, and try to be distinctive in ways that will allow their own survival in a world where five-year associate turnover rates exceed 80 percent.

The third cause is that the profession is a win-lose game. This phenomenon is inherent to the adversary system.

Seligman offers tactics from positive psychology that might help, such as recognizing and then rebutting catastrophic thoughts, preventing pessimism from becoming pervasive, and organizing the day to gain more personal control over it. Unfortunately, he sees no antidote for the zero-sum, win-lose nature of legal work: "For better or for worse, the adversarial process, confrontation, maximizing billable hours, and the 'ethic' of getting as much as you can for your clients are much too entrenched."

To Seligman's list of contributors to attorney dissatisfaction, add another for those working in big law firms: the transformation of most such institutions into businesses focusing on the bottom line. This orientation is exacerbating the psychological plight of their attorneys. The worse news is that even though such firms employ only 15 percent of all lawyers, they exert outsized influence over the legal profession and the society at large. Most have evolved in a troubling direction.

CHAPTER 5

THE TRANSFORMATION OF BIG LAW FIRMS

*The real problem of the 1980s was the lax
admissions standards of associates of all firms to partnerships.
The way to fix that now is to make it harder to become
a partner. The associate track is longer and more difficult.*
—Bradford Hildebrandt, founder of Hildebrandt Inc.,
a law firm management consulting firm, speaking in 1996

IN 1976, MOST OF MY FELLOW LAW STUDENTS and I regarded large firms as the place to be. That had been true long before I became an attorney, and it's been true ever since. Because the nation's largest 250 law firms today employ only about 15 percent of all practicing lawyers, it may seem odd that they occupy such a revered position, but they do. The reasons are many, and the influence of big firms is profound.

In substantial part, the importance of large law firms is a function of economics. Virtually all of the nation's largest corporations rely upon lawyers in big firms for advice and representation—and they pay handsome sums. Most firms have full-service capabilities: corporate counseling, mergers and acquisitions, litigation, tax advice, lobbying, and estate planning for the wealthy. Corporations also draw most of their own in-house attorneys from such firms.

Big-firm lawyers also move through the revolving door that leads into and out of government. For example, the typical biography of a top white-collar criminal defense attorney includes prior experience as a prosecutor. Likewise, over the years many partners in large law firms have moved into the highest echelons of government and back. The cumulative influence of what the profession calls "big law" is enormous. So is its power.

As previously observed, the tentacles of big law reach deeply into law schools, too. Their subliminal messages to students pervade campuses, where firm names appear on classrooms, legal aid clinics, student lounges, and even entire buildings. Deans want their graduates to take jobs with big firms because that will make their schools' employment numbers look good to prospective applicants, especially if they can make the *National Law Journal*'s annual list of "go-to schools"—the ones that place the most graduates in the nation's biggest law firms.

The firms themselves make enticing offers. Along with generous compensation packages to debt-ridden students comes the promise of equally valuable nonmonetary benefits: clients present cutting-edge issues; mentoring comes from the profession's leading figures; training and experience at a large firm open up additional career options; big firms provide opportunities for exposure to diverse personalities and practice styles. The list of advertised attractions is long, although, as discussed later, the reality today often diverges dramatically from what many firms present in their recruiting materials.

The pervasive power and influence of big law firms earn them a special place that also deserves a special scrutiny. In that respect, former Yale Law School dean Anthony Kronman's prescient observations two decades ago still resonate: "The large corporate firm continues to exercise an influence, both within the profession and outside it, that far exceeds its numerical strength. However influence and power are measured—whether in raw economic terms or in subtler, political ones—these firms remain the leaders of the bar. In that respect, their position is little different from what it was a generation ago, or even earlier."

Big law firms have never been eleemosynary institutions. But in 1993, Kronman lamented what he called their growing hostility to the lawyer-statesman, the devoted citizen who is intelligent and wise and who cares about the public good, not just about private ends such as making money. When I was at Kirkland & Ellis, one senior lawyer, Elmer Johnson, especially exemplified this tradition.

Johnson joined the firm immediately after graduating from the University of Chicago Law School in 1957. As head of the firm's corporate practice during the 1970s and 1980s, he advised leaders of industry and commerce. He served as general counsel of General Motors from 1983 to 1988 before returning to private practice. But he was also the primary author of the Commercial Club of Chicago's twenty-first-century update of Daniel Burnham's 1909 Plan of Chicago. From 1999 to 2002, he served as president of the Aspen Institute. In a 1994 interview, Johnson said, "My historical perspective indicates that what accounted for the success of the market system was the ability of corporate managers to act primarily not out of self-interest but as fiduciaries."

When it comes to running their own law firms, few of today's senior partners relegate self-interest to such a secondary status. That's one reason that life in big firms has deteriorated since Elmer Johnson left Kirkland & Ellis in 1999. Kronman anticipated the decline. Many of the traditional benefits that once came with joining a large firm have disappeared. Mentoring young attorneys to develop a firm's human assets is increasingly rare, as are meaningful opportunities for hands-on training that involves real clients and cases. Big firms have become far bigger than Kronman imagined, and while they still lead the profession in every economic measure, their leadership has turned to a focus on business-school-type data that undermine the essential attributes of any true profession. This is evident from surveys showing that the most lucrative big firms have the least satisfied lawyers.

That is not to say that visionaries can no longer be found in any big firms. Many attorneys in large firms perform charitable and civic work and, as already noted, move seamlessly into and out of government service. But Kronman properly identified three troubling developments that have accelerated since he wrote about them in 1993. They reflect and reinforce firms' changing priorities, which make any individual attorney's desire to serve the public good even more difficult to achieve today.

The first factor is sheer size. In 1960, the largest firm in the United States had 169 lawyers; in 1988, it had 962 attorneys. By 2012, DLA Piper had more than 4,200 lawyers in seventy-seven offices throughout the world. Twenty-one other firms had more than 1,000 attorneys. Explosive growth has taken a toll on community and collegiality. Size also makes more difficult the task of assessing individual attorney merit. It becomes tempting for firm managers to settle on quick and easy numerical solutions—in particular, metrics that chart a lawyer's contribution to yearly profits. Other professional values that can't be quantified, such as mentoring and encouraging the intergenerational transition of clients, get lost in numbers that also carry the deceptive illusion of objectivity.

The second factor that concerned Kronman twenty years ago was money and the intense desire of most big-firm partners to make more of it. Today, the incomes of such firms' equity partners—those who together own the firm and share its profits—far exceed any expectations they had in law school. But you wouldn't suspect it from the way most of them now run their firms. They allow the obsessive pursuit of quick profit to override the well-being of those who actually generate their wealth. Such behavior begins to explain widespread associate dissatisfaction.

The third factor is the decline in human values that numeric indicators can't measure. As a consequence, the transformation of most big law firms from central players in a noble profession to a collection of profit-maximizing enterprises has produced an unfortunate culture. Most of those now leading the profession have been charting an errant course.

OVER THE PAST THREE DECADES, big-firm leaders have moved steadily away from partnership ideals and toward what they euphemistically call the "business model" now dominating private practice. Large law firms haven't been alone in this corporatization of America. Medicine, higher education, journalism, and other professions that earlier generations viewed as callings to a special kind of service have suffered a similar fate at the hands of bean counters. Defenders point to the upside: greater efficiency, more precision in measuring inputs and outcomes, and, for lawyers in big firms, much more money. But the downside reveals itself in conditions for which there is no metric, because none bears directly on short-term profitability. One of those is the growing epidemic of career dissatisfaction among attorneys, especially in large firms.

Two earlier developments helped lay the groundwork for a transformation of big firms that accelerated during the 1990s and beyond. The first came with a United States Supreme Court decision in 1975. In the 1960s, a law firm's invoice to a corporate client might consist of one line: "For services rendered." That changed dramatically when hourly billing for actual time spent became more prevalent. In 1975, the Court hastened that development: it outlawed minimum legal fee schedules as an antitrust violation.

The case didn't involve corporate law firms directly, but its impact did. Under minimum fee schedules, attorneys had been paid set amounts based on the particular service performed. A simple will might cost $100, a court appearance might be $200, and so on. The schedules had originated in the nineteenth century as maximum fee charges or caps. In the 1930s and 1940s, state bar associations used them to set the minimum amounts that attorneys should charge for their work. The organizations imposed penalties on lawyers who charged less than the stated requirements.

When the Supreme Court's 1975 ruling threw out the schedules as unlawful attempts to fix prices, most law firms that hadn't already adopted hourly billing for their services did so. Lawyers everywhere, including those in corporate law firms (which were much smaller in those days), likewise began to think more concretely about the process of converting their time to money. Clients also started asking more questions about the actual lawyer activities that were behind the one-line invoices.

A second facilitator of big law's transformation came in 1978 when Yale Law School graduate Steven Brill founded the *American Lawyer*. Whereas previously the country's eminent law journals had focused on recent developments in the law, practice tips, and scholarly analyses, Brill's magazine covered inside stories about the firms themselves. If a senior partner suddenly left his or her firm after working there for many years, Brill kept digging until he found the real reasons behind the move. If firms underwent internal power struggles, Brill would identify and interview the antagonists for his magazine. Disaffected lawyers in particular seemed eager to answer his questions—sometimes off the record. But one way or another, previously kept secrets were revealed. The *American Lawyer* wasn't a supermarket tabloid, but, beginning with the first issue in February 1979, it rattled a staid profession. That issue's lead story about Skadden, Arps, Slate, Meagher & Flom's name partner, "Flom Takes Over as Top Money Maker in '78," embodied what would become its ongoing focus: the money that partners at big law firms made.

Brill blew open a topic that had always been off-limits in polite company: partner compensation in the nation's largest law firms. Prior compilations of such information had been closely guarded secrets. Some big firms participated in an annual survey that the large accounting firm now known as PricewaterhouseCoopers gathered. But it wasn't comprehensive, and firm leaders limited the circulation of that information to a very small group at the top.

By 1985, the *American Lawyer* had persuaded partners in many of the nation's largest firms to talk about their financial performance, as well as what they knew about other firms. That year, Brill published the first listing of the Am Law 50. Almost twenty years later, his successor as editor in chief, Aric Press, launched another ranking: the A-List. In addition to revenue per lawyer, it considered firms' diversity, pro bono service, and associate satisfaction. Perhaps he intended the A-List as a partial antidote to the myopic financial behavior that the equity partner rankings had spawned. Firms would compete to get on the A-List, too, but not with the intensity of mission that characterized their quest for a spot on what by then had become the Am Law 100—the list of the country's biggest and richest law firms.

BRILL'S INNOVATION allowed attorneys to discover how much other big-firm lawyers were earning elsewhere. As a reporter at the time observed, "Lawyers, seeing what their colleagues were making, began to move around. A new era in law practice had begun."

Every year, firm managers could compare their average profits per partner with those of competitors. The public consumption of all this information didn't make lawyers better human beings; in most respects, it made them worse. But it also made some of them rich because senior leaders focused on management techniques that would move their firms up in the annual rankings. And so while in 1985 the overall average partner profits for firms on the inaugural list of the Am Law 50 was $300,000 ($625,000 in 2011 dollars), average partner profits for the top fifty firms in the Am Law 100 in 2011 had grown to $1.6 million.

More than a quarter century after *Am Law* published its first list, Aric Press argued that the transparency resulting from the *Am Law* rankings had been a positive development. He suggested that the discussion of commerce and earnings "in the top echelon of the profession . . . makes for a healthier marketplace." Press also observed that providing more people with greater access to such financial information empowered them to question their firms' strategies and achievements without fear that they'd be branded as traitors or heretics.

Press had a point. But he also acknowledged, "Information turned loose on any environment has the power to warp it, and law firms proved as susceptible as other human enterprises." Anyone attending a big law firm's equity partner meeting after 1990 could attest to the impact of the *Am Law* rankings. For the past twenty years, moving a firm up the list has been regarded as a badge of honor for the managing partner who could achieve it.

The rankings were an ironic development for members of a profession who regularly counseled corporate clients agonizing over legally required public shareholder disclosures. One might have expected that the outside attorneys advising those clients would have steadfastly resisted volunteering their own secrets. For a time they did. Well into the 1980s, many firms saw the wisdom of discretion—meaning silence—in these matters. Some law firms operated so privately with respect to the division of their economic wealth that a nonmanaging partner knew only the size of his or her share. The question of relative compensation even within a single firm was left to speculation, gossip, and ad hoc information-sharing arrangements among colleagues. Associate attorneys didn't know what their compatriots were making, either.

Not anymore. Over the decades since the first appearance of the *Am Law* list, data reported from all firms have become more comprehensive and irrevocably public. Brill's gathering and dissemination of financial information was not itself the cause of the profession's current predicaments; rather, as Press noted, the problem was what decision makers have done with it.

Brill had intended that his principal audience would be those considering jobs at large firms. "The idea was simple," he later said. "People who were deciding on careers and looking at law firms as business institutions ought to have some means of comparison." In an interview discussing law firms' responsive behavior since he'd first published the Am Law 100 twenty-five years earlier, Brill observed in 2012, "No one is forcing them to look at the rankings and just be hell-bent on doing something—anything—to improve the ranking." But hell-bent they have been.

For example, the *American Lawyer* has no way to verify independently the data that firms give it. That creates a potential for mischief that is analogous to how some law schools manipulate *U.S. News & World Report* rankings. In that respect, the fact that firms have been caught fudging the numbers they submit to the *American Lawyer* is a testament to the power of the rankings themselves.

Recently, Citi Private Bank Law Firm Group suggested that a surprising number of big firms were inflating the profit numbers that they provided to the *American Lawyer*. Citi has a unique line on many firms' confidential financial information because it's a major lender to law firms and their partners. Additionally, Citi compiles an annual survey of law firms' financial performance that it disseminates to managing partners of participating firms. Reporting on profitability, capitalization, staffing, and mobility, it tabulates results according to firm size. But Citi doesn't name firms individually, and it has a long record of maintaining the confidentiality of each law firm's data. Unlike submissions to the *American Lawyer*, firms have no incentive to exaggerate the numbers they provide to Citi and every reason to assist its compilation of an accurate survey.

In August 2011, the *Wall Street Journal* reported on a Citi presentation to "an audience of chairmen and managing partners of many of the world's biggest or most profitable law firms." According to an attendee, Citi said that 22 percent of the top fifty firms overstated their 2010 profits per partner by more than 20 percent. An additional 16 percent inflated their numbers by 10 to 20 percent. Another 15 percent inflated their profit numbers by 5 to 10 percent. Cumulatively, the variances involved more than half of the nation's top fifty law firms.

Many of those discrepancies may have resulted from the different definitions of "partner" that Citi and the *American Lawyer* used. But even that reconciliation still left a 10 percent variation involving firms that had overstated their profits to *Am Law*. As he explained away much of the controversy, ALM editor in chief Aric Press committed the publication to additional efforts that would reduce "the possibility for mischief, intended or otherwise."

But continuing mischief there was. Less than a year later, another highly public scandal over the reliability of a law firm's submission to the magazine erupted. In April 2012, the *American Lawyer* publicly announced its retroactive revision of Dewey & LeBoeuf's earlier reported revenue and profits for 2010 and 2011. It moved the numbers downward after *Bloomberg News* quoted the firm's management about earnings that were far below what the firm had told the *American Lawyer*. Instead of average equity partner profits of $1.8 million in 2011, the revised number was $1.04 million—a stunning drop. The average for 2010 also went down, from $1.6 million to $980,000. A Dewey & LeBoeuf spokesman told the *American Lawyer* that the discrepancy resulted from methodological differences between the firm's internal financial accounting and the numbers it submitted to the magazine, "which we assume is the case for every law firm that participates in your survey." The editors of the publication didn't buy that excuse, but as Chapter 8 explains, the controversy over those revisions was among the least of Dewey's problems at the time.

THE LEGAL WORLD took a decidedly unfortunate turn when even honest law firm managing partners used Brill's data in a manner far different from his stated intent. At about the same time that the *U.S. News* rankings embedded themselves into the psyches of law school deans, the annual Am Law 100 rankings began to assume a seminal significance for those running big law firms. Competitive by nature, lawyers accepted the implicit challenge that Brill's new disclosures offered: achieve the highest possible Am Law 100 ranking. The men who governed the most prestigious law firms—few, if any, women had significant management roles at that time—found themselves teaching to the *Am Law* test.

Two numbers increasingly dominated the new strategies that endure to this day, although firms differed in the weight they placed on each. The first was overall firm revenue, presumably because some leaders believed (as many still do) that size itself was a worthwhile distinction. That's ironic because there are no economies of scale in private law practice. Law firm management consultant firm Altman Weil reports that the thirty-year experience of its *Survey of Law Firm Economics* explains why: "Larger firms almost always spend more per lawyer on staffing, occupancy, equipment, promotion, malpractice and other non-personnel insurance coverages, office supplies and other expenses than do smaller firms." Although that conclusion seems counterintuitive because larger firms should be able to spread fixed costs over a greater number of lawyers, Altman Weil observes that such an assumption doesn't take into account the added costs necessary to support growth.

Another consultant estimates that the optimal size for a law firm is around 100 lawyers. Even the managing partner of a large New York firm, Davis, Polk & Wardwell, acknowledged, "Unlike many other industries, there aren't the economies of scale leading law firms inexorably toward growth."

A second *Am Law* metric is more important for most big-firm leaders: average profits per partner. Presumably, the belief is that free-market forces will cause the best and brightest of attorneys to make the economically rational decision to work where the pay is highest. But maximizing dollars in the near term imposes longer-run costs on the culture of most big firms. Too many attorneys eventually discover that money isn't everything.

Managing partners admit publicly that they run their firms to maximize instant profits for the relatively few. For example, a *Chicago Tribune* front-page story about Chicago-based Sonnenschein, Nath & Rosenthal (later SNR Denton after its 2010 merger with a large UK-based firm) in early 2008 observed, "The firm hoped to boost its profits per partner, a key benchmark, from about $800,000 in 2005 to $1.4 million by 2008. In 2007, the firm's profits per partner had been $915,000, according to *American Lawyer* magazine." To achieve its goal, the firm was laying off thirty-seven lawyers and eighty-seven other employees. The managing partner explained, "We have to take the steps necessary to make sure we are competitive for talent and achieve the profitability our lawyers expect. A small group of firms are positioning themselves to pull away from the pack [in terms of profitability]. We intend to be in that small group." And that was before the financial crisis hit in September 2008.

(Spoiler alert: The firm didn't make its goal. In 2008, its average profits per partner dropped to $805,000. By 2011, it had become larger through a transatlantic merger, but overall average partner profits for the combined entity were down to $700,000.)

IN THE DRIVE to increase equity partner profits, Sonnenschein joined many large law firms in adopting a model that Cravath, Swaine &

Moore and other New York City firms had used for decades. It consists of a three-legged stool: leverage, hourly rates, and billable hours.

A firm's leverage is the ratio of all attorneys to the equity partner owners. The higher the leverage, that is, the more salaried lawyers per equity partner, the more money equity partners as a group make. Firms create leverage by hiring far more entry-level associates than they ever intend to promote into the equity partnership. Thanks to the other two legs on the three-legged profits stool—high hourly rates and billable hours—the equity partners make a lot of money on those associates during the years preceding the up-or-out equity partnership decision.

The second leg is hourly rates. Before the onset of the Great Recession in 2008, big firms increased their rates by 6 to 8 percent annually from 1998 to 2007. At most big firms, a typical third-year associate billing $150 an hour in 1998 cost $400 or more in 2009. Although many firms froze rates in 2009, soon thereafter the rise continued. In 2012, rates were moving up at an overall 5 percent clip, but the nation's largest twelve firms were increasing rates by more than 7 percent.

The resulting arithmetic for calculating equity partner profits is straightforward. By 2012, top firms typically paid first-year associates a salary of $160,000 a year, plus a year-end bonus averaging less than $10,000. The average base salary and bonus for all midlevel (third-through fifth-year) associates was $204,000. Meanwhile, those firms charged clients an average of $400 an hour for associate time while requiring them to bill at least 2,000 client hours a year. (In 2011, actual average billable hours for all third-, fourth-, and fifth-year associates were 2,037.) That's $800,000 in gross revenue from someone whom the firms paid only one-fourth of that amount—not a bad markup.

But things become even more lucrative when firms can charge more than $500 hourly for senior associates' time, because those attorneys' total compensation typically remains below $300,000. Better still for the equity partners are associates who bill more than the 2,000-hour minimum. Even allowing for other associate costs, including overhead, benefits, training, and the like, the model produces enormous wealth for the firm's owners, that is, the equity partners.

The regime yields predictable results. Only large client matters will support associates' high hourly rates. Small cases and disputes that enabled an earlier generation of lawyers to develop courtroom and client experiences have dropped away. As an associate during the early 1980s, I was the lead attorney in several jury trials; in today's big firms, associates rarely get such opportunities. Those smaller cases are far less profitable than behemoth matters on which any single attorney has only a small slice of the work and little sense of the whole. But in addition to hands-on training, those client matters provided autonomy that is important to maintaining high morale and promoting job satisfaction. They allowed attorneys to perform tasks that were closer to what they'd expected being a lawyer to mean. In short, the pursuit of short-range profits has contributed to the growing gap between expectations and reality that is creating more dissatisfied attorneys.

Meanwhile, beyond the relentless tedium of the work itself, partners demanded that associates do even more of it as they exploited the third leg of the equity partner profits stool—billable hours. In the continuing search for metrics that can help them maximize quick gains, law firm leaders have turned the world upside down. Specifically, they've used billable hours to measure productivity when, in fact, the behavior that maximizes hours is antithetical to true productivity.

Productivity is the "relative measure of the efficiency of a person [or] system . . . in converting inputs into useful outputs." But the relevant output for an attorney shouldn't be total hours spent on tasks; it should be useful work product meeting a client's needs. Total elapsed time without regard to the quality or usefulness of the result reveals nothing about a worker's value. More hours often mean the opposite of real productivity. No one inside most big firms questions this perversion because leadership's primary goal is increasing equity partner wealth. More is better, and the misnomer "productivity" persists.

The notion defies common sense. Effort on the fourteenth hour of a day can't be as valuable as that exerted during hour six. Scientific research has repeatedly demonstrated that fatigue compromises effectiveness. That's why, for example, the US Department of Transportation relies on studies demonstrating the effects of exhaustion on the human mind and body in imposing mandatory rest periods after interstate truckers put in prolonged stints behind the wheel. After working seventy hours during an eight-day period—an average of just under nine hours a day—over-the-road drivers must rest for thirty-four consecutive hours. Ask big-firm lawyers working at that pace (or even longer per day) if they then go thirty-four straight hours without looking at a smartphone for messages or talking with clients and colleagues, much less returning to the office.

THE OBSESSION WITH billable hours has contributed to an apparent paradox: increasing big law firms' incomes amid growing career dissatisfaction. In fact, the very concept of billable hours is a relatively recent invention. In 1958, an ABA pamphlet suggested that lawyers were not good businesspeople and should keep better records of their time and activities. It recommended that lawyers strive to bill 1,300 hours annually. That would qualify as part-time, non-partner-track employment today.

As recently as the early 1980s, few law firms had minimum hours requirements. Today, most large firms expressly set them at 1,900 to 2,000 hours a year. That's the range appearing most often in the NALP directory—the official guide that students use to learn about all law firms. The largest of the big firms—those with more than seven hundred attorneys—have the highest billable hour requirements.

Two thousand hours a year may not sound onerous. After all, that's just a forty-hour week for fifty weeks a year. Except the key word is *billable*, and—even more important—the number is a minimum. Associates take the hint. They understand that their futures depend on measured output—hours billed to clients. In the culture of most firms, success requires many more hours than the firm-stated base number.

But even 2,000 hours a year is a lot. Yale Law School's brochure *The Truth About the Billable Hour* outlines hypothetical workdays leading to various total annual hours scenarios. It should be required reading for any lawyer contemplating a career in a big firm. When lunch and bathroom breaks get included, billing an honest 2,000 hours means working weekdays from 8:00 A.M. until 7:00 P.M. and all day Saturday (excluding commuting time).

The caveat about honesty is important. Besides pitting the attorney's self-interest in billing more time against the interest of the client who pays the bills, the regime also encourages lawyers to "pad" their time. That's lawyer-speak for fraud. Because attorneys self-report their client hours, time billed but not actually worked usually goes undetected. Webster Hubbell, a former chair of the Arkansas Bar ethics committee and state supreme court chief justice before becoming a high-ranking official in the US Department of Justice during the Clinton administration, was a partner in a prestigious law firm when he billed clients for time he never worked. Eventually he went to prison for it. Another partner in a prominent Chicago firm got into trouble when someone wondered how he could bill almost 6,000 hours annually over four consecutive years. The answer was that he couldn't. Still another lawyer was caught adding hours of bogus time to a bill before sending it to a client. The problem is sufficiently widespread that many companies specialize in auditing outside law firm invoices to clients. When they discover fraud, they'll even provide expert testimony about their findings.

Understanding the actual time that a lawyer must put in over the course of a year in order to bill even 2,000 honest hours provides perspective on a major law firm management consultant's recent missive to the profession: "The high point of law firm productivity was in the late 1990s, when average annual billable hours for associates in many firms were hitting 2,300 to 2,500." If astronomical numbers of billable hours are what is called productivity, what happened after consultants advised firms to increase it? "The negative growth in productivity, even during the 'boom' years preceding the current downturn when demand was growing at a healthy rate, was driven to some extent by associate pushback on the unsustainable billable hour requirements at many firms."

THE MOST SINISTER and least publicized feature of the big-law business model is associate attrition. The law firm pyramid with associates at the base and equity partners at the top requires a remarkable thinning of ranks on the road to a partial ownership interest in the firm, that is, equity partnership. Just prior to the Great Recession, the five-year rate of associate attrition exceeded 80 percent. That is, after five years a typical starting associate class of fifty would be down to ten. Even more striking and meaningful, fewer than five of those would become equity partners many years after that.

That's much worse than it used to be. Except at places such as Cravath and a few other New York City firms, the odds against success in a big firm were not always that daunting. Instead, most firms offered young lawyers a reasonable chance at a lifetime career. Implicit in the demanding work was the promise of an eventual reward, namely, admission to the partnership and the security that came with it. Now, subject only to a handful of exceptions, becoming an equity partner almost anywhere is a long shot. The emphasis on increasing equity partner profits in the near term incentivizes greed that produces concentrated wealth at the top of most big firms. Over time, reducing the number of new entrants into equity partnerships has enhanced that wealth. That's how, as previously noted, average equity partner profits for the top fifty firms in the Am Law 100 went from $300,000 in 1985 to $1.6 million in 2011.

Even so, firms seeking to achieve an optimal attrition rate don't have an easy task. In the decade preceding the Great Recession, what law firm management consultants called "associate pushback" at 2,500 billable hours a year was driving away young lawyers that the firms wanted to keep. According to the NALP Foundation, the average associate attrition rate in 2002 for firms of 500 or more attorneys was 15 percent—the same as the average of all NALP categories (under 100 lawyers, 101–250, 251–500, and over 500). Over the next five years, the rate for the largest firms cruised past all others—to 20 percent. For every ten associates they added to the payroll in 2007, seven departed.

As a result, big firms began adopting strategies to "keep the keepers," as described in the title of one NALP Foundation publication. As recently as January 2008, large firms in particular were taking steps to stem the growing tide of associate dissatisfaction that produced more and earlier attrition than firms wanted. Some firms, including Cravath, used money and awarded associates special bonuses of up to $50,000 on top of regular bonuses ranging from $35,000 to $50,000. The New York City firm of Sullivan & Cromwell began a program of encouraging partners to say "thank you" and "good work" to subordinates. Milwaukee-based Quarles & Brady expanded parental leave to twelve weeks for women and six weeks for men and eliminated billable hour requirements. Dallas-based Strasburger & Price reduced associate minimum billable hour requirements from 1,920 to 1,600, albeit with an asterisk: new attorneys were asked to spend 550 hours yearly in training sessions and shadowing senior lawyers. Chicago-based Chapman & Cutler announced a two-tier pay structure: either bill 2,000 hours a year and get paid accordingly, or drop to 1,850 and earn less. More than half took the reduced schedule.

Such accommodative efforts became unnecessary after the financial crisis in 2008 and the ongoing Great Recession decimated the demand for new lawyers in big firms. For example, in contrast to the 2009 story that it had eliminated minimum billable hours requirements, Quarles & Brady's 2012 NALP directory entry reported a minimum billable hours expectation of 1,800, with bonus eligibility requiring 1,900 base hours, "assuming satisfactory performance." The special bonuses have shrunk, too, although equity partner incomes haven't.

Of course, associate attrition can sometimes lead to decent outcomes for those who leave their initial firms. In a survey of twenty-five hundred associates who departed from big firms in 2011, almost 40 percent took jobs as associates in another firm, while 22 percent became corporate in-house attorneys and 7 percent took government jobs.

A SINGLE METRIC tells the tale of many large-firm transformations: between 1985 and 2010, the average leverage ratio for the Am Law 50 doubled from 1.76 to 3.54. In addition to pulling up the ladder and leaving many more young lawyers behind, firm leaders used another technique to maximize leverage and the resulting immediate profits: adding years to the survivors' trek. Students searching through law firm recruiting materials or the NALP directory won't find meaningful information about a firm's track record in promoting its new hires to equity partnership. Nor will they have any clue that, if the past is prologue, the rules will continue to change in their disfavor after they enter that race to the top. For example, Chicago-based Kirkland & Ellis made the path to equity partner longer as the firm's average equity partner profits increased from $400,000 in 1985 to more than $3 million in 2011.

Over time, more firms adopted another strategy that Kirkland originally pioneered to ensure that only the highest-quality attorneys advanced: two-tier partnerships. In its original form, the system was a proving ground. Associates advancing to the first tier, non-equity partnership, had no assurance of promotion to the second, equity partner. But they had the opportunity over the subsequent three or four years to prove their value. Thereafter, they received either promotion to equity partner or a reasonable period of time to find a new job elsewhere.

Compared to the forty-four firms in the 1994 Am Law 100 that had two tiers, there were seventy-seven in 2003. But increasingly, firms haven't followed an up-or-out approach. Instead, they began to see non-equity partners as a profit center. During the decade from 1999 to 2009, the number of attorneys in the largest 100 firms nearly doubled. But as the number of non-equity partners grew threefold, the number of new equity partners grew by less than one-third. The creation of a large cadre of permanent non-equity partners can result in big problems for a firm.

One difficulty is that such lawyers become second-class citizens. They know it, and everyone else in the firm knows it. They may be decent, hardworking people. But once they receive the scarlet letter of permanent non-equity status, their morale plummets—and understandably so. After all, throughout their lives they succeeded at everything they tried, achieving an outstanding college record and good grades at a top law school. They're intelligent and ambitious; otherwise, firms wouldn't have hired them in the first place. But then, after years of hard work, they learn that they won't reach the next level and never will. Only magical thinking can wish away the demoralizing impact of that message.

Even worse, any firm creating a permanent subclass of such attorneys takes an individual problem and makes it an institutional one. If permanent non-equity partners do meaningful and fulfilling work, they'll deprive younger attorneys of those increasingly scarce opportunities. That expands the morale problem into the senior associate ranks.

Conversely, allowing permanent non-equity partners to perform tasks that other attorneys avoid can create another set of difficulties. Some observers note that non-equity partners sometimes "take on non-billable leadership positions . . . involving pro bono, diversity, recruiting, training, and professional development." Unfortunately, there's no better way to send a message of management's indifference to such pursuits than by putting the second team in charge.

Another defense of a permanent non-equity partner level is that such a track enables firms to "retain some whiz-bang lawyers who have young children they want to spend more time with or who just want to get off the equity partner treadmill." A better approach could be to rethink the wisdom of a system that produces that unhappy treadmill in the first place.

THE LAW SCHOOL BUBBLE that creates a surplus of new attorneys each year serves the prevailing big-law model well. But law schools that brag when they make the *National Law Journal*'s annual list of "go-to schools"—those placing the greatest number of associates in the nation's largest 250 law firms—should rethink that boast. In light of remarkable rates of associate turnover and the gauntlet leading to equity partnerships, an old saying seems apt: for many students who land jobs in big firms, the experience is similar to winning a pie-eating contest where first prize is more pie.

Why do students do it? In their book *Freakonomics,* Stephen J. Dubner and Steven D. Levitt examine the universal lure that accompanies the unlikely prospect of hitting it big. They offer drug dealer gangs as an example. The behavior of the gangs' foot soldiers is economically irrational: legions of them work the streets hoping to become kingpins someday, but they know that few will. The phenomenon explains the behavior of many young lawyers in big firms, too.

For example, in its 2012 article about "go-to schools," the *National Law Journal* noted the continuing decimation of the big-law-firm market for new graduates. In 2007, the top twenty law schools sent 55 percent of their graduates to big firms; in 2011, that figure was down to 36 percent. Even so, most of that year's forty-four thousand law graduates would count those big-firm new hires as winners because they had landed the most desired, well-paying jobs. But recent data on associates at big firms who were promoted to non-equity partner in 2011 provide insight into the long odds against success in those places.

In 2011, forty-seven Harvard graduates in large law firms were promoted from associate to partner. That sounds like a lot, except that five years earlier—in 2006—Harvard sent 338 graduates into those big firms. (The resulting 15 percent promotion rate in 2011 assumes that Harvard graduates who advanced to partner that year came from an original group of Harvard associates that was approximately the same size as the 2006 group. Given stable hiring patterns during the mid-2000s, it's a reasonable assumption.) Even fewer will survive to make equity partner—which can take several more years at some two-tier firms.

Other top schools' graduates face similar odds. For the following law schools, the number of new partners at big law firms in 2011 compared to the number of new associates that big firms hired five years earlier was: Columbia Law School, 31 new partners in 2011 versus 313 associate hires in 2006; Northwestern, 14 partners in 2011 versus 143 associates in 2006; University of Pennsylvania, 15 partners in 2011 versus 187 associates in 2006.

As already observed, not all of this attrition leads to bad outcomes. But the larger point is that few pre-law students give much thought to the prevailing culture of big law firms. By the time they graduate from law school, some are more knowledgeable, if not downright cynical. Before taking new associate positions, many accept the fact that their prospects for advancement to equity partner are sufficiently remote that it's not a realistic ambition. For them, a job at a big law firm means they can retire their student loan debt and then move on to pursue the dreams that took them to law school in the first place. Or perhaps they'll find other positions that weren't part of their original career plans but are professionally satisfying.

The real problem involves another group: law school graduates who join big firms as prisoners of their own confirmation bias. They think they'll continue to be among the handful of winners in the equity partner sweepstakes. For too many of them, the disappointment can be profound. As firm leaders lengthen the equity partner track, reduce the relative number of new equity partners, increase leverage ratios, and run their firms to maximize wealth at the very top of the pyramid, they undermine institutional morale and worsen intergenerational tensions.

Senior partners who are changing the rules that governed their own rise through the ranks rationalize that, as a group, today's younger lawyers are inferior. They complain that today's associates act as if they are entitled and that they are unwilling to work as hard as today's leaders believe they themselves once did. For any particular person, there may be something to such criticisms. All young attorneys are well advised to conduct themselves in ways that either avoid those complaints or render them patently ridiculous. But the sweeping generalization about an entire generation is simply wrong. It's also doubly ironic, considering the legions of baby boomer attorney leaders who act entitled, too. Behavior follows incentive structures. If some of today's young lawyers sometimes behave as if they don't have a reasonable shot at winning the big-law equity partner tournament, it's because they don't—and they've figured that out.

FOR MOST BIG LAW FIRMS TODAY, the keys to success are hiring large new associate classes each year and getting young lawyers to put in long hours during the time preceding the equity partnership decisions about them. That strategy keeps equity partner wealth growing. With the assistance of management consultants who are not lawyers, most leaders of large firms have pushed their firms away from their professional ethos and toward the outer limits of their potential as profit-generating enterprises. Only a relatively few partners at the top have benefited. The resulting personal costs imposed on those working at all levels in today's big firms are difficult to quantify, but they are painfully real.

The intense competition for status as measured by the *Am Law* rankings has eaten away at the internal fabric of professionalism and increased attorney career dissatisfaction. The result has been a fundamental change in the very culture of many—perhaps most—large law firms. This should surprise no one. What manager wouldn't want his law firm to maintain its position or move up the most important *Am Law* list? There was and is one way to accomplish that feat: increase the firm's average profits per partner. How to achieve that? The prevailing model requires increasing leverage ratios, hourly rates, billable hours, or—even better—all of them.

Every year presented a new challenge and a new opportunity for each firm. Managing partners sought the highest possible position on what became a prestigious listing that increasingly drove decisions about attorney workload, promotion, and compensation. But every economically rational firm was striving to better its ranking, too. The good news for the survivors was that partner profits for the Am Law 100 continued climbing, reaching an overall average of $1.4 million in 2011.

The resulting culture of a large firm also reveals itself in the criteria applied in making its most important decisions, those involving who will become part of the firm's future. There the Am Law 100 has also done great damage. It invited managing partners to focus on a single question: what is the current business case supporting a particular attorney for promotion or compensation? To maintain its position on the *Am Law* list, a firm had to answer this question "correctly" as to each partner or potential partner. Otherwise, average partner profits would decline and the firm's relative ranking would fall. Each and every year mattered for that *Am Law* year alone. As the value of the partnership increased over time, it became more difficult for prospective partners to make the case to management that they deserved these ever-loftier entry levels of equity partner compensation. The vicious circle was in place. Moreover, existing equity partners found themselves at the mercy of managing partners' compensation formulas, which required a similar self-justification exercise annually, lest they lose their own equity positions in the firm.

As the *American Lawyer*'s editor in chief, Aric Press, said in his introduction to the 2007 Am Law 100: "Profits-per-partner [is] the key metric that has turned law firm managers into contortionists. . . . This Law Firm Golden Age has been fueled by surging demand for high-end legal services and unrelenting annual rate hikes. Partners reaped the benefits of hard work—and of pulling up the ladder behind them. Stoking these gains has been a dramatic slowdown in the naming of new equity partners."

Admittance to the equity partner club didn't offer much job security, either. In early 2007—before the Great Recession began—Chicago-based Mayer Brown announced the firing of forty-five equity partners, 10 percent of its worldwide total. The firm's incoming chair defended the action: "We have objectives to make sure our stock price stays high."

Other firm leaders likewise boasted about new agendas to maximize immediate results. At most firms, numbers told the story. For example, the *American Lawyer* ranked the New York firm of Cadwalader, Wickersham & Taft fifty-fourth in total revenues for 1995. It earned half a million dollars in average partner profits, good enough for eighteenth on the *Am Law* list. With 268 lawyers and 76 equity partners, its leverage ratio was about 3.5.

At that point, the firm was two years into the reign of Robert O. Link Jr., who had led a group of young partners in taking control of the firm. He transformed it into what Link called a meritocracy. Partners who brought in business made more money, and less productive partners were cut. A decade later, Cadwalader still had only seventy-five equity partners, but its total attorney count had almost doubled to more than five hundred attorneys, producing a stunning leverage ratio of almost 7. Its 2005 average partner profits of $2.5 million placed it third on the Am Law 100 list, and its leverage ratio bested all others. Cravath's was 4.5; Sonnenschein's was just under 4; Mayer Brown's was just over 3. By the end of 2006, Cadwalader had added only one additional equity partner, for a total of 76, even though total head count had grown to 555; average partner profits soared to almost $3 million.

In a February 2007 interview, Link saw only blue skies ahead: "Are we going to have difficulty sustaining this? No, short of some cataclysmic event that hits everyone else, too." Ironically, the article also noted that "the engine of the firm is its asset-backed structured finance practice. . . . It is a specialized area that, in its most basic form, involves the issuance of tradable securities tied to fixed assets or revenue streams, most commonly residential mortgages." That sector of the economy would be at the center of a cataclysmic event that Link had been unable to envision.

Link also complained that the profession continued to attract too many people unsuited to his firm's corporate practice. His remarks illustrate pervasive intergenerational tensions throughout many large firms: "There's a big imbalance in terms of expectations of law graduates and law firms. It's all these history majors who found out they couldn't get jobs in history and decided to go to law school." He bragged that his firm no longer recruited at Yale because "they don't seem to produce the kind of lawyer we want."

He remained confident about the firm's course, noting that the profession had widely recognized and embraced Cadwalader's high-leverage business model: "If you look at the last ten years, you probably have more change in the legal industry than at any other time," he observed, while offering a governing principle that resonated throughout the world of large law firms: "Everyone should wake up in the morning and feel a little vulnerable."

When the Great Recession arrived less than a year later, Link himself probably felt a little too vulnerable. By the end of 2007, the firm hadn't added to its equity partner ranks, even though its total attorney head count had swelled to 645 and its leverage ratio had increased to 8.5 (compared to Cravath's 4.5). But average partner profits had declined to $2.7 million. New initiatives immediately followed as the firm's profit engine ("asset-backed structured finance") stalled in the wake of a subprime mortgage crash—the "cataclysmic event" that Link had so glibly dismissed as impossible.

In January 2008, the firm announced the layoff of thirty-five lawyers, mostly associates. The asset-based mortgage practice that had catapulted the firm from relative obscurity to its place among the top moneymakers had disappeared. Still, a firm spokesperson expressed confidence that there would be no more layoffs in the future.

A month later, a new chair replaced the fifty-three-year-old Link, who remained a managing partner until November, when he wasn't included on the slate of candidates for the management committee. Meanwhile, ninety-six lawyers received their walking papers in July as the firm announced that it would continue to shrink so that, "in September 2008, the firm will have 580 lawyers, the same number we were in January 2006."

But that wasn't the end of the story. When dollars alone drive the culture of a partnership, firm leaders sometimes forget that the individual partners themselves act accordingly. On January 16, 2009, the firm announced that its 2008 average partner profits had slid to $1.9 million—down 30 percent from the prior year. A week earlier, seven of its eleven London partners and twelve associates who may have suspected the upcoming bad news had defected to a New York–based competitor, Paul Hastings, which later reported partner profits comparable to Cadwalader's newly reduced level. After resolving a threatened lawsuit with Paul Hastings, Cadwalader then turned to the task of cutting even more associates from the London office—raising in part the suggestion that the defectors should have taken more associates with them. A few days after losing most of that office, another Cadwalader partner in New York left to join Mayer Brown.

Cadwalader survived, bouncing back to a reported $2.4 million in average equity partner profits for 2010 with an Am Law 100–leading leverage ratio exceeding 7. Profits declined slightly in 2011 as total attorney head count continued dropping to 464. No one is calling it a bailout, but government money helped Cadwalader's recovery. After January 2009, the firm received almost $24 million in legal fees for its work on the US Department of the Treasury's Troubled Assets Relief Program (TARP). Other big firms earned significant fees on the collapse, too. But Cadwalader's take was the biggest, and it's especially ironic. The firm's lucrative asset-based structured finance practice had produced stunning profits for Cadwalader in the years before those markets—and the firm's related legal practice—collapsed.

Looking back on his tenure as the firm's leader, former chair Link later said that he was proud of his efforts: "There's no question we had to make adjustments, that we were hard hit by the recession in the capital markets . . . [but the firm now] is in a position to go forward."

In a sense, it may look as if Cadwalader wound up in 2012 where it had begun in 2007. But that facile conclusion masks the disruption to almost 200 Cadwalader attorneys (plus staff) who lost their jobs as the firm became smaller—from 645 lawyers in 2007 to 464 in 2011. It also ignores another comparative statistic that sheds more light on the internal disruptions associated with the firm's apparent rejuvenation. According to the *American Lawyer*, Cadwalader had 76 equity partners and 23 non-equity partners in 2006. Five years later, the *American Lawyer* reported that Cadwalader had 21 *fewer* equity partners (55) and 23 *more* non-equity partners (46). Finally, another data point provides insight into the associate ranks: in the *American Lawyer*'s annual survey of mid-level associates' career satisfaction, Cadwalader placed 102nd out of 126 large law firms in 2011. It dropped to 125th out of 129 in 2012.

THE CENTRAL FEATURES of the prevailing big-firm model—leverage, hourly rates, and billable hours—create conditions that decrease opportunities for advancement and are hostile to any attorney's search for a balanced life. That seems obvious. After all, an emphasis on billable time as a key metric for success displaces other worthwhile activities. Less apparent is a closely related problem: the model's most important metrics also fail to value diversity because its bottom-line impact is not readily apparent in the short run.

One corporation's general counsel who had worked for many years in a big firm provided this insight as a former insider: "The call on law firms to up their diversity efforts may not be effective unless it affects their bottom line and/or their client base. Therefore, if law firms are satisfying their clients' needs without having a diverse work force, the law firms will have little reason to be as responsive to a call to up their diversity efforts, unless their clients demand that they institute diversity and inclusion policies and/or programs." The attitude described helps to explain why, although women and minorities achieved significant law school gains after 1970, they have lagged far behind in large law firms.

In 1963, 4 percent of law students were women; by 2012, women accounted for almost half of all law students. On law school faculties, female representation increased from 15 percent in 1980 to almost 40 percent in 2005. Minorities constituted 8 percent of law students in 1980; since then, their representation has tripled.

For women and minority lawyers who didn't become professors, the story has been different, especially in big law firms. In 1952, when former United States Supreme Court associate justice Sandra Day O'Connor graduated third in her class at Stanford Law School, she received a single law-related job offer: legal secretary. Until the 1960s, the places for women practicing law included domestic relations and probate, not corporate boardrooms or in front of judges and juries. Today women remain overrepresented in some practice areas—government, private industry (in-house counsel), legal aid/public defender. More women than men are also sole practitioners. But in most large law firms, the percentage of female equity partners has hovered around 15 percent for the last twenty years.

Likewise, minorities have been less likely to obtain judicial clerkships or join private practice and more likely to start their careers in government or public service jobs. They are grossly underrepresented in the top private sector jobs, such as corporate general counsel and law firm partner. Less than 5 percent of equity partners in NALP firms are minorities.

History looms large as an obstacle to changing important social institutions. Overcoming long-standing behavioral patterns in the nation's top law firms has presented especially formidable challenges. For corporate clients and their lawyers, the interpersonal fit created a comfortable inertia: when white males dominate the corporate world, it's natural for them to seek demographically compatible legal advisers. Moreover, winning the confidence of a significant corporate client can take years, but those relationships ultimately become an important criterion in partnership promotion decisions. All of that creates a long lag time between setting a meaningful diversity objective for the composition of a law firm partnership and achieving it. But even taking such considerations into account, the lag in most large law firms has been remarkable, as has been the reluctance of senior partners to disclose the absence of progress.

Although most large law firm leaders would prefer not to discuss their diversity failures publicly, the age of transparency is working against them. For example, Yale Law Women (YLW) now identifies annually the "Top Ten Family Friendly Law Firms." YLW's 2011 report expressed concern "about the low rates of retention for women, the dearth of women in leadership positions, the gender gap in those who take advantage of family friendly policies, and the possibility that part-time work can derail an otherwise successful career."

According to YLW's survey methodology, family-friendliness is mostly a function of big firms' attention to particular issues that affect women more than men. There's nothing wrong with that, but it shouldn't be confused with what really undermines the family-friendliness of any big firm—its devotion to billable hours as a primary measure of success. Among additional problems, the regime provides little incentive for mentoring; there's no way for partners to bill that time. These and other difficulties aren't gender-specific.

Still, the numbers (and some big firms' unwillingness to divulge them) tell an unfortunate tale with respect to the advancement of women. YLW's 2012 survey found that, on average, 43 percent of associates at responding large law firms were women, but they accounted for only 17 percent of equity partners and 12 percent of firm executive management committees. Only 30 percent of newly promoted partners in 2011 were women. Even worse, that's just the report from firms that provided information. Because the data aren't flattering, most big firms don't want to divulge their lack of progress in promoting women and minorities.

Well into the twenty-first century, the vast majority of large law firms resisted NALP's call for more transparency about the composition of their equity partnerships. In December 2009, NALP announced plans to obtain a detailed breakdown of equity/non-equity partner data from firms as part of its annual survey for the NALP directory. When some big firms balked at providing the data—a few threatened that they wouldn't fill out the form at all if NALP required such diversity information—the organization "backpedaled," as executive director James Leipold put it. The legal employer directory "represents an important revenue source for us," he said.

A prominent group of judges, professors, and attorneys wrote a public letter criticizing NALP's retreat. Their principal point was that assessing a firm's true diversity requires knowing who the real partners are. The breakdown of equity versus non-equity partners matters because only equity partners share in a firm's profits and the road to equity partnership has become longer and more difficult. As already noted, the number of non-equity partners tripled between 1998 and 2008, but the number of equity partners increased by only one-third. In 2009 and 2010, the number of equity partners in big firms actually declined; in 2011 it remained essentially flat. Mushed together—as NALP's equity/non-equity partner data were—the numbers became meaningless (except for increasingly rare one-tier firms).

Meanwhile, the *American Lawyer* jumped into the breach. Using responses to its annual diversity survey, the publication compiled data on the seventy firms in the Am Law 100 that were willing to provide it. Eventually NALP asked their member law firms for such information, but those accounting for about half of the partners in two-tier firms refused to answer its equity/non-equity partner questions. The firms that supplied data revealed how slowly the most prestigious and lucrative segment of the profession has progressed with respect to gender, race, and ethnicity. Among the respondents included in NALP's November 2011 reports, 84 percent of equity partners were men, 16 percent were women, and 5 percent were racial or ethnic minorities. A 2012 survey of the largest 250 law firms found that women accounted for 19 percent of all partners (equity and non-equity) and 15 percent of equity partners—about the same as a decade earlier. White males have monopolized big firms' equity partnerships, and they still do.

Behind the numbers are important questions about internal law firm dynamics. Why have big firms lagged so far behind law schools in promoting women? One response points to women who have taken themselves off the equity partner track to have children and raise families. That's a factor and there's nothing wrong with female attorneys who make that choice, but it's not a complete explanation. For women lawyers who want to have children, biological imperatives will always create a necessary interruption. Even if they choose to stay home with their kids for an extended period of time, that break from the practice of law need not impair their legal careers permanently. Nevertheless, in many firms, it does.

Some women have fought back. Prior to the economic downturn that began in late 2007, a few law firms began serious efforts to accommodate women who had left the practice and wanted to return. In 2006, two partners at New York's Skadden, Arps, Slate, Meagher & Flom began a project, Back to Business Law, whereby women who had left the profession temporarily went through a reeducation process that covered recent developments and reintegrated them into legal practice.

"The goal," said a female partner at Skadden who was the incoming chair of the ABA's business law section and started the project, was to "provide a little bit of a lifeline for those not practicing—to be aware of developments at a high level. And while no firm has enough alumni who are no longer practicing to do a program, the ABA can help us band together to put together some top programs."

"We can't have this pool of talent and let it evaporate," explained another female Skadden partner heading the effort. "We need to nurture them. We don't know if it's the right way or the only way but certainly one means to accomplish our goal."

Unfortunately, it was a great idea whose time apparently came and went. According to the ABA website in 2012, the "Back to Business Law project has been sunset."

Meanwhile, the rise of a few female lawyers into positions of power and influence hasn't reversed the overall trend at most law firms. Part of the explanation is that many of these women embody the paradox of success. Women who moved to the top of big firms over the past two decades were among the first females ever to reach senior leadership roles in their firms. But some of these successful female attorneys seem determined to prove that they have all the toughness of their male mentors—maybe more. They then become younger women attorneys' harshest critics. Perhaps this results from acculturation that was necessary for them to succeed in what has been and still is largely a man's world. Perhaps they feel compelled to prove their uniqueness by preventing other women from replicating their successes. Or perhaps it's just who these particular people always were and will be. Better female role models wrestled with the competing demands of home and office, giving hope to future generations of young women attorneys that career and family need not be mutually exclusive.

The underrepresentation of minorities presents a similar problem: without mentors, advancement is impossible. Of course, mentors for minorities need not be minorities themselves. But the foregoing numbers—fewer than 5 percent minority equity partners—demonstrate the absence of a related cohort: minority partner role models. A young attorney's ability to identify with a successful partner makes a difference to his or her approach to practicing law, especially in a large firm. Even for me, a white male, finding what was and is a relatively unusual role model in a big firm—a partner whose success hadn't precluded the balanced life to which I aspired—was important.

Meanwhile, an institutional culture that allows young lawyers to develop a sense of community is increasingly at odds with the prevailing big-law business model that values immediate results. In other words, life is becoming more difficult for everyone in such firms, regardless of race or ethnicity. The resulting environment doesn't foster diversity because there's no metric that measures its contribution to short-term profits. The *American Lawyer* A-List offers some incentives for diversity, but it didn't exist until 2003 and it's not enough. For example, according to the 2012 NALP directory, one of the firms mentioned earlier, Cadwalader, Wickersham & Taft, had 452 lawyers, 104 of whom were partners. Ninety-one of those partners were men; thirteen were women. Of the men, five were Asian American, one was Latino, one was Hawaiian/Pacific Islander, and one was American Indian/Alaska Native; none was African American. All of the women partners were white, except for one Asian American. There's no breakdown between equity partners and non-equity partners.

Clients can exert a powerful influence on law firm behavior, and they're adding pressure on diversity issues. Microsoft's general counsel, Brad Smith, summarized the practical case: "We believe that diversity in our legal teams is a business necessity. The better we can understand and appreciate the interests and needs of the incredibly diverse array of individuals who make up our stakeholder groups, the more effective we can be. If we can't understand how other people are thinking, there's a greater likelihood that we'll fail to address their needs or persuade them of our position. In this sense, diversity is not simply something that would be nice for us to have; it's a prerequisite for our success."

In 2004, the general counsel of seventy-two major corporations signed a "call to action" that Sara Lee general counsel Roderick Palmore had created and promoted. Following up on an earlier "statement of principle" that BellSouth general counsel Charles Morgan had written and circulated in 1999, Palmore took things a step further: "I didn't want a long detailed document that talked about how to go about designing a program and that sort of thing." Rather, he wanted his fellow top in-house lawyers and their companies' outside law firms to focus on results. Firms failing to comply with diversity benchmarks risked a loss of business.

One signatory to Palmore's "call to action" outlined the business reasons for the efforts: "As a global corporation, we benefit tremendously from a broad spectrum of perspectives that can be achieved by having people from as widely diverse backgrounds as possible working with us. After all, we serve a global population. How can we hope to understand the needs and concerns of customers around the world without incorporating their views into the very fabric of our operations?"

Likewise, another general counsel added, "To position ourselves to receive the best ideas, the best resources, and the best people, it is essential that we include a mix of ideas and perspectives." Still another senior legal officer offered this analysis: "We want our workforce to reflect and represent our customers and the communities where we engage in business. The obvious extension to that is having our vendors, suppliers, consultants, and advisors, including law firms, reflect and represent the same thing."

All of this raises a question about what diversity really means and the value it provides. Its aim could be to capture differences that produce meaningful competition among ideas arising from varied perspectives and approaches. In that regard, objective attributes—such as gender, race, or ethnicity—are relevant, but they're often insufficient to achieve the most important diversity objectives. If the only women or minorities who succeed are those who share the essential values, behavior, characteristics, and outlooks of their white male mentors, they can offer no counterbalance to the worst elements of that world.

IN SO MANY WAYS—including career satisfaction, balance, and diversity—the profession has now become the principal casualty of its transformation. The short-run maximization of annual profits has morphed into the most important long-run goal, too, and few senior partners ever reconsider it. Meanwhile, partner profits and attorney dissatisfaction have risen in tandem as big firms' lawyers make more money and enjoy it less. Those twin developments are not coincidental.

Some results were predictable. Many of these firms' partners achieved staggering wealth. But other consequences may not have been expected: the free-agency system of lateral partner hiring destabilizes firms; the climate of widespread uncertainty undermines morale; depression and job dissatisfaction among lawyers are pervasive. All of the added income carries with it an assumed obligation to work harder; client expectations and demands become greater as they pay more for legal services; lawyers' personal lives are often lost in the shuffle; and the partnership prize at the end of it all seems ever more elusive, if it was worth the effort at all. These developments begin to explain why the practice of law is filled with unhappy attorneys and why lawyers in large firms are among the most dissatisfied.

The problem of depressed, overworked attorneys is growing, and the transformation of large law firms from a professional to a business model is an unambiguous contributor. Steven Brill and the *American Lawyer* are not to blame for everything—or perhaps anything—that's gone wrong with most of the profession's large firms. In 2012, Brill's successor, Aric Press, argued that other forces would have caused change: the surge in demand for high-end legal services, market segmentation among law firms, client mobility, the growth of recruiters. Maybe the legal profession was just a late arrival to the kind of transparency that had already reached other occupations.

But being a lawyer is supposed to mean membership in a special club, making it different from holding other jobs. In that respect, the flow of information about law firm profitability that Brill single-handedly broke loose almost thirty years ago has contributed to profound and, in many respects, troubling changes. All attorneys in big law firms are making far more than they would have earned thirty years ago. If they answered honestly, those lawyers would tell you that when they were students, never in their wildest dreams did they imagine income of the magnitude they now enjoy. And if they were honest, a disturbingly large number of them would also acknowledge that money has not bought them happiness. Some would relinquish a portion of their income to work less and achieve a more balanced life, if they thought that option was available to them. For many, their work remains a persistently depressing experience, largely because it seems unfulfilling, unrelenting, or both.

CHAPTER 6

SURGING INCOME INEQUALITY

What are you going to do about the growing
disparity of wealth in the United States of America?
—Jim Lehrer, television commentator and author, when asked in October 2011
to frame the most important question he'd pose to candidates in the 2012
presidential election; however, a year later, as moderator of the first debate
between President Barack Obama and Governor Mitt Romney, he didn't.

I ADMIT IT: practicing law became far more lucrative than I'd ever
dreamed possible when I was a new associate with a starting salary of
$25,000 in 1979. Today, starting salaries at my old firm are $160,000 and
every equity partner in just about every big law firm is comfortably
among America's 1 percenters. But astute observers correctly note that,
in the larger economy, the real action has been even higher—among
those in the top one-tenth of 1 percent of the country's socioeconomic
pyramid. A similar concentration of wealth is undermining large law
firms. The greed of those at the top, together with growth agendas that
have fueled widespread lateral partner hiring and unwise law firm mergers, is making the inequality problem worse. As these trends destabilize
many big law firms, some institutions that everyone assumed were too
big—and too successful—to fail are now gone. More bad news is ahead
because others will follow them. In that respect, Karl Marx may have
been correct when he wrote that history repeats itself, "first as tragedy,
then as farce."

In some ways, the 2011 complaints of Occupy Wall Street protesters
about growing income inequality resonated with anyone paying attention

to the ongoing redistribution of wealth within large law firms. In 1985, top equity partners in a typical big firm earned three times more than their lowest-paid fellow equity partners. In many firms today, that internal top-to-bottom equity partner multiple is more than ten and growing. But the continuing glut of lawyers means that no one has any sympathy for an attorney with a job requiring a legal degree, much less one that pays a six-figure salary.

So far, rich lawyers in big firms have avoided the kind of public outrage directed toward bankers, even though the top 1 percent of attorneys doubled their share of America's income—from 0.61 to 1.22 percent—between 1979 and 2005. In 1986, the Am Law 100 partner average annual income was approximately eleven times that of the average American employee; in 2010, it was more than twenty-three times that benchmark. Even so, the less publicized gap—in society and within large law firms—is inside the ranks of the privileged, and it has been growing. By one estimate, the top one-tenth of 1 percent of Americans captured half of all gains going to the top 1 percent over the last three decades.

Nobel laureate Joseph Stiglitz and Northwestern University professor Jeffrey Winters are among many academic observers who suggest that today's oligarchs use wealth to preserve power. One effective tactic is to encourage the pursuit of dreams that, for most 99 percenters, are largely illusory. A *New Yorker* cartoon captures the point with a bar scene that shows a scruffy man in a T-shirt telling a well-dressed fellow patron: "As a potential lottery winner, I totally support tax cuts for the wealthy." For today's young attorneys, one largely illusory dream has become an equity partnership atop a big law firm's leveraged pyramid.

How has this happened in big law firms and why is it occurring now? Meritocracies are vital and valuable, but for nations as well as for institutions, extreme income inequality reveals something untoward about the culture that produces it. In large law firms, exploding inequality has become one symptom of a profound ailment: the singular focus on compensation that rewards bad behavior—hoarding clients, demanding more billable hours, raising leverage ratios. As the prevailing model creates amazing wealth for a few, it encourages attitudes that poison working environments and diminish the profession. In the process, it often destabilizes the law firms themselves.

Measured by their average equity partner profits, all large law firms have become lucrative, stunningly so. No one feels sorry for any equity partner anywhere. But even the remarkable average is misleading because it masks the internal distribution of wealth within an equity partnership. Except for a few firms retaining lockstep compensation systems in which partners enter and progress through the equity partnership together, the gap between the top and bottom of the pyramid has expanded dramatically in recent years. In that respect, big firms have mirrored American society: the rich have become a lot richer.

Some leaders rationalize this ongoing redistribution of big law wealth with interesting rhetorical positions. For example, K&L Gates chair Peter Kalis defended the widening internal equity partner gap as the product of geography. Explaining why his firm's pay spread rose from about five to one to as much as nine to one during the past decade, Kalis said, "Houses cost less in Pittsburgh than they do in London."

London is certainly a more expensive city than New York, and New York is more expensive than Pittsburgh—K&L Gates's headquarters. Some firms consider cost-of-living differences when setting compensation; some apply formulaic across-the-board geographical adjustments. But none of that addresses the equity partner income inequality issue, which involves a widening internal range and not the relative cost of comparable talent across offices.

In fact, the article quoting Kalis proves that something other than geography has been at work: "A small number of elite firms, such as Simpson Thacher & Bartlett and Cravath, Swaine & Moore, still hew to narrower compensation bands, ranging from 3-to-1 to 4-to-1, typically paying the most to those with the longest service." Cravath has a London office. Simpson Thacher has offices in Beijing, Hong Kong, London, Los Angeles, New York, Palo Alto, Sao Paolo, Tokyo, and Washington, D.C. Yet they have avoided the surging top-to-bottom equity partnership pay gaps that Kalis attributes to geography. Even so, the chair of Seattle-based Perkins Coie, Robert Giles, echoed Kalis's comments in defending his 850-lawyer firm's base salary spread of eight to one. He just used different cities to make Kalis's unpersuasive geography argument.

The most common defense of the growing wealth gap in big firms is the stated need to attract and retain high-priced talent. Certainly, not all lateral partner hiring is pernicious. In fact, a firm can serve itself and its clients when it identifies and acquires an attorney to meet a particular need. The best firms—even the historically closed family of Cravath, Swaine & Moore—have sometimes turned to the lateral market to fill a special opening. When they recruit laterally on a limited basis, firms can usually absorb a new partner into the firm's culture.

But as firm leaders have increasingly adopted the goal of simply purchasing books of business that include the attorneys servicing the clients they bring with them, a much different phenomenon has overtaken many large firms, especially since 2000. As usual, firm managers are loath to acknowledge the downsides. One has been growing income disparities within equity partnerships: they compromise the profession's traditional values and destabilize firms. For example, the morale effect can be immediate. As a legal consultant explains, "A majority of big law firms have begun reducing the compensation level of 10% to 30% of their partners each year, partly to free up more money to award top producers."

An additional complication can also lead to serious problems: ascertaining the truth about a so-called top producer isn't easy. As firms turn to the market in their endless search for lateral partner rainmakers, they often bid up the price of such attorneys to levels far beyond those lawyers' true value. Sometimes the behavior is fear-driven, such as the firm that seeks to counter revenue losses from its own departing partners by finding replacements so as to avoid a death spiral of additional defections. A firm that thinks it can assess and bid away stars from a competitor often finds disappointment when it discovers that it paid far too much. Even so, incoming laterals get a grace period to prove themselves. After all, the leaders who recruited them are reluctant to admit mistakes, especially prominent ones.

Managing partners of firms most active in the lateral hiring market suggest that money has been important to some partners they have acquired. But they also argue that other factors mattered, such as the desire for a global platform. For example, Frank Burch, co-chair of DLA Piper, acknowledged that enticing a lateral hire requires that the money offered be comparable. But he also said that his firm "did a lot of hiring from firms that reported higher profits per partner" than DLA Piper, including Paul Hastings, Skadden, Arps, Slate, Meagher & Flom, White & Case, and Morgan, Lewis & Bockius.

Burch was able to make this claim because a firm's average partner profits are just that—an average—and have little relationship to what the most promising lateral partners will make at their new firms. They're interested in the high end of the range because, as one former managing partner of a big firm observed, "Over the last few years there has been a dramatic change in the balance of compensation, to a large degree undisclosed, in which increasing numbers of partners fall below the firm's reported average profits per equity partner (PPP). . . . Typically, two-thirds of the equity partners earn less, and some earn only perhaps half, of the average PPP."

A firm's average partner profits aren't luring high-powered laterals; the money at the very top is. Perhaps the desire to provide clients with a better global platform plays a role in some decisions, but firms that experienced the highest number of lateral partner departures in 2011 were already worldwide players. In fact, four—DLA Piper, K&L Gates, Jones Day, and SNR Denton—were simultaneously on both the most-departures and most-hires lists.

There have been many recent high-profile examples of expensive lateral hires. In 2011, Jamie Wareham became big law's latest $5 million man when he left Paul Hastings to join DLA Piper. It's unlikely that the move improved his ability to serve clients. But another question is far more important to his new firm: has Wareham been worth it? No one at DLA Piper would know for sure until he'd been there for a while. Equally significant, it's a good bet that the few who obtained that information would never disclose it publicly if it reflected unfavorably on the wisdom of the original hiring decision. In 2015, Wareham moved to another firm, Fried Frank.

The burgeoning lateral hiring phenomenon exacerbates the worst aspects of the prevailing big-law model. Except for increasingly rare lock-step systems (such as Cravath's), eat-what-you-kill compensation schemes already pit partner against partner in seeking credit for billings. As a consequence, each partner builds individual client silos so that others can't claim a portion of billings that determine annual compensation. There's no incentive to share client relationships; indeed, the contrary is true. Hoarding maximizes a partner's lateral options and therefore makes his or her exit easier, if not more likely.

In these ways, the lateral imperative further compromises traditional partnership values and, in turn, contributes to the broader destabilization of a firm. It discourages mentoring and the institutionalization of client relationships. Training young attorneys and sharing clients might pay dividends for a firm in the future. But most senior partners regard the long run as someone else's problem. Anyone inclined to consider truly partner-like conduct pauses to ask: *What if, someday, I have to justify my economic worth to a new set of partners elsewhere?*

As economic incentives produce predictable human behavior, the combined actions of individual partners over time create a firm's culture while simultaneously destabilizing the firm itself. The contest for laterals accelerates the race around that vicious circle and, with each new addition from outside, diminishes a sense of community and shared purpose. How long can anyone reasonably expect the center to hold when the only shared partnership objective is making money? Only for as long as profits keep rising.

That puts pressure on firms to continue increasing each year's profits to keep the rainmakers happy. Such a strategy gives them their best shot at keeping the designated "best people" while enticing others to sign on. But such a culture can fuel rapid departures when the money stops flowing. The 1987 failure of the Finley Kumble law firm proved that in spectacular fashion, although some would argue that apart from the desire to make money, that firm never had any culture at all.

THE SEVEN-HUNDRED-LAWYER FIRM that by 1987 had become known simply as Finley Kumble began as the dream of Steven Kumble almost twenty years earlier. It eventually became his enduring nightmare. From aggressive lateral hiring to enormous income gaps within so-called partnerships to the public obfuscation and dissembling of leaders as the firm came apart, Finley Kumble's lessons resonate today. But few senior partners in big law firms seem interested in them.

After receiving his undergraduate degree from Yale, Kumble graduated from Harvard Law School in 1959 and went to work at a small New York City firm, Goldstein, Judd & Gurfein, where he quickly acquired a reputation that some described as "predatory." A year later, he and two Goldstein partners joined another small firm. After Kumble made $50,000 as his share of the fee on his first big client deal there, he quit his job, moved to Florida, and in six months reportedly blew all the money on bad investments. Returning to New York, he joined Amen, Weisman & Butler.

In 1968, Kumble and sixty-one-year-old Leon Finley, a prominent lateral hire who had become a name partner in the Amen Weisman firm, took control. They renamed the firm for themselves and three other lawyers who had sided with them in the power struggle: Finley, Kumble, Underberg, Persky & Roth. It had eight partners and a single office in New York City.

The firm's letterhead changed frequently after 1968 to reflect lateral partner stars whom Steven Kumble hired to attract business. High-profile recruiting was central to his strategy—the principal aim of which was to make money. As Kumble himself later put it, "In Finley, Kumble, money may not have been everything. But it was close."

In 1970, Kumble brought in noted litigator Norman Roy Grutman as a name partner to head the fledgling firm's litigation department. But egos have always abounded at the top of the profession, and in 1976, Grutman left after a falling-out with Kumble. When name partner Robert Persky was convicted in 1973 for filing false statements with the Securities and Exchange Commission, Kumble hired Andrew Heine, who had a reputation as one of the top young corporate lawyers in the city, to head the corporate department in his place. In 1975, former New York City mayor Robert Wagner became a partner whose name would immediately follow Finley's and Kumble's because the Wagner family had long been a New York institution.

Thirty-eight-year-old Marshall Manley became Kumble's most consequential lateral hire when he joined the firm as a name partner in 1979 after leaving the Los Angeles office of Manatt Phelps, which he'd helped to build. Manley was a remarkable business generator, but he was as brash as his ego was large. A straight talker, he defied convention when speaking his mind during a 1978 interview with Steven Brill, who had not yet founded the *American Lawyer*. When Brill's article appeared in *Esquire* magazine, Manley's vulgar candor cost him his job at Manatt Phelps.

"We come up against older guys who interviewed us for jobs when we were coming out of school and we kick the shit out of them," Manley told Brill. "Our clients see that. They see that we're goddam smarter than the old firms. They see our adrenaline. . . . I have no qualms about stealing lawyers and clients from other firms. It's the keystone of our program."

When the article appeared, Manley was on a business trip in Hawaii. While he was away, the twenty-three Manatt Phelps partners decided unanimously that they wanted him out. But on later reflection, they feared the loss of the business that Manley had brought to the firm and proposed various compromises in an attempt to keep him. Unmoved, Manley gathered up his clients and opened the Los Angeles office of Finley Kumble, by then the fastest-growing firm in New York City.

The acquisition of Manley was a continuation of Steven Kumble's aggressive approach to growth. When a fellow partner suggested that a better ambition might be for the firm to become the best, Kumble answered, "When you're the biggest, everyone will think we are the best."

In addition to prominent hires that preceded Manley, in 1977 Kumble persuaded the New York District Council of Carpenters that his politically connected firm (with former Mayor Wagner on the roster) was a perfect fit for labor negotiations with the city. When Kumble made his pitch, the firm didn't have a labor lawyer, so he acquired one. Likewise, when Robert Casey, a name partner of another firm—Shea, Gould, Climenko and Casey—developed personality conflicts with two of his other name partners, Kumble persuaded him to move his tax practice to Finley Kumble in 1979; Casey's clients went with him. Such moves became a template for future growth, though they irked the firms that Kumble victimized. By 1979, the New York office had seventy attorneys.

Kumble's next step was geographic expansion to accompany the marquee names that the firm kept adding to the partnership list. He traveled the country pitching new clients and seeking new high-profile partners regarded as having the charisma to attract new engagements. Among other prominent hires were former United States senator Joseph Tydings (by 1981 merger of the forty-four-lawyer Washington firm that Tydings managed), former New York governor Hugh Carey (1983), and, for a reported $1 million each, retiring United States senators Paul Laxalt and Russell B. Long (1986). In what must have been an especially interesting match of personalities, Donald Trump's organization also became one of the firm's clients.

During the early 1980s, Finley Kumble grew exponentially, establishing offices throughout the country and in London with the goal of cross-marketing over many locations. By 1984, Manley had built the firm's California office to 150 lawyers. The firm's Florida presence grew to 140 attorneys in four offices. Geographically dispersed, Finley Kumble partners were united in the common belief that they could make more money at the firm than anywhere else, something that Kumble regularly reiterated at partner meetings.

Rewarding the salesmanship that brought in business, Kumble didn't place a similar premium on quality lawyering or efforts to build an enduring institution. As he later put it, "The amount of business a lawyer brought in the door was dominant in setting compensation and was a good barometer of power and influence as well." The internal spread between the highest- and lowest-paid partners grew to seventeen to one. The big names and the business generators made the most money, even if they did little or no actual legal work on the matters that they brought into the firm.

Finley Kumble seemed to be on an unstoppable roll. It promoted itself as a national firm in which merit—measured exclusively in dollars—governed. The more business a lawyer generated, the more money he took home. In 1984, Steven Kumble predicted that the firm would have seven hundred lawyers in a year or two and embody a new kind of legal institution: "a total meritocracy." At the same time, Marshall Manley boasted, "Come back in a few years and see if this system isn't working. If it doesn't work . . . we'll all be gone. Our partners came here by voting with their feet, and they'll leave the same way." Only three years later, they would.

By 1986, the firm's cash flow wasn't keeping up with the funds that flowed out for overpaid lateral partner stars, office expansions, and a commission-like structure that rewarded partners for originations rather than their substantive contributions to actual legal work. In 1986, Marshall Manley received $1.2 million for generating $14 million in billings, even though he'd left Finley Kumble in 1985 to become president of an insurance and financial services firm. Officially he was still a Finley Kumble partner in 1987, seeking a six-figure share of billings that reportedly didn't include a single hour of his time.

Meanwhile, the firm also suffered from a complete lack of transparency. One former partner said that he and others placed their names on the firm's mailing list so they could find out when and where Finley Kumble had opened new offices, as well as the names of new partners who had joined the firm. Any sense of shared community or common purpose—beyond making money sooner rather than later—was missing.

Lost altogether—if ever it had existed at all—was anything that resembled institution building for the long run: mentoring, promoting collegiality or encouraging intergenerational client continuity. In such a culture, it's no surprise that questionable financial practices developed to mask fast-and-loose accounting schemes. Most partners knew that firm leaders obsessed over monthly cash collections, but they had little awareness that the firm was borrowing to make partner distributions. In early 1987, partners learned through the receipt of individual K-1 partnership income forms that 44 percent of their partnership draws for 1986 had been borrowed money. Outsized egos had always fueled personality conflicts and power struggles among the firm's leaders, but now the real uprising began.

Money had been the glue holding Finley Kumble together, and as profits and collections retreated, partners with portable books of business began to leave. As one senior partner observed, "What brought most people in was money. And I think that as soon as they got scared or nervous that the money would not be there, the lack of foundation and lack of loyalty led them to do what people who have no sense of loyalty always do: think about themselves."

For a time, Finley Kumble's leaders fought back with a strategy that other failing firms would later employ: a public relations campaign. At the same time that Steven Brill was writing about Finley's imminent demise for the September 1987 issue of the *American Lawyer*, the *New York Law Journal* carried a contrasting front-page story: "Finley Kumble: Success, Change, Some Pain." The *Journal* reported, "The firm is making adjustments to accommodate its fast growth and its success. Although Finley Kumble's rivals might relish a juicy divorce, it doesn't appear to be forthcoming. Although there is room for improvement, even the most unhappy partner did not suggest that Finley Kumble was anywhere near the brink of disaster." Except it was.

Two months later, the *New York Times* picked up the story: "Torn by dissension and debt, its pieces are coming apart. Unlike those firms it liked to tweak, Finley Kumble will never make it to its 20th birthday." Although Steven Kumble no longer ran the firm, he still presented himself to the media as its public face. According to the *Times,* he acknowledged that since June, 22 of its 250 partners had left, the London office was being closed, and smaller US offices were being shut down. But Kumble insisted that "much of what is happening is an outgrowth of a decision to 'streamline the firm.'" Likewise, fellow name partner Hugh Carey insisted, "Regardless of how many torpedoes hit the ship, the firm is going forward."

When the end became obvious as partners throughout the country left the firm, no one at the top demonstrated leadership. Steven Kumble later explained that he essentially checked out after losing a power struggle in early 1987. In that way, he absolved himself of responsibility for the firm's continuing disintegration as the year progressed. He later wrote about that time as if he'd been a disinterested bystander rather than a central player in the firm's fate: "Looking back on it now, it is still painful. It was as though a bomb had exploded and all the leaders had died. Rumors were rampant. No one was communicating with anyone. There was no control, no head, no one person or group who knew what was going on and could explain it to our clients, our trade creditors, our banks, and, most importantly, to the younger lawyers and the staff. Careers were up in the air."

Steven Kumble formally withdrew from the firm on December 15, 1987. Two weeks later, the remaining partners voted to dissolve it. On February 24, 1988, the banks forced Finley Kumble into bankruptcy.

TOO MANY LAW FIRM LEADERS learned the wrong lessons from Finley Kumble. Most important, they rationalized away the firm's failure as irrelevant to other firms. Future United States secretary of state Warren Christopher was chair of Los Angeles–based O'Melveny & Myers when he offered his assessment of Finley's demise: "From the outside, it appears that their problem was overexpansion. The lesson is the obvious one that overexpansion is a real danger, along with a tendency to equate size with quality."

Such simplistic characterizations rendered Finley Kumble a failure of execution rather than of fundamental vision. If the firm had been better managed, most observers reasoned, it would have continued to thrive. If other firms wanted to avoid Finley Kumble's fate, they should just grow more slowly.

In truth, the lessons of Finley Kumble were far more profound, or at least they should have been. In 1990, Steven Kumble himself offered other clues that remained unheeded by later generations of big law firm leaders. He described the internal compensation spread between the highest- and lowest-paid partners—seventeen to one—as "staggering" at a time when other firms' compensation spreads were between three to one and five to one. "Ultimately," he wrote, "that disparity was part of the reason people in the firm ran for the exits when they learned about our broader troubles. Behind the disparity lay greed and the desire for power."

Likewise, he admitted, "There was far too much emphasis on who brought in the business." Partners went to extraordinary lengths in preserving their "client origination" credit for business. "Over time," Kumble wrote, "'making the numbers' got out of hand. Methods of computing compensation entitlement drifted more toward business origination. And as business origination grew to be the major determinant of compensation, other distortions crept in. Concurrently, greed took over and pushed senior people to demand increasingly outrageous amounts of money."

But the most important lesson went to the very core of Finley Kumble itself. Steven Kumble observed that his firm "lacked the social fabric and the institutional glue that might hold another firm together in times of financial stress." He continued, "Finley, Kumble fell apart because it was never really together. At the top, there were too many strong egos, too many 'maximum leader' types, and too little institutional glue."

There should be a message in all of this for today's law firm managers who have become obsessed with lateral hiring, but they seem not to notice it. In the 2011 annual survey of law firm chairs and managing partners, 80 percent said they planned to add lateral hires in litigation, 75 percent expected to add corporate practitioners, and 60 percent planned to supplement their partnerships with intellectual-property specialists. Meanwhile, lateral hiring also led these current leaders' lists of biggest disappointments in 2011 (e.g., "lack of sufficient success in attracting laterals"). None of them remembers the tragedy of Finley Kumble.

The recession of 1990–1991 reinforced another lesson that some firm leaders had drawn from Finley Kumble: insofar as profits are at least part of the glue that holds any partnership together, it's critical to safeguard them, but how? As the managing partner of a large Philadelphia law firm admitted in 1991: "Lawyers are not exactly the shining stars of the management world—and now we're confronted with having to manage organizations that were never designed to be managed in the fashion that we're managing them. It's an interesting challenge."

Many firms met the challenge by hiring outside management consultants who brought with them business-school concepts to help partners run their businesses. One of the early pioneers in this newly developing cottage industry was Bradford Hildebrandt, who headed a prominent consulting firm bearing his name. He observed, "In most firms, current management has never operated within a recession and really didn't know how to deal with it." Over the next two decades, Hildebrandt and others would make a lot of money offering business-oriented suggestions to those firms.

One proffered metric connected directly to the bottom line: a firm's leverage ratio. The arithmetic was simple: fewer equity partners meant more profits for those who were. In 1996, Hildebrandt outlined principles that undoubtedly echoed the advice he gave many of his large law firm clients throughout the 1990s: "The real problem of the 1980s was the lax admissions standards of associates of all firms to partnerships. The way to fix that now is to make it harder to become a partner. The associate track is longer and more difficult, and you have a very big movement to two-tiered structured partnership."

The drive to maximize quick profits became a perfect fit for business-school-type metrics: leverage ratios, client billings, billable hours. There was another benefit, too: such data became a supposedly fair and objective way to measure any attorney's value. "Just look at the numbers" became the answer to any partner's complaint about his or her compensation. Behavior that didn't contribute to the bottom line dropped out of the calculus by which law firm leaders assessed their partners. What's the immediately quantifiable value of collegiality, mentoring, developing a sense of community, and encouraging intergenerational transition of clients?

Meanwhile, the Am Law 100 became a more powerful and ready reference by which every big firm could measure its relative performance. One firm—Heller Ehrman—expressly abandoned its successful and long-standing culture in an effort to move up the profitability list.

TWENTY-FIVE YEARS after the failed experiment of Finley Kumble, the story of Heller Ehrman proved again the fragility of such a business model. The difference between the two firms was that Finley Kumble never had a culture to lose; money drove everything from the beginning. Heller Ehrman descended from a nobler position, so its tragic story should seem more familiar to the leaders of today's big law firms.

In 2006, for the first time in its 118-year history, the six-hundred-lawyer San Francisco–based firm crossed the million-dollar threshold in average equity partner profits; two years later, the firm dissolved. In an effort to keep up with the rest of big law's transformation into a collection of profit-maximizing businesses, Heller Ehrman lost its identity.

For decades prior to its final phase, Heller Ehrman's unique culture had attracted many talented law school graduates. A mock coat of arms inside its offices illustrated the relaxed culture that pervaded the firm: a laurel wreath, the scales of justice, and a Latin phrase, *elvem ipsum etiam vivere*—"Elvis lives." For most of its history, profits were spread more evenly among the firm's equity partners (called shareholders) than at the eat-what-you-kill firms with which it competed for clients and talent. Business generation mattered, but so did citizenship, collegiality, and quality of lawyering. The firm's partners made less money than their peers at other San Francisco–based firms, but they didn't care. In 2001, most regarded the average partner profits of $645,000 as enough. But in the mid-2000s, the firm became more oriented toward its bottom line because it feared losing ground to others taking that approach.

"There has been a philosophical adjustment to how we reward our people," said firm chair Matthew Larrabee in 2008. "We are allocating more to our biggest producers." When asked what accomplishment had given him the greatest pride during his three years as chair, Larrabee said, "Having the shareholders rally around what we are doing to make us a more competitive business."

But that rally would end quickly. Less than a year later, Larrabee presided over the firm's bankruptcy filing. Former Heller Ehrman partners have suggested that the firm's downfall began in 2003 when it took the first steps away from its unique culture. At that time, Heller Ehrman's six hundred lawyers placed it in the midsize category. Worried about a future in which it feared that only a few megafirms would survive, Heller acquired a sixty-lawyer corporate firm, along with several more lawyers from the dying Brobeck, Phleger & Harrison firm. Then, in 2005, a merger with Boston-based Goodwin Procter broke down because Goodwin reportedly sought significant reductions in Heller's attorney head count (partners and associates), increases in billable hours, and changes in management structure. When the discussions terminated, Goodwin instead opened four new offices in California and hired several Heller partners to staff them.

Heller then made changes that Goodwin had requested and that some longtime Heller partners later deemed fatal. Seeking to increase average partner profits, the firm changed its compensation structure and pushed dozens of partners out the door. Others defected because the culture that had lured them to the firm in the first place had disappeared; they no longer had any reason to stay for less money than they could earn elsewhere. As one former partner put it, "Now that they have made money [their] number one [priority], I don't know why they are surprised when people leave to make more money."

Additional attempted mergers with larger Chicago-based firms failed during the summer of 2008, first with Baker & McKenzie and then with Mayer Brown. In the latter case, leaders of Heller's highly profitable intellectual-property group weren't sure they'd be happy at Mayer Brown, so in late August they announced that they were leaving for another firm, Washington, D.C.–based Covington & Burling. Two weeks later, Mayer Brown said that "various issues, including client and practice conflicts," had brought discussions to an end. In September, Heller's banks notified the firm that it was in default on its operating loans.

Banks sometimes step in because partner departures trigger a firm's borrowing covenants. Lenders like it when a partnership grows, but downsizing is another matter entirely. Typically, standard language in loan agreements for operating funds limits the speed and extent to which any large law firm can get smaller, whether voluntarily or involuntarily. But there's additional fallout for many banks that have extensive relationships with individual partners in a troubled firm: many of those partners have outstanding personal loans for capital paid into the firm, home mortgages, and private credit lines. Some law firms' banks also manage hundreds of millions of dollars in the partners' and employees' pension funds.

Two weeks after the bank's notice to Heller Ehrman, the partnership voted to dissolve the firm. On December 29, 2008, it sought bankruptcy protection under Chapter 11. By then, most of Heller's partners had found jobs, but more than three hundred former employees, mostly nonlawyers, were reportedly still out of work as the broader economy careened toward a deepening recession.

In revamping the firm so that more money went to the rainmakers, the firm's leadership lost two battles and the larger war. Heller's unique culture disappeared in its effort to retain stars. When the firm's financial condition worsened, the stars became nervous, as did some longtime partners. As Heller attorneys discovered that they could make comparable money elsewhere in a more certain economic environment, they left. Eventually the firm itself folded.

Heller's last chair missed the essential lesson of his management failures. Concluding that he should have worked faster and more furiously on the very strategic plan that destroyed his firm, Larrabee observed, "We worked extraordinarily hard to grow our business and improve our performance because we needed to generate more work in an increasingly competitive market . . . we might have been better served by starting that effort even earlier."

Another former partner offered a different diagnosis: "There were tensions between the imperative of growth and the core values of the firm."

BOTH FINLEY KUMBLE and Heller Ehrman went beyond hiring individual partners and executed the ultimate lateral hiring event—the acquisition of other law firms. Such transactions can be more problematic than the individual acquisition of so-called stars. In recent years, the focus on growth for growth's sake has produced a frenzy of law firm merger activity, some of which involves the combination of two already large law firms. As previously described, leverage is a moneymaker for equity partners, but there are no economies of scale in the practice of law.

Nevertheless, merger mania is rampant and the stated motivations seem curious. For example, Sonnenschein, Nath & Rosenthal's partner profits remained far below its chair's enthusiastic 2007 hopes of a $1.4 million average by 2008. The recession intervened, but as other firms held their ground, Sonnenschein's average partner profits dropped—

from $915,000 in 2007 to $780,000 in 2009. In September 2010, it merged with Denton, Wilde, Sapte, a UK firm with even lower average partner profits. The combined firm became a Swiss *verein*, that is, not a traditional law firm but a voluntary association whose structure facilitates centralized management over a group of entities that maintain their local legal identities and financial independence. In 2011, the firm's SNR side (Sonnenschein) reported average partner profits of $880,000 for its US operations. Meanwhile, its UK side (Denton) had suffered a 36 percent drop in average partner profits to $368,000 in 2010; though preliminary figures for 2011 showed improvement to $525,000, the figure still remained well below SNR's stand-alone performance.

Notwithstanding such ambiguous financial results, SNR Denton's global CEO, Elliott Portnoy, nevertheless declared the merger a success. In fact, he said, the firm wasn't done growing: "All of this expansion is driven by our clients and our sectors and not by geography. It is important strategically that partners understand that the SNR/Denton merger was not a destination but a part of the journey."

Whether that journey leads the firm to a better place remains to be seen. It also depends on who makes that judgment and how. The reported combined average partner profits number for SNR Denton for 2011 was $700,000—making it ninety-second on the Am Law 100 list that year. For 2010, the final year preceding its merger with Denton, Sonnenschein's profit margin was 26 percent. SNR Denton's 2011 profit margin was lower, at 22 percent. Meanwhile, its ranking on the *American Lawyer*'s 2011 Midlevel Associate Satisfaction Survey was 115th out of 126 firms. (In 2012, it improved to 88th out of 129 firms.)

Washington, D.C.–based Hogan & Hartson (1,100 lawyers) joined with the UK firm Lovells to become a 2,300-attorney Swiss *verein* in May 2010. At the time of the announcement, Hogan's chair described the transaction as a "quantum leap that we never could have achieved by bringing in partners from smaller firms." A quantum leap to what is unclear. Hogan Lovells's reported average equity partner profits in 2010 and 2011 remained close to the $1.2 million that Hogan alone had averaged over the prior three years. During 2009—the final full year before its merger with Lovells—Hogan & Hartson's profit margin was 37 percent. For 2011, Hogan Lovells's profit margin was 36 percent. The combined firm's ranking on the 2011 Midlevel Associate Satisfaction Survey was slightly better than SNR Denton's, 112th out of 126 firms, but it improved to 76th in 2012.

Boston-based Edwards, Angell, Palmer & Dodge joined with Chicago's Wildman, Harrold, Allen & Dixon in May 2011. Boasting that clients would "benefit from the expanded range of services and larger geographic reach," the combined firm's first appearance on the Am Law 100 list for 2011 showed 65 fewer lawyers (585) than the number at the time of the merger announcement (650). The combined firm's leverage ratio exceeded 10; it finished last (at number 100) in profit margin (10 percent), and ranked 89th in average partner profits ($730,000) for its fifty equity partners.

Getting reliable information with which to assess the results of these and other mergers isn't easy because the senior partners orchestrating the transactions have a vested interest in making them look good. So do the ubiquitous law firm management consultants cheering them on. Once they undertake a merger strategy, everyone involved takes herculean steps to vindicate it.

This leads management and outside consultants to define success in deceptively simple terms: getting bigger and/or growing equity partner profits in the short run, whichever reflects more favorably on the merger decision. One problem is that growth alone doesn't create value. Nor is enhanced profitability automatic. That doesn't make all law firm mergers a bad idea. But any significant merger has a potential for future instability that is sometimes unseen, rarely quantified, and often ignored—until it's too late.

IN THE END, most merger proponents pander to a simplistic hope: synergy of the combined entity will produce value greater than the sum of its parts. If that happens, it can be a good deal economically for the survivors at the top, at least for a while. But many others may find themselves on the wrong side of a merger's "restructuring opportunities"—a euphemism for shrinking the new equity partnership.

For example, eighteen months after the October 2007 merger that created Dewey & LeBoeuf, the firm had cut the compensation of sixty-six partners. By 2010, the combined firm that once numbered over thirteen hundred lawyers had trimmed away three hundred of them. But as a later chapter describes, its troubles were just beginning.

When Indianapolis-based Baker & Daniels (320 lawyers) merged with Minneapolis-based Faegre & Benson (450 lawyers) in early 2012, Faegre's chair, Andrew Humphrey, a transactional attorney who became the combined Faegre Baker Daniels chief executive partner, said the new firm would have a "unified compensation structure." He planned to manage "partner expectations" and "incentivize people the right way." As he melded Baker & Daniels's two-tier partnership with Faegre & Benson's single-tier one, some people probably didn't like the results.

Mergers that involve both US and overseas firms can result in pay cuts for attorneys in the foreign firm when the combined entity links pay more closely to productivity measures such as leverage and billings. As a merger specialist in a law firm management consulting firm observed, "That can create very unhappy people, very quickly."

As with high-profile lateral partner hires, mergers put pressure on leaders to push everyone harder. They want to show increases in client billings, billable hours, and leverage as proof that the new institution is better. However, even instant increases in partner profits don't prove the long-term value of the transaction.

But mergers continue because lawyers excel at a skill that can become their undoing: dismissing or reframing adverse precedent that fails to suit the position they want to take. They delude themselves into thinking that somehow their firms are immune from the fundamental human tendencies and larger societal trends that will continue to bring great firms down. Pre-law students with a confirmation bias that tilts them toward legal careers grow up to be senior partners who still suffer from that affliction.

A CORE PROBLEM inside the growing merger and lateral partner bubble is a loss of community and shared sense of purpose. Lawyers united solely in the mission of boosting current-year profits present daunting challenges to law firm leaders attempting to combine highly individual firm cultures.

K&L Gates is a recent example of a law firm that has experienced remarkable growth. It has resulted from a series of mergers that began when Kirkpatrick & Lockhart combined with London-based Nicholson, Graham & Jones in 2005. That created a single firm of 826 attorneys by the end of 2006. In 2007, it added Seattle firm Preston, Gates

& Ellis—home of Microsoft founder Bill Gates's father—giving K&L Gates 1,400 attorneys. In January 2008 it added Hughes & Luce in Dallas. Six months later it picked up North Carolina–based Kennedy, Covington, Lobdell & Hickman. In March 2009, it added Chicago-based Bell, Boyd & Lloyd. By the end of 2010, the firm's attorney head count approached 1,800—almost 1,000 lawyers more than K&L itself had in total after its London merger only four years earlier.

On December 30, 2010, K&L Gates chair Peter Kalis reportedly sent an email that revealed the unseen challenges associated with his firm's merger craze. The legal blog *Above the Law* reproduced his message, in which Kalis reminded fellow partners to get their outstanding client bills paid before the end of the firm's fiscal year. There's nothing wrong with such exhortations. In fact, managing partners of every firm offer them all the time—as they should. But assuming the accuracy of *Above the Law*'s reporting, Kalis's communication to his partners revealed the firm's challenges following its explosive growth through acquisition. After correcting typos purportedly in the original, it read:

> Let me be clear about a couple of things. First, partners and administrators at this law firm are expected to run through the tape at midnight on December 31. Many of you came from different cultures. I don't care about your prior acculturation. We didn't conscript you into service at this law firm. You came voluntarily. What we are you are as well. And that brings me to my second point. We are a US-based global law firm. US law firms operate on a cash basis of accounting. Our fees must be collected by midnight within the fiscal year in which they are due. You don't get to opt out of this feature because it doesn't appeal to you. Again, I couldn't care less whether it appeals to you. It is who we are and therefore it is who you are. Get us paid by tomorrow.

In response to *Above the Law*'s request, Kalis declined to comment on the memo. But assuming its validity, the message acknowledged an unintended consequence of the prevailing big-law business model: law firm mergers erode what were once distinct firm cultures. Two sentences make the point: "Many of you came from different cultures. I don't care about your prior acculturation."

Like any service business, a firm is simply the sum of its people added to the accumulated franchise value of its brand. As senior partners make lateral moves or merge into what become new and different equity partnerships for everyone involved, what does the culture of that new firm become? Does it coalesce around the single common goal of raising current-year profits as high as possible? Is there room for other, nonmonetary values that traditionally have attracted some young lawyers to the profession, and if so, how do firms encourage their survival?

The answers matter because, as Kalis's email emphasizes: "What we are you are as well." What passes for culture in too many big firms is his message's final line: "Get us paid by tomorrow."

Before it merged with the Preston Gates firm, Kirkpatrick & Lockhart's 2007 profits per partner averaged $800,000 and its profit margin was 26 percent. By 2011, partner profits averaged $890,000, but its profit margin had dropped to 22 percent—among the year's worst in the Am Law 100. Meanwhile, K&L Gates ranked 105th out of 126 firms in the *American Lawyer*'s 2011 Midlevel Associate Satisfaction Survey. The firm dropped to 115th out of 129 firms in 2012.

PERHAPS THE POSTER CHILD for recent big-law merger mania is DLA Piper. (Some observers, including K&L Gates's Kalis, insist that DLA Piper and other Swiss *vereins* aren't really law firms.) DLA Piper resulted from the combination of several large firms that were once independent enterprises based in the United Kingdom, Baltimore, Chicago, and San Diego. The firm grew from 2,700 lawyers in January 2005 to 4,200 by 2012. The attorneys it *added* during that period would equal one of the twenty largest firms in the world. Then again, so would the 1,000 attorneys that K&L Gates added during the four years ending in December 2010.

DLA Piper made news in late 2011 when it hired outsider Tony Angel to be the firm's new co-chair. The whirlwind courtship between Angel and the firm began with a May 2011 breakfast meeting that included incumbent global chair Frank Burch and others on the leadership team. Six months later, Angel got the top spot.

"He's got great values and he believes in what we're trying to do and he shares our view of what's going on in the world," Burch said as he described the person with whom he would now share DLA Piper's global chair. "So, we didn't hesitate for a second and worry about the fact that the guy was not in the firm."

When Burch commented that Angel has "great values," "believes in what we're trying to do," and "shares our view," what did he mean? DLA Piper's press release offered this hint: "Tony will work with the senior leadership on the refinement and execution of DLA Piper's global strategy with a principal focus on improving financial performance and developing capability in key markets." In other words, Angel's job was to make DLA Piper bigger and its surviving equity partners richer.

At the time of the announcement, law firm management consultant Peter Zeughauser said that Angel was a hot property: "It's hard to get a guy that talented. There just aren't that many people out there who have done what he has done." Zeughauser was referring to Angel's management of UK-based Linklaters from 1998 to 2007. By the time he left, it had a global presence and average partner profits of $2.4 million. Although DLA Piper's 2010 average partner profits exceeded $1.1 million in 2010, Angel's job would be to take them even higher. Presumably, one way would be to improve the firm's profit margin, which had dropped from 30 percent in 2007 to 25 percent in 2011, even as the firm's leverage ratio increased from 5 to more than 7.

Ignored in the financial shorthand and the discussion of profit miracle workers are questions no one asks. For example, most big firms prospered wildly during big law's go-go years, which began in the mid-1990s and continued into the twenty-first century. Does the person at the top deserve all the credit? The partners who bring in clients, orchestrate deals, and win trials might think otherwise. Conversely, by 2010 Linklaters's average profits per partner had slipped to $1.8 million. Did that happen because Angel had left three years earlier? The financial crisis is a more likely culprit. And perhaps most important, what gets sacrificed in the quest for growth and instantaneous profits? That is becoming clearer: things that aren't easily quantified, including a sense of community and a culture in which mentors would groom home-grown talent to develop a firm's future leaders. What does it say to (or about) other DLA Piper partners that not a single one of them was deemed as qualified to lead the firm as an outsider?

Rather than consider the heresy implicit in such questions, the spin zone focuses on what legal headhunter Jack Zaremski called a "brave move" that "might very well pay off." Pay off, indeed. In the *American Lawyer*'s 2011 Midlevel Associate Satisfaction Survey, DLA Piper ranked 99th out of 126 firms. In reviewing their shared values and vision, did Angel and his new DLA Piper partners discuss the rewards that might come with addressing the firm's attorney dissatisfaction rate? Probably not. After all, Linklaters ranked 108th in the same survey. To its credit, DLA Piper improved to 53rd out of 129 firms in 2012; Linklaters dropped to 124th.

LOW LEVELS OF JOB SATISFACTION among associates are one of many burdens that leaders of big firms are willing to inflict as they grow their firms and their personal wealth. Other collateral damage became apparent as the Great Recession began. But what some big firms did to many of their partners and associates merely revealed the fragility of the prevailing business model. For a few firms, the model has been their undoing.

CHAPTER 7

CONTINUING DESTABILIZATION

We have met the enemy, and he is us.
—*Pogo*, 1971

EXTERIOR SHOCKS CAN EXPOSE internal weaknesses. In 2008, the economy soured and the demand for legal services that had contributed to the exponential growth of big firms and their equity partners' profits waned. Corporate transactional lawyers found that they had nothing to do except to reinvent themselves as bankruptcy-related attorneys who worked on the restructuring of dying clients. Litigators found that their clients had become more eager to settle matters sooner rather than later, thereby avoiding the legal fees that a prolonged battle generated. And so it was that the average number of hours billed in firms of more than five hundred lawyers dropped by more than 5 percent from 2007 to 2009. That may not sound like a lot, but the bottom-line implications were significant, all the more so when considering that, in the aggregate, firms were shedding associates by the thousands.

During earlier downticks in the business cycle, law firms sought to avoid publicity about employees whom they were jettisoning due to lack of business. Such press sent bad messages to two constituencies: law students who were thinking about joining a firm and clients who might use a firm's excess capacity as a way to extract price concessions. Their victims embraced the low-profile approach because it minimized individual shame and they could seek other employment without media attention. But in the new millennium, as law firm management consultants and law firm leaders with MBAs continued to transplant business school jargon into the legal profession, big firms began using a term that was already familiar to most American workers: *layoffs*.

The Internet forced candor. It allowed associates from different firms to create virtual communities. Their anonymous tips to *Above the Law* opened new windows into large law firms. No longer able to finesse rumors about associate and partner departures, many law firms went public with the information themselves. Firms that had adhered previously to "no comment" as a response to press inquiries were making announcements and issuing press statements about their draconian and unprecedented actions.

Such transparency revealed ugliness in many big law firms. As the global economy collapsed, employees in other industries agreed to work fewer hours so that more of their colleagues could remain on the payroll. Some countries, including Germany, did this on a national scale and achieved enviable unemployment rates because everyone shared the burden. America's big-firm partners turned the screw in the other direction, concentrating the first waves of pain at the bottom. Mass layoffs of associates became necessary so that attorneys who kept their jobs could fill the days and nights productively. The survivors had to maintain sufficiently high billable hours to sustain record equity partner profits.

Firm leaders also used the public announcements of layoffs to send a message to their potential lateral partner audience that they weren't afraid to make the hard decisions, run their institutions as businesses, and continue growing profits. In an era of senior leadership's fears and abundant associate supply, present and future associates took a backseat to prospective rainmakers. Even in hard times, extraordinary profitability remained. Throughout the darkest days of the Great Recession, average partner profits for the Am Law 100 never dropped below $1.25 million a year—less than 5 percent from the all-time high in 2007.

THE GREAT RECESSION exposed the worst aspects of many firms' cultures. The effort to preserve equity partner wealth resulted in one day—February 12, 2009—that immediately became known as "Bloody Thursday." In a few hours, a half dozen large law firms that previously had weathered difficult economic times without large layoffs announced the termination of eleven hundred attorneys and staff. One of the largest firms in the country, DLA Piper, trimmed eighty of its fifteen hundred lawyers while also dismissing one hundred nonlawyers.

Such steps might look like a typical business response to difficult economic times. But that implies that the practice of law should be a typical business. Even more important, it assumes that equity partners are entitled to grow their individual wealth, regardless of underlying economic conditions and the toll that their actions take on others or the profession. For DLA Piper and other big firms that were kicking the best and brightest legal minds of the next generation to the curb, layoffs weren't about trying to save the firms in the long run. Rather, they were about trying to preserve equity partners' million-dollar incomes for the upcoming year and beyond.

Then again, some leaders probably feared that a significant decline in partner profits—even in the midst of the worst recession since the Great Depression—would leave their most productive partners vulnerable to lateral poachers from other firms. In that respect, they had made themselves victims of circumstances that they had helped to create.

Whatever the motives, it was an interesting turn of events. When times were good, equity partners everywhere had always defended their staggering incomes on the grounds that they'd assumed an owner's risk and were entitled to reap the profits. Now, rather than carry excess capacity, allow average billable hours to continue dropping back to levels that many of them had worked when they were associates, and risk erosion of equity partner profits into the high six-figure range (where they'd been prior to 2005), they blithely shifted those risks to the firm's non-owner attorneys and staff, who lost their jobs. A day after its cuts, DLA Piper announced a 4 percent increase in its 2008 revenue and a rise in average profits per partner, to almost $1.3 million. A year later, that average was still around $1.2 million. It dropped to $1.135 million in 2010 before moving back above $1.2 million in 2011.

Other law firms had already taken similar steps, as each day's new headlines amply demonstrated:

- "Wilson Sonsini blames downturn for 113 layoffs"
- "MoFo [Morrison & Foerster] cuts 201 jobs in latest round of layoffs"
- "McDermott lays off 149 across US network"

For many firms, their actions were a dramatic about-face from previously announced positions. For example, Latham & Watkins's chair had announced a no-layoffs policy in March 2008, after a year in which, according to the *American Lawyer*, its average equity partner earnings soared to almost $2.3 million. Discussing the firm's record financial success in 2007, he said that the firm had erred in dismissing associates during the 1990 recession. He emphasized that profitability later suffered from the shortage of capable associates when the economy recovered. "There will be no layoffs," he proclaimed. "The subject was not even on the table for discussion."

A year later, in February 2009, the *American Lawyer* reported that Latham's 2008 partner profits dropped to $1.8 million. Three weeks after that, the firm's no-layoffs policy went out the window as 190 associates and 250 staff lost their jobs.

Latham wasn't alone. Throughout the country, firm leaders worked feverishly to preserve their equity partners' million-dollar paychecks. San Francisco–based Orrick, Herrington & Sutcliffe fired a hundred lawyers and twice as many staff after earning $1.3 million in average partner profits in 2008. Los Angeles–based O'Melveny & Myers terminated 90 attorneys and 110 staff a few days after reporting a 7 percent decline in partner profits to $1.5 million. After earning average partner profits of $1.4 million in 2008, Chicago-based Sidley & Austin cut loose 89 associates and 140 staff, and served notice on those in its London office that many of them were next. On and on and on it went.

In a world where astronomical profits alone held many large law firms together, most firm leaders perceived themselves as having few options. The not so distant past when average equity partner earnings were a paltry half million dollars was less than a distant memory; it was as if those days had never existed at all. Managing partners behaved as though their firms would disintegrate unless they took drastic steps to preserve equity partners' stunning wealth. The sad truth is that many of them might have been correct.

The few firms that resisted such short-termism may have reaped rewards. Some appeared on the *American Lawyer*'s 2011 A-List, which took into account associate satisfaction, diversity, and pro bono activities in addition to revenue per lawyer. Hughes, Hubbard & Reed avoided mass layoffs during the Great Recession and led the A-List in 2011 and 2012 after a second-place finish in 2010. Debevoise & Plimpton likewise kept extra associates on the payroll throughout the Great Recession as its average partner profits dropped below $2 million in 2009, but it ranked third on the A-List in 2010, fifth in 2011, and eighth in 2012 (by which time its average partner profits were back above $2 million again). Munger, Tolles & Olson has been a top A-List finisher since 2008, when it became the first firm outside New York City to be ranked number one—a position it held for three years before finishing second in 2011 and third in 2012.

Then again, perhaps associates who survived layoffs at their firms developed a new sense of career satisfaction from that fact alone. That might explain why some of the previously mentioned firms imposing significant 2008 and 2009 layoffs also made the 2010 A-List, including Latham & Watkins, Morrison & Foerster, O'Melveny & Myers, and Orrick, Herrington & Sutcliffe. Two of those firms, O'Melveny and Orrick, didn't make the 2011 list because their associate satisfaction scores dropped significantly in the late 2010 survey. O'Melveny's improved associate satisfaction scores in 2011 returned that firm to the A-List in 2012, when it placed seventh. Orrick's 2011 association satisfaction showed gains, too. In the end, the real lesson of the A-List is that most firms' desire to make it will never trump managing partners' short-range economic self-interest.

THE REACTION OF MOST big-law-firm leaders to the economic downturn did more than put many employed lawyers out of work. It also blocked newcomers' entry into that segment of the profession. Graduates from top law schools in 2009, 2010, and 2011 became members of the "lost classes" because summer intern programs and new hiring had plummeted dramatically, too. As firms revoked or deferred previous offers of full-time employment that third-year students had accepted, only 71 percent of 2009 law school graduates secured any job requiring bar passage. The class of 2010 fared even worse—68 percent. For the class of 2011, the drop continued, to 55 percent.

The ripple effect on the future will be even more profound. When the most lucrative 15 percent of the profession hangs out a Not Hiring sign, many other new lawyers feel it. Graduates who otherwise would have taken big-firm jobs apply for less remunerative positions that in prior years went to others.

As previously noted, before the Great Recession began, the Bureau of Labor Statistics estimated that there would be a grand total of 98,500 additional lawyer positions of all kinds during the *entire decade* ending in 2018. In 2012, the BLS revised that number downward to 73,600 for the decade 2010 through 2020. But insofar as either estimate assumed big law firms would resume growth at their recent historical rates, even the reduced number will turn out to be wildly high. From 2005 to 2008, the NLJ 250—the 250 largest US law firms—grew at a net annual rate of 4 to 5 percent. But at the end of 2011, the NLJ 250 employed a total of 126,000 lawyers—7,000 fewer than three years earlier. At that rate, employment in the big-law-firm segment of the profession wouldn't return to its 2008 level until at least 2015, and net increases beyond that would be even further away. Meanwhile, the spectacular failure of some large firms is making things even worse.

LIKE FINLEY KUMBLE two decades earlier, Heller Ehrman's demise demonstrated the speed with which a seemingly secure institution can unravel because focusing on the near future leaves it fragile and vulnerable. So did the death of two other venerable firms, Thelen in 2008 and Howrey in 2011.

Formed by merger in 1998, Thelen, Reid & Priest consisted of two predecessor firms—Thelen, Marrin, Johnson & Bridges and Reid & Priest—dating to 1924 and 1935, respectively. San Francisco–based Thelen Marrin specialized in large construction projects, including the Hoover Dam and the Golden Gate Bridge. New York's Reid & Priest was known for its electric utility expertise. Together, the new firm had 350 lawyers.

Eight years later the Thelen firm, now with 390 lawyers, merged with Brown, Raysman, Millstein, Felder & Steiner, a twenty-seven-year-old New York firm that was best known for its corporate and technology practices. The combination was the largest law firm merger of 2006 and resulted in a single entity of more than six hundred attorneys. Its 2007 leverage ratio exceeded 6 and its average partner profits were more than $800,000.

Integrating the two firms became problematic, as the firm lost more than two hundred lawyers, including name partners Peter Brown,

Richard Raysman, and Jeffrey Steiner, during the two years immediately following the merger. Observers noted that "Thelen became bogged down in Brown Raysman's debt, and Thelen's marquee construction group did not meld well with Brown Raysman's technology and finance practices."

As with Heller Ehrman, the excessive loss of partners triggered the firm's bank loan covenants restricting the number of such departures permitted in any twelve-month period. The firm sought to find a willing merger party that would thereby boost head count and stem additional defections. Those efforts failed and partners voted for dissolution in October 2008.

In an announcement to all employees, Thelen Reid management said: "The decision to dissolve the firm was precipitated by several economic factors, including recessionary pressures and numerous partner departures over the past year, both of which have negatively impacted firm revenues. . . . Thelen management wishes to thank those who have been part of the Thelen family over the firm's many years of service to its clients." In contrast, a former Thelen chair blamed the absence of strong leadership for the firm's collapse.

FORTY FORMER THELEN LAWYERS, including the firm's final chair, Stephen O'Neal, found a new home at Washington, D.C.–based Howrey, only to have their new firm fail as quickly as Thelen's had. Its sudden downfall came as a surprise, too. As recently as May 19, 2008, a Washington publication, *Legal Times*, had honored Howrey chair Robert Ruyak as one of the profession's "visionaries." By February 1, 2011, he was hoping that Chicago-based Winston & Strawn would hire most of Howrey's partners as the firm collapsed.

It was a remarkable reversal of fortune. When Ruyak became chair in January 2000, the Howrey firm with its 325 attorneys ranked near the middle of the Am Law 100, with average profits for its eighty-nine equity partners of $575,000. Not content with the firm's reputation as a premier antitrust litigation practice (its motto was "In Court Every Day"), Ruyak led his institution on a quest for a higher profile. As the *Legal Times* observed when honoring him in 2008, "To achieve that vision, Ruyak knew that the firm had to be bigger, so Howrey went on a merger spree." He led Howrey on a binge that picked up a Houston-based patent firm, acquired the antitrust practice of another firm, and opened offices in London, Amsterdam, Brussels, Paris, Munich, and Madrid.

For a while the strategy seemed to work. By 2006, Howrey had 555 attorneys and its 127 equity partners averaged $1.2 million. After profits dropped in 2007, they soared by almost 30 percent in 2008—the biggest percentage gain in the Am Law 100 that year. Howrey's 2008 profits were $1.3 million per equity partner—an all-time high.

Even as the economy faltered, the firm didn't change direction. In November 2008 Ruyak brought in the former chair of the failing Thelen firm, along with thirty-nine of its construction litigators. In July 2009, Howrey acquired a twenty-six-attorney intellectual-property Silicon Valley boutique.

As Ruyak continued to paint a rosy picture of the firm's performance during tough economic times, partners were surprised to learn in early 2010 that profits had actually plunged by 30 percent the previous year and that they would receive only two-thirds of their previously budgeted compensation. The firm's overseas partners were especially unhappy, and the head of the European intellectual-property group resigned from the executive committee. Within six months, he would leave and take almost all of Howrey's European intellectual-property practice with him.

Ruyak and the executive committee developed a plan to cut costs. In early spring, the firm began to push people out. More than sixty partners would be gone by July. Meanwhile, partners had learned in March that the firm had overpaid the previous year's distributions to cover taxes and that they owed the firm money because it had performed so poorly relative to its budget. The partner departures continued, and the firm's primary lender, Citibank, became restless. Still, in November 2010, Ruyak and newly appointed vice chair Sean Boland assured partners that Howrey could still reach 75 percent of its target for 2010, which was $1 million in profits per partner. A decade earlier, Boland himself had been a high-profile lateral hire.

Meanwhile, Ruyak and Boland were secretly working on a merger with another firm in an effort to bail Howrey out of its mess. As the two men met with Winston & Strawn chair Dan Webb and managing partner Thomas Fitzgerald, Boland took a page from Steven Kumble's media playbook. Asked about the wave of departures that most recently had included vice chair Henry Bunsow to Dewey & LeBoeuf, Boland insisted that Howrey was optimistic about its prospects after a "difficult" restructuring process in 2010 and was in a "much better position for 2011." Boland continued, "The amount of costs taken out of the firm at all levels—which include leases, partners, associates, and the like leaving the firm—have [sic] made the firm much more efficient. It's done wonders for our cost structure, such that we're going to see some major advantages in 2011. We're very encouraged by the cost cutting that we've done." Six weeks later, Boland resigned and took forty-five Howrey attorneys with him to another large firm, Houston-based Baker Botts.

During January 2011, Howrey's merger discussions with Winston & Strawn devolved into a collection of individual offers that it made on February 1, 2011. Winston wanted only certain Howrey groups: global antitrust, the Washington, D.C., office, the intellectual-property practice, the entire Houston office, and global litigation. Of the eighty-one offers it extended to partners, about half were accepted.

On March 9, 2011, Howrey announced its dissolution. If prior law firm failures are any indication, bankruptcy proceedings involving Howrey, its partners, and its partners' new law firms will continue for years. For most partners, the firm's once-proud motto—"In Court Every Day"—has assumed a new and unpleasant meaning.

In subsequent interviews, Ruyak's partial explanation of the firm's collapse was that the financial success of 2008 had been aberrational (on the high side) but had created expectations. Large contingency receipts accounted for much of that year's nonrecurring spike, and the firm was still "figuring out how to do [alternative fee arrangements] well." Of course, that simplistic notion ignores a more fundamental problem: the revolution of rising expectations is unforgiving. Ruyak got closer to the mark when he later put it this way: "Partners at major law firms have very little tolerance for change."

By that, he really meant that his partners had very little tolerance for a decline in earnings. But that culture existed for a reason. Aggressive growth by acquisition produced partners who didn't know each other and therefore had more difficulty trusting each other. Ruyak had helped to create a firm that became more profitable in the short term but lost the cohesion and shared purpose needed to bind it through adversity for the long haul. Once profits declined, institutional allegiances became tenuous and the firm itself became fragile. The leadership's failures of transparency and communication caused a drop in earnings to come as a surprise to the vast majority of partners. The partners' loss of confidence in each other made the firm's subsequent collapse especially swift.

In 2000, Howrey had a clear identity and average equity partner profits of almost $600,000—seemingly sufficient to keep partners satisfied and the firm stable. A decade later, disappointing projections that the firm might reach only 80 to 90 percent of its $940,000 target for average equity partner profits (in other words, $750,000 to $850,000) fed rumors and led to the firm's disintegration.

As the firm failed, efforts at public relations didn't help. Law firm management consultant Peter Zeughauser served as Howrey's adviser from the time Ruyak hired him in 2000. He attended all but one of the annual partner retreats over the next decade and was responsible for setting up the late November 2010 dinner at which Ruyak and Boland met with Winston & Strawn's chair, Dan Webb, and managing partner Thomas Fitzgerald to discuss Howrey's search for a merger partner. As Howrey was failing and its practice group leaders were heading for the exits, Zeughauser remained a loyal spokesman, echoing vice chair Sean Boland's assurances that all was well and that Howrey had a plan. The firm was "getting back to its strengths," Zeughauser said. "Look, in today's world you're going to lose people you don't want to lose. But Howrey is very focused on continuing to strengthen its practice and that's what they're doing. What's happening at Howrey is largely by design."

After the firm failed, Zeughauser offered a more candid analysis. What happened at Howrey "was in no small part attributable to a number of leaders not owning responsibility and, indeed, walking away from their partners when they needed them most." Those leaders, all Ruyak-era lateral transfers who had been put in trusted positions, "often had legitimate complaints, but . . . instead of doing the heavy lifting, they walked away."

THE DEMISE OF HOWREY previewed an even more momentous law firm collapse. But big firms' leaders dismissed Howrey's fate as irrelevant to their firms; pernicious and pervasive trends continued unabated. Meanwhile, a powerhouse Wall Street institution began to stumble on its way to an infamous fall.

CHAPTER 8

DEWEY & LEBOEUF: A CASE STUDY

If the direction we're taking the firm in was somehow disapproved of,
then the reality is that there ought to be a change in management.
But I don't sense that.
—Dewey & LeBoeuf chair Steven H. Davis on March 22, 2012,
two months before the firm filed for bankruptcy

DEWEY & LEBOEUF IS A CASE STUDY in disasters that occur when prevailing big-law trends combine with leaders' hubris and an unwillingness to accept facts that contradict preconceived views. It illustrates the capacity of firm managers to obfuscate and dissemble when truth becomes harsh and unpleasant. And it demonstrates that at times of true crisis, when leadership is most needed, some so-called leaders really aren't. To be sure, some aspects of Dewey & LeBoeuf's failure are unique. Managing partners of other firms focus on them as reasons to dismiss Dewey as aberrational. That's a mistake.

The partners running large law firms are talented lawyers. They're smart and they know it. They're adept at rationalizing away adverse precedent that doesn't buttress whatever argument they want to make. They analyze why failed firms dating back to Finley Kumble are different from their own, rather than considering the fundamental characteristics they share.

Those in charge of Dewey & LeBoeuf were no exception. But great strengths can become tragic flaws. The talents that took Dewey & LeBoeuf's leaders to the pinnacle of the profession combined with a capacity for self-delusion to crush their firm and upset the lives of everyone associated with it. Dewey & LeBoeuf's managers ran the firm in ways that most lawyers would never recommend to a client. They ignored the fragility of the big-law business model and its intolerance for missteps. Whatever they might have learned from earlier disasters involving big law firms, it's too late to help them now. The question is whether leaders of other firms have learned anything from Dewey & LeBoeuf.

THE DEMISE OF DEWEY & LEBOEUF sent unprecedented shock waves throughout the legal and business worlds in early 2012. Only five years earlier, the profession had experienced a much different surprise when the white-shoe establishment of Dewey Ballantine merged with the somewhat stodgy LeBoeuf, Lamb, Greene & MacRae. For different reasons, the chair of each firm thought he'd seen in the other firm a perfect fit for his institution's needs. What they created instead became a monumental failure. Dewey Ballantine wanted more stability, greater visibility, and enhanced financial security. LeBoeuf Lamb was looking for the cachet that came with a venerable Wall Street firm name and a mergers-and-acquisitions (M&A) practice. When the firms combined in October 2007, Dewey & LeBoeuf had more than thirteen hundred lawyers in twenty-seven offices throughout the world. According to the *American Lawyer*, its average equity partner income in 2008 exceeded $1.5 million a year. On Memorial Day 2012, it filed for bankruptcy.

Dewey, Ballantine, Bushby, Palmer & Wood was named after Thomas E. Dewey, the former governor of New York and Republican presidential candidate who lost decisively to Franklin D. Roosevelt in 1944 and almost beat Harry Truman in 1948. But its origins dated to 1909. At the time of the October 2007 merger, the Am Law 100 ranked it sixty-sixth in gross revenues and twenty-ninth in average equity partner profits.

LeBoeuf, Lamb, Greene & MacRae was formed in 1929 and became known for its utility, energy, and insurance practices. Its pre-merger rankings and average partner profits were similar to Dewey Ballantine's: forty-ninth in gross revenues and twenty-eighth in average equity partner profits.

In 2006, Dewey Ballantine's chair, Morton A. Pierce, had pursued widely publicized merger discussions with San Francisco–based Orrick,

Herrington & Sutcliffe. Dewey's M&A practice had been a big attraction for Orrick. But as the negotiations proceeded, several of those Dewey partners left for other firms, so the deal fell apart. The exercise left Dewey Ballantine weaker.

Meanwhile, Steven H. Davis had become chair of LeBoeuf Lamb in 2004 and sought to expand the firm beyond the specialties for which it was known. To that end, he began looking for prominent lateral hires, starting with Ralph Ferrara, a partner at New York–based Debevoise & Plimpton and a former top lawyer at the Securities and Exchange Commission. LeBoeuf Lamb reportedly promised to pay Ferrara $2 million a year and supposedly assume responsibility for his pension, a liability valued at $16 million. The legal community celebrated Davis's hiring of Ferrara because he raised the firm's profile in Washington, D.C., and positioned LeBoeuf Lamb to represent corporate clients in securities cases. But that early coup also encouraged Davis in a strategy that the firm followed to an unfortunate extreme.

Davis wanted LeBoeuf Lamb to get bigger and believed that a high-powered M&A practice was the way to give the firm a global presence. A New York–based legal recruiting firm reportedly received $2 million for bringing together LeBoeuf Lamb and Dewey Ballantine. Those discussions began during a May 2007 breakfast in midtown Manhattan between Davis and Pierce.

Davis was enthusiastic about the prospect of merging with Dewey Ballantine. Normally, selling such an idea to the rest of any big firm's partners wouldn't be easy or quick. But Davis had previously consolidated power after another partner group launched an unsuccessful challenge to his leadership. In the process, he allegedly acquired a reputation such that, as one partner later said, "If you voted against the transaction, it would be career suicide." On September 28, he assembled the firm's New York partners in the firm's cafeteria where a consultant from McKinsey & Company—which had analyzed the merits of the merger for a reported $1.3 million—read aloud each partner's name and recorded the votes. It was unanimous.

After the merger in October 2007, Davis became chair of the combined firm; Pierce and Ferrara became vice chairs. In an unusual move, many partners of each firm received four-year contracts that guaranteed their compensation, regardless of the firm's performance. According to Martin Bienenstock, a high-profile bankruptcy partner who joined the firm shortly after the merger and sat on the firm's executive committee through the firm's demise, the point of that tactic was "to be sure that the business generators remained in place. Some people's contracts guaranteed money no matter what the firm's income was." Bienenstock reportedly got a long-term deal, too.

When the full force of the 2008 recession hit, the firm missed its profits target: instead of a 25 percent increase from 2007, profits dropped 15 percent. Bienenstock later described Dewey management's response to the problem: "The firm dealt with not being able to pay the income that it wanted to pay many partners by promising to pay it in future years as the money was earned." In other words, Dewey & LeBoeuf mortgaged its future.

BY EARLY 2009—eighteen months after the merger—the compensation of sixty-six partners had been cut, some by as much as 80 percent so that they were paid less than senior associates. Davis also thinned the ranks throughout 2009 and into 2010, as the total number of Dewey & LeBoeuf lawyers dropped by 300. Staff cuts totaled another 300.

Dewey pursued a "barbell" approach to partnership compensation. One end of the barbell consisted of the senior partner rainmakers who controlled clients and billings; the other end included the so-called service partners who did most of the work. Partners who controlled billings received the lion's share of the firm's profits. Some partners were making $300,000 a year; others were pulling down $6 million to $7 million. Still, it's unpersuasive to pin the entire rap on Davis as a rogue player who operated without the backing of senior partners on the good end of the barbell.

In April 2010, the firm issued a $150 million bond offering, a rare action for a US law firm. Insurance companies bought the bonds, which provided a lower interest rate than Dewey's banks were charging. The bonds matured—meaning that principal repayments would be required—three to ten years from issuance, that is, starting in April 2013. Again, Dewey & LeBoeuf's management bet on the future to bail the firm out of its increasingly urgent difficulties.

What was that $150 million for? According to the firm's private placement memorandum for the bonds, it was "to refinance existing debt and for general Firm purposes." The memorandum didn't disclose that some partners had multiyear, multimillion-dollar guaranteed-compensation deals. But it noted that the firm had already "made several high-impact lateral hires." In addition to paying those partners, the bond proceeds also helped to fuel the next leg of Dewey's business plan: an even more aggressive pursuit of rainmakers via lateral hires.

For the next three years, the firm told the *American Lawyer* that average equity partner profits were hovering around $1.5 million—near the level that each firm had achieved separately just before the merger. As Dewey & LeBoeuf won awards for its diversity and moved up in associate satisfaction surveys, the firm made the 2011 *Am Law* A-List, which was based on a combination of qualities that include not only revenue per lawyer but also diversity, pro bono work, and associate satisfaction. From all outward appearances, the firm seemed to be doing everything right.

Dewey accelerated its lateral hiring of expensive partners, some with multiyear compensation deals. It became one of the top-ten firms in 2011 lateral partner hiring, picking up thirty-seven, five of whom were refugees from the Howrey firm as it failed. A February 2012 article in the *American Lawyer* quoted Davis's description of the firm's shift in emphasis: "Now, we're moving into a new part of the cycle for the firm where we're concentrating on building up key practice areas and offices and meeting strategic needs for our clients."

MEANWHILE, in an October 2011 partner meeting, Davis reported that the firm wasn't meeting its revenue projections. But partners who didn't have compensation guarantees discovered another unpleasant fact: about a hundred of the firm's lawyers had special deals. Collectively, some individuals would receive millions before other partners saw a dime beyond monthly draws against their share of profits.

On January 27, 2012, Davis summoned partners to a meeting in New York at which he told them that the firm had $250 million in profits for 2011, but half of that was already committed to pension obligations to retired partners and to guaranteed-compensation partners who had taken firm IOUs for the prior two years. A committee would devise an allocation plan whereby partners would share what was left.

"You have to own this problem," Davis reportedly told stunned partners.

On February 13, the highest-paid twenty-four partners met at the firm's offices in New York. Again Davis explained that Dewey couldn't pay all it owed partners in deferred and current compensation. The meeting became acrimonious, but soon thereafter the committee that had been working on the allocation plan announced that most of the highest-paid partners had agreed to cap their own compensation at $2.5 million for 2012. Its long-range proposal was to repay about half of partners' previously deferred compensation over the next ten years and write off the remainder. With that, Dewey's leaders would add another long-lasting burden that future partners would eventually bear, assuming the firm survived.

All of that came too late to stop the firm's unraveling. As partners listened to headhunters about other opportunities and evaluated their options, Davis issued a firmwide memo on March 2, 2012, explaining that media rumors about Dewey's problems were baseless. Nevertheless, he said, the "press stories on U.S. legal blogs" required that he announce cost-cutting measures earlier than he'd planned. More than fifty of the firm's eleven hundred attorneys would see the exit, along with some partners whose earlier departures were supposedly consistent with the firm's strategic plan to "ensure the firm's competitiveness." The memo didn't explain why several of the partners who had already left included firm practice leaders and managing partners.

While all of that was happening, senior partner Richard Shutran, the chair of Dewey & LeBoeuf's global finance group, acknowledged that the firm was in discussions with its banks over its $100 million revolving credit facility, describing the negotiations as standard. Meanwhile, the firm was in the process of drawing $75 million of it—another debt that would have to be repaid or renegotiated by April 30, 2012.

The hemorrhaging of talent continued as Dewey lost dozens of partners—twelve from its elite insurance group in a single day, six more a few days later, and a managing partner in its Houston office a day after that. Davis sought to assuage his troops with a memo that acknowledged and regretted the loss of "long-term colleagues and successful practitioners . . . for many years," but noted that his initial assessment was that the departures "will not have a financial impact on the firm." He didn't instill confidence when he offered this reason for not fretting about the firm's future bond repayment obligations: "Our first debt payment is in April 2013, and it would be odd to say in 2012 we're in default."

In late March, Dewey hired a prominent public relations crisis manager, Michael S. Sitrick, whose clients included Paris Hilton. Shortly thereafter, *Fortune* magazine published a lengthy interview in which Davis explained that the firm was in good shape: revenues were up compared to 2011, and rumors of the firm being in financial straits were "utterly and completely bogus." In fact, he said, "our fundamental objective and priority was to create an elite global firm. We are closer to that today than we have ever been."

Dewey's continuing media campaign might actually have fed fears about the firm's fate. After all, crisis management requires a crisis. Perhaps Dewey's management team thought that the media had created its problems and that employing the person whom the *Los Angeles Times* had called "The Wizard of Spin" would solve them.

No public relations magician could neutralize what happened shortly after Davis's *Fortune* interview in which he'd explained, "If the direction we're taking the firm in was somehow disapproved of, then the reality is that there ought to be a change in management. But I don't sense that." Less than a week later, Davis lost his chairship, the firm adopted a new five-person "office of the chairman" (which included Davis, but only briefly), and a corporate partner in the London office took over day-to-day operations.

To allay concerns over the continuing departures, a new approach emerged: of the firm's more than two hundred remaining partners, only seven were key to its survival. It was a dubious proposition at best, but evidently someone forgot to tell the seven so that they could keep their stories straight. When reporters asked them individually about the meeting at which these key partners supposedly had pledged continuing loyalty to the firm, two said they were committed to the firm's success; another said that he hadn't abandoned Dewey but was fielding calls from other firms that were interested in hiring him. A fourth—vice chair Morton Pierce, who'd been an architect of the 2007 merger—offered this response to questions about whether he was part of a reported "consensus" that partners were "pulling together" to do what they could for the firm: "There was a meeting and I was there." The remaining three refused to respond to messages seeking comment. By the end of April 2012, Dewey had lost more than seventy of the three hundred partners with whom it started the year in January and Davis was no longer a member of the five-man office of the chairman or the firm's executive committee.

As the initial payment on the firm's $150 million in bonds remained due in April 2013, the pool of partners who would someday write those checks continued to shrink. In echoes of statements that Howrey's leadership had made a year earlier, Dewey's now four-man office of the chairman insisted that the departures would "not have a negative impact on the firm" because Dewey was becoming smaller by design. The furor intensified, further undermining Davis's earlier comments about the firm's financial strength, when the *American Lawyer* announced that it was revising the firm's earlier reported revenue and profits numbers downward for 2010 and 2011. Instead of average equity partner profits of $1.8 million in 2011, the revised number was $1.04 million. The prior year's average was also revised—from $1.6 million to $980,000 in 2010.

Dewey's general counsel responded with the suggestion that other law firms used internal numbers that differed from those submitted for purposes of the *Am Law* rankings, too. Senior corporate partner Richard Shutran, who by now was a member of the four-man office of the chairman that had taken over for Davis, similarly dismissed the issue: "They're just not comparable numbers. That's something people like to pick on." The *American Lawyer*'s new editor in chief responded that Dewey & LeBoeuf management had provided the numbers upon which the publication had relied previously, and she stood by the new revisions.

ONE PROMINENT DEWEY & LEBOEUF PARTNER, John Altorelli, spoke publicly about his firm as he was leaving it in early April 2012. Altorelli personified the lateral-hiring business model prevailing among big law firms. After graduating from Cornell Law School in 1993, he made his way through four law firms in fourteen years: LeBoeuf, Lamb, Greene & MacRae, then Paul Hastings, then Reed Smith, then Dewey Ballantine (shortly after Dewey's failed attempt to merge with Orrick, Herrington & Sutcliffe and six months before it joined forces with his original firm, LeBoeuf Lamb).

On his way out of Dewey and into his fifth stop, DLA Piper, Altorelli tried to explain why his position on Dewey & LeBoeuf's executive committee didn't make him in any way responsible for the firm's troubles. In fact, he seemed to think that no one was culpable because it was all a matter of "unfortunate timing." It hadn't had anything to do with developing a post-merger strategic plan that undermined morale with rapid downsizing, implementing quick compensation cuts for sixty-six partners (some by as much as 80 percent), mortgaging its future by issuing bonds, giving IOUs to partners when the firm under-performed, and rolling the dice with its institution's stability by guar-anteeing multiyear compensation to some lateral hires. Rather, Altorelli thought that management just needed more time than it had to "run off the expenses of the merger."

Altorelli then described a kind of magical thinking that evidently had infected the Dewey & LeBoeuf business plan. "If we didn't have this long of a recession," he said, "we wouldn't be having this conversation. The firm was going strong, the people are too good. It crept up on us. We kept thinking it'll get better tomorrow, then it doesn't get better. The next thing you know, it's been four years."

Yet somehow, Altorelli suggested inconsistently, his time at Dewey & LeBoeuf—which began only months before the October 2007 merger—were five of the best years of his career. He and the firm pros-pered. When he turned to the question of Dewey's future, he adopted the stance of a disinterested observer. It was as if he'd had nothing to do with whatever had gone wrong with his firm, even though he'd served on its executive committee.

"I'm not sure how they can weather the departures," he said. "It doesn't take a rocket scientist to say, I don't know how many more they can suffer. . . . [T]here could be a survival path to a smaller Dewey. I don't know how that would work. They seem to have a strategy. Or the firm will be busted up into a bunch of little pieces and survive in the hearts and souls of a lot of good people."

Like many others who gained immediate benefits from the lateral-hiring frenzy, Altorelli's approach seemed to have worked well for him personally. His move out of Dewey came with a seat on DLA Piper's twenty-four-member executive committee.

ON APRIL 12, MANY OF DEWEY'S current and former partners were un-pleasantly surprised to receive revised K-1 partnership income forms for 2011, some of which differed dramatically from the ones they'd received in January. A cover letter from the firm's accountants, Pricewaterhouse-Coopers, said cryptically, "Updated allocations provide a more equitable basis for connecting taxable income with cash received."

The firm's next public relations move didn't help, either. An April 21, 2012, article in the *New York Times* carried this headline: "A Bankruptcy Lawyer Ministers to His Firm." One of the country's most prominent bankruptcy attorneys, Martin J. Bienenstock, moved to the center of the action to face "perhaps the most challenging assignment of his career: the restructuring of his own law firm." The article touted his credentials, which included "part-time professor at Harvard Law School and the author of a well-known treatise on bankruptcy reorganizations."

Principles of legal ethics complicate any lawyer's effort to counsel his own partnership, but Bienenstock's new role came with a special irony. He'd been one of the first big lateral hires that Dewey & LeBoeuf had made in November 2007—a month after the merger that created the firm. He was also an ongoing member of the firm's partnership within a partnership. That is, there were players at the top, and there was everyone else; he was one of the players. That very notion is difficult to reconcile with fundamental legal principles of partnership law, which include a fiduciary duty owed equally to all fellow partners, accountability, and sharing of risk and rewards.

For thirty years Bienenstock had worked at Weil, Gotshal & Manges. In April 2012 he was probably wishing he'd stayed there, even though for a while he'd been a big beneficiary of the Dewey & LeBoeuf lateral-hiring push and the related barbell approach to partner compensation. The internal top-to-bottom partner income gap had reportedly exploded to more than twenty to one. But as Dewey unraveled, Bienenstock reportedly became one of twenty-five partners who'd agreed to cap their personal earnings at $2.5 million in return for IOUs from the firm.

The *Times* also quoted Dewey's wizard of spin, Michael S. Sitrick: "We are considering various paths, including continuing to operate as an independent global law firm and a strategic combination with another leading law firm, the latter of which could take many forms. Nothing, however, is definite at this point." That expression of uncertainty and indecision provided no comfort to any of Dewey's constituencies— lawyers, clients, creditors, and lenders.

If Dewey's leaders thought that better press could solve the firm's crisis, they had reversed the relationship between public relations and crisis management, which is simple: manage a crisis properly and the resulting story will write itself. There's an obvious corollary: manage the firm properly and there will be no crisis to handle. But perhaps some leaders' real goal was media distraction that bought time while some top partners arranged for soft landings in other firms.

Things got worse with reports that Manhattan district attorney Cyrus Vance Jr. was investigating whether Dewey's former chair Davis had misled partners and the firm's bankers about firm finances. As if to put an exclamation point on the disintegration of any true partnership culture within the firm, Vance's investigation reportedly began because "a group of Dewey partners presented evidence to the district attorney about supposed financial improprieties by Mr. Davis." Once notified, Dewey's management initiated its own internal investigation.

By the end of April, Dewey's managing partners no longer controlled the firm's fate. Rather, Dewey was reliving the final days of Finley Kumble, Heller Ehrman, Thelen, and Howrey. The ongoing defection of partners coincided with insufficient current cash from clients. Dewey's banks were now controlling the end game.

IN MAY, DEWEY & LEBOEUF'S situation deteriorated rapidly. Former employees filed suits alleging violation of the federal Worker Adjustment and Retraining Notification (WARN) Act, which requires sixty days' notice in the event that a business intends to close. At the same time, the federal Pension Benefit Guaranty Corporation took over Dewey's employee pension plan because it was allegedly underfunded by more than $80 million. Victims in such circumstances typically include retired employees for whom potential federal replacement funds are just a small fraction of what the firm had promised them. Other losers are retired partners in Dewey's unfunded pension plan, many of whom hadn't shared in the outsized profit years after 2000. There's no federal backstop for their pensions.

Then reports surfaced that Dewey & LeBoeuf's original 2010 bond offering materials might have misled those investors. The specter of misrepresentation claims added a new dimension to a questionable strategy that had attracted outside funds. As bondholders watched the value of their Dewey bonds plummet, it became conceivable that if the firm had made misrepresentations in connection with the original offering, some partners might have additional financial exposure.

ALL ALONG THE WAY, Martin Bienenstock proclaimed that the firm had "no plans to file bankruptcy and anyone who says differently doesn't know what they're talking about." He didn't say that he had a plan for the firm's survival. The Greenberg Traurig firm had engaged in discussions about acquiring pieces of Dewey, but those conversations had ended with the news of the Manhattan district attorney's investigation, a few days before Bienenstock's statement. In asserting that the firm had "no plans to file bankruptcy," Bienenstock was trying to explain away a line in the April 30 memo that the firm's four-man office of the chairman—including him—had sent to global partners: "All partners, including EC [Executive Committee] and OC [Office of the Chairman] members, are encouraged to seek out alternative opportunities for themselves or groups of partners, as appropriate."

His fellow members in the four-man office of the chairman were already well along in their own relocation plans. Within two weeks, all of them would be gone. On May 9, the first two left on the same day. Jeffrey Kessler, the chair of the firm's global litigation department, had joined Dewey Ballantine in 2003 after spending his career at Weil, Gotshal & Manges. He was a noted sports lawyer and had served on Dewey & LeBoeuf's executive committee for years. Perhaps reflecting the celebrity clients that pervaded his practice, Kessler was an unabashed cheerleader for Dewey's barbell compensation system: "The value for the stars has gone up, while the value of service partners has gone down," he said. Steven Kumble must have shuddered when he read those words in the *New York Times*. Fewer than two weeks after signing the April 30 memo from the office of the chairman, Kessler left Dewey to join Winston & Strawn.

On the same day, a fellow member of the office of the chairman, Richard Shutran, left Dewey & LeBoeuf for O'Melveny & Myers. He'd been co-chair of the firm's corporate department and chair of its global finance practice group. A day after Kessler and Shutran departed, Bienenstock announced that he was heading to another New York firm, Proskauer Rose.

That left only L. Charles Landgraf as the sole remaining member of Dewey & LeBoeuf's office of the chairman. Unlike Martin Bienenstock, Jeffrey Kessler, and Richard Shutran, Landgraf hadn't been among those listed in the "Company Senior Management" section of Dewey

& LeBoeuf's 2010 private placement memorandum. Nor had he been singled out for special treatment as one of the seven key partners supposedly vital to the firm's survival when the Dewey public relations machine took that tack. He had never been one of the many faces of Dewey & LeBoeuf as it used a crisis management expert to spin some way out of its problems.

Rather, Landgraf had been a longtime LeBoeuf Lamb partner before its merger with Dewey Ballantine. His biography describes a loyal company man who answered his firm's call to service whenever it came. When LeBoeuf Lamb needed a partner to bolster its London office insurance practice or help start a Moscow outpost, Landgraf went. When he returned to Washington, D.C., he became a leading insurance industry lobbyist and eventually headed that office. When Dewey & LeBoeuf's top management needed someone to "spearhead" the plan to repay guaranteed-compensation partner IOUs with 6 percent of the firm's annual income for six or seven years beginning in 2014, Landgraf pitched in with Jeffrey Kessler to sell it.

Landgraf may be like many longtime big-law partners who have watched their firms morph into something that now seems quite foreign to them. They defer to others when they shouldn't, and become victims of their own loyalty. In an interview that Landgraf and Martin Bienenstock gave jointly to the *Wall Street Journal* after Bienenstock had already resigned from the firm, leaving Landgraf behind, he still let Bienenstock do all of the talking. The interview transcript ran seven pages; Landgraf's contribution barely consumes a half page.

But Landgraf's few words during that interview suggest that those who led the Dewey & LeBoeuf partnership within a partnership might have hoodwinked him, too. He told the *Journal,* "The technique of using guarantees of all forms, especially in the recruitment of laterals and retention of key business users, is pretty widespread throughout the industry."

It's not. For a limited duration involving the recruiting of select lateral partners, such promises have become useful devices. But multiyear, multimillion-dollar deals for legacy partners? Special arrangements for a hundred members of a three-hundred-partner firm? Not for anything that calls itself a partnership.

Two days after that interview, Landgraf decamped for Arnold & Porter. And then there were none, at least at the top. In eerie irony,

Steven Kumble's description of his failing firm twenty-five years earlier described what was happening during the final weeks at Dewey & LeBoeuf: "Here was a business with 2,000 people on the payroll and their lives and careers were suddenly in shambles. They had mortgages to pay, bills to meet, kids to send to school. And nobody was talking to them. Nobody knew what was going on. It was confusion. It was hysteria."

ON MEMORIAL DAY, MAY 28, 2012, Dewey & LeBoeuf filed for bankruptcy. The firm listed debts of $315 million to more than five thousand creditors. The firm's banks and bondholders held most of the secured debt—about $225 million. The petition listed the Pension Benefit Guaranty Corporation, which had taken over the firm's employee pension plan, as the largest unsecured creditor, owed $80 million. It listed cash assets of $13 million and accounts receivable of $255 million, although any bankruptcy filing makes receivables worth much less than their face value.

In a remarkable testament to the pervasive and persistent confirmation bias that afflicts almost everyone, on the same day that the *Wall Street Journal* ran the Dewey bankruptcy filing story, two Brookings Institution fellows who were not lawyers suggested on the paper's op-ed page that overregulation of attorneys had produced the firm's downfall: "Dewey's collapse has been attributed to the firm being highly leveraged and unable to attract investment from businesses outside the legal profession." Apparently the authors hadn't been paying much attention to what was actually happening to the firm after the 2007 merger that created it, including the $150 million from outside investors.

By the summer of 2012, Dewey & LeBoeuf's presence a year earlier on the *American Lawyer*'s A-List had become a distant memory. In the July 2012 issue, which included the current year's list, the *American Lawyer* ran a cover story on the death of the firm: "House of Cards." Of course, the magazine's retroactive revision of the firm's financial performance for 2010 and 2011 raises the question of whether it ever belonged on the A-List at all. The answer is probably no.

Three-term New York governor Thomas E. Dewey had been right when he reportedly put in his will a clause requiring that after his death (which occurred in 1971) the firm bearing his name cease using it. The firm persuaded his estate otherwise, but with a perverse caveat that the late governor would have hated even more: the Dewey name should always come first. Until the next failure of a big law firm eclipses Dewey & LeBoeuf's, in any discussions of law firm disasters, that name certainly will.

CATALOGING ALL OF THE DAMAGE that results from the collapse of a firm such as Dewey & LeBoeuf is a daunting task. Some casualties are obvious, including creditors that will never get paid and innocent employees who lose their jobs. Less sympathetic are partners who watch their capital investment in the firm evaporate. For each Dewey partner, it was 36 percent of the most recent annual target compensation—amounting to a six- or seven-figure forfeit. Many still owed seven-figure personal loans for their capital contributions to the firm. In fact, when Citibank sued one former Dewey partner to collect on that debt, he responded that the bank and his former firm had conspired to defraud him.

Loss of previously contributed capital is just the beginning. Former partners need their own lawyers to deal with a myriad of additional claims, including those brought by bankruptcy trustees to "claw back" monies that partners received from the firm as it failed. The bankruptcy estate could be entitled to recover a portion of the firm's distributions to partners from the time a court determines that the firm first became insolvent. Likewise, partners who took their client silos with them to other firms will find themselves and their new firms facing "unfinished business" claims for work begun at the failed firm but continued at the new one. The bankruptcy trustee for Heller Ehrman chased that defunct firm's unfinished-business assets until forty of the law firms that hired former Heller Ehrman partners as it died eventually agreed to pay $8 million to settle some of the claims. Other firms unwilling to settle are still fighting the rest.

Coincidentally, on May 24, 2012, a United States district court judge in New York City issued a major opinion involving another firm's failure and the unfinished-business doctrine. The case involved ten of the nation's largest law firms—including K&L Gates and DLA Piper—that had hired partners from the failing Coudert Brothers law firm in 2005. The plan administrator for the Coudert Brothers bankruptcy sued those partners and their new firms to recover monies relating to alleged unfinished business that the partners had taken with them. The new firms sought dismissal, arguing on various grounds that they weren't subject to such claims involving their once-promising lateral hires. The court rejected the law firms' arguments. It ruled that former Coudert Brothers partners had to account for profits that their new firms had received on continuing client matters originating at their long-defunct former firm.

The New York ruling followed a well-developed line of cases dating from a 1984 California Court of Appeals decision. But this ruling came from a federal court in New York—home to some of the world's biggest law firms. On September 4, 2012, another judge in the same court came to a different conclusion, namely, that a dissolved firm's pending hourly fee matters aren't the property of the defunct firm. Depending on the appellate court's resolution of the question, former Dewey partners and their new firms could collectively spend millions on lawyers to litigate these and other disputes relating to a law firm's collapse. If they lose, they'll write even bigger checks to the winning bankruptcy trustee.

Apart from such ongoing hardships to former partners, some of whom deserve little sympathy because they were responsible for Dewey's collapse, failing firms worsen the overall lawyer bubble. Even with the unfinished-business doctrine and other swords hanging over their heads, senior partners with books of business secure seven-figure compensation packages elsewhere, courtesy of the lateral-hiring craze. But many young lawyers are left behind. Collectively in the case of Dewey & LeBoeuf, they produced what one legal recruiter called a "massive disruption" in the New York attorney job market.

Likewise, new graduates who thought they were among the relatively few big winners as new Dewey & LeBoeuf hires received an April 2012 email deferring their start dates to January 2013, but that was just a prelude to the withdrawal of all offers a couple of weeks later. Second-year students who had accepted Dewey summer internship positions had no idea where to turn as the firm fell apart; the firm didn't formally cancel its summer program until April 27, 2012. NALP couldn't help any of them.

The cascade of falling dominoes doesn't end with a troubled firm's lawyers and prospective attorneys, either. As anxiety grew over Dewey's worsening fate, one of the firm's seasoned paralegals sent a missive to *Above the Law*. Its most poignant passages resonated far beyond that firm: "I know these facts do not necessarily make for sexy headlines but I do ask that you report on the following. While some laugh and play their lyre as the city of Rome burns, it will be well over one thousand staff members who will also be gainfully unemployed."

ONE OF DEWEY & LEBOEUF'S most prominent lateral-hire partners was a living example of the pervasive big-law-firm trend and its attendant dangers. As the Howrey firm was failing in January 2011, Dewey hired that firm's former vice chair, Henry Bunsow, allegedly with a two-year compensation guarantee of $5 million annually. In the early 1990s, Bunsow had been a partner at Brobeck, Phleger & Harrison—a large San Francisco–based firm that failed in 2003.

After Dewey collapsed, Bunsow sued several of his former Dewey & LeBoeuf partners for fraud on the grounds that they persuaded him to join the firm at a time when, Bunsow alleges, leaders were running it as a Ponzi scheme. Bunsow also pointed to Am Law 100 profit numbers as "typically the first and most important information relied upon by potential lateral partners in making decisions about joining other firms."

DEWEY & LEBOEUF had some unique problems, including multiyear compensation packages to legacy partners of the merged firms and massive debt that included millions in outside investor bonds and outstanding IOUs to partners when the firm failed to meet annual profit targets. But it was also a vivid example of ubiquitous trends in big law firms: growth for the sake of growth; combining firms without respect for their differing cultures; concentrating wealth and power at the top within so-called partnerships; eroding a middle class of equity partners who might bring more accountability to their firm leaders; using client silos as definitive measures of value; offering expensive guaranteed contracts as part of an aggressive lateral hiring approach that undermines collegiality and community. It's a long and unfortunate list of self-inflicted wounds.

Typically, those at the helm of faltering institutions initially deny any problems. Downsizing is by design; the firm remains strong; financial performance is unaffected by departures; the press is to blame; enemies and competitors are circulating rumors and falsehoods. It, too, is a long list, and it always sounds the same. Often they hire professional public relations firms in the hope that better press will solve their problems. When the end finally comes, they place blame for the disaster elsewhere—the economy, problems with novel fee arrangements, waiting too long to implement a strategy that they still refuse to recognize as a failure, press-induced panic, inflexible banks pulling credit lines. Usually there's not even a hint of willingness to accept personal responsibility for mismanagement.

A month after Heller Ehrman went bust, its final chair, Matthew Larrabee, said, "We worked extraordinarily hard to grow our business and improve our performance because we needed to generate more work in an increasingly competitive market. . . . [W]e might have been better served by starting that effort even earlier." Another possibility: not starting that effort at all.

Six months after Howrey's partners voted to dissolve the firm, its final chair, Robert Ruyak, told an interviewer that he'd had little time to reflect on what, if anything, could have been done differently to prevent his firm from going under but that, all things considered, "I don't have any regrets." Three months later he told another interviewer that he'd done the best he could: "I have no regrets."

After his exile, Dewey & LeBoeuf's former chair Steven H. Davis told his partners that he did his best "to navigate the firm through challenging and turbulent times." He expressed regret at his firm's troubled situation but took no responsibility for how his actions had produced it. In fairness, Davis was probably following the advice of his recently retained counsel to refrain from any admission of culpability. After all, the Manhattan district attorney's office had an ongoing investigation into his stewardship of the firm.

Morton A. Pierce served as Dewey Ballantine's chair at the time it merged with LeBoeuf, Lamb, Green & MacRae in 2007 and had been a principal architect of the transaction. After the merger, he was vice chair of Dewey & LeBoeuf and negotiated a multiyear compensation deal that supposedly paid him $6 million annually. At age sixty-three, he reportedly negotiated a new one in 2011 that upped his income to $8 million for a few years more before dropping back to $6 million. Throughout 2011 and into 2012, Dewey & LeBoeuf's website introduced his biographical page with these two sentences: "Morton Pierce is a Vice Chair of Dewey & LeBoeuf and co-chair of the Mergers and Acquisitions Practice Group. He is also a member of the firm's global Executive Committee." As the firm's road became rockier in mid-April 2012, Thomson Reuters identified Pierce as one of the seven key partners on whom Dewey & LeBoeuf's very survival depended. But Pierce refused to commit himself to the firm's future.

Less than a month later, the Dewey veteran distanced himself completely from any role in his firm's disintegration. Eating soup while packing up for his new gig at White & Case, seven blocks down Avenue of the Americas, on May 3, 2012, he said that he actually hadn't been actively involved in management for years: "I think the executive committee did the best job that they could under the circumstances."

Pierce also observed that as he searched for a new place to work, several firms had been "great and welcoming." In fact, he wished he could combine them all into one and move there. Then the man who'd been at the top of Dewey Ballantine and had helped orchestrate its disastrous merger with LeBoeuf Lamb in 2007 added a bit of gallows humor: "Although looking at the Dewey & LeBoeuf merger, maybe mergers aren't such a good idea."

Without taking any personal responsibility for the firm's collapse, he told the *New York Times* the same day, "I am sorry about what happened"—as if some external event or third-party actor had been the real culprit. In his interview, Pierce didn't mention that his resignation letter that day reportedly covered one more item: he claimed that Dewey & LeBoeuf owed him $61 million.

Martin Bienenstock, the rainmaker whom Dewey & LeBoeuf had hired away from Weil, Gotshal & Manges, was part of the four-man office of the chairman that replaced Steven Davis. He'd served on Dewey's executive committee since joining the firm in November 2007. As he presided over the firm's final days, a reporter asked him what had caused it to fail. He blamed Davis ("might be guilty of optimism"; "the chairman had the right to give contracts"), the economy ("in 2008 and 2009, every Wall Street law firm suffered"), and the press (the early departure of the insurance M&A group "was an optical nightmare because the press was all over it and made a very big deal of it"). He saw culpability in everyone and everything but himself: "I think the world changed after the merger in October 2007, and maybe some of the contracts given to people were not as prudent in the new world. And no one saw the new world coming." According to the Harvard Law School website, Bienenstock taught the school's corporate reorganization course in the spring 2012 term.

Maybe the behavior of these former big-firm leaders is just another aspect of the lawyer personality in full bloom. Or maybe it's the transformation of these attorneys' great strength into a tragic flaw: their persuasive powers extend to self-delusion and they actually believe what they're saying. Whatever the cause, their comments are ironic on another level, in that many members of their generation—senior partners in big firms across the nation—complain that today's younger attorneys fail to take responsibility for mistakes and consequences.

The transformation of most big firms has been achieved at the expense of values that don't come with a metric. One of those values is a shared sense of purpose that generates the willingness to weather difficult times. Too many firms now expect annual K-1 partnership income statements to hold everything together. Finley Kumble, Heller Ehrman, Thelen, Howrey, and Dewey & LeBoeuf illustrate how the focus on maximizing growth and profits in the near term can threaten important values that are vital to the very survival of the institution. Dewey & LeBoeuf wasn't the first victim of the prevailing big-law strategies or the hubris that fed them. And it won't be the last.

PART III
DEFLATING
THE BUBBLE

CHAPTER 9

LAW SCHOOLS

I can no longer ignore that, for a very large proportion of my students, law school has become something very much like a scam.
—University of Colorado School of Law professor Paul Campos in his first (and anonymous) blog post on *Inside the Law School Scam*, August 7, 2011

THE LAWYER BUBBLE IS ARTIFICIAL, and law school deans are uniquely positioned to put the profession on a path to unmaking it. More thoughtful government policies could encourage them to do so. Likewise, the managing partners of the nation's influential big law firms could improve a culture that they have created. Perhaps most important, prospective law students could spend productive hours challenging assumptions about themselves and the profession. They could ponder more carefully their own suitability for a legal career and learn more about what life as a lawyer really means.

Most of the key players in the current system won't want to entertain ideas such as these, which clash with the pursuit of their own short-term self-interest. Too many deans are wedded to running their schools as businesses for which *U.S. News & World Report* rankings supply the definitive means of evaluation. Too many special interests relating to the lending and debt collection industries make a lot of money off the growing lawyer bubble. Too many senior partners in big firms have become accustomed to extraordinary incomes and are unwilling to emphasize long-run values that don't contribute to the current year's bottom line. Too many individual pre-law students find comfort in seeing only what they want to see as they move toward law school and beyond. But the current situation is unsustainable. Whether embraced or resisted, the future will arrive.

A PLETHORA OF SUGGESTIONS for structural reform in legal education have recently circulated inside and outside the academy. Some are unrealistic; others offer more promise. In the end, the most effective way to shrink the lawyer bubble is by attacking its source, that is, by reducing the number of law school applicants. An important first step is eliminating the economic incentives that encourage deans to play fast and loose with their prospective students' lives. Law schools could add transparency beyond the ABA's bare-minimum statistical requirements. They could then encourage enrolled students to consider career options that won't yield the lucrative starting salaries that big law firms promise. And they could conduct themselves in ways that some already do: reminding everyone that the law is, indeed, a vital profession for which they are worthy gatekeepers.

Legal faculty self-criticism. Notwithstanding the heavy hand of law schools in creating the lawyer bubble, legal academics have not been entirely without a conscience. One law school professor who expressed public regret over his role as a facilitator and beneficiary of the law school bubble was Paul Campos. After graduation, he spent a year working as an associate in the Chicago office of Los Angeles–based Latham & Watkins before leaving to teach at the University of Colorado School of Law. In 2011, he was a tenured professor there when he went rogue, writing that for many of his students, law school had become a scam: a combination of overpaid law professors and deans shamelessly promoting legal degrees as gateways to a prestigious career amid job prospects that were and are bleak.

Campos received mixed reviews for his whistle-blowing, if that's what it was. Although his first blog post (excerpted at the beginning of this chapter) was anonymous, University of Chicago Law School professor Brian Leiter seemed to know who had authored it. For years Leiter has been a vocal critic of *U.S. News & World Report* rankings methodology, but he characterized the as yet unrevealed Campos as a "failed academic who has done almost no scholarly work in the last decade, teaches the same courses and seminars year in and year out, and spends his time trying to attract public attention, sometimes under his own name, this time anonymously . . . just doing what he always does, trying to surf the wave of the latest fad and attract attention to himself."

In sharp contrast to such condemnation, the widely read legal blog *Above the Law* named Professor Campos its 2011 "Lawyer of the Year."

Another academic voice rose to condemn the state of American legal education in June 2012, when Washington University School of Law professor Brian Z. Tamanaha published *Failing Law Schools,* a book he'd found "difficult to write." That difficulty stems from his central argument: tenured law school faculties are the key villains behind the oversupply of lawyers, the overcompensation of law professors, and a generation of young graduates with staggering student loan debt and limited job prospects. While chiding deans who pander to *U.S. News & World Report* rankings and game that system, Tamanaha also sees the ABA Section on Legal Education as an example of regulatory capture: law schools control the organization that sets the rules governing their behavior.

Tenured faculty members are an important constituency in any effort to reshape legal education. Without support from professors who recognize the problems and demand a remedy, meaningful change becomes almost impossible. Self-awareness is an essential first step toward broader institutional progress.

On the other hand, self-criticism that borders on the absurd serves little purpose. Two professors at Emory University School of Law urged that a federal investigation might yield sufficient evidence to put many law school deans in jail. In a seventy-seven-page article, they outline theories such as mail and wire fraud, racketeering, conspiracy, and false statements. Predictably, another law professor at Emory immediately responded that he'd already written an article explaining why such prosecutions weren't appropriate.

Another impractical suggestion came from a Northwestern law professor who coauthored an opinion piece in the *Wall Street Journal* with a young associate at Kirkland & Ellis. They urge allowing undergraduate colleges to offer law degrees. Their analysis starts from the premise that there's a lawyer shortage, arguing that some lower- and middle-income Americans are underserved. The authors believe that allowing colleges to offer undergraduate law programs would reduce law school tuition to zero (for such students), produce more lawyers, enable some attorneys to charge lower fees, and thereby ensure broader access to legal services for those who currently can't afford them. There's no reason to analyze the untested assumptions that underlie their analysis because, like too much legal scholarship and academic thought, the idea is insufficiently tethered to the real world of possibilities.

Other legal scholars' proposals are equally unrealistic. As previously noted, University of Iowa College of Law emeritus dean N. William Hines would eliminate *U.S. News* rankings for all law schools below a certain level—perhaps twenty-five or fifty—rather than the current ordering that ends at 145 and relegates the rest to unranked nether regions. Assuming that the magazine gave advance notice of such a plan, the resulting frenzy to make the cut for a newly limited rankings range would boggle the mind. So would the race to get included in subsequent years. Here again, the inquiry is completely academic because *U.S. News* has no reason to reduce the number of schools it ranks. After all, the vast majority of students who believe the magazine's assessments attend schools ranked *below* the top twenty-five or fifty. The only effective cure for the *U.S. News* rankings is for prospective law students to ignore them in making one of the most important decisions of their lives. Perhaps then law school deans and other senior administrators in higher education will ignore them, too.

Many law professors not only are self-aware but also exhibit courage in expressing public concern about the growing lawyer bubble. Campos and Tamanaha are two recent and highly public examples, but one of the pioneers in speaking truth to power has been Indiana University Maurer School of Law professor William Henderson—a persistent and constructive voice for many years. Readers who study the notes at the end of this book will find his work cited frequently. Although our views sometimes diverge, Henderson has provided the best kind of academic thought and legal scholarship to a troubled profession. Some examples are included in the discussion that follows.

Financing legal education. Professor Tamanaha suggests making private student loans eligible for discharge in bankruptcy. That's a good start. But because such loans account for only a small slice of total law student loan debt, federal loans are a bigger burden and present a larger problem.

Several reforms might help to break the current cycle whereby student borrowing for law school is too easy while getting a job upon graduation is becoming too difficult. One step would be a return to pre-1976 rules whereby bankruptcy discharged educational debt. Such a move won't create jobs for unemployed attorneys, but it could open a safety hatch for some of them. As financial adviser Mark Kantrowitz observed, "In the coming years, a lot of people will still be paying off their student loans when it's time for their kids to go to college." Allowing automatic discharge in bankruptcy (as happens with most other debts) might also help restore accountability to private lenders, although the bigger challenge of government-issued loans requires a different solution.

For that problem, Tamanaha would tighten federal loan eligibility requirements and cap loan totals by school. Although neither of those suggestions deals with the existing debt bubble, he's on the right track in seeking a way to increase law school accountability.

Removing the current bankruptcy exemption for all educational lenders, including nonprofit institutions and the federal government, would be an important start. But adding one more twist might achieve even better outcomes: allowing the federal government to recover guarantee losses from a law school (and its university) whenever a student loan became the principal contributor to an alumnus's later bankruptcy—a finding that the bankruptcy court could make. (It could be a simple formula, such as whenever outstanding educational loans exceeded 50 percent of a bankrupt's total indebtedness.) Such a step could encourage law school administrators to rethink their current efforts to sell a legal education. Customers who have the option of refusing to pay *after* they've purchased a product that turns out to be worth far less than advertised present sellers with a qualitatively different risk compared to those without such recourse.

This approach may carry unintended consequences. In particular, holding law schools accountable for their students' unpaid loans could create admissions bias in favor of those who can afford to pay. But requiring need-blind admissions for all students as a prerequisite to a school's participation in any federally backed loan programs might counteract that temptation. This much seems clear: until law schools themselves underwrite all student loans or otherwise become financially responsible for them directly, deans will remain removed from meaningful accountability, which is the only real cure for the present mess.

Today's system isn't even close to such a paradigm of law school responsibility. Rather, the system insulates schools financially from the adverse long-run implications of their agendas and decisions. Too many deans focus on maximizing tuition receipts without regard to how students fund those payments. If federal money backed billions of dollars in law school loans that were later discharged in bankruptcy, law schools might be subject to some of the scrutiny that for-profit colleges have recently begun receiving. If the schools (and their parent universities) became financially responsible for losses that caused some of their graduates to declare bankruptcy, some might stop remitting 20 to 30 percent of revenues back to their universities. Over time, some might reduce their exposure by lowering tuition. Others might shrink the size of their entering classes and/or cease operation altogether. Any of those outcomes would be an improvement.

Revise the third year. The organized bar and law schools could perform a great service to the profession by lobbying for the elimination altogether of law school's third year, as Tamanaha also urges. But he thinks that not all schools would jettison the third year. Instead, he believes that the profession would evolve into a differentiated legal system comprised of "research-oriented law schools [that] coexist alongside law schools that focus on training good lawyers at reasonable cost." In his view, "some degree programs will be two years, others will remain at three, with clinical components."

His prediction may be correct, but it seems more likely that student preferences for lower costs and quicker degrees would force virtually all schools of comparable quality to offer two-year programs exclusively once any significant number of them did. That prospect makes the task of implementing such a change far more daunting. Deans understand that their schools' financial interests cut the other way, in favor of retaining a third year of tuition revenues (especially because administrators expect law schools to return part of revenues to their universities). That's a key reason that today's accelerated JD programs often persist in pricing the degree rather than the time spent getting it. But eliminating the third year altogether would set up the possibility of lower costs.

More realistic is the prospect of making the third year of law school more meaningful. As shrinking government budgets crush legal assistance programs for the poor, law schools could accomplish the win-win of giving students real-life client opportunities that enhance their practical skills while making the profession—and the world—a better place.

To his credit, former Northwestern dean David Van Zandt encouraged such experiential learning. His final strategic plan for the school recommended that third-year students have "an opportunity for a semester-long, faculty-supervised, full-time experience in which they can put into practice their prior learning."

Many opportunities to implement such changes already exist. For example, the Legal Services Corporation (LSC) endured a nearly 20 percent cut in funding between fiscal years 2010 and 2012, necessitating a reduction of almost six hundred lawyers and eight hundred paralegals; the prospects for its immediate future are even worse. LSC has local complements in almost every city where there's a law school, and all would welcome sophisticated student help. They'd also need supervisors. If insufficient tenured and tenure-track faculty were qualified or interested, practicing lawyers could assist—as many already do, to their great personal and professional satisfaction.

But everyone should be honest about those efforts, too. As previously explained, what students learn in clinical programs won't help most of them get jobs. It also won't have much relevance to the mundane junior associate tasks that those who later work in large law firms perform. Most of that work requires no specialized training at all; too much of it doesn't even require a legal degree. But the vast majority of the nation's forty-four thousand annual law school graduates won't get positions in big firms anyway, and most of those who do won't stay at their initial firms very long. It makes sense to give all students practical legal skills that they can use in their continuing efforts to make a living—whether in a law firm, as sole practitioners, or otherwise.

Training programs for recent graduates. Some law schools have worked with local bar associations to develop incubator programs that train sole or small-firm practitioners who want to help underserved populations. The premise of such programs is that, despite the general oversupply of lawyers in America, a vast proportion of the population remains without access to essential legal services. Law school legal aid clinics can't pick up all of the slack, so some schools are working with local bar associations to develop pilot programs that train new graduates for that untapped market. The magnitude of that potential demand remains unknown and, therefore, a largely untested assumption of such programs.

Even so, in 2007 CUNY School of Law began its Incubator for Justice program as an outgrowth of a 1998 collaborative whose purpose was to support graduates working solo or in small-group practices serving the poor. Over an eighteen-month period, it provides training "in basic business issues such as billing, record-keeping, technology, bookkeeping and taxes while, at the same time, facilitating incubator participants' involvement in larger justice initiatives and in subject-based training in immigration law, labor and employment and other topics that will arise continually as these attorneys build their practices." With the help of the Missouri Bar Association, the University of Missouri–Kansas City School of Law launched a similar program in 2011. Charlotte School of Law is working on one, as are the Columbus Bar Foundation, the Boston Bar Association, and the Chicago Bar Foundation.

Until the price of a legal education comes down, financial concerns will complicate graduates' efforts to serve those lacking the means to pay what most lawyers charge. But incubator programs that offer the realistic promise of a sole practice or small-firm career might look better to unemployed young lawyers than waiting tables or working as a barista at a coffee shop. In fact, many may find that such work actually fits their expectations of what being a lawyer would mean. There could even be an added benefit: surveys suggest that such practitioners are more likely to be satisfied with their careers than many of their counterparts in big firms.

Reduce supply. Some might worry that the economic effects of the foregoing proposals could make the lawyer bubble worse. After all, won't any reduction in the cost of legal education increase student demand? Won't allowing graduates to discharge their student loans in bankruptcy encourage people to attend law school because they know that eventually they can avoid tuition costs? Such questions assume that leaders who helped to create the current problems are powerless to help remedy them.

The ABA hasn't required law schools to increase enrollments; deans have made those decisions. Collectively, the profession would benefit if others followed the lead of Frank Wu, chancellor and dean of the University of California Hastings School of Law. On May 2, 2012, he announced that starting in fall 2012, his school would admit 20 percent fewer students: "The critics of legal education are right. . . . There are far too many law schools and there are too many law students and we need to do something about that."

A handful of other deans have announced similar plans to reduce the sizes of their entering classes. George Washington University's former dean, Paul Schiff Berman, hoped to reduce first-year enrollment below 450. Albany Law School, Creighton University School of Law, and Touro College Jacob L. Fuchsberg Law Center also reduced their 2011 incoming classes. Northwestern University Law School's new dean, Daniel Rodriguez, announced that he's thinking about reducing class size. (Rodriguez is dealing with the residue of his predecessor's actions, including aggressive solicitation of transfer students and implementation of an accelerated JD program—both of which contributed to an increase in the number of Northwestern degrees awarded annually.)

Downsizing isn't easy. Another law school dean, Jim Chen at the University of Louisville, explained why Wu's approach at Hastings will have difficulty gaining traction elsewhere: "I'm totally understanding of what Hastings is trying to accomplish and I'm very sympathetic to the idea that you don't want to admit more people into a declining [job] market. How you manage to do that without the revenue is going to pose a very formidable challenge for most American law schools."

The challenge for the profession as a whole becomes even greater when some deans acknowledge that they don't care about the broader implications of their actions. The largest law school in the country, Thomas M. Cooley, continues to expand in the face of a dismal market for attorneys. Cooley's associate dean, James Robb, said that his school "isn't interested in reducing the size of its entering class on the basis of the perceived benefit to society." Nine months after graduation, only 38 percent of Cooley's 999 graduates in the class of 2011 had full-time long-term jobs requiring bar passage.

Continue trends toward greater transparency. With or without the ABA's assistance, leaders in higher education could combat the growing over-supply of lawyers with better information. For starters, they could follow the lead of their students. In 2009, two Vanderbilt University law students founded an organization called Law School Transparency because they realized that existing law school employment and salary data were oversimplified and misleading. Law schools resisted their efforts to obtain information, but the ongoing pressure from students concerned about finding law jobs eventually moved the ABA and some schools in the direction of greater candor.

In April 2012, the Law School Transparency website unveiled a comprehensive database of law-school-specific information. It includes the real full-time legal employment rate, underemployment score, and prospective students' total projected law school loan burden. Still, the database is limited because it relies on four sources: the ABA, *U.S. News & World Report*, individual schools' websites, and the schools' NALP reports. (Law schools could withhold their NALP reports from the project, and 75 percent of them did.)

The ABA can do more, such as requiring law schools to report all relevant salary and employment information for their graduates. Even if the ABA doesn't mandate it, law schools could provide comprehensive job and salary information. Some already do, including the University of Chicago's four-year summaries showing salaries for various employment categories according to class percentiles (25th, median, 75th, and mean). Stanford Law School reports similar information for its most recent three years of graduates.

Provide prospective students with reality therapy. In the end, even comprehensive disclosure of financial information about debt and job prospects won't neutralize one of the biggest contributors to the lawyer bubble—the attitudes of prospective law students themselves. The battle against selective perception and confirmation bias is endless. But law schools could help reduce student demand and thereby slow the growth of the lawyer bubble if they simply focused on selling an honest message to prospects.

At no point in the admissions process do law schools ask students to consider a typical lawyer's life. If they did, fewer would apply and graduates would suffer less disappointment when they encountered the challenges of a legal career, beginning with their efforts to earn a living with a law degree. Such prophylactic counseling suggests a starting point for reform.

Most entering students don't know what lies ahead, and those who do resist the truth with a powerful corollary: bad things happen only to someone else. Their career expectations come from idealized images that bear little resemblance to the daily work of most attorneys. In real life, *The Good Wife*'s Alicia Florrick and the lead characters on *Law & Order* are few and far between, but try telling that to a prospective one-L.

Nevertheless, that's what law schools and undergraduate colleges could do—starting before students begin their expensive journeys. Legal studies is a popular pre-law major and a natural venue for courses that could enlighten prospective law students. Even schools that lack a formal legal studies program typically have a pre-law adviser who could establish smaller versions of a full-blown course. Concentrated reality therapy for juniors and seniors could go a long way toward helping them make better choices that will yield lifetime benefits.

Finding instructors for such sessions should be easy, particularly as practicing attorneys line up for adjunct teaching positions that combine prestige with the possibility of meaningful service to society. Each year at New York University School of Law, several hundred attorneys typically apply for a handful of adjunct positions relating to specialized areas of the law. Many would be qualified to conduct classes and seminars aimed at the profession's larger problems—oversupply, declining morale, and the growing gap between prospective students' expectations about what being a lawyer will entail and the much different reality of most practicing attorneys' lives.

On their websites, top law schools can brag about sending half of their graduates to big firms with six-figure salaries. But rather than pretending that such a result is unambiguously positive, law schools could tell their applicants more: how few graduates start their careers in such firms, and how high attrition rates are. Why not describe what life and work are really like in most of those places? The goal wouldn't— and shouldn't—be to talk anyone out of law school. But before any student makes the fateful decision to embark on a legal career, law schools could encourage every student to consider whether such a career fits an aspirant's personality and ambitions.

Once law school classes begin, the focus could turn to the various paths within the profession; no single one suits every individual. Many students get caught up in the social status hierarchy that assumes big firms must become their first choice because they're prestigious and offer the biggest starting salaries. Even students who don't ask could hear law schools answer this question for them: what are the other practice options and their career satisfaction rates?

A first-year curriculum in the top law schools could include penetrating analysis of big-firm realities from a young attorney's perspective. This would raise crucial questions: How do law firms—even large ones—differ from each other in ways that matter? What tasks do associates perform? What kind of lifestyle is possible at firms that expect associates to bill 2,100 hours or more a year?

For all students, the overriding inquiry would become: How does any particular new attorney think about the fit that's best? As Professors William Henderson and David Zaring observe, "Law professors now write novels about lawyers and analyze surveys of lawyers and law firms using basic tools of social science. In both cases, the goal is to explain what law firm life is really like. Perhaps the teaching part of legal education should develop similar aspirations."

Such a project is analogous to moving sex education from the whispers and misconceptions of the playground to a clearheaded exposition in the classroom. For those valuing the long-run fate of human beings thrust into an unexpected and unwelcome reality, it's equally important. Is there a metric by which to measure the success of such efforts? How about higher rates of attorney career satisfaction in the years ahead? Or is that an externality that the law-school-as-a-business model labels irrelevant to its bottom line and therefore ignores?

An attack on high rates of attorney dissatisfaction could target the front end of the profession's pipeline. Educators could perform an important service by forcing prospective students to overcome their own assumptions; some might realize that they don't want to be lawyers after all. Law schools can equip students with the knowledge necessary to resist pressures that put most of them on the big-law track before they understand where it leads. Without such knowledge, inertia will result in too many students stuck in unfulfilling careers. If only half of today's practicing lawyers enjoy their work, then the profession's most vital mission is to help the others either refrain from entering it in the first place or find more individually compatible positions once they arrive.

Which schools will go first? A variant of what economists call the prisoner's dilemma poses an obstacle to any voluntary disclosure proposal. A law school that pursues such brutal candor risks losing applicants to schools that obfuscate. Nevertheless, moving in the direction of greater transparency should improve the quality of law schools that have the courage to try. Any educational institution is only as good as its essential human assets: students and faculty. Better information to all prospective lawyers could shift their preferences from big-firm starting salaries and elusive equity partner wealth to longer-range considerations of what they really want from a legal career. A school that similarly moved its emphasis away from favoring the large-firm track and toward a more balanced mission that included big law firms as constituents without allowing them to dwarf all others could attract a broader range of students and faculty. That would make the school stronger. The elite law schools have the least to lose in taking such a leadership role.

There's also a more powerful reason to act, which is that it's the right thing to do—for students, for the profession, and for society. Deans can pretend that none of this is their job and that they're just minor players in a large market beyond their control. They can argue that the task of informing those who buy a law school education is someone else's responsibility, even as they encourage the pursuit of big-firm jobs that are disappearing. But if law schools aren't obliged to play fair with their own students, who is?

This suggests a new and simple guiding principle that all law school deans could consider: treat prospective and actual students as if they were their own kids. In the ways that matter most, they are.

CHAPTER 10

BIG
LAW FIRMS

*Everyone should wake up in the morning
and feel a little vulnerable.*
—Robert O. Link Jr., chair of Cadwalader,
Wickersham & Taft, February 2007

*Lawyers and firms that operate as though [profit is the only
value or measure by which a firm should measure itself] have
only themselves to blame for their choices—and their
pernicious influence on lawyers at large.*
—Aric Press, ALM editor in chief, May 2012

T HE FAILURE OF LAW FIRM LEADERS to think beyond the current
business model that they have constructed has produced catastrophic consequences. Undeterred by the experiment of Finley Kumble
twenty-five years earlier, managing partners at Heller Ehrman, Thelen,
Howrey, and Dewey & LeBoeuf persisted along an ultimately fatal
path. Without a meaningful course correction, similarly unhappy outcomes lie ahead for firms that follow the same road.

Apologists for big firms argue that firm leaders aren't to blame for the
profession's worst trends and the resulting disasters. Rather, they say,
leaders simply responded rationally to external forces thrust upon them.
For example, law professors Bernard Burk and David McGowan explain
away today's pernicious trends as inevitable: "These developments are not

the result of narcissism, venality or sociopathy in the elite bar; they are normal and predictable human and institutional responses to changes in the marketplace over which the bar has no control."

Such excuses for aggressively selfish behavior let too many people off the hook. To protest that the leaders of big law firms are merely rational actors responding to forces beyond anyone's control misses a central point: leaders have choices. The cumulative impact of senior partners' actions determines an institution's culture. Absolving those at the top of responsibility for their decisions implies a deprivation of free will that understates their power and disserves the profession.

Law firms are collections of people. Some have gathered and remained together in pursuit of a single goal: quickly expanding individual personal wealth. For them, the prevailing big-firm model is working well. They regard the continuing skyward march of equity partner earnings, combined with the growing inequality gap within their partnerships, as conclusive proof of their own success.

But the prevailing model isn't the only model, and, as the failures of Dewey and others have shown, it may not even be sustainable. The lawyers at the top of all big firms have the power to improve their attorneys' lives, enhance the long-range health of their partnerships, and restore nobility to the profession. For true visionaries, this governing principle could become powerful: create a culture that transcends the current year's partner earnings. What follows are some possibilities for those who are willing to question the dominant approach that has contributed to the profession's current crisis.

These ideas are aspirational insofar as few existing large firms are likely to adopt them in their entirety. For starters, they require firms' leaders to acknowledge that long-run interests should sometimes trump greed. Current trends make that no easy feat. In that respect, the principles set forth below may be better suited to a new firm. But leaders possessing the will to buck popular trends will find important constituencies that embrace change. In fact, some suggestions come from the actual experiences of a few successful and highly regarded firms. But they are exceptions. For many others, the prevailing model will produce more spectacular failures. Even so, analogizing to economist Joseph Schumpeter's hypothesis of creative destruction, the demise of such firms will create opportunities for their former members to remake the profession.

Rethink and revise the billable hour system. Nothing requires leaders to use the billable hour regime that causes so much misery, but almost all big firms and many others have adhered to it. That's a choice, and it's not a good or even obvious one. Clients detest its perverse rewards for inefficiency; associates crumble under its pressures. Even at large law firms, perceptive partners acknowledge the toll it has taken on the culture of their firms and the profession. With every recession, the billable hour takes another public relations hit and law firm leaders scramble to appear responsive. Periodically over the past twenty years, optimists have declared its imminent demise. Yet it survives.

Long ago, clients should have rebelled. For some reason, they still don't. An October 2010 survey of in-house corporate counsel reported that 75 percent of client payments were pursuant to alternative fee arrangements (meaning something other than a firm's standard hourly rate), but 80 percent of those weren't really "alternative"—they were simply hourly rate discounts. Another survey found that alternative fee arrangements accounted for only 16 percent of revenues at the nation's largest law firms in 2010. To date, the billable hour seems to be weathering yet another onslaught, as a July 2012 analysis confirmed: "The results suggest that the billable hour remains entrenched, despite widespread reports that clients are dissatisfied with the practice."

Why do clients put up with the hourly rate regime and the remarkable amounts that lawyers make from it? Only they know the answers. One factor is inertia: the billable hour has now been around long enough to provide a comfortable familiarity. Another factor is perceived certainty: number of hours times hourly rate is a simple formula, and in-house lawyers find reviewing invoices for approval and payment to be a straightforward exercise.

Perhaps the most important reason is that certain attorneys command market power with respect to certain types of legal work, and the spillover effect benefits many more. If the stakes are high, corporate general counsel seek the best lawyers to obtain the best result. There may be an oversupply of lawyers generally, but the number of top practitioners is finite. That allows them to reap outsized rewards for their services, as well as for those younger lawyers who are part of the total representation package. The same oligopoly pricing power accounts for the ability of some attorneys to charge hourly rates that bear

a surprising consistency across top firms. Bankruptcy fee petitions—
where, as discussed below, judges have held the billable hour regime
sacrosanct—facilitate information exchange contributing to behavior
that economists might describe as conscious parallelism. (It happens
with the firms' acquisition of associate talent, too. Starting salaries at all
of the top firms have moved together for decades.)

Of course, none of this means that general counsel for large corporate
clients are giving big firms' attorneys a blank check. Requiring outside
law firms to prepare budgets for a client's legal matters rarely occurred
twenty-five years ago; now it's commonplace. Many corporations now
use "requests for proposal" to solicit competitive bids on their legal work
before awarding it. For routine matters susceptible to commoditization,
fixed fees have become useful cost-savings mechanisms that reward efficiency. But even here, clients have to overcome the nagging concern
that an attorney might devote insufficient time to their matters, cutting
corners to stay within the agreed price for services rendered.

Assuming the continued intractability of the billable hour system, an
incremental commonsense improvement could help: clients could reduce payments for lawyers who work unproductively long hours. Almost every attorney experiences periods when billing fifty or more hours
a week is unavoidable for a limited duration. But extraordinarily high
billable hours over months or years should result in client compensation
penalties for any firm that permits an attorney to work them. Unfortunately, the prevailing economics of big law firms dictate—and reward—
the opposite. Clients routinely refuse to pay for first- or second-year
associates on the grounds that their work product doesn't justify their
high hourly rates. They should be equally skeptical of the value that anyone billing extraordinarily high hours delivers.

To implement this partial cure, a straightforward mechanism—
indeed, a new metric—could turn the billable hour system against itself.
Rather than mislabel attorney billables as measures of productivity, it
would expose the true effects of excessive hours: declining attorney effectiveness and increasing career dissatisfaction. As already described,
the scientific basis connecting excessively long workdays to poor results
(along with reduced health and morale) is overwhelming. Clients could
put that learning to work for them. Every invoice could include each attorney's rolling twelve-month billed hours for all clients. That could lead

to interesting discussions about systematic discounts based on reduced value for some lawyers who have made working long hours a central element of their lifestyle.

On a macroeconomic scale, each firm could develop a new Working Culture Index that revealed a firm's environment to clients and recruits. Attorneys now accept as given the 2,000-hour threshold that most firms maintain, even though most current big-law leaders faced no such mandatory minimum level when they were associates. Although there's little chance of turning the clock back from that now pervasive requirement, a firm's Working Culture Index could provide incentives for senior leaders to move away from hours as a defining metric.

One construction of the Working Culture Index (WCI) would start with attorneys who bill fewer than 2,000 hours annually (including pro bono work and genuine firm-related activities such as recruiting, training, mentoring, client development, and management). Lawyers in this category wouldn't count toward their firm's WCI. But at each 100-hour increment above 2,000—that is, 2,100, 2,200, 2,300, and so on—the percentage of attorneys reaching each successively higher numerical category would add to the firm's overall WCI. To reflect the increasing lifestyle costs of marginal billable hours, attorneys with the most hours would count at every 100-hour interval prior to their own. That is, an attorney billing 2,400 hours would have been included in the firm's index at the 2,100-, 2,200-, and 2,300-hour levels, too. Separate indices could exist for associates (AWCI) and partners (PWCI), and for each office of a firm.

The Working Culture Index would reveal distinctions that firmwide averages blur. For example, Firm A might have an AWCI of 125, calculated as follows:

50 percent of associates bill fewer than 2,000 hours = 0 AWCI points

50 percent bill more than 2,000 hours = 50 AWCI points

40 percent bill more than 2,100 hours = 40 AWCI points

25 percent bill more than 2,200 hours = 25 AWCI points

10 percent bill more than 2,300 hours = 10 AWCI points

No associates bill more than 2,400 hours

Total AWCI for this firm: 125

Firm B's AWCI of 315 would describe a much different place:

10 percent of associates bill fewer than 2,000 hours = 0 AWCI points
90 percent bill more than 2,000 hours = 90 AWCI points
75 percent bill more than 2,100 hours = 75 AWCI points
60 percent bill more than 2,200 hours = 60 AWCI points
45 percent bill more than 2,300 hours = 45 AWCI points
30 percent bill more than 2,400 hours = 30 AWCI points
15 percent bill more than 2,500 hours = 15 AWCI points
No associates bill more than 2,600 hours
Total AWCI for this firm: 315

For recruits, the advantages of such information seem clear. Some would prefer firms with a high WCI; most wouldn't. A WCI above 300 might prompt questions about the physical health of a firm's attorneys; a WCI of 0—no one working more than 2,000 hours—might prompt questions about the health of the firm itself. Big disparities between partners (PWCI) and associates (AWCI) would be revealing, too.

Included with the Working Culture Index could be firm-specific attrition rates by class year, from starting associate to first-year equity partner. NALP's last report before the 2008 financial crisis showed big law's five-year associate attrition rates skyrocketing to more than 80 percent overall—and they had returned to that level by 2011. But significant differences existed among firms.

Increasingly, these issues are becoming important to clients, too. General counsel at major corporations have begun to understand that balance in the lives of their outside lawyers can be an important factor in their companies' bottom line: "No other company would treat its most important commodity poorly enough to cause a turnover rate of 85 percent for first year lawyers who are gone by the sixth year. Why are you doing it? How can you get away with that?" Another general counsel suggests: "We are looking at retention issues, training, and flex time. They are all creeping into the alternative fee discussion." And still another notes that the absence of balance contributes to high associate attrition rates in large law firms and that attrition, in turn, imposes costs that result from the loss of institutional knowledge and continuity.

Susan Hackett, former senior vice president and general counsel of the Association of Corporate Counsel, makes a broader point: "The lesson is that the work is just beginning once you've made a hire. The greatest investment in any new lawyer is not in the cost of hiring, but in developing the culture, support mechanisms and leadership initiatives that will ensure a lawyer's future success. In addition to the payoff you get by way of 'return' from the hires who stay with you, the larger benefits of cultivating a better work environment will rain down on everyone in the firm."

Hackett also explains that the synergistic relationships among balance, diversity, values, and outcomes have likewise become evident to clients: "What's good for minority and women hires—meaningful training, mentoring, challenging work, an equal chance to make mistakes and be reprimanded (and forgiven), client development opportunities, balanced life options and the like—is good for every lawyer working in the firm. Address the issues that your minority lawyers are talking about, and you'll address the issues that will help your overall attrition figures improve."

As one senior in-house counsel similarly observes, "We look for our law firms to institute linkage to balanced work arrangements to retain female counsel. We want our outside law firms to work hard to retain women who need alternative relationships."

Many corporations already require outside counsel to follow formal written guidelines ranging from billing invoice detail to a commitment to diversity. They could encourage the development of a big-law-firm Working Culture Index. Along with attrition rates, it could be an interesting addition to the *American Lawyer*'s A-List criteria. Imagine an equity partner meeting that included this agenda item: "Reducing our Working Culture Index and attrition rates." Big law is filled with free-market disciples who urge better information as a panacea. Consistency should prompt them to embrace these two new measures.

Challenge courts to reconsider the billable hour's sacrosanct status. The courts are in a position to help undo the billable hour's stranglehold, but so far they've made things worse by entrenching the regime. A recent example came when the lawyers in *Perdue v. Kenny A.* sued on behalf of children in Georgia's state-run foster care program. After eight years, the trial court awarded attorneys' fees under the federal statute permitting winning plaintiffs to recover from the losers. In its April 2010 ruling, the United States Supreme Court adopted a rule that, ultimately, would reduce that monetary award by several million dollars.

Writing for a five-justice majority (Roberts, Alito, Scalia, Thomas, and Kennedy), associate justice Samuel Alito took offense at the suggestion that the prevailing civil rights lawyers should "earn as much as the attorneys at some of the richest law firms in the country." More important, the Court rejected the argument "that departures from hourly billing are becoming more common." It observed that "if hourly billing becomes unusual, an alternative to the lodestar method [hours worked times billing rate] may have to be found. However, neither the respondents nor their amici contend that that day has arrived."

The Court's ruling made it less likely that that day will arrive anytime soon. In 1983, it first adopted the lodestar calculation—hours worked times billing rate—as a useful starting point for fee awards. Now, in its first significant ruling on the issue in almost thirty years, the Court stripped away everything but the lodestar as the method for determining a lawyer's permissible compensation in many federal cases. Room for practitioners to experiment away from hourly billing is nowhere to be found in the majority opinion.

In fact, the Court's analysis extends beyond civil rights cases to "virtually identical language in many of the federal fee-shifting statutes." That covers any federal court evaluating any kind of fee request, including bankruptcy petitions, regardless of whether it involves fee shifting. State courts will continue to use the lodestar approach in probate, divorce, and other proceedings. As a result, lawyers continue to maximize their chances for court approval of fees by adhering to hourly billing. Innovators experiment at their peril because, depending on the type of matter, they risk not getting paid at all.

The Supreme Court's recent imprimatur on the billable hour regime helps that regime to endure and reinforces what lower courts have already been doing for years in bankruptcy proceedings. Particularly in large, high-profile cases that big firms handle, the result has been a kind of trickle-up economics, where a debtor's estate in bankruptcy becomes a vehicle for channeling more wealth to some lawyers who already have plenty. During the Great Recession, large firms found bankruptcy to be an especially lucrative practice area. That's because federal judges have acquiesced to lawyers exploiting the billable hour regime.

For example, in a 2011 article in the *Wall Street Journal* about senior partners who command four-figure hourly rates from clients, Weil, Gotshal & Manges's bankruptcy department leader Harvey Miller was quoted: "The underlying principle is if you can get it, get it." A year earlier, Miller—widely regarded as the dean of the bankruptcy bar—was resisting discount requests from court-appointed monitors in the Lehman and General Motors bankruptcies: "If you had cancer and you were going into an operation, while you were lying on the table, would you look at the surgeon and say, 'I'd like a 10 percent discount'? This is not a public, charitable event."

That comment was as ironic as it was offensive, considering that his firm had already billed $16 million on its way to $45 million in fees for the GM bankruptcy, which public taxpayer money did indeed fund. Although taxpayers didn't finance Lehman's bankruptcy, the final attorneys' fees petition for three and a half years of work in that proceeding sought more than $400 million in compensation for Harvey Miller and his colleagues at Weil, Gotshal & Manges—more than forty of whom billed $1,000 an hour. In 2011, Weil Gotshal's average equity partner profits reached an all-time high of more than $2.4 million. No one expects Miller or any other lawyer to work for nothing. But his cases—big corporate bankruptcies—illustrate how dysfunctional and socially expensive the billable hour regime can be, even as it makes some wealthy lawyers even richer.

Bankruptcy cases differ from other matters in an important respect: the client's role with respect to attorneys' fees. By definition, the bankrupt debtor lacks sufficient assets to cover all liabilities. Filing a bankruptcy petition puts control of the debtor's business into the hands of a bankruptcy judge. As the case proceeds through federal court, separate attorneys represent different stakeholders, namely, the debtor and its creditors. The court's role includes protecting the assets of the bankrupt's estate for the benefit of creditors and then distributing those assets fairly among creditors entitled to share in it. When the court has finished its carving up, the pie is gone. In that important respect, attorneys working on bankruptcy cases don't confront either the specter of client accountability or the promise of future work associated with continuing client relationships.

A debtor's bankruptcy lawyers get the first shot at the debtor's income and assets. That is, they're paid ahead of everyone else. Such a rule makes sense because otherwise no lawyer would take on the work for an insolvent client. But the problem is that those attorneys' fees are largely free of the oversight that typically comes with a traditional representation. Although the debtor is supposed to review and approve its bankruptcy lawyers' fee requests, the judge (in conjunction with the US Department of Justice Trustee Program) has the final word in evaluating fee petitions.

That's where the system goes awry. Courts aren't equipped to second-guess how attorneys spend their time—amounting to tens of thousands of hours in complex bankruptcies. As to hourly rates, approving fee petitions theoretically requires courts to determine whether they're reasonable and customary for the services performed. If law firms in the select club of the nation's top bankruptcy practices keep rates high and moving higher, the fees based on those rates pass the court's threshold standard of acceptability. What most lawyers in big firms charge becomes the standard for reasonable and customary. As for hours billed, no one responsible for reviewing attorneys' fee petitions feels comfortable second-guessing the time that individual lawyers devote to particular tasks. They defer to the self-appointed experts doing the work, that is, the lawyers themselves.

The issue isn't so much the rate of a top adviser such as Harvey Miller, whose skill and experience may be worth every penny that clients pay him, or the time he spends personally offering strategic advice. That's equally true for other areas of the law. No corporate general counsel wants to tell a board of directors that a bet-the-company case was lost because he or she had a chance to save a few bucks on the hourly rate of whoever tried the case. In that respect, not all lawyers are fungible. The best attorneys in any field properly command outsized rates for their work in matters where the stakes are high. But armies of attorneys and other billers come with them. The top large firms charged more than $500 an hour for an average associate and almost $900 an hour for an average partner. As previously noted, more than forty of Miller's partners at Weil Gotshal billed $1,000 an hour during the Lehman bankruptcy.

When the Justice Department's US trustee recently suggested reforms to the current fee system, big firms united in opposition. Among the US trustee's concerns was the possibility that some firms might have different hourly rate schedules for their attorneys working on bankruptcy matters than for those working on matters for other clients. It worried that a partner whose $1,000 hourly rate might show up in a petition for fee approval might be charging non-bankruptcy clients $800 or less for that same hour. In a letter objecting to proposals for greater transparency concerning hourly rates, the head of the restructuring practice at Miller's firm, Weil, Gotshal & Manges, wrote, "Disclosure of confidential rate information is unprecedented. Competitors . . . may use the disclosed information to gain unfair advantage."

Ironically, an attorney who had been the liquidating trustee for the Finley Kumble bankruptcy and was lead counsel for Dewey & LeBoeuf when it filed for bankruptcy on May 28, 2012, offered a comment that seemed to support the US trustee's request. "Big law firms, which can throw scores of lawyers at a single case, cannot help but splurge on a major bankruptcy," said Albert Togut, the managing partner of a boutique law firm specializing in bankruptcy. "It's in their DNA that, when they approach a project, they bring every resource at their disposal to the project." He urged the trustee staff to make a change that would encourage greater use of small, specialized law firms. At the time, Togut's firm had nineteen lawyers.

Reconsider size. Growth for the sake of growth isn't a strategy for success; it's a dubious path to an unknown destination. The myth that law firms benefit from economies of scale is exactly that—a myth. One hundred attorneys may be too few for a firm to achieve optimal size, but two thousand is certainly too many. Firms that perceive the need to be global will continue to grow, but no economic imperative drives that mission. Some firms use their burgeoning size as a way to increase short-term leverage and equity partner profits: they add bodies, increase gross revenues, and reduce or limit the number of equity partners. Life can become good financially for the relatively few winners.

Apart from pervasive career dissatisfaction throughout the ranks, many such firms will become the victims of circumstances that they themselves are creating—as Howrey and Dewey & LeBoeuf did most recently, and as Finley Kumble did twenty-five years ago, with a host of other fatalities in between. Others will survive with a culture that makes attracting law schools' best and brightest graduates increasingly difficult. Larger firms produce less cohesive workforces. Building a sense of community isn't easy when lawyers attending their annual partnership meetings don't recognize most of the people in the room. Especially in big firms that keep getting bigger, the corporatization of the profession is exacerbating individual isolation and alienation. Building community and a shared sense of purpose loses out to maximizing profits.

The principal beneficiaries of large law firm growth are obvious. A handful of firm leaders at the top drive an agenda that enhances their personal prestige. Law firm management consultants make big money by helping firms develop and pursue strategic plans to become larger. Headhunters earn a living by spinning lawyers through the lateral-transfer revolving door.

But many of today's most respected lawyers practice in firms that have fewer than three hundred attorneys. Some firms are among the Am Law 200; some don't care if they ever make that list. In some cases, talented lawyers left their big firms to create smaller ones. Leaders of large law firms could think about the kind of workplace that they'd want to join right out of law school today. They could even try to recall what they most enjoyed about their own firms when they started out two or three decades ago. If senior partners ruled in accordance with their fondest memories of earlier years as practicing attorneys, many large firms would look much different—starting with size.

Reduce leverage. Between 1985 and 2010, the average leverage ratio for the Am Law 50 firms doubled, from 1.76 to 3.54. As with the explosive growth of many big firms, no economic imperative drove that destructive trend, either. Many successful, profitable, and even elite firms thrive with leverage ratios far below the current average. Notable examples appearing on the *American Lawyer*'s A-List for the last three consecutive years (2010 to 2012) are Covington & Burling (leverage ratio in 2011: 2.07), Wilmer, Cutler, Pickering, Hale & Dorr (1.98), and Gibson, Dunn & Crutcher (2.79). I have no detailed knowledge about life inside any of these firms, but the fact that their associate satisfaction and other relevant scores land them perennially on the A-List is probably not an accident. And it's a safe bet that the income these firms' equity partners earn still exceeds their wildest law school expectations.

Recruit thoughtfully. Rather than tolerating five-year associate attrition rates exceeding 80 percent, law firms could approach recruiting with a different attitude: that they are finding new family members. They could seek people who appear to have the potential to become fellow law partners someday—and remain with the firm for a long time thereafter. Senior partners could become more active in interviewing law students, even on campus. Among other advantages, it would vest those who have the power to help young attorneys succeed with a personal interest in that outcome. This usefully leverages the reluctance of most big law firms' senior partners to admit that they were wrong.

No recruiting process is perfect. But to optimize results, firms could proceed with greater transparency. They could calculate and publish their Working Culture Index number; they could reveal attrition rates; they could acknowledge that fewer than one in ten new hires will advance to equity partner after a decade of hard work (assuming that the firm's track record in that respect is similar to most large law firms and they don't adopt my suggestion to deleverage). Young attorneys will make better decisions if they have more information about the lives they are likely to lead.

Dissatisfied lawyers are demoralizing to the institutions employing them. Not all hopes can become reality, and some attrition on the road to partnership will remain a feature of every great law firm. Nevertheless, more truth in recruiting can force students to confront their own unrealistic ideas. They could better understand the daunting odds against success and, perhaps, reconsider how they're defining it. They might make more-informed decisions that better serve them, their firms, the profession, and society.

The magnitude of this educational mission became clear from a comment by one of the second-year law students who thought they were going to spend the summer of 2012 working as Dewey & LeBoeuf interns at $3,000 a week. A month before some of the thirty selected students were scheduled to begin work, Dewey told all of them that there would be no summer program. Indeed, it appeared increasingly likely that there would be no firm by the time the summer began.

Talking to a reporter for the *New York Times*, an Ivy League student expressed hope that other firms would step up and give these abandoned students jobs: "A firm may look like a corporation, yes, but we're all part of a fraternity of lawyers. Next year one becomes a member of the bar association, a linked structure. The firms may be competitors, but at the end of the day this is still the greater legal field. I hope this sensibility that we are part of a profession will also be in the minds of people as they consider us." Such a naive triumph of hope over reality reveals the magnitude of the task required to educate prospective lawyers about the path ahead.

Provide associates with meaningful work. Pro bono activities can replace the small cases that previously gave young attorneys real experiences involving real clients. In 1962, 11 percent of all civil cases went to trial; by 2002, the percentage had dropped to under 2. The proportion of criminal cases going to trial went from 15 percent to 5 percent. Occasionally there are local aberrations, such as the doubling of Chicago federal jury trials from 2006 to 2011 (the number went from 59 to 127). But the general trend has been downward. Pro bono cases could fill some of that void. Likewise, if firms were willing to reduce their usual hourly fees, they could take on small matters that young attorneys could handle on their own.

Virtually all big firms encourage their attorneys to perform pro bono activities, and many firms have outstanding track records. In 2011, fourteen Am Law 200 firms averaged more than 100 pro bono hours per lawyer for the year. They were Jenner & Block; Paul Hastings; Covington & Burling; Hughes, Hubbard & Reed; Milbank, Tweed, Hadley & McCoy; Patterson, Belknap, Webb & Tyler; Dechert; Robins, Kaplan, Miller & Ciresi; Arnold & Porter; Orrick, Herrington & Sutcliffe; Gibson Dunn; Foley Hoag; Morrison & Foerster; and O'Melveny & Myers.

Disconnect associate compensation from billable hours. Implementing the previously outlined Working Culture Index would give clients leverage in negotiating lower hourly rates for some attorney time, but it won't break the back of firms' corrosive billable hours culture. That requires changing most law firms' existing incentive structures for associates. No firm penalizes associates for working outrageous hours. In fact, many firms expressly reward such behavior. Every lawyer understands that client emergencies can require an unusually large time commitment for a limited period. But the key word is *limited*. Associates who bill more than 2,200 hours year in and year out are doing themselves, their clients, their firms, and their profession a disservice—they just don't realize it. Neither do the partners for whom they work.

If associates knew that they wouldn't get a single additional bonus or salary dollar for any billed hour above, say, 2,100 in a calendar year, several things could happen. Some might still work excessive hours because that's who they are. But there's no reason for that behavior to set the tone for an entire institution. Others might work long hours without billing all of their time. Partners could tell them to stop on the grounds that they are undermining the firm's environment. Most associates would find other productive ways to use their new freedom. Some might even go home for dinner and stop working most weekends. Imagine a law firm culture that encouraged attorneys to spend time with their spouses and children—and opened windows of time for them to do it.

Provide true and honest associate review. Without billable hours as the definitive (and easy) metric for associate evaluation, partners would actually have to assess the quality of young lawyers' work. Even the best recruiting efforts will yield mistakes and mismatches. Firms could adopt meaningful and transparent review processes that deliver the message the moment it becomes clear that a young lawyer won't advance to the next level. Salary differences among associates in a class could make the point unambiguously. Telling people where they stand relative to their peers could give them the information they need to make better decisions about their futures.

In the current model, senior associates are profit centers. If there's work on which they can bill time, partners have a financial incentive to keep stringing them along until the up-or-out decision about their entry into equity partnership. Lockstep associate compensation systems keep associates' hopes high but allow partners to leave them in the dark for too long.

Eliminate two-tiered partnerships. Like senior associates, non-equity partners are cash cows for big firms. Although some firms have used them as a kind of probationary period during which attorneys either prove their value as potential equity partners or fall by the wayside, adhering to that principle requires leadership discipline that has disappeared in many firms. Rather than dismissing attorneys who will never become equity partners, the more lucrative approach for senior leaders is to keep them around. As a consequence, managing partners are doing two things: they're adding years to the equity partner track and allowing non-equity partners to remain indefinitely. As previously explained, both behaviors disserve a firm and most of the lawyers in it.

Send the equity partner elevator back down. Actor Jack Lemmon said that those who succeeded in his business had an obligation to send the elevator down for others. Senior partners could adopt a similar attitude. That requires firm leaders to abandon the desire for instant gratification that too often dictates their decisions. In particular, those at the top have the power to transcend their own greed by removing the artificial constraints on entry into equity partnership pyramids. Quality need not suffer if firms move the focus away from maintaining arbitrary leverage ratios. Such a culture could motivate promising young attorneys from the very beginning of their careers. Greater commitment to their work could produce better performance and output. Promoting all deserving candidates can grow partner profits. If it costs equity partners some profits in the short run, they can afford it—and their firm will benefit in the long run.

As a closely related strategy, a firm could hold partners accountable for mentoring, collegiality, and intergenerational transition of the firm's clients. These and other attributes of a true partnership make a firm stronger. But here's the challenge: there's no metric by which the currently prevailing model can incorporate the resulting enhancements in institutional loyalty and stability. Perhaps this question will suffice as a temporary proxy: what's the survival of a law firm worth?

Shrink the gap. Once firms become true to the quality commitment that could govern the consideration of all equity partner candidates, they could implement the next step toward enhancing the institution's strength and stability: shrinking the yawning internal equity partner income gap and adopting lockstep compensation for equity partners. If law firms had the checks and balances that complete corporatization typically provides—namely, an independent board of directors and shareholders—the result would be preferable to the worst of both worlds that currently characterizes many of them. The senior partners at the top of most big firms don't face the restraining forces of shareholders or an outside board of directors. The trend toward greater concentration of wealth and power at the very top of equity partnerships has reduced the size of the group just below them. But those midlevel equity partners once acted as a check and balance, holding law firm leaders to some degree of accountability.

In most big law firms today, top leaders are accountable to no one besides each other. This dangerous model results in a partnership of real players within a larger group that is a partnership in name only. It allows the hubris, arrogance, and poor judgment of a few to ruin the lives of many and to destroy the firm itself. Genuine lockstep systems with no discretionary profit pools to distribute at year-end create certainty, restore a middle class of equity partners, and ameliorate the effects of self-interested behavior that undermines the notion of partnership.

Several of the country's most prominent and successful firms have adhered to lockstep partner compensation systems (or a modified version of them). Most such traditionalists are in New York: Cravath, Swaine & Moore; Cleary, Gottlieb, Steen & Hamilton; Davis, Polk & Wardwell; Debevoise & Plimpton; Simpson, Thacher & Bartlett; and Wachtell, Lipton, Rosen & Katz, to name a few. As Cleary Gottlieb's managing partner, Mark Walker, said in 2007, "My view is that if someone says I'm not going to Cleary Gottlieb because (another firm) is guaranteeing me a salary of X, then they don't belong at our firm anyway." When asked if Cravath's partners would stick around if the firm didn't make so much money (more than $3 million a year in average partner profits at the time of the 2007 interview), the firm's presiding partner, Evan R. Chesler, answered, "I don't know the answer to that. I think there is more glue than just money."

Adopt mandatory retirement policies. The last stage of a lockstep compensation system, declining income for partners beyond a certain age, could become a down ramp on the way to the exit. For many attorneys, contemplating life after the practice of law means a difficult encounter with their own mortality. The challenge is particularly daunting for those in a profession that requires great sacrifice to succeed. The problems of transition aren't limited to big law firms or even lawyers, but the large-firm setting brings them into sharp focus. The issue is not and never has been whether lawyers who want to work into their dotage should be able to do so. Nor is the issue whether they should receive payment for doing so. Rather, the question is whether at some point they should cease sharing equity partner profits.

As the drive to maximize profits and enhance competitiveness continues, law firms "restructure"—a euphemism for firing the less productive partners. At Chicago-based Sidley Austin, some affected attorneys filed age-discrimination suits. After the firm stripped thirty-two partners of their partnership status in 2005, the Equal Employment Opportunity Commission sued on behalf of the victims. Sidley defended on the grounds that, as former owners, law firm partners were not employees for purposes of the age discrimination laws. The federal district and appellate courts ruled against the firm's position. When the United States Supreme Court refused to take the case, Sidley settled. In a consent decree, the firm agreed that "each person for whom the E.E.O.C. has sought relief in this matter is an employee." The thirty-two former partners received a collective $27.5 million.

Sidley was especially vulnerable to age-related claims because its self-perpetuating executive committee ran the firm. One former partner called it "apostolic succession." Partners had little involvement in the issues that mattered most. As the EEOC saw it, that made them employees. Today, that's become true of most big law firms.

In real partnerships, age discrimination laws wouldn't apply and mandatory retirement policies would be safe. That's important because such policies address the daunting challenge that aging equity partners present to a firm's long-term stability, especially at the top of the pyramid. They reap great financial rewards, sometimes despite low contributions to the firm's productivity, and aren't eager to relinquish wealth or power. These individuals become roadblocks to intergenerational transitions in a world of sacred leverage ratios. They are one reason that, in 2007, half of US law firms with more than fifty lawyers had mandatory retirement ages for partners. Since then, firms have backed away from such policies. Some blame (or credit) the government, but the self-interest of affected senior partners who eliminated those policies also warrants a closer look.

In 2010, the EEOC again brought an age-bias case against a law firm—this time on behalf of a Kelley, Drye & Warren partner who claimed that the firm's policy of de-equitizing partners at age seventy was unlawful. Eugene D'Ablemont's dispute with his longtime firm began in December 2000 when he composed a letter describing the bonus he thought he'd earned in his first year as a "life partner." That was the designation that Kelley Drye gave its partners the year after they turned sixty-nine and no longer held equity in the firm.

"This is the time of year when," he wrote, "as a life partner, I begin to worry whether my sainted wife Mary will have to wear her threadbare cloth coat for another year." Surely he was being sarcastic. Kelley Drye's average equity partner profits during his final year as an equity partner, 1999, were $575,000.

Bolstering D'Ablemont's claim to a big bonus, two of his clients had earlier written that the firm's action created "a rather difficult situation for our company as we move forward" because his personal involvement since the 1970s had caused them to remain at Kelley Drye. They expressed dismay that D'Ablemont would no longer be allowed to take the lead on their matters. Earlier in 2000, D'Ablemont had also requested an increase in his client development allowance—from $10,000 to $20,000—in part to cover entertainment expenses at the Westchester Country Club, the Metropolitan Club, and the club at Seabrook Island, where clients "have come to expect to be entertained."

Although D'Ablemont received a pension as a life partner and annual bonuses that ranged from $25,000 to $75,000, he later claimed that the bonus amounts were one-seventh to one-twentieth of what he would have earned if he'd remained an equity partner. Defending itself after the EEOC filed suit in 2010, the firm asserted that during the late 2000s D'Ablemont billed a yearly total of between 195 and 324 hours. Even so, he claimed credit for millions of dollars in client billings.

The case reignited the debate over whether law firm partners are employers—and therefore exempt from age discrimination laws—or merely employees who have little control over their fate at the hands of managing partners. That legal issue went unresolved when the case settled in April 2012. D'Ablemont got $574,000—$450,000 for the years 2001 to 2010, plus $124,000 for 2011, plus 12 percent of fees collected from certain client matters after 2011.

The dispute highlights the worst flaws in the prevailing big firm model. An aging senior partner's clients worry about continuity of representation when that partner retires because the senior partner has failed to solidify relationships between those clients and younger protégés. A senior partner hangs on to client relationships and billings because year-to-year survival in the equity partnership turns on the metrics that have become the basis for valuing all talent. Equity partners who have already pulled up the ladder on the next generation remain big winners. Losers include clients and younger lawyers. The firms themselves become victims when the failure of elders to achieve intergenerational transition of clients destabilizes the institutions.

Long before it settled the case, Kelley Drye had eliminated the mandatory retirement provision from its equity partnership agreement. In 2007, the New York State Bar Association recommended eliminating all mandatory retirement ages in law firm partnership agreements. The ABA House of Delegates voted similarly to recommend against mandatory retirement policies for law firms. Many firms quickly followed the organized bar's recommendations, including Dewey & LeBoeuf and Cadwalader, Wickersham & Taft. K&L Gates's chair, Peter Kalis, announced: "Our partners concluded that age-based limitations on partner status are anachronistic and out-of-step with enlightened views of productive older lawyers."

Everyone assumed that these big-firm leaders' motives were noble— that they were honoring an aging group of elders for whom eighty was becoming the new sixty-five. Perhaps the alignment of such actions with these partners' personal self-interest was coincidental. But without the change, managing partners who favored eliminating these rules would have been swept away in the next wave of mandatory retirements. No one mentioned that removing this so-called restriction on senior partners was exacerbating the larger problems of intergenerational transition.

Combined with the eat-what-you-kill business model, the absence of mandatory retirement is allowing aging baby boomers to block the advance of younger attorneys. The prospect of forced exit from equity partnerships at a definite age offered some counterweight to embedded senior leaders who have been pulling up ladders within their equity partnerships. The absence of a fixed departure point coupled with the ability of aging partners to continue enhancing their personal fortunes produces a predictable outcome: tension between those who hang on and the younger group waiting for its turn. As that wait gets longer, antagonisms intensify. Artificial constraints—especially leverage ratios—prevent the promotion of well-qualified candidates after years of personal service and sacrifice. If there's not economic room at equity partner decision time, their efforts will have been for naught. In sacrificing the talents of one generation in order to keep enriching another, the firm itself becomes the ultimate victim.

The United Kingdom is smarter about this issue. In April 2012 it dismissed a former partner's challenge to his firm's compulsory retirement age of sixty-five. An argument that the firm offered in defense of its policy—and that the court accepted—was the need to clear the path for associates and junior partners to advance.

Develop exit platforms for aging partners. Until America's big-firm leaders become wiser about all of this, aging baby boomers will continue to face an unhappy dilemma: embrace marginalization or hog opportunities. How they resolve it has profound implications for attorneys of all ages and their firms.

"In my experience, it is much harder for older partners to maintain their position if their billable hours decline," an employment lawyer observed recently. For the person who worries about maintaining his or her compensation, one law firm consultant had simple advice: "Very few people are so skilled that they can't be replaced by a younger, more current practitioner. You've got to be so connected to important clients that the firm is going to fear your departure." In other words, aging partners should avoid giving younger lawyers a chance to develop client relationships. That works well for someone who wants only to maximize profits as rapidly as possible and never contemplates life after the law, but for everyone else in the firm and for the profession generally, it's disastrous.

A firm's health and prosperity don't turn on a succession of close-range financial successes. Stability requires farsightedness. But those running firms under the prevailing big-law model abhor that suggestion. Meanwhile, young attorneys learn by example. "Firm clients" cease to exist; they're absorbed into jealously guarded fiefdoms that become transportable business units. Traditional partnership principles of mutual respect and support yield to unrestrained self-interest. Eventually, everyone loses. Young attorneys resent older ones; wealthy equity partners erect futile defenses against their own inevitable decline in influence to an unhappy place; firms lose the stability that comes with loyal partners and clients.

There may be a way out of this conundrum: encouraging partners to redirect their skills. For example, the New York Legal Aid Society program Second Acts taps into the growing army of retired lawyers. As Miriam Buhl, pro bono counsel at Weil, Gotshal & Manges, put it, "The point is not to have distinct phases of working life and after-working life, but to meld the two by having pro bono work be part of a lawyer's career. Therefore, when lawyers retire, they can somewhat seamlessly slip into meaningful volunteer work."

Another illustration is the Advanced Leadership Initiative at Harvard University. "The idea is to produce people who can have an impact on society, who can imagine solutions to big problems in a big way," according to business school professor Rosabeth Kanter. She and others at Harvard conduct a year of multidisciplinary seminars and classes for fellows who develop ideas and leave with an action plan. A retired partner at the New York firm Debevoise & Plimpton became a key member of an International Senior Lawyers Project team that helped Liberia's new government negotiate contracts with multinational corporations for access to that country's resources. The retired chair of Chicago-based McDermott, Will & Emery used experiences from his health care practice to help a nonprofit organization deal with end-of-life issues.

Solutions start with recognizing that behavior follows economic structures and the incentives they create. In most big law firms, the singular emphasis on a handful of indicators—hourly rates, attorneys' billable hours, and leverage ratios—has produced blinding wealth for a few. But those metrics lose their luster when they become organizing principles of life. The profession's daily demands leave all lawyers with precious little time to reflect on what their lives after practice might be. Most successful partners eventually will need help finding a path that reshapes their self-identity while preserving their dignity. For firms that care, the challenge is to permit disengagement with honor.

Firms could do a great service and improve their own stability for the long haul if they encouraged aging colleagues to do the right thing. But it requires thinking beyond today's calculations that determine a partner's current-year compensation. It requires valuing what can't be measured easily and embedding it in a firm's culture so that reaching retirement age isn't a shock, it's a blessing. It requires empathy, compassion, and leadership.

It's possible for the profession's leaders to test these and other ideas by seeing how well they accord with a single overriding principle: seek to leave the firm and the profession as a whole better than they found it. Someone once did that for them.

Think outside the box. The most important challenge for big law firm leaders is also the most difficult: embracing innovation. Forces outside the control of big firms will shape the profession; many will be surprises. Thirty years ago, firms maintained significant in-house law libraries where associates toiled for hours on legal research projects. The most sophisticated firms on the cutting edge of technology had dial-up Lexis terminals. Today's associates can perform the same tasks on a laptop computer in a fraction of the time. Outsourcing, contract attorneys, and computerized document review systems didn't exist in the 1970s; now they're commonplace. The list of developments that revolutionized the way lawyers work is long.

No one can predict what will come next, but thoughtful observers have some ideas that the leaders of big firms ignore at their peril. Indiana University Maurer School of Law professor William Henderson offers the example of Novus Law, a private company that specializes in electronic discovery, which can remove the drudgery—along with the lucrative billable hours—of work that associates would otherwise do.

Henderson also cites Axiom, an organization through which attorneys can hire themselves out for limited projects at an agreed price. ALM editor in chief, Aric Press, calls it "a textbook example of an outfit entering a market at a low place on the value chain, prepared to move up as its bigger and wealthier competitors withdraw." Axiom founder Mark Harris was an associate at Davis, Polk & Wardwell when he realized that he was billing out in one month an amount equal to his entire annual salary. In 2000, he started a "new kind of law firm with no partners, no billable-hour rat race, and no pricey overhead." Axiom matches attorneys with clients on a free-agency basis for a specific project at a set price. Each attorney on the roster is free to decline work. Axiom is attracting some of the nation's top young attorneys, who "run the gamut from parents who want to spend more time with their children to people who want to write the next great American novel, work from home or at their clients' offices." By 2012, Axiom was a nine-hundred-person firm, serving nearly half of the Fortune 100 through eleven offices and four global delivery centers.

Press describes the potential implications of Axiom's business model for some large law firms: "[Axiom's] projects are notable for a few reasons. The work is repetitive. It can be broken down into steps. Lawyers don't have to be involved throughout. And, perhaps most importantly for these purposes, this work used to be done by private law firms or inhouse departments." Press acknowledges that it's low-end work, but "so was making rebar steel . . . the rough beast that slouched toward Bethlehem Steel is now headed this way."

Whether it's through piecemeal innovators such as Axiom, Novus Law, or something else, the high-end legal delivery system will continue to evolve. Big firms could benefit from heeding Henderson's advice: "Retain profits and use those funds to build better recruitment and training systems and create better (and proprietary) work processes that enable a firm to grow organically by taking market share from its pennywise, pound-foolish peers." Yet, as he correctly predicts, "for better or worse, this strategy is unlikely to be embraced by many firms." Quoting Richard Susskind, Henderson laments, "It's hard to tell a room full of millionaires that their business model is broken."

As a temporary measure until leaders implement more enduring changes, Press suggests a partner protection plan. He starts from the correct premise that recent law firm failures have at least two common denominators: "really poor leadership . . . and partnerships filled with lawyers who refused or failed to act as owners." Noting that "having a spine might help," Press offers a structural fix that might better protect the interests of those who are unwilling to voice dissent—or even ask for copies of their firms' financial statements. He would put in place a "cross between an outside director and an ombudsman, someone appointed and paid by the partners who has access to the executive and comp committees and only one job: keeping track of the firm leaders and calling fouls as necessary." Most managing partners will recoil from the proposal, but wise firms would consider it seriously.

Apart from the larger trends over which law firms themselves may have little control, there are living examples of an alternative model that emphasizes community and other immeasurable values over the focus on the near term that now dominates the profession's large firms. Los Angeles–based Munger, Tolles & Olson led the *American Lawyer's* A-List for three years in a row before finishing second in 2011 and third in 2012. But most big-firm leaders would regard some of its numbers as mediocre at best and would consider its positive attributes irrelevant to the prevailing large law firm business model:

- The 180-lawyer firm isn't among the Am Law 100. Its gross revenues placed it in the middle of the Am Law 200 in 2011.
- Average equity partner profits in 2011 were $1.35 million—well below those of many other top firms.
- It has a single-tier partnership structure—equity partners only.
- Leverage is nonexistent; the ratio of associates to partners is one to one.
- Its 2012 NALP directory entry reports that the firm has no minimum billable hours requirement.
- Almost half of the firm's associates and 20 percent of its partners are women; 30 percent of associates and 18 percent of partners are minorities.
- Attrition is relatively rare: almost 50 percent of the lawyers who have joined Munger Tolles over the past twenty years are still there.

Less quantifiable and even more important in understanding the firm's continuing success is what one observer calls "a strong identity, loyal clients, and happy lawyers." Some partners have offices on the same floors as litigation support staff attorneys. Associates participate in firm decisions about lateral hires. In fact, associates sit on all of the firm's committees except partner compensation and associate review. Even the firm's most powerful body, the fifteen-lawyer policy committee, includes three associates. When there are votes, they "just raise their hands. It's not like the partners get two votes and the associates get one," according to an associate who co-chaired the pro bono committee at the time of her 2008 interview. In 2012, managing partner Sandra Seville-Jones told the *American Lawyer*, "We have not changed anything to be near the top [of the A-List]. We're just being us."

It's not surprising that such a culture attracts some of the best graduates from the nation's elite law schools. As of 2012, 70 percent of the firm's attorneys had clerked for federal judges; eighteen of them clerked for justices on the United States Supreme Court. From early in their careers, associates get training and opportunities to do the things lawyers do—take depositions, write briefs that actually get filed, and participate in strategy sessions. Munger Tolles makes a real effort to close the gap between expectations and reality that plagues so many other big firms.

The firm doesn't have a mandatory retirement policy, probably because one of the firm's founders still sets the tone. Seventysomething name partner Ron Olson says, "We try to hire the very best available. We believe, over time, the best lawyers get the best results, and the best results attract the best clients."

Longtime client Warren Buffett agrees: "They're very responsive. They get results, and they get them fast. You are dealing with extraordinarily high-quality people."

Although primarily a litigation shop, Munger Tolles also has a vibrant corporate practice. In addition to Buffet's Berkshire Hathaway, the firm's clients include Oaktree Capital Management LP, Abbott Laboratories, Verizon Communications, Shell Oil Company, and Boeing. Pro bono activities and community involvement are built into its culture, as is the firm's commitment to increased diversity.

Munger Tolles doesn't disclose its internal distribution of equity partner compensation, but everything else known about the firm suggests that firm leaders have not allowed so-called macroeconomic imperatives to determine the firm's culture. All big law firms should take the lesson. They need not grow into the thousands. They don't have to demand a minimum of 2,000 billable hours from their associates or convey the clear message that advancement requires many, many more. Nothing in the structure of any firm limits the number of new equity partners so that the incumbents' seven-figure incomes will be even higher next year—and the year after that.

IT'S IRONIC THAT THE BABY BOOMERS running today's big firms complain about younger attorneys behaving as if they're entitled to wealth and success. They have it backward. Those in charge have developed a sense of entitlement; they behave and compensate themselves accordingly.

The law is a service profession. A law firm is, and will remain, only as good as the best new attorneys that it can attract. As young lawyers decide how they want their lives to unfold, many of the future's best and brightest will reject the cultures that pervade most large law firms and opt for something that more closely resembles Axiom or Munger Tolles. Perhaps those who don't will be sufficiently talented to keep the pipeline full, even for firms whose cultures seem hostile to attorney career satisfaction. But firms whose leaders don't recognize the ways that the attitudes of the next generation differ from their own will create opportunities for the firms that do.

Those willing to replace a myopic focus on the near future and business-school-type metrics with a longer vision and reasoned judgment could value things that cannot easily be measured. Community, collegiality, mentoring, a shared sense of institutional purpose that extends beyond the current K-1 partner income statement, and many more are there for the taking. Those willing to bet on the future can change the face of the profession for the better.

CHAPTER 11

PROSPECTIVE LAWYERS

More than any other time in history, mankind faces a crossroads.
One path leads to despair and utter hopelessness. The other to total
extinction. Let us pray we have the wisdom to choose correctly.
—Woody Allen, *Side Effects*

WITH RECENT PUSHES toward greater transparency, those thinking about attending law school today have the tools necessary to make an informed decision. The question is whether they'll use them. Undergraduates are well advised to approach the issue with a seriousness of purpose that may be foreign to most of them. A timely investment in skeptical self-assessment along with critical inquiry into available data can yield lifetime rewards and avoid enduring mistakes. Candor from law schools and transparency from big law firms—even the educational equivalent of pre-law boot camp—are useless if students ignore them.

Thoughtful consideration of any individual's suitability for the legal profession could begin years before a prospective attorney applies to law school, but usually it doesn't. The exercise could start with introspective analysis, add reliable information about a legal career, and then consider the fit, but that seldom occurs, either. Throughout such an inquiry, one thought could dominate: the personal stakes and the cost of a miscalculation are extraordinarily high. But the impulse to see the world in a particular way minimizes the ability to see the potential for bad outcomes and distorts decisions. Notwithstanding these challenges and more, the most effective path to a better profession requires a focus on young people who think they want to be lawyers but haven't yet applied to law school. For prospective attorneys, a conscientious search for better information will empower them to make better decisions.

As for the particular type of practice setting that might best suit any individual once he or she graduates from law school, there's no magic formula or universal solution. But finding the right spot is important. Remaining alert to changes that might render an initial choice uncomfortable is even more vital. Anyone who doubts the latter proposition should read the story of Mark Levy.

On April 29, 2009, the fifty-nine-year-old Kilpatrick Stockton partner took his own life. By all accounts, he'd done everything right—summa cum laude from Yale College, honors from Yale Law School, a long and distinguished career as one of the nation's leading appellate court advocates. The day after his firm announced layoffs that included Levy, a colleague who stopped by to say good-bye found his body. He'd shot himself with a gun that no one knew he owned. A few months later, the *ABA Journal* ran a lengthy article on his impressive life and terrible death.

His wife declined to be interviewed for the story, but the *Journal* found friends that offered some insight. They said that Levy was deeply invested in his work and had few other interests besides his family. In earlier years he'd struggled with depression.

The article's description of Levy applies to many lawyers today: "[He] loved the practice of law, but he struggled with the business of law. Without a firm stable of paying clients, he grew vulnerable in a world where rainmaking is often valued over skill and judgment. For all his prestige, he had little real power behind his formidable stature. To some his final act was a rebuke to what his beloved profession had become—a statement made in the very office he had been told to vacate."

Levy's death was only the beginning of a terrible period for the legal profession. Not surprisingly, it coincided with the deepening Great Recession. A month after Levy's tragic end, two more attorney suicides from two different large firms made the news—an associate who had been laid off and a partner who had lost a major trial. Then in January 2010, a forty-five-year-old partner in Baker & Hostetler's Houston office apparently shot himself on a Galveston beach.

Additional tragedies followed. On July 15, 2010, a Chicago subway train struck and killed Stewart Dolin. He was a partner working in the

Chicago office of Pittsburgh-based Reed Smith, a global firm of fifteen hundred attorneys. A week later, the Cook County medical examiner confirmed that the fifty-seven-year-old father of two had intentionally placed himself in harm's way. Since 1989, Dolin had worked at a medium-sized law firm, Sachnoff & Weaver. It had grown to 140 attorneys by 2007, when it merged with Reed Smith. Dolin had become head of the combined firm's US corporate and securities group, but shortly before his suicide, Reed Smith promoted another lawyer to co-head the group. Connecting any of those recent events in Dolin's life to his untimely death is now impossible.

Everyone has encountered unhappy attorneys, and reports of a lawyer taking his or her own life have been rare. But that made the wave that began in early 2009—as the economy hit bottom and big-firm layoffs at all levels peaked—especially alarming. Maybe government lawyers, attorneys in small or midsized firms, or those in other positions have been committing suicide, too, but receiving less media attention. For example, when a sixty-four-year-old Connecticut sole real estate practitioner hanged himself in November 2009, press coverage was minimal.

Most of the attorney suicides that the national media covered in 2009 and 2010 included accomplished big-law partners in their forties and fifties. No single set of shoulders bears the blame, and only the leaders of the respective firms know whether or to what extent their firms' evolving culture might have contributed specifically to these final acts. But firms adhering religiously to metrics such as client billings, billable hours, and associate partner leverage as fundamental criteria for lawyer evaluation have become less collegial and more unforgiving. Even in good times, having to justify one's economic existence anew during every review cycle can be unsettling or worse. For some, the feared loss of income or status can be powerfully unpleasant.

Does the fact that a few lawyers committed suicide mean that they should not have gone to law school? No one should jump to that conclusion, either. But their lives and untimely deaths are important reminders that human beings sometime lose sight of their own fragility. The unique challenges of a legal career—especially in recently transformed big law firms—haven't helped, especially as they have played out during times of general economic distress. If those who met a terrible end at their own hand had started their legal careers with better knowledge about themselves and the path ahead, or if the devolution of most big firms hadn't made that world increasingly harsh, perhaps some of the stories would have ended differently.

ONE OF THE MOST TRAGIC big-law stories of 2011 involved a young associate at Skadden, Arps, Slate, Meagher & Flom. Lisa Johnstone graduated from Northwestern Law School in 2004 and joined Sidley Austin in New York. She accepted Skadden's offer in 2007. As the economy stalled, she took advantage of the chance to defer her start date for a year, during which she drew half salary of $80,000.

Johnstone worked in Skadden's corporate transactions department in Los Angeles. After she failed to arrive at her office on a summer Monday morning in 2011, her body was found in her condominium. She had last been seen on the prior Saturday afternoon, when she contacted a friend about dropping off her dog because she planned to be at her desk by 4:00 A.M. Monday. She never made it.

The responding officer at the scene interviewed Johnstone's mother, who said that her daughter "worked herself very thin" and "worked over 80 hours a week." Johnstone's brother told the investigator that his sister "sounded more frazzled than usual" and "was getting off work extremely late" when he had spoken with her a few weeks earlier. A full toxicology report found no indication of drugs or alcohol in her system.

Skadden's legendary reputation for its attorneys' long hours and hard work caused many in the legal blogosphere to blame the firm for working her to death. No one can say whether that's true, but the culture of most big law firms has become brutal. Whatever the cause of Lisa Johnstone's untimely end at age thirty-two, her story provides a poignant reminder of the slender threads that tether every person to this earth—including young people who sometimes misperceive themselves as indestructible. It also emphasizes the importance of making the best possible choices whenever they arise.

However unpleasant Skadden's culture may be for some, plenty of firms are worse. Skadden ranked 69th out of 126 firms in the *Am Law* 2011 Midlevel Associates Survey and 7th on *Am Law*'s A-List. (It dropped to 15th on the 2012 A-List—still a commendable performance—

but its associate satisfaction rank fell to 89th out of 129 firms.) According to published reports, Skadden has another favorable metric: unlike other firms that have grown their internal equity partner income gaps, the top-to-bottom spread at the firm was only five to one in 2012.

NO ONE SHOULD RELY ON others to resolve the problems that have accompanied the lawyer bubble and the corporatization of the legal profession. In the final analysis, each individual must make a series of personal decisions, starting with the wisdom of pursuing a legal career. Analyzing the forces that have brought the profession to its current crisis may provide useful background information, but the most important lesson is clear: even as fortuity plays a key role in outcomes, individuals still have the power to make decisions that shape their lives.

Anyone who thinks his or her life as a lawyer will resemble media images of attorneys is naive. Anyone who uses law school to buy three years of time is writing an expensive check to avoid a decision about the future. Anyone who abandons independent judgment in deferring to *U.S. News & World Report* rankings risks error of monumental proportions. Anyone who blindly follows the money into a big law firm because it promises wealth and prestige should enter carefully and proceed cautiously. All of these decisions are important, and no one else can make them.

EPILOGUE

If we measure the wrong thing,
we will be tempted to do the wrong thing.
—Nobel laureate in economics Joseph E. Stiglitz,
The Price of Inequality: How Today's Divided Society Endangers Our Future

HAVE THINGS DEGENERATED SIGNIFICANTLY from what has always been true about the grueling demands of a legal career? For any lawyer, the road to success is tougher than it was thirty years ago, and no relief is in sight. The negative impact is probably greatest on those at the margin—attorneys who didn't choose the right career but feel trapped in it. Their decisions would have been different if they'd known more about the futures awaiting them. Lawyers who never should have gone to law school in the first place have been around for a long time. But there's nothing inevitable about such a fate.

After graduation in 1919, Archibald MacLeish practiced for four years and then traveled to Europe to pursue his true passion: poetry. Failing to make a career of his literary dreams, MacLeish thereafter continued to write poems while settling for a distinguished life of public service. He didn't return to the law until 1958, when he secured poet Ezra Pound's release from an insane asylum.

When MacLeish left private practice in 1923, he complained, "The law is crowded—interesting—full of despair. It offers its own rewards, but none other. As a game there is nothing to match it. Even living is a poor second. But as a philosophy, as a training for such eternity as the next hour offers, it is nowhere—a mockery of human ambitions." The essential point of his remarks could have come from last week's comments to an *Above the Law* post.

Another timelessly unhappy group consists of lawyers who wind up in large firms but should have gone elsewhere to practice law. Charles Halpern joined Arnold & Porter in 1965 but left a few years later. His personal crisis of conscience came when a ride in Paul Porter's Cadillac after Martin Luther King Jr.'s assassination caused him to wonder about "some of the incongruities of the life" he was leading. The new and deprecating phrase "limousine liberal" hit him too close to home. Shortly thereafter—and this was in the late 1960s—Halpern worried about what a lifetime of work in a firm like his would mean.

"I looked around at the senior partners and I did not see anyone I wanted to be like," he later wrote. "They lived with the insecurity of having to continually prove themselves in this highly competitive environment, both by turning out a great deal of highly polished work and by attracting corporate clients."

In 1969, Halpern co-founded the Center for Law and Social Policy. His pioneering work in the public interest law movement continued as he started the Mental Health Project (now the Bazelon Center for Mental Health Law) in 1971 and the Council for Public Interest Law (now the Alliance for Justice) in 1976.

So in some respects, the contemporary complaints aren't new. They come from people who erred in their initial career choices and later regretted their decisions. MacLeish and Halpern personify what many of today's big-law-firm partners would label recruiting mistakes.

MacLeish exemplifies an error that wasn't the fault of his firm or his profession. His passion was poetry, not the law. He never should have gone to law school. By his own admission, he'd chosen law as a default solution when he wasn't really sure what he wanted to do after college. An earlier and more complete consideration of the profession might have kept him from committing the mistake that thousands of undergraduates still make every year.

Halpern's miscalculation was different: he chose the right profession but initially the wrong place in it. Although Arnold & Porter was small by today's standards—the Washington, D.C., firm had thirty lawyers when he joined in 1965—its prestige made it the next logical step on his path after Yale Law School and a federal judicial clerkship. Today, others follow Halpern's path into much larger firms every year. With better information about the experiences that await them, many might make different career choices and become more satisfied attorneys.

As an aside, the year 2010 marked the eighth consecutive year that Arnold & Porter was on *Fortune* magazine's list of the "100 Best Companies to Work For," so maybe Halpern would have different observations about his old firm today. It may suffer from many of the problems that afflict big-law-firm cultures generally, but its presence on *Fortune*'s list probably wasn't an accident.

Even for Arnold & Porter, the trend line is interesting. Relying on any metric is fraught with peril, and the firm still garners many awards related to diversity, pro bono work, and family-friendliness. But in 2008, it was nineteenth in *Fortune*'s "Best Companies to Work For" rankings; in 2009, it was twenty-first; in 2010, it was sixty-fifth. In 2011, it dropped off the list. Meanwhile, the firm's average partner profits went up, from $910,000 per partner in 2008 to $1.4 million in 2011.

Perhaps a young lawyer in any legal setting today could do worse than apply Halpern's test: try to find senior attorneys who lead lives to which they can aspire. If there aren't any, it may be time to move on— after repaying student loans, that is.

IT WOULD BE A MISTAKE to regard all of the current problems associated with the legal profession in general and large law firms in particular as entirely new. After all, in 1829 Joseph Story, an associate justice of the Supreme Court and the first Dane Professor at Harvard, observed, "The law is a jealous mistress." One can only imagine what his class on work-life balance would have been like if he'd taught one. Story loved the law and belonged in that career. So did one of my Kirkland & Ellis on-campus interviewers at Harvard, Fred H. Bartlit Jr., although he eventually left the firm he persuaded me to join.

Bartlit was in charge of Kirkland's litigation group when he interviewed me in 1977. Not long after I arrived at the firm, he called me into his office. A new client from California had called and needed a lawyer to handle a small case in Chicago.

"I'm going to call this guy back with you on the phone and tell him you're the lawyer they want," he said. That was fine with me.

Bartlit made the call and the client followed his advice, although I think it helped that they couldn't see how young I was. I went to work on the client's problem and got a good result. A few months later, when the client contacted me directly with a request to handle all of its cases in Chicago and Washington, D.C., I sent Bartlit a short memo letting him know.

In his distinctive blue felt-tip pen (he always taught his protégés to use blue for good news in jury presentations, red for bad news), Bartlit wrote back, "Great—this is the way it's supposed to work." From the outset, he designated me as the billing attorney for the client.

Fred Bartlit was one of several important mentors I had at Kirkland & Ellis. He couldn't charge clients for the time he spent training me and other young attorneys, but he didn't care. He took pride in building the firm rather than billing clients. The result was a cadre of extraordinarily successful trial lawyers who still carry the baton of excellence that he passed along to us. He led by example in living the professional life that had propelled most of us to law school in the first place—counseling clients, trying cases, making a difference. In the process, Bartlit created value for his firm and its clients. But the metrics in common use today can't begin to capture the kind of value that a partner like Fred Bartlit provides to a law firm.

Bartlit was still in charge of Kirkland's litigation department when he left the firm in 1993 to form his own highly successful litigation boutique. He developed the view that the billable hour model was stupid. To no one's surprise, his new firm largely jettisoned that system in favor of alternative fee arrangements that, as the Bartlit Beck firm website explained, "reward success and efficiency." In 2009, the *American Lawyer* named his firm "Litigation Boutique of the Year." As this book goes to print, he is still trying cases well into his seventies; among the most recent distinctions on a long list of career accolades, he served as George W. Bush's counsel in *Bush v. Gore* and as chief counsel to the presidential commission investigating the Deepwater Horizon Gulf Coast oil disaster in 2010.

In 2011, the editors of the *ABA Journal* asked Bartlit to identify a book that he thought every lawyer should read. He suggested Martin E. P. Seligman's *Flourish: A Visionary New Understanding of Happiness and Well-Being* because, he said, Seligman "explains how happiness comes from achievements—not from the money that comes from achievements, but the pure joy of succeeding at very hard missions. And he explains that today's parents are teaching 'learned helplessness' to their kids, which will preclude most of them from succeeding.

He also describes how people with failures in their lives end up as the biggest successes, because they are hardened by surviving failure."

That's consistent with a theme he expressed often in the practical application of his work: "Show me a lawyer who's never lost a case and I'll show you a lawyer who's never tried a case."

Today, attorneys as prominent as Bartlit don't typically conduct on-campus interviews. His law school recruiting efforts say something about him and the firm that he and others were trying to build. Years after Bartlit left Kirkland & Ellis, he remained proud of his old firm and, I think, retained it as part of his identity. That also says something about the community that Kirkland and most big firms once were. One more thing about Bartlit is certain: he chose the right profession.

So did I.

IT'S A DIFFERENT PROFESSION TODAY, but some perceptions of its nobility endure. Before Nitin Nohria became dean of the Harvard Business School in 2010, he had looked hopefully to the law as an alternative model for a business world in shambles. Along with many colleagues, he regretted the loss of integrity that business suffered after the pursuit of self-interested short-term goals led to the near-collapse of the financial system in 2008.

"I believe that management education has been overly focused on the principles of management," he said after Harvard's announcement that he would become the business school's next dean. James Ellis, dean of the University of Southern California's Marshall School of Business, echoed similar concerns: "We taught our students how to look for cracks in the economy and we taught them how to exploit [those cracks]."

Nohria identified the law as an example of a profession that business might emulate. His goal was to develop a more ethical core transcending attitudes that had come to dominate MBA programs. He even pushed for a lawyer-type MBA oath. Since then, students at some top schools, including Harvard, Columbia, and the Wharton School of the University of Pennsylvania, have taken one.

It was a nice gesture. But Nohria, his fellow business school deans, and their erstwhile students seem not to have noticed that short-termism and misguided business-school-type metrics have infected the legal profession, too.

THE GREAT TRANSFORMATION of the legal profession isn't over. So far, it has produced a dangerous lawyer bubble—from law schools to the top of the profession at America's big corporate law firms. Rather than providing what economists call equilibrium solutions, this bubble will continue to create instability.

The resulting turmoil will produce opportunities. In charting their own destinies, future generations of lawyers could use the fragility of the currently prevailing model to reshape the legal profession for the better, starting with individual decisions that could enhance their own psychological well-being. Knowledge is power; forewarned is forearmed.

In the end, it comes down to personal choices. Life isn't one big decision; it's the accumulation of small ones. The baby boomer generation now in charge of almost everything has done some things right, but it has made a mess of the legal profession. Time and again, the focus on shortsighted metrics has sacrificed long-term vision. Nothing made that approach inevitable; choices made it happen. Better choices can fix it.

AFTERWORD

T HE MORE THINGS CHANGE . . .
Three years after initial publication of *The Lawyer Bubble*, unfortunate trends persist. From law schools to the big firms at the pinnacle of the profession, short-termism still drives most leaders to the wrong destinations. Despite progress in some areas, challenges have become even more daunting. As the cost of attending law school has risen faster than inflation, average student loan debt for today's graduates has grown to $127,000 for private law schools and $88,000 for public ones. Since 2006 alone, law student debt has surged at inflation-adjusted rates of 25 percent (private schools) and 34 percent (public schools), respectively.

Perversely, as law school tuition has increased at rates exceeding those of college and medical school, the supply of new lawyers continues to outpace demand. Law schools are still producing almost twice as many new attorneys as the market can absorb. That's because too many deans and administrators—especially at schools where a majority of new graduates are unable to find decent jobs requiring a JD—exploit the system's failure to hold them accountable for those poor employment outcomes. Once students use federal loans to pay tuition, the school has no incentive to help them find a job. Far too many students mortgage their futures for an elusive dream.

Likewise, leaders at big law firms remain largely unresponsive to client concerns and worker morale. Although equity partners at big firms make more money than most of them ever dreamed of earning when they were in law school, income inequality *within* partnerships is increasing. As a consequence, a relatively small, insular, and self-interested group—a "partnership-within-the-partnership"—presides at the top of most firms. And the insidious billable hour system endures because, however heinous clients and associates find it, the regime is lucrative for law firm equity partners. Other short-term metrics encourage senior lawyers to maximize current profits by limiting advancement opportunities for the next generation. Meanwhile, most leaders engage in the ongoing frenzy to attract partners from other firms—lateral hires who promise portable books of client business to the highest bidder but often can't deliver them. Taken together, law firms' compensation, profit, and growth strategies create work environments that continue to foster pervasive attorney dissatisfaction.

Aggressive lateral partner and inorganic growth strategies are also making big firms' stability increasingly dependent upon current partner profits. As I predicted three years ago, the spectacular collapse of Dewey & LeBoeuf in 2012 was not the last big firm failure. Other law firm leaders ignored the lessons that Dewey should have taught them. As a result, their venerable and seemingly healthy institutions followed that firm's path to extinction. Even the subsequent criminal indictment and trial of Dewey & LeBoeuf's former chairman had no discernible impact on the willingness of other firms' managers to follow his misguided strategy of aggressive inorganic growth.

When it comes to promoting broader societal goals—such as diversity within the profession and legal representation of the needy—most big firms still earn a failing grade. Because diversity lacks an easy metric by which to measure its contribution to short-term profits, it generates lip service but little substantive progress. To their credit, many firms have recognized the importance of pro bono efforts to help those who cannot afford a lawyer. But for society generally, the profession is not providing middle- and lower-income Americans with access to essential legal services.

Anyone waiting for market forces to correct this perilous tilt will wait a long, long time. In some instances, government rules prevent the market from getting a chance to operate at all. For example, federally backed student loans fund law school tuition without holding schools accountable for their graduates' poor employment outcomes. In other cases, the behavior of those in power is contrary to rational economic decision making. The best illustration is big-firm leaders who continue to pursue aggressive inorganic growth and lateral partner hiring, even in the face of empirical evidence that the strategy is often a financial loser. In still other instances, society is unwilling to fund its most basic constitutional promises, particularly the provision of legal services to those who cannot afford them.

PART I OF *The Lawyer Bubble* discussed student attitudes and law school behavior. To their credit, undergraduates seem to be doing their part to reduce the oversupply of new attorneys. Since 2012, increased transparency about recent graduates' inability to secure employment that actually requires a law degree has produced a significant drop in law school applicants, especially at marginal schools where the employment outcomes are horrific.

Back in 2004, schools saw a record number of applicants—100,000. As business schools gained in popularity, the number of law school applicants declined steadily—to 83,000 by the fall of 2008. But when the Great Recession hit, some undergraduates decided that law school was a good place to wait for the economy to improve. By 2010, the number of law school applicants had increased to 88,000.

In 2010, first-year law school enrollment peaked at 52,500. But that was also the year that the ABA finally responded to public pressure and required schools to report meaningful employment data for their most recent graduates. Rather than counting any short-term or part-time job as if it were a well-paid, full-time position at a big law firm, transparency began to reveal the ugly truth: nine months after graduation, only about half of all law graduates had obtained full-time, long-term employment requiring bar passage. By the fall of 2014, the total number of *applicants* for the entering class had plummeted to a modern-day low of 55,700.

Some deans and law professors hailed that drop as proof that the market was correcting itself. Professor Theodore Seto of Loyola University School of Law in Los Angeles even predicted a *shortage* of new law graduates by 2015: "Beginning in fall 2015 and intensifying into 2016 employers are likely to experience an undersupply of law grads, provided that the economic recovery continues." But contrary to Seto's prediction, the job market for new lawyers has languished. In fact, ten months after graduation, only 231 of 396 of 2014 graduates from Professor Seto's law school had obtained full-time, long-term, JD-required jobs (excluding nine who got law school–funded positions).

A functioning market would have self-corrected. As demand for new lawyers plummeted, law schools would have reduced quickly the supply of new graduates, starting with dramatic declines in student admissions. Schools with the least success in placing their graduates would have felt the impact most profoundly. At the weakest schools, tuition would have gone down, not up—and some of them would have closed.

None of that happened because the legal education market is dysfunctional. Some law schools have exploited the resulting moral hazard. Deans, administrators, and faculty members have failed to heed the obvious message that the declining number of applicants conveyed. Instead of shrinking the size of entering classes, most schools adopted an easy fix to preserve revenues: increase acceptance rates to keep classrooms filled and tuition revenues flowing from federal student loans. In 2004, the overall law school acceptance rate was just over 50 percent. For the class entering in the fall of 2014, that rate had soared to almost 80 percent. Some schools have eliminated LSAT exam requirements, waived application fees, and adopted the equivalent of open enrollment. Today, anyone who wants to attend law school can do so somewhere.

That doesn't mean everyone entering law school will graduate or pass the bar, much less get a JD-required job. Professor Aaron Taylor of St. Louis University School of Law studied trends in applicants and admissions since 2010. He found that low-end law schools in particular were successfully recruiting less-qualified students, especially minority candidates. Schools with the lowest median LSAT scores for incoming students now rely disproportionately on African American and Hispanic students to fill their classrooms.

The cynical secret is that these schools are enrolling far too many students who won't graduate, will fail to pass the bar, or are unlikely to get a JD-required job that pays enough to retire their staggering law school debts. For example, the schools in the lowest quintile (based on median LSAT scores) accounted for more than half of all 2013–2014 attrition from law schools. Those schools also have the worst graduate bar-passage rates (74 percent average for 2013) and accounted for one-third of all 2013 graduates who were unemployed and seeking work. Rather than a harbinger of future diversity gains in the profession, the behavior of bottom-feeder law schools bolsters preexisting racial stratification. The weakest schools are using the rhetoric of diversity (along with federal student loans) simply to survive, not because their deans experienced some epiphany prompting them to lead the profession toward a noble societal objective.

IN 2014, THE US Department of Labor's Bureau of Labor Statistics (BLS) adopted a new methodology for projecting lawyer demand. The change emboldened Professor Seto and others who denied the existence of a law school crisis. Unfortunately, those projections are almost certainly wrong.

During the Great Recession, the BLS's earlier methodology resulted in downward revisions of its ten-year lawyer employment projections. In 2008, it anticipated an increase in the total net number of legal jobs by 98,500 through 2018. In 2012, it reduced that projection to 74,800 through 2022. Taking into account retirements, deaths, and other attrition, the BLS separately estimated that the profession could absorb about 20,000 new graduates annually for the subsequent decade. Meanwhile, schools have been producing new law graduates at about twice that rate—40,000 a year.

Remarkably, the new BLS methodology more than doubles the anticipated number of new legal jobs over the next ten years. Rather than annual absorption of about twenty thousand new lawyers from 2012 through 2022, the BLS now projects room for more than forty-one thousand a year. Overnight, demand caught up with what had been a chronic and widely observable oversupply of attorneys. To understand the absurdity of the BLS's new conclusion, simply apply the new methodology retroactively to previous years. The result: the obvious glut of new lawyers that became painfully obvious during the Great Recession never existed at all!

The technical and analytical flaws in the BLS's new methodology are too numerous to detail here. But a few problems are apparent. For example, since 2011, ABA-required law school disclosures have revealed a persistent full-time, long-term, JD-required employment rate of approximately 55 percent for new graduates. That's close to the projections that the BLS's old methodology produced for a long time. The new approach amounts to saying that, somehow, all of those unemployed graduates must have been finding law jobs after all. As the old joke goes, endless digging in a roomful of manure was worth the effort; there was indeed a pony to be found—with the help of a little regression analysis.

Likewise, actual employment numbers for the legal services sector of the economy are a stark contrast to the BLS's optimistic trend line. At the end of December 2014, employment in all legal services (including nonlawyers) was 1.120 million—about the same as a year earlier and down more than 60,000 jobs from its May 2007 peak. During that seven-year period, law schools produced more than 300,000 graduates. The BLS's new forecast would suggest a stunning rate of lawyer attrition (to make room for those 300,000 new attorneys), raise serious questions about the state of the profession generally, and should cause many prelaw students to wonder whether law school was the right choice.

Sometimes the most obvious answer is also the correct one. The actual employment rates for new law school graduates tell a straightforward story. Almost a year after graduation, only about half of recent graduating classes are finding full-time, long-term jobs requiring a JD. Total employment in the legal services sector remains far below 2007 peak levels. Recent data are not encouraging: between December 2013 and December 2014, actual legal services–sector employment *decreased*.

Some law school deans and professors are particularly defensive about all of this.

Professor Seto, whose 2014 prediction of a lawyer shortage by 2015 was wildly off the mark, used the new Bureau of Labor of Statistics projections to declare that they could portend an imminent lawyer shortage—this time by 2016. He's wrong about that one, too.

Another law professor in denial, René Reich-Graefe, teaches at Western New England School of Law where almost two-thirds of his school's 2014 graduates failed to find full-time, long-term, JD-required employment within ten months of graduating. Nevertheless, he urged everyone involved with legal education to "Keep Calm and Carry On"— the title of his upbeat article. He wrote that "recent law school graduates and current and future law students are standing at the threshold of the most robust legal market that ever existed in this country—a legal market which will grow, exist for, and coincide with their entire professional career [*sic*]."

Professor Reich-Graefe didn't offer to make loan repayments on behalf of graduates who could not find jobs requiring a JD. For his school alone that would have been a big undertaking because 92 percent of Western New England School of Law's 2014 graduates had student debt averaging more than $130,000.

There are other examples of law-school-crisis denial—from admissions officers to prominent deans. But the most egregious offenders run schools that have especially abysmal records of placing their recent law graduates in meaningful JD-required jobs.

For example, in March 2015, the president and dean of Western Michigan University–Cooley Law School, Don LeDuc, wrote, "The time of the law school critics has passed. Now is the time for those whose dream is to become a lawyer to disregard the blog-fog and look at the clear employment picture that the Bureau of Labor Statistics has painted. That dream's future is now." The dream remained elusive for most 2014 graduates of President LeDuc's school; only 30 percent of them obtained full-time, long-term jobs requiring a JD. Average student debt for his school's September 2013 graduates with law school loans exceeded $128,000. Perhaps President LeDuc meant that nightmares qualify as dreams.

ALL OF THESE academic efforts to wish away serious problems embody the self-interested triumph of hope over reality. They are also disingenuous because they ignore a basic fact about the law school market: it is not a single market at all. Not every law school provides the same potential job opportunities. And pervasively sloppy analyses disregard this reality. Stated differently, the actual employment market for new law school graduates is a collection of several distinct submarkets. Those submarkets produce dramatically different outcomes for particular law schools and their graduates.

The same analytical flaw—ignoring the different law school markets—colors a recent study purporting to measure the incremental value of a JD degree. The authors, Professors Michael Simkovic of Seton Hall University School of Law and Frank McIntyre of Rutgers Business School, originally titled their article "The Million Dollar Degree," based on their argument that the average lifetime value of a JD degree is a million dollars. Understandably, law school deans and admissions officers embraced that headline. But even the authors of the study acknowledge, "We also cannot determine the earnings premium associated with attending a specific law school."

In journalism, that's called burying the lead. Each year, 10 to 15 percent of law graduates land jobs in big law firm jobs that pay the

Distribution of Reported Full-Time Salaries

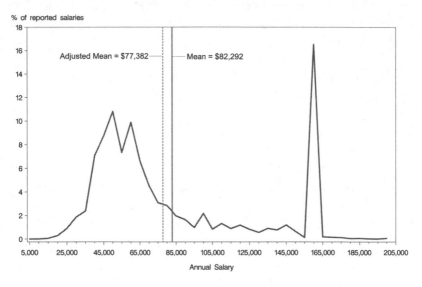

Note: Graph is based on 22,095 salaries reported for full-time jobs lasting a year or more. A few salaries above $205,000 are excluded from the graph for clarity, but not from the percentage calculations. The left-hand peaks of the graph reflect salaries of $40,000 to $65,000, which collectively accounted for about half of reported salaries. The right-hand peak shows that salaries of $160,000 accounted for about 17% of reported salaries. However, more complete salary coverage for jobs at large law firms heightens this peak and diminishes the left-hand peaks—and shows that the unadjusted mean overstates the average starting salary by just over 6%. Nonetheless, as both the arithmetic mean and the adjusted mean show, relatively few salaries are close to either mean. For purposes of this graph, all reported salaries were rounded to the nearest $5,000.

© NALP 2015. www.nalp. org. Graph reproduced with permission.

most—six-figure starting salaries of up to $160,000 a year. But in 2013, only 24 of 201 ABA-accredited schools placed 20 percent or more of their graduates in one of those positions. In graphical terms, the resulting bimodal distribution of new attorney starting salaries looks like the chart above.

This distribution highlights a problem with concluding too much from the "million-dollar degree" study. In particular, any average has more probative value if the distribution of values follows a bell-shaped curve—that is, a few values at the low end, most data points near the middle, and a few at the high end. But lawyer incomes do not fit such a curve; rather, the distribution of incomes among lawyers is skewed: a vast majority at the low end, a few scattered throughout the middle, and a very few at the extremely high end. For such a distribution, the median (or midpoint) better conveys a sense of actual outcomes. To illustrate the point, consider how the average wealth of middle-class workers in a room changes if Bill Gates is added: the average becomes meaningless in describing the other members of the group. More useful for any analysis would be the median—that is, the wealth of the person in the middle of a distribution that identified Bill Gates as an extreme high-end outlier.

Even accepting all of the assumptions of the "million-dollar degree" study, the authors concede that their average is not a *net* number; it's a gross value that does not take into account income taxes or law school tuition. Using their data and methodology, the incremental net present value of a JD at the *median* of their limited sample is $330,000 over an entire forty-year career. At the low end of the income distribution for attorneys the value is negative. But that headline would not help marginal schools promote the value of their JD degrees.

The actual distribution of starting salaries requires a detailed consideration of employment outcomes for graduates of the 177 nonelite schools, which fall into two groups. For 2013 graduates, one group would have included 88 regionally dominant law schools where more than 55 percent of graduates (which was the overall 2013 average for all law schools, excluding law school–funded positions) found full-time, long-term, JD-required employment. That's not great, but it's a lot better than the group of 89 schools that did worse. Among those institutions, 34 schools placed less than 40 percent of 2013 graduates in such positions, and 13 placed less than one-third.

The story gets worse. Even as every submarket for new lawyers plummeted during the Great Recession and its aftermath, most schools actually *raised* tuition. In addition to increasing their acceptance rates, some schools even expanded enrollments to maximize student loan revenues. A poster child for this phenomenon is Infilaw, a private-equity-owned consortium of three for-profit law schools: Arizona Summit (formerly known as the Phoenix School of Law), Charlotte, and Florida Coastal. Between 2011 and 2014, the Infilaw schools increased the size of their combined graduating classes from 679 to 1,223. But only 36 percent of their 2014 graduates found full-time, long-term, JD-required jobs. Meanwhile, Infilaw burdened their students with average debt exceeding $140,000.

WHY DOES SUCH disequilibrium persist? Because graduates' inability to find JD-required employment has no impact on continued federal funding of student loans that keep marginal schools alive. The current system of financing legal education insulates schools from the financial risk that their students will fail to obtain the jobs for which they are supposedly training them. The weakest schools are the biggest beneficiaries of this multidimensional protective cover, which includes federal guarantees at the front end and nondischargeability of educational debt in bankruptcy at the back end. Students and federal taxpayers are the biggest victims.

Simply put, the market is not self-correcting because market forces never get a chance to operate. Many of the schools with the worst employment outcomes leave their graduates with the highest levels of law school student debt. Consider this list of the student debt leaders along with the full-time, long-term, JD-required employment rates for their 2014 graduates:

School	Average debt (2014 grads)	FT-LT-JD (2014 grads)
Arizona Summit	$187,792	40%
Thomas Jefferson	$172,445	30%
New York Law School	$166,622	43%
Northwestern University	$163,065	78%
Florida Coastal	$162,785	35%
American University	$159,316	45%
Vermont Law School	$156,713	48%
Touro College	$154,855	57%
University of San Francisco	$154,321	33%
Columbia University	$154,076	87%
California Western	$151,797	48%
Whittier College	$151,602	27%

Only two elite schools that placed a significant number of graduates in high-paying big law firm jobs appear among the leaders in average student debt for 2014—Northwestern and Columbia. That makes some sense. More than half of those graduates begin their careers in big law firm jobs with starting salaries as high as $160,000 a year. They will be able to repay their law school loans. Of the ten other schools on the list of the top dozen in average student debt, three placed *one-third (or fewer)* of their students in full-time, long-term, JD-required positions. That schools with placement rates ranging from 27 percent to 87 percent appear on the same list of institutions creating the most debt for their students makes no sense at all.

Examples of schools at the low end of employment outcomes and near the high end of student law school debt include:

School	Average debt (2014 grads)	FT-LT-JD (2014 grads)	% with debt (2014 grads)
Thomas Jefferson	$172,445	30%	91%
Florida Coastal	$162,785	35%	93%
Whittier	$151,602	27%	91%
Golden Gate	$146,288	25%	88%

Compare those results to schools that have *lower* average student debt, dramatically *higher* employment outcomes, and *fewer* students with debt, including:

School	Average debt (2014 grads)	FT-LT-JD (2014 grads)	% with debt (2014 grads)
University of Virginia	$132,182	85%	78%
University of Pennsylvania	$130,002	91%	74%
Stanford	$128,137	85%	78%
Duke	$125,406	88%	80%

My recent article for the *American Bankruptcy Institute Law Review* outlines a proposal to remove some of the current obstacles to a functioning law school market. The plan starts with a fixed maximum loan amount for tuition and living expenses (say, $55,000 a year) and then creates a sliding scale of law school accountability. Students borrowing money to attend schools where a majority of recent graduates failed to find full-time, long-term, JD-required employment could still obtain loans, but the federal guarantee would not apply to the entire $55,000 annual maximum. The federally guaranteed portion would slide downward in accordance with the school's employment outcomes.

For example, students attending a school that placed only 45 percent of its most recent graduates in full-time, long-term, JD-required jobs might qualify for only half of the annual $55,000 maximum federal guarantee amount. That law school would be forced to reduce tuition and/or the student would have to look elsewhere to fund any gap between the cost of law school (tuition and living expenses) and the federally guaranteed amount. If a school opted to make up any shortfall by making direct loans to students, those loans would be dischargeable in bankruptcy without the showing of undue hardship currently required to wipe out any higher education debt.

Tying the benefits of federal student loan guarantees to graduates' JD-required employment outcomes would begin to create law school accountability. The resulting market forces should produce meaningful price differences based on a school's results for its students. That is not happening now. In California, class of 2014 law graduates from schools with dismal placement rates—Golden Gate University, Whittier, and California Western—incurred debt exceeding that of their more successful counterparts at Stanford and UC-Berkeley. In Boston, the 2014 graduates of Suffolk University (47 percent placement rate in full-time, long-term, JD-required employment) incurred debt almost identical to that of students at Yale and more than students at Boston College and Boston University—all of whom had far better job prospects than Suffolk graduates. In New York, 43 percent of the 2014 graduates of New York Law School found full-time, long-term, JD-required employment. Average student debt at graduation was $166,622—higher than Columbia and NYU, where placement rates were more than double that of New York Law School.

Without meaningful reform, recent history demonstrates that market solutions will remain elusive. Compared to the fall of 2008—just before the Great Recession began—the number of 2014 law school applicants dropped by almost thirty thousand, but first-year enrollment during that period declined by only about twelve thousand. During that period, not a single ABA-accredited law school closed and the ABA approved six new ones.

AS FOR THE ABA's role in all of this, the problem of regulatory capture persists. For example, beginning with the graduating class of 2014, the ABA moved backward in the effort to promote law school accountability. In particular, it extended the period for reporting the employment status of every school's most recent graduates. Rather than nine months after graduation—that is, as of February 15 in the year following a student's graduation—the new rule lengthens the period to ten months.

In July 2013, Professor Deborah Merritt of the Ohio State University–Moritz College of Law provided the ABA with persuasive objections to the proposed change. She argued:

- the evidence did not support the principal argument for the change—namely, that schools in states reporting bar examination results later than other states were at a disadvantage because their graduates have a more difficult time getting a job without the credential of bar passage;
- moving the cutoff date would impair the ability to make yearly comparisons at a time when the profession is undergoing dramatic transformation;
- prospective students would not have the most recent employment information as they decided where to send their tuition deposits in April; and
- the change would further diminish public trust in law schools and the ABA.

Her objections were sound but unavailing. The March 15 cutoff rule passed the ABA committee by a ten-to-nine vote.

The new ten-month rule didn't help most law schools anyway. Because the graduating class of 2014 was smaller (by 6.5 percent), schools collectively reported a slightly higher overall employment rate—58.7 percent (up from 55.9 percent for the nine-month data for the class of 2013). However, the absolute number of graduates employed in full-time, long-term JD-required positions (excluding law school–funded jobs) fell from 25,762 for the class of 2013 to 25,344 for the class of 2014—about 2 percent. At 58 of 203 ABA-accredited schools, the employment rate for 2014 graduates was still below 50 percent.

THE ABA'S RESPONSE to the student debt crisis has been equally weak. In May 2014, it appointed a special Task Force on the Financing of Legal Education. Its chairman, former ABA president Dennis W. Archer, was an unfortunate choice because he also chaired the National Advisory Board for Infilaw—the private-equity-owned consortium of three for-profit law schools that survive on federally backed loans, burden their students with stunning levels of student debt, and report some of the worst placement rates of any law schools in the country. Even with the new ten-month rule, none of the Infilaw schools could get their 2014 full-time, long-term, JD-required placement rates above 40 percent (Arizona Summit, 39.9 percent; Florida Coastal, 34.5 percent; Charlotte, 34.1 percent).

Archer wasn't the only problematic appointment to the Task Force, but he was the most prominent. And he was particularly unlikely to guide the group toward the tough, impartial message urging dramatic change that the profession sorely needs. That became clear on June 17, 2015, when the Task Force released its final report. It found that 25 percent of law schools receive at least 88 percent of revenues from tuition and that inflation-adjusted tuition had increased even as law graduates' job prospects remained bleak. But the Task Force decided that any attempt to wrestle with such obvious market dysfunction was beyond its charter because all of higher education confronted similar challenges. Instead of meaningful solutions, the Task Force offered these superficial proposals:

- law schools should offer students better debt counseling;
- the US Department of Education should develop "plain English" disclosure information about student loans;
- the ABA should collect and disseminate information about how law schools spend their money; and
- the ABA should encourage law schools to experiment on curriculum and programs.

In the end, Archer's Task Force is just another example of how insularity prevents the ABA from advocating and implementing necessary reform. It shows how regulatory capture remains a persistent and sometimes disabling condition for the organization that is supposed to guide the profession forward.

BOTTOM LINE: the crisis has not yet prompted viable long-term solutions. But the reform movement is making inroads. The larger debate about students' educational debt generally has produced legislative attempts to fashion relief. Bills aimed at even partial solutions—such as allowing students to refinance their school loans as they would a home mortgage—have provoked a public discussion, even if congressional paralysis ultimately squashed them.

Similarly, many schools have revisited the structure and curriculum of legal education itself. In the summer of 2013, President Obama entered the fray when he gave voice to what most practicing lawyers have known for a long time: the third year of law school is not worth its cost. But for reasons that *The Lawyer Bubble* describes, the third year will not go away any time soon. For starters, it contributes one-third of almost every law school's annual revenue stream.

The most meaningful positive impact on legal education is likely to come from two external forces. The first is the adoption of a mechanism that ties law school funding to outcomes. Until schools have some financial accountability for their graduates' poor employment results, many of them will exploit the current regime's inherent moral hazard. Lacking any economic incentive to consider likely job prospects for their recruits, some schools will continue focusing their efforts on filling classrooms to maximize revenue. At the weakest schools where graduates confront the most difficulty finding jobs, the trend toward open enrollment—law school for anyone who wants to attend—will persist. As that happens, no one should be surprised as bar passage rates for new graduates continue to decline.

The second external force is the next generation of prospective students themselves—a group with whom I've become especially familiar over the past decade. Some of them are adjusting their expectations to fit the reality of what being a lawyer will really mean. A better awareness of that reality may lead others away from law school altogether. But to be clear, *The Lawyer Bubble* was never intended as a brief against attending law school; to the contrary and beginning with my advanced undergraduate seminar at Northwestern University that inspired this book, my goal has been to inform, enlighten, and challenge. For too many undergraduates, law school remains, as I wrote, "the last bastion of the liberal arts major who couldn't decide what to do next."

That option is appealing until reality rears its head. What prospective attorneys expect as they fill out their law school applications often bears little resemblance to the actual practice of law. To bridge the gap between expectations and reality, *The Lawyer Bubble* remains a straightforward exposition of the world as it is rather than as undergraduate prelaw students with confirmation bias and understandable youthful optimism would like it to be. The vast majority of students taking my course have gone on to law school, but they have a better understanding of where it will lead. Their realities will more closely align with their expectations.

The book's driving impulse—transparency—has produced dramatic declines in the number of law school applicants. If that trend continues, eventually schools will run out of even unqualified and poorly informed prospective law students to exploit. The loss of student debt–revenue generators will imperil marginal institutions, and at long last, perhaps something resembling a functional market in legal education will emerge.

PART II OF *The Lawyer Bubble* described modern destructive trends at most big law firms. Those have accelerated, too. To be clear, it was never my thesis that all big law firms will disappear—that won't happen. Some of them are home to the best and brightest legal talent clients can buy. Those lawyers' unique services can command premium prices anywhere. But that does not mean the future is bright for *all* big firms.

A few firms have resisted the prevailing business model, but most have embraced it. The billable hour still accounts for the vast majority of big firm revenues even though clients decry its inefficiency and abuses. Hourly billing rates continue to rise. Even during the Great Recession, rates at the largest two hundred firms increased an average of 3 percent annually. Likewise, most law firm leaders have been increasing their firms' leverage ratios—the number of non-equity lawyers to the number of equity partner owners—because higher leverage means more profits for relatively fewer equity partner owners. To accomplish that objective, they have been reducing the number of equity partners and creating a growing subclass of second-class citizens—namely, non-equity partners. In 2004, 24 percent of all partners in the Am Law 200 were non-equity partners; by 2013 the percentage had increased to 40. Here is another way to describe that phenomenon: an entire generation of big law firm leaders is still pulling up the ladder on its own kids. That has long-term implications for morale, client transition, and institutional stability.

Likewise, growth for the sake of growth continues. Along with law firm mergers, most law firm leaders are fueling a frenzied market for lateral partner hires as the quickest way to achieve that growth. They seem indifferent to scholarly studies proving that the strategy is a financially losing proposition for most firms.

A few top partners acknowledge publicly that aggressive lateral partner hiring is fraught with peril. Ed Newberry, co-global managing partner of Squire Patton Boggs (the product of a 2014 merger to be discussed below) told *Forbes*, "Lateral acquisitions, which many firms are aggressively pursuing now . . . is a very dangerous strategy because laterals are extremely expensive and have a very low success rate—by some studies lower than 50 percent across firms."

Ironically, even leaders of big law firms admit that the ongoing rush to recruit partners with portable books of business often fails to pay off for the firms that do it. In a 2013 survey, managing partners said that only 60 percent of laterals were better than break-even economically. In 2014, the percentage dropped to 57. In 2015, it dropped again, with managing partners reporting that only 54 percent of their lateral hires exceeded their own undisclosed definition of "break even." If senior leaders are willing to admit that their decisions to hire expensive new partners have such high failure rates, imagine how much worse the truth must be. And that doesn't even begin to consider the detrimental non-financial impact that can result when lateral partners who barely know each other reshape a firm's culture.

Mergers are not always what they seem, either. Firms seeking to avoid Dewey & LeBoeuf's fate—sudden and spectacular implosion—have pursued "survival" or "liquidating" mergers. Such events occur when a troubled firm is in such desperate financial straits that it sacrifices its identity as partners disappear into a potential savior willing to extend a lifeline. The respected Patton Boggs firm was headed for oblivion until Squire Sanders came to the rescue in July 2014. The fate of the combined institution, Squire Patton, remains uncertain. But in the immediate aftermath of that merger, the Patton Boggs component suffered a number of high-profile departures, including its former chairman, a prominent white-collar criminal defense attorney, and eight former members of the firm's thirteen-person executive committee.

IN 2014, BINGHAM McCutchen looked for a survival merger, too, but failed to find one. The wounds taking the firm to that unfortunate point in its illustrious history were self-inflicted.

Jay Zimmerman became Boston-based Bingham, Dana & Gould's chairman in 1994. Over the next fifteen years, he orchestrated ten mergers or combinations with other firms, opened eleven new offices, and increased firm revenues tenfold—to $800 million. Zimmerman began his aggressive growth strategy in 1997 when the firm absorbed a New York City firm to gain a foothold there. In 1999 and 2001, it merged with two more New York firms. But the really big event came in 2002 when Bingham combined with the three-hundred-lawyer San Francisco–based McCutchen, Doyle, Brown & Enersen to form the eight-hundred-lawyer Bingham McCutchen. Under Zimmerman's direction, the combined entity then added more law firms, including one in Tokyo. In 2009, it absorbed two-hundred-lawyer McKee Nelson, pushing its total attorney headcount to over one thousand.

Characterizing those results as proof of a successful growth plan seemed self-evident. After all, as a 2011 Harvard Law School case study put it, the firm had evolved "from a 'middle-of-the-downtown-pack' Boston law firm in the early 1990s to a preeminent international law firm by 2010 . . . by following a strategy of sequential mergers, or 'combinations.'" Looking to the future, Zimmerman said, "For the first time since I've been in this job, we have all the pieces we need to do our job." As Zimmerman gave that interview, outward prosperity masked his firm's inner weakness.

After Bingham's merger with McCutchen, Doyle, Brown & En-
ersen, cultural differences loomed large over the combined organization,
but Zimmerman persevered in growing the firm. He boasted that his
mergers and lateral hires had produced a "management committee . . .
from all over. You don't have to have been at Bingham Dana forever to
lead at the firm." But he failed to focus on how too many highly paid
partners parachuting into the top of a firm can compromise firm culture,
concentrate power in the hands of a relative few, and create a problematic distribution of partner compensation—a partnership-within-a-partnership that presides at the top of a firm. When Bingham began to
unravel in 2013, the spread between its highest- and lowest-paid partners was twelve-to-one.

Nor did Zimmerman consider the morale problems that resulted
when Bingham acquired McKee Nelson in the largest law firm merger
of 2009. To retain important McKee Nelson partners, Bingham provided multiyear compensation guarantees of $4 to $5 million each—
putting some of them at the top of Bingham's pay scale. As the firm
stumbled in 2014, former partners said that "the size and scope of the
McKee Nelson guarantees led to internal fissures . . . that caused at least
some partners to leave the firm."

In early 2014, the firm revealed that 2013 revenues had dropped by
almost 13 percent and profits by almost 10 percent. Bingham began
losing partners. In a management shake-up, Zimmerman relinquished
day-to-day responsibilities to Steven Browne, whose search for a
merger candidate was nothing like his predecessor's earlier efforts.
Bingham needed a lifeline from a larger institution—and it needed
one quickly.

Several firms took a look and backed away. Eventually, discussions
with Philadelphia-based Morgan, Lewis & Bockius proceeded to a final
proposal. Browne publicly urged his fellow partners to approve the deal,
offering the not-so-subtle message through the media that Bingham's
bankruptcy remained an option if they didn't.

On November 10, 2014, Bingham partners approved the merger, but
a few days later Morgan Lewis decided on a different approach. Rather
than merge, the firm undertook the largest lateral-hiring effort in history,
making offers to 227 of Bingham's 307 remaining partners. Eventually,
Morgan Lewis agreed to take on another 525 Bingham lawyers, legal

professionals, and staffers. Thereafter, Bingham said it would liquidate voluntarily. Otherwise, the remnants of Bingham McCutchen—a 125-year-old Am Law 100 firm that two years earlier boasted average equity partner profits of $1.7 million—would find a final resting place in bankruptcy court.

Why did Bingham collapse? A partnership cobbled together through a series of lateral hires and mergers with ten different firms over the prior fifteen years could not weather a 10 percent drop in average profits for the firm's 130 equity partners—to a mere $1.475 million in 2013. That says something about what that partnership—and so many others like it—had become. Bingham's inglorious end became more proof that the prevailing big law firm business model is fragile. Yet the underlying behavior producing that disaster—including the pursuit of aggressive inorganic growth, overpaying lateral hires, and increasing the top-to-bottom income spread within the partnership—is pervasive. When money is the glue that holds partners together, it should come as no surprise that allegiances remain only as strong as current-year profits or the absence of better lateral movement opportunities for individual firm partners who increasingly have one eye on the exit at all times.

In the end, Harvard Law School's 2011 case study originally touting Bingham's success has become a postmortem on catastrophic failure that occurred only three years later.

BIG FIRM LEADERS' pervasive urge to increase the size of their institutions is somewhat perplexing. As far back as 2003, law firm management consultant Altman Weil reported that its thirty years of survey data proved the absence of scale economies in the practice of law. In fact, as firms get bigger, the report continued, maintaining the infrastructure to support continued growth becomes more expensive. Whether it is individual laterals, group laterals, or the ultimate lateral hiring event—a law firm merger—why does the dubious growth strategy persist? For the answer, look at the explanations of the people who orchestrate them: law firm leaders and their management consultants.

For example, *The Lawyer Bubble* cited the 2011 merger of Edwards, Angell, Palmer & Dodge with Wildman, Harrold, Allen & Dixon as an example of the uncertain financial consequences of a big law merger.

In late 2014, the newly combined firm, Edwards Wildman, entered that market again. Then-chairman Alan Levin candidly admitted he was a "bigger is better" guy: "Size matters, and to be successful today, you really have to be in that Am Law 50"—the nation's largest fifty law firms based on total gross revenues. Levin went on to explain that he had commissioned a study to identify potential merger partners before settling on Texas-based Locke Lord. For him, it was all about getting bigger, regardless of the flaws in that guiding principle.

But recent studies have echoed Altman Weil's earlier conclusion about the perils of unfocused expansion. In 2014, the Georgetown Law Center and Thomson Reuters Peer Monitor devoted their annual Report on the State of the Legal Profession to the topic of inorganic law firm growth. The report concludes that "growth for growth's sake is not a viable strategy in today's legal market." It debunks "the notion that clients will come if only a firm builds a large enough platform or that, despite obvious trends toward the disaggregation of legal services, clients will somehow be attracted to a 'one-stop shopping' solution." The report urges managing partners to follow a simple principle: "Strategy should drive growth and not the other way around." But it also notes that most big law firm leaders ignore that central tenet.

In its final passages, the report offers a damning indictment, asserting that much of the recent growth activity at big firms "masks a bigger problem—the continuing failure of most firms to focus on strategic issues that are more important for their long-term success than the number of lawyers or offices they may have." In other words, some firm managers are hiding behind the rhetoric of growth to distract their partners' attention away from the absence of a real strategy.

Will law firm leaders pay any attention to these and similar warnings from neutral, unbiased experts expressing genuine concern about the profession's trajectory? Based on their behavior to date, the answer seems to be no.

DOES SUCCESS REQUIRE a place on the Am Law 50 list? If size is the only measuring stick, then the tautology holds. Big = successful = big. But if something else counts, such as profitability or stability, then the answer is no. The varied financial performance of firms within the Am Law 50 disproves the "bigger is always better" hypothesis. The 2014 profit margins of those fifty firms ranged from a high of 66 percent (Quinn Emanuel) to a low of 15 percent (Squire Sanders, which merged with Patton Boggs in June 2014). Some of the biggest firms in 2014 were among the lowest in profit margin, including DLA Piper (3,702 lawyers; 27 percent profit margin), Dentons (2,285 lawyers; 26 percent profit margin), and K&L Gates (1,952 lawyers; 18 percent profit margin).

Conversely, Cahill, Gordon & Reindel ranked fourth in profit margin (59 percent), and it's not even a member of the Am Law 50. But that firm's equity partners were not complaining about its 2014 average profits per partner (PPP): $3.6 million—good enough for fifth place on the PPP list. Among the fifty largest firms in gross revenues, twenty had profit margins placing them in the *bottom* half of the Am Law 100. Becoming bigger assures neither becoming better nor becoming more profitable.

Many big law leaders simply want to preside over growing empires. To assist their efforts in justifying a questionable growth strategy, they hire law firm management consultants who have developed special language to reinforce a mindless "size matters" mentality. Kent Zimmermann, a law firm management consultant for the Zeughauser Group, said that Morgan, Lewis & Bockius's contemplated merger with Bingham McCutchen in 2014 "may be part of a growing crop of law firms that feel they need to be 'materially larger' in order to increase brand awareness, [which is] viewed by many of these firms as what it takes to get on the short list for big matters."

Zimmermann's underlying assumption that bigger would be better for Morgan Lewis does not withstand scrutiny. In the 2014 Am Law rankings, Morgan Lewis itself was twelfth in gross revenues and twenty-fourth in profit margin (44 percent). It didn't need to "increase brand awareness." That concept might help sell toothpaste; it does not describe the way sophisticated corporate clients actually select outside lawyers.

Similarly, when a Bingham-Morgan merger was still a possibility, Zimmermann said that he had "seen firms with new leadership in place look to undertake a transformative endeavor like this [Morgan Lewis-Bingham McCutchen] merger would be." If his overall observation about firms with new leadership is true, then those leaders should be asking themselves: transform to what? Acting on empty buzzwords risks a "transformative endeavor" to institutional instability, if not oblivion.

In contrast to the misguided "size matters" approach, major corporate clients are offering words of caution. In late 2013, IBM general counsel Robert Weber told the *Wall Street Journal*, "I'm pretty skeptical about the value these big mergers give to clients. . . . I don't know why it's better to use a bigger firm." Weber should know because before joining IBM, he spent thirty years at Jones Day—one of the largest law firms in the world.

Is anyone listening? IBM's longtime outside counsel, Cravath, Swaine & Moore, is. Based on size and gross revenues, Cravath does not qualify for the Am Law 50, but its clients don't care. The firm has been among the few to resist "eat-what-you-kill" partner compensation (discussed at length in *The Lawyer Bubble*) in favor of a lock-step system that emphasizes quality work, encourages collaboration, and promotes institutional stability. Cravath's average partner profits for 2013 and 2014 exceeded $3.3 million.

ONE FIRM PROFILED in *The Lawyer Bubble* has now set the standard for the pursuit of relentless growth. In January 2015, Dentons combined with Asia's largest firm, Dacheng Law Offices, to create the biggest law firm in the world—6,600 lawyers. Each firm was itself the product of rapid inorganic growth. Dacheng was founded in 1992 and grew to more than four thousand lawyers worldwide, mostly though the cobbling together of many smaller firms in Asia, especially China. Dentons resulted from transactions that combined four large law firms—Sonnenschein, Nath & Rosenthal; Denton Wilde Sapte (UK); Salans (France); and Fraser Milner Casgrain (Canada)—into an organizational form known as a Swiss verein, where each firm maintains its own profit pool but shares strategy, branding, IT, and other core functions. One year after that four-way consolidation, Dentons's profit margin was 26 percent, placing it among the bottom fifth of Am Law 100 firms.

By the time of the Dacheng deal, 2,600 lawyers carried the "Dentons" brand. But a brand is not a business, and any brand is only as good as its underlying product. Law firms have a single product to sell: the talent of their personnel. Inorganic growth imperils a firm's ability to deliver consistent quality and preserve a culture reinforcing that ethic. In that regard, law firms have precious little room for error.

In responding to anticipated questions about the impact of the Dacheng merger on quality, Dentons's global CEO Elliott Portnoy said, "We know our competition will suggest that this dilutes profitability and will raise questions about quality control. But the simple truth is that we're going to be able to generate more revenue, increase our profitability and position ourselves as a truly multicultural firm."

Portnoy framed an important question and then ducked it. Sound bites about multiculturalism do not answer a central inquiry: What will the culture of the combined organization become, and how will it promote quality attorney work product? In particular, the practical differences between Dentons and Dacheng are enormous. According to the *American Lawyer*, average revenue per Dacheng lawyer in 2013 was $78,000. Dentons's 2013 revenue per lawyer was $505,000. Even with separate revenue and profits pools, integrating these two giants will be daunting.

Remarkably, only three months after completing the Dacheng deal, Dentons added the 420-lawyer McKenna, Long & Aldridge to the North American arm of its verein. The two firms had discussed merging in late 2013, but a significant number of McKenna Long partners balked and the deal died. Because the prevailing big law firm model does not value dissent, it is no surprise that during the next twelve months McKenna Long suffered a massive partner exodus: fifty-nine departures totaling more than 22 percent of the partnership—a greater percentage loss than any other big firm that year.

Some dissenters stayed until the deal became a reality. For many years, McKenna Long's government contracts practice was one of the largest, oldest, and most prestigious of its kind. A month after the announcement of the Dentons–McKenna Long merger, most of that group—nineteen out of twenty-three lawyers—moved to another firm, Covington & Burling. The departing McKenna Long attorneys had successfully opposed the 2013 merger, so when discussions with Dentons resumed in 2015, they voted with their feet. As one of the group's leaders explained, "[Dentons] is going to become a different firm. We thought if we're going to become a different firm, we would take a look around and become a firm of our choosing."

With its absorption by Dentons, Atlanta-based McKenna Long disappeared. But lest anyone doubt the self-interest that motivates many big law leaders, McKenna Long's last chairman, Jeffrey Haidet, landed on his feet: he became a co-CEO of Dentons US—the North American arm of the global verein.

At the time of the McKenna Long merger, Portnoy spoke about the firm's future growth plans: "There is no logical end." Dentons's global chairman Joseph Andrew echoed that sentiment: "We compete with the largest firms in the world and the smallest law firms." That mission statement sounds exactly like the type of growth plan that the 2014 Georgetown/Thomson Reuters report cautioned big firm leaders not to follow.

Whether such an attempt to be all things to every kind of potential client is a viable long-term business strategy for any law firm remains to be seen. At best, the strategy places little or no value on a firm's culture. It also sacrifices any meaningful sense of firm identity other than for leaders of the enterprise to say that they have built something big.

Does adding size enhance quality and add client value? Does it make an institution more nimble in coping with a changing environment? Does it enhance morale, collegiality, and long-run firm stability? Does aggressive inorganic growth improve or worsen profit margins?

Many firm leaders are not even asking those questions. If they don't, fellow partners should. After all, they have skin in this game, too.

PARTNERS OUTSIDE THE leadership circle are not posing these and other challenging questions because of another accelerating trend: income spreads *within* equity partnerships continue to get bigger. A few firms (typically lock-step institutions such as Cravath) still retain a top-to-bottom compensation gap of as little as four-to-one within their equity partnerships, but they are among a vanishing breed. At some firms, the gap has exploded to more than twenty-to-one. The median in 2014 for all partners (equity and non-equity) among the 103 responding Am Law 200 firms was eleven-to-one. A corollary to this growing gap is the disappearing middle class of equity partners. At most firms, the resulting distribution of compensation creates a small group at the top—a partnership-within-a-partnership—and a much bigger group at the bottom. The danger is that leaders will pursue misguided agendas as they ignore client desires and the best interests of fellow partners outside the leadership circle. The evidence proves that this danger is becoming a reality.

Every year, Altman Weil publishes a survey of chief legal officers (CLOs)—that is, the people at large corporations who are responsible for hiring outside law firms. The survey asks the CLOs to evaluate outside counsel and, each year since 2009, has posed this question:

In your opinion, on a scale of 1 to 10, how serious are law firms about changing their legal service delivery model to provide greater value to clients (as opposed to simply cutting costs)?

Eighty-five percent of CLO respondents gave outside firms a rating of 5 or below. Every year since 2009, the median score has been 3. In another recent survey, big law leaders listed their priorities for their firms. In rank order, they were (emphasis added):

- Increasing revenue
- New business
- Growth
- Profitability
- Management succession
- Cost management
- Attracting talent (lateral partner hiring)
- *CLIENT VALUE*
- Improving efficiency
- *LAWYER PERFORMANCE*

To accomplish the top-priority items—the very ones clients say they do not want their firms pursuing—lateral hiring and mergers remain the growth vehicles of choice. Meanwhile, as partner morale declines, leadership knows this and does little to respond. According to an Altman Weil survey, 40 percent of law firm leaders reported that their partners' morale in 2013 was lower than it had been in 2008—and those are the "lucky" lawyers who survived the big law firm purges and layoffs during the Great Recession. Likewise, a 2013 *American Lawyer* annual survey revealed that law firm leaders thought that only 56 percent of their firms' partners were "somewhat optimistic" in 2013, down from 63 percent a year earlier.

Corporate clients are also noticing that, as the prevailing business model maximizes current profits at the expense of everything else that matters, diversity in big law firms has stagnated. African Americans and Hispanics comprise 26 percent of the US workforce but less than 10 percent of the country's lawyers. Minority representation among equity partnerships at large firms has languished around 5 percent for more than two decades. Fewer than 2 percent of big law firm partners are African American. Women constitute one-third of the profession, but for more than twenty years the percentage of female equity partners has hovered around 15 percent. Today, only seven of the nation's largest one hundred firms have a female chair or managing partner. Mary Snapp, deputy general counsel of Microsoft, spoke for many of her corporate colleagues when she discussed the diversity gap in the legal profession: "If people are going to have faith in a judicial system . . . it's essential that those people represent the diversity of the population."

TOO MANY BIG law firm leaders are increasingly distant from these and other concerns of clients and fellow partners. Believing its own press releases, the partnership-within-a-partnership at the top has become impervious to internal criticism and dissenting voices. There is an unwillingness to rock the boat, even among those who fear it may be developing leaks. Partners outside the leadership circle are reluctant to pose questions that could be perceived as failing to behave as "team players." Just ask any equity partner who has attended a recent big firm partnership meeting. I know the answer, both from personal experience and from confidential discussions with partners at firms throughout the country. "Keep at it," big firm partners everywhere tell me. "You are saying what everyone else is thinking but afraid to say."

Simultaneously with the release of *The Lawyer Bubble* in April 2013, one of the profession's leading international observers, Richard Susskind, wrote, "Most law firm leaders that I meet have only a few years to serve and hope they can hold out until retirement. . . . They are more focused on short-term profitability than long-term strategic health."

In the two years since publication of my book, short-termism continues to rule the day. But what was once the long term is not as far away.

THERE IS NO shortage of cheerleaders willing to defend the legal profession's unfortunate trends. Once a cottage industry, law firm management consultants have made millions of dollars offering big law firm leaders plenty of bad advice over the years: increase leverage, use billable hours to measure productivity, maximize leverage ratios by tightening equity partner admission requirements to increase current profits, expand geographic footprints, and adopt a host of other business-type metrics that have transformed the profession into a collection of short-term, profit-maximizing businesses. They warned leaders of midsized firms to merge or die. As the prevailing model that they sold now reveals its flaws—sometimes through the dramatic collapse of the institutions they once advised—many of these consultants have pivoted to denial.

Brad Hildebrandt, founder of Hildebrandt Consulting, offered these comforting words to his law firm constituents in 2014: "Large law firms are weathering the storm of the past five years and continue to transform their businesses to operate with efficiency and agility amid a new set of client expectations." Every relevant survey of big firm leader attitudes and strategic plans proves Hildebrandt wrong.

Likewise with respect to law schools, UC-Irvine School of Law dean Erwin Chemerinsky, who appears regularly on the *National Jurist*'s annual list of the "Most Influential People in Legal Education," coauthored a recent *New York Times* op-ed chastising anyone who suggested that a crisis in legal education existed. He argued that "as recently as 2007, close to 92 percent of law-school graduates reported being employed in a paid, full-time position nine months after graduation. True, the employment figures had dropped by 2012, the most recent year for which data is available, but only to 84.7 percent. . . . And with the economy improving and law-school enrollments shrinking, there will be more jobs available for new law graduates."

But the 2012 data on which Dean Chemerinsky relies include law school–funded positions and "JD-Advantage" jobs—the latter being a catchall that allows law schools unrestrained and unaudited discretion to include accountants, risk managers, human resources employees, and many others who have positions that do not require an expensive law degree. Moreover, Chemerinsky's 2012 data include only those graduates "for whom employment status was known." Nine months after graduation, only 57 percent of all 2013 graduates had full-time, long-term jobs (including law school–funded positions) requiring bar passage.

Finally, like most academic defenders of the current legal education system, Chemerinsky ignores the multiple law school submarkets. As previously discussed, top schools have little difficulty placing their graduates; far too many schools at the bottom have abysmal employment rates. His school is somewhere in between. Ten months after graduation, 63 percent of UC-Irvine School of Law's 2014 graduates (fifty-nine out of ninety-three, excluding ten who held law school–funded positions) had full-time, long-term, JD-required jobs.

Still another ardent defender of the current regime—of both law schools and the prevailing big law firm model—is Professor Richard A. Epstein, who teaches at the University of Chicago and New York University Law Schools. As an example of the hostility that the professoriate can exhibit toward teachers with real-world experience, *The Lawyer Bubble* mentioned briefly Professor Epstein's resistance to Elena Kagan's desire to resume her tenured position on the University of Chicago Law School faculty after her service as US solicitor general under President Bill Clinton. The vote against Kagan's return went Epstein's way; Harvard stepped in, offered her a job, and eventually made her dean.

In Professor Epstein's review of *The Lawyer Bubble* for the *Wall Street Journal*, he offers these reassuring words: "Is the 'Profession in Crisis,' as the subtitle of *The Lawyer Bubble* has it? The answer is no." Where a person stands depends on where he or she sits. The elite law schools at which Professor Epstein holds endowed chairs—the University of Chicago and NYU—are not in crisis and never will be. Likewise, although large law firms have retained him as an expert witness on client matters, that role provides no insight into a practicing attorney's life in one of them. Perhaps that accounts for his doubts about the evolution of those institutions. Understandably, anyone who has not personally experienced the dramatic transformation of such places would have difficulty believing how quickly their dominant culture has deteriorated.

Most legal educators and practicing lawyers who have commented on *The Lawyer Bubble* have reaffirmed its central themes. Such reviewers characterized it as a "must-read," "essential reading," and "an important book, carefully researched, cogently argued and compellingly written." Some suggested that I had "a complete mastery of his subject matter, both from an economic and legal perspective" and had written "the perfect book for a terrible time." Those accolades are gratifying, but they don't answer the burning question: Will the people in a position to change the profession's troubling trajectory use their power and influence to do so?

MORE THAN TWO hundred years ago, Thomas Paine wrote, "A long habit of not thinking a thing wrong, gives it a superficial appearance of being right, and raises at first a formidable outcry in defense of custom. But the tumult soon subsides. Time makes more converts than reason." So it will be for the legal profession.

Only grudgingly will embedded interests yield to forces beyond their control. Formidable as those interests sometimes seem, they will have no choice. Prospective law students are becoming more sophisticated; transparency is giving them the weapons to make informed choices about their futures in what must remain a noble profession. The resulting pressure on law schools will increase. Things would move more quickly toward equilibrium if the federal government overhauled the mechanism for funding legal education. Until it does, too many law schools will exploit the resulting moral hazard, and the profession will suffer—as will far too many law students who become unemployed JD degree holders with massive educational debt.

Likewise, vested interests that benefit from the short-termism dominating most big law firms will yield eventually to continuing client pressures. The trend toward disaggregation of legal services will see large corporate clients moving tasks to less costly providers, including in-house staffs. Technology has been a great disrupter and a powerful leveler, enabling small and medium-sized firms to compete with large firms for complex corporate work. The Thomson Reuters Peer Monitor "Mid-Size Law Firm Report" observes that "mid-size firms (as well as Am Law Second 100 firms) are clearly advantaged by client focus on efficiency and cost effectiveness and by the increasing willingness of clients to 'disaggregate' or 'unbundle' matters, both litigation and transactional. . . . [S]maller firms often exhibit a flexibility in responding rapidly to client needs that can be more difficult for larger organizations."

These developments are not hypothetical; they are already happening. An analysis of 2 million invoices for 300,000 corporate client matters totaling more than $10 billion in outside legal fees showed that from 2010 to 2013 clients were already voting with their pocketbooks. For all matters, the market share of megafirms—those with more than 750 attorneys—declined from 26 percent to 20 percent. But even more telling, on high-fee matters generating more than $1 million, the "big enough" firms of 201 to 500 attorneys increased their market share from 22 percent to 41 percent. Many practitioners are also finding that the shift from big law to not-so-big law is rewarding in nonmonetary ways, such as increased collegiality and a greater sense of community.

ALL OF THIS takes us back to the prelaw undergraduates who were my principal motivation for writing this book. As they consider law school, the vast majority of them have noble ambitions about what they will do with a legal degree. First and foremost, they want to help people.

In that respect, *The Lawyer Bubble* mentioned briefly an increasingly important issue for our society of haves and have-nots: access to legal representation. In the 1963 landmark case of *Gideon v. Wainwright*, the US Supreme Court unanimously ruled that criminal defendants have a constitutional right to counsel at state expense if they cannot afford one. Fifty years later in courts throughout the country, that right still goes unrealized. As two commentators recently observed, "Governments have failed to adequately fund defense systems, many judges tolerate or welcome inadequate representation, and the Supreme Court has refused to require competent representation, instead adopting a standard of 'effective counsel' that hides and perpetuates deficient representation."

There is no comparable right to counsel in most civil cases. The National Center for Access to Justice at Cardozo Law School reports, "In our states, more than 80 percent of the litigants appear without lawyers in matters as important as evictions, mortgage foreclosures, child custody and child support proceedings, and debt collection cases."

A complete exposition of the access problem could fill another book, but for the larger themes of *The Lawyer Bubble*, one point in particular resonates: prelaw students who attend law school expecting to become Atticus Finch are finding that, in the real world, society increasingly is unwilling to pay for the services he renders.

Measured in constant 2013 dollars, funding for the Legal Services Corporation, the largest federal legal aid organization, has declined from $866 million in 1979 to $341 million in 2013. In the past ten years alone, LSC's funding has shrunk 40 percent (adjusting for inflation). *That* translates into thousands of attorneys no longer available to assist the poor. The National Center for Access to Justice estimates that there is one legal aid lawyer for every 8,893 Americans who qualify for legal aid. At the individual state level, relative access to civil legal aid attorneys is greatest in the District of Columbia—almost 9 per 10,000 people in poverty. But from there the drop is dramatic: New York is second highest with 3.48 per 10,000 impoverished citizens. Texas is lowest: 0.43 per 10,000.

The high cost of legal education that creates growing student loan debt exacerbates the access problem. For reasons discussed in *The Lawyer Bubble,* income-based repayment plans offer only limited relief. Even worse, the attitudes behind current trends against funding the Legal Services Corporation seem likely to inflict future pain on IBR programs as well. Here, as elsewhere, those in a position to make a difference—notably political leaders—must change their behavior. As with law school deans and big law managing partners, that will require a generational turnover to those who have no allegiance to bad ideas that are not working.

ACROSS THE PROFESSION, change will continue. The question is: Who will be smart enough to see the resulting opportunities and seize them? Some will; some won't. But those who think we are all merely victims of life's vicissitudes miss a crucial lesson: individuals making choices created the current mess; better choices can clean it up. The choice for those who enter the profession is clear: make yourself part of the solution or remain part of the problem. There is no longer any safe middle ground. It turns out there never was.

STEVEN J. HARPER
Wilmette, Illinois
2016

ACKNOWLEDGMENTS

T HE THINGS THAT MATTER most in my life begin with my wife, Kit. She made everything else possible—the most important being our three children, Ben, Pete, and Emma. Emma was my first editor in the early phase of this project. Her valuable insights advanced it to the next level, where my literary agent, Danielle Svetcov, of Levine Greenberg Literary Agency helped me to craft a successful proposal. Danielle's relentless efforts then put the manuscript in the care of a gifted editor, Tim Bartlett, and his outstanding assistants, Sarah Rosenthal and Kaitlyn Zafonte, at Basic Books (Perseus). Project editor Collin Tracy and copyeditor Sue Warga guided the manuscript to its successful completion.

I owe a special debt to a handful of distinguished reviewers whose critiques of an early draft made this book far better than it otherwise would have been. Daniel Bowling III (former senior vice president, Coca-Cola Enterprises, and senior lecturing fellow, Duke Law School), Robert Helman (former chair of Mayer Brown LLP and lecturer in law at the University of Chicago), Steven Lubet (Williams Memorial Professor of Law, Northwestern University), and James Sandman (president of the Legal Services Corporation and former managing partner, Arnold & Porter LLP) bear no responsibility for any aspects of the book that others may find erroneous, objectionable, or offensive; any such faults are mine alone. But these illustrious attorneys deserve great credit for important improvements over what this project might have been. We conducted the process so that each reviewer could provide candid feedback anonymously to my editor. In fact, they didn't even know the identities of fellow reviewers. Their helpful insights pervade the final product in ways that they themselves will recognize.

I am also grateful to many friends in the legal profession. In particular, *American Lawyer* editor in chief Aric Press provided a forum that amplified my voice in 2010 when he began publishing my blog posts on the *American Lawyer*'s website, Am Law Daily. My regular readers will notice that this book continues many themes that first appeared there. Editor Dimitra Kessenides assisted that effort. Upon Aric's promotion to editor in chief of the ALM parent organization, his successors, Robin Sparkman and Kim Kleman, and editors Ed Shanahan, Pia Sarkar, and David Bario, continued publishing my views, some of which were and are heretical. My friends and former colleagues at my firm of thirty years, Kirkland & Ellis, contributed to a satisfying and successful first act as a trial attorney that made possible my second act as an author, educator, and critical commentator on a profession that I love. Northwestern Law School professor Steven Lubet first drew me into teaching when he invited me to serve as an adjunct in his trial advocacy course almost twenty years ago. His fellow Northwestern Law professor Robert Burns then added me to his team of adjunct faculty teaching the legal ethics component of that program.

In 2007, the dean of Northwestern University's Weinberg College of Arts and Sciences (and later university provost) Daniel Linzer persuaded me to offer an undergraduate seminar on any topic of interest to me. My thanks to the many Northwestern University undergraduates who dared to take my course on the legal profession. They allowed me to challenge their fundamental assumptions about themselves and the careers that they planned to pursue. Most went on to law school. They inspired me to write this book in the hope that future generations of attorneys might benefit from it.

—S.J.H.

NOTES

INTRODUCTION

xi   *Recent surveys report that six out of ten:* Stephanie F. Ward, "The Pulse of the Profession," *ABA Journal,* Oct. 2007.

xi   *Sometimes those stories even make the front page:* See, e.g., P. Lattman, "Once an Ambitious Law Firm, Reduced to Grim Dispatches," *New York Times,* May 1, 2012.

xii   *The number of JDs awarded annually:* "Enrollment and Degrees Awarded, 1963–2011 Academic Years," ABA Section of Legal Education and Admissions to the Bar, www.americanbar.org/content/dam/aba/administrative/legal_education_and_admissions_to _the_bar/statistics/enrollment_degrees_awarded.authcheckdam.pdf (accessed Sept. 7, 2012); J. Palazzolo, "Law Grads Face Brutal Job Market, *Wall Street Journal,* June 25, 2012.

xiii *To paraphrase the* American Lawyer'*s editor in chief:* A. Press, "Change You Can Believe In," *American Lawyer,* Dec. 2010.

xiii *Among the two hundred largest firms in 2000:* V. Li, "This Time It's Personal," *American Lawyer,* Feb. 2012, 53; D. Combs, "No Place to Hide," *American Lawyer,* June 2010, 73.

xiv   *While rainmakers offered . . . record low levels:* After years of steady decline, the *American Lawyer* Midlevel Associate Survey for 2012 reported an improvement in associate morale (*American Lawyer,* Sept. 2012). That could reflect associates reconciling themselves to a world in which any well-paying job in a depressed economy is itself sufficient reason to be satisfied, or it could be a one-time departure from an embedded trend, or it could reflect the possibility that more large-firm leaders have begun to regard associate satisfaction as a priority.

xv   *From 2010 to 2011 it dropped:* N. Koppel, "Bloom's Off the Law School Rose," *Wall Street Journal,* Sept. 28, 2011.

xv   *Likewise, the Law School Admission Council reported:* Law School Admission Council, "LSAC— Data—Tests Administered," www.lsac.org/LSACResources/Data/lsats-administered.asp (accessed Sept. 1, 2012).

xv   *For the class entering in the fall:* Law School Admission Council, "LSAC Volume Summary," www.lsac.org/lsacresources/data/lsac-volume-summary.asp (accessed Sept. 1, 2012).

xv   *The popular explanation for these phenomena:* D. Segal, "For 2nd Year, a Sharp Drop in Law School Entrance Tests," *New York Times,* Mar. 19, 2012.

xv   *In fact, the reduction in the number:* Law School Admission Council, "LSAC—Data—Tests Administered."

xv   *To put that in historical perspective:* Ibid.

xv   *The bottom line is that:* J. Palazzolo, "Law Grads Face Brutal Job Market," *Wall Street Journal,* June 25, 2012.

CHAPTER 1: TRACKING THE BUBBLE

4   *Today there's a lawyer for every 265 Americans:* American Bar Association, "National Lawyer Population by State," www.americanbar.org/content/dam/aba/migrated/marketresearch/ PublicDocuments/2011_national_lawyer_by_state.authcheckdam.pdf (accessed Sept. 1, 2012); G. Priest, "Lawyers, Liability, and Law Reform: Effects on American Economic Growth and

Trade Competitiveness," Yale Law School, Faculty Scholarship Series no. 624, 1993, http://digitalcommons.law.yale.edu/fss_papers/624 (accessed Sept. 1, 2012).

4   *In 2012, after the Great Recession:* United States Department of Labor, Bureau of Labor Statistics, "Lawyers," *Occupational Outlook Handbook*, 2012, www.bls.gov/oco/ocos053.htm (accessed Sept. 1, 2012).

4   *Another prediction considered attrition:* Estimated annual openings through 2015: 26,239; 2009 bar exam passers: 53,508; lawyer surplus: 27,269. Economic Modeling Specialists, Inc., www.economicmodeling.com/2011/06/22/new-lawyers-glutting-the-market-in-all-but-3-states, highlighted in C. Rampell, "The Lawyer Surplus, State by State," *New York Times,* June 27, 2011.

4   *Fewer than half of 2011 graduates:* Association for Legal Career Professionals, "Law Grads Face Worst Job Market Yet—Less Than Half Find Jobs in Private Practice," press release, June 7, 2012, www.nalp.org/2011selectedfindingsrelease (accessed Sept. 1, 2012).

4   *Nine months after graduation:* J. Palazzolo, "Law Grads Face Brutal Job Market," *Wall Street Journal,* June 25, 2012.

4   *Along with their degrees . . . almost $100,000:* W. Henderson and R. Zahorsky, "The Law School Tuition Bubble," *ABA Journal,* Dec. 27, 2011.

4   *Average law school debt for the graduating class of 2011:* S. Favate, "Law Students, How Much Debt Do You Want?" *Wall Street Journal Law Blog,* Mar. 23, 2012, http://blogs.wsj.com/law/2012/03/23/law-students-how-much-debt-do-you-want (accessed Nov. 2, 2012).

5   *One-third of respondents to a survey:* Veritas Prep, "Inside the Minds of Law School Applicants," executive summary, Oct. 25, 2011, www.lawschoolpodcaster.com/wp-content/uploads/2010/10/FINAL_Executive-Summary_2011-Law-School-Applicant-Survey.pdf (accessed Sept. 1, 2012).

5   *For example, no pre-law student . . . the mob:* J. Grisham, *The Firm* (New York: Doubleday, 1991).

5   *Psychologist Daniel Kahneman:* D. Kahneman, *Thinking, Fast and Slow* (New York: Farrar, Straus & Giroux, 2011); D. Kahneman, "Don't Blink! The Hazards of Overconfidence," *New York Times Magazine,* Oct. 23, 2011.

6   *But if prospective lawyers allow themselves:* N. Koppel and V. O'Connell, "Pay Gap Widens at Big Law Firms as Partners Chase Star Attorneys," *Wall Street Journal,* Feb. 8, 2011.

6   *Nine months . . . salary of $72,000:* Association for Legal Career Professionals, "Median Private Practice Starting Salaries for the Class of 2011 Plunge as Private Practice Jobs Continue to Erode," press release, July 12, 2012, www.nalp.org/classof2011_salpressrel; Association for Legal Career Professionals, "Employment and Salary Trends for New Law Graduates, 1985–2000," NALP *Bulletin,* June 2001, www.nalp.org/2001junemploymenttrends (accessed Sept. 18, 2012).

6   *That may not sound bad, but . . . misleadingly high:* W. Henderson, "Distribution of 2006 Starting Salaries: Best Graphic Chart of the Year," Empirical Legal Studies, Sept. 4, 2007, www.elsblog.org/the_empirical_legal_studi/2007/09/distribution-of.html (accessed Sept. 1, 2012); W. Henderson, "The End of an Era: The Bi-Modal Distribution for the Class of 2008," Empirical Legal Studies, June 29, 2009, www.elsblog.org/the_empirical_legal_studi/2009/06/the-end-of-an-era-the-bimodal-distribution-for-the-class-of-2008.html (accessed Sept. 1, 2012).

6   *For all law firms, the median starting salary:* Association for Legal Career Professionals, "Median Private Practice Starting Salaries for the Class of 2011 Plunge as Private Practice Jobs Continue to Erode," press release, July 12, 2012, www.nalp.org/classof2011_salpressrel (accessed Sept. 1, 2012).

6   *The median annual income of all practicing lawyers:* United States Department of Labor, Bureau of Labor Statistics, "Lawyers," *Occupational Outlook Handbook*, 2012, www.bls.gov/oco/ocos053.htm (accessed Sept. 1, 2012).

6   *Professor Herwig Schlunk:* H. Schlunk, "Mamas, Don't Let Your Babies Grow Up to Be . . . Lawyers," Vanderbilt Law School, Law and Economics Working Paper 09-29, http://online.wsj.com/public/resources/documents/SSRN-id1497044.pdf; H. Schlunk, "Mamas 2011: Is a Law Degree a Good Investment Today?" Vanderbilt Law School, Law and Economics Working Paper 11-42, http://papers.ssrn.com/sol3/papers.cfm?abstract_id=1957139## (accessed Sept. 1, 2012).

7   *"After graduating as a political science major":* A. Keh, "For Satin, a Mets Farmhand, 1 Hit, 1 Run, Plenty of Thrills," *New York Times,* Sept. 4, 2011.

7   *Prior to 1890, no other law school:* D. Garvin, "Making the Case—Professional Education for the World of Practice," *Harvard Magazine,* Sept.-Oct. 2003.

8   *For example . . . Clarence Darrow:* C. Darrow, *The Story of My Life* (New York: Da Capo Press, 1996), 29–30.

8   *"be able to apply them":* Garvin, "Making the Case."

8   *From 1890 to 1916, the number of law schools:* A. Reed, *Training the Public for the Profession of Law* (New York: Carnegie Foundation for the Advancement of Teaching, 1921), 193, 443.

8   *As recently as 1963 . . . had doubled:* American Bar Association, Section of Legal Education and Admissions to the Bar, "Enrollment and Degrees Awarded, 1963–2011 Academic Years," www.americanbar.org/content/dam/aba/administrative/legal_education_and_admissions_to _the_bar/statistics/enrollment_degrees_awarded.authcheckdam.pdf (accessed Sept. 1, 2012).

8   *On a per capita basis:* Priest, "Lawyers, Liability, and Law Reform."

9   *Recently the Maryland Department of Legislative Services:* K. Sloan, "Law School 'Tax' at Baltimore More Than Twice What University Claimed," *National Law Journal,* Feb. 28, 2012.

9   *For private schools . . . gross revenues:* Ibid.

9   *In 2003, there were more than ninety-eight thousand:* Law School Admission Council, "LSAC Volume Summary," www.lsac.org/LSACResources/Data/LSAC-volume-summary.asp (accessed Sept. 2, 2012).

9   *Average annual tuition:* K. Sloan, "Tuition Is Still Growing," *National Law Journal,* Aug. 20, 2012.

9   *Since then . . . enrollments have steadily risen:* American Bar Association, "Enrollment and Degrees Awarded, 1963–2011."

9   *By 2010, there were more than 1.2 million:* American Bar Association, "National Lawyer Population by State," www.americanbar.org/content/dam/aba/migrated/marketresearch/Public Documents/2011_national_lawyer_by_state.authcheckdam.pdf (accessed Sept. 1, 2012).

9   *In the United Kingdom . . . in Germany:* "NZ World Leader in Per Capita Lawyer Stakes," *New Zealand Herald,* July 15, 2010.

10   *The law school business model:* Henderson and Zahorsky, "The Law School Tuition Bubble."

10   *The origins of the government student loan program:* R. Shireman, "Straight Talk on Student Loans," Center for Studies in Higher Education, University of California, Berkeley, Research and Occasional Paper Series CSHE.10.04, 2004, http://cshe.berkeley.edu/publications/docs/ ROP.Shireman.Loans.10.04.pdf (accessed Sept. 6, 2012).

11   *In 2011, the US Department of Education:* A. Martin, "Debt Collectors Cashing In on Student Loan Roundup," *New York Times,* Sept. 8, 2012.

11   *"I couldn't believe the accumulated wealth":* J. Ashton, "A Love Letter from Your Student Loan Bill Collector," InsideARM.com, Feb. 23, 2011, www.insidearm.com/opinion/a-love-letter -from-your-student-loan-bill-collector (accessed Sept. 9, 2012).

11   *"new oil well":* M. Russell, "Student Loans: The ARM Industry's New Oil Well?" Inside ARM.com, Oct. 20, 2011, www.insidearm.com/obs-in-focus/student-loans-the-arm -industrys-new-oil-well (accessed Sept. 9, 2012).

11   *"the closest thing to debtor prison":* Martin, "Debt Collectors Cashing In."

11   *It wasn't always so:* National Consumer Law Center, "No Way Out: Student Loans, Financial Distress, and the Need for Policy Reform," June 2006, www.studentloanborrowerassistance .org/blogs/wp-content/www.studentloanborrowerassistance.org/uploads/File/nowayout.pdf (accessed June 27, 2012).

12   *No data supported the suggestion:* H.R. Rep. 95-595, 1st Sess. 1977, 19978, 1978 U.S.C.C.A.N. 5963, 6094, 1977 WL 9628.

12   *"more myth and media hype than reality":* T. Collins, "Forging Middle Ground: Revision of Student Loan Debts in Bankruptcy as an Impetus to Amend 11 U.S.S. Sec. 523(1)(8)," *Iowa Law Review* 75 (Mar. 1990): 733.

12   *"After a surge in former students":* "You Don't Owe That," *Wall Street Journal,* July 25, 2012.

12   *In 1997, the Bankruptcy Reform Commission:* D. Chen, "Student Loans in Bankruptcy," CRS Report for Congress, July 26, 2007, http://assets.opencrs.com/rpts/RS22699_20070726.pdf (accessed Aug. 20, 2012).

12   *"How in the world":* "Private Student Loans Should Be Dischargeable in Bankruptcy Courts, Senator Says," *The BLT: The Blog of Legal Times,* Mar. 20, 2012, http://legaltimes .typepad.com/blt/2012/03/private-student-loans-should-be-dischargeable-in-bankruptcy -courts-senator-says.html (accessed June 27, 2012).

12   *Nonfederal loans accounted for only 7 percent:* J. Mitchell, "Trying to Shed Student Debt," *Wall Street Journal,* Apr. 28, 2012.

12   *But now . . . some have theorized:* Ibid.

13   *"ever break the grip of autism":* J. Clark, "Bankruptcy Judge Lets Woman with Asperger's Discharge Student Loans," Total Bankruptcy, May 29, 2012, www.totalbankruptcy.com/ bankruptcy-news/bankruptcy-laws/aspergers-student-loans-800191912.aspx (accessed Aug. 27, 2012).

13   *"at the end of her 'rope'":* J. Caher, "Rare Discharge Is Granted in Case of Student Loan Debt," *New York Law Journal,* July 17, 2012.

13   *"What I say to the judge":* R. Lieber, "Last Plea on School Loans: Proving a Hopeless Future," *New York Times,* Aug. 31, 2012.

14   *"It's a noose around my neck":* Mitchell, "Trying to Shed Student Debt."

CHAPTER 2: THE ROLE OF THE ABA AND *U.S. NEWS* RANKINGS

15   *In a recent survey, 86 percent:* K. Sloan, "Survey Suggests Prospective Law Students Still Have Stars in Their Eyes," *National Law Journal,* June 19, 2012.

16   *By 2012, the magazine was ranking:* "Methodology: Law School Rankings," *U.S. News & World Report,* Mar. 12, 2012. Current methodology posted at www.usnews.com/education/ best-graduate-schools/top-law-schools/articles/2012/03/12/methodology-law-school -rankings; L. Edwards, "The Rankings Czar," *ABA Journal,* Apr. 2008.

16   *In 1997, virtually every law school dean:* R. Morse, "A Visit with Northwestern's Law School Dean," *Morse Code: Inside the College Rankings,* July 24, 2007, www.usnews.com/education/ blogs/college-rankings-blog/2007/07/24/a-visit-with-northwesterns-law-school-dean (accessed Sept. 2, 2012).

17   *"Millions of dollars":* D. Segal, "Is Law School a Losing Game?" *New York Times,* Jan. 8, 2011.

17   *Quality assessment is the biggest contributor:* Complete methodology at R. Morse, "Law School Ranking Methodology," various dates from 2008 through 2012, www.usnews.com/articles/ education/best-graduate-schools/2008/03/26/law-methodology.html; www.usnews.com /education/best-graduate-schools/articles/2011/03/14/law-school-rankings-methodology -2012?PageNr=1 (accessed Sept. 2, 2012).

18   *As a matter of statistical theory . . . numerous deficiencies:* M. Cloud and G. Shepherd, "Law Deans in Jail," Social Science Research Network, Feb. 24, 2012, http://papers.ssrn.com/sol3/ papers.cfm?abstract_id=1990746 (accessed Sept. 2, 2012).

18   *"were asked about Princeton Law School":* J. Hoffman, "Judge Not, Law Schools Demand of a Magazine That Ranks Them," *New York Times,* Feb. 19, 1998.

18   *"As I recall, they ranked Penn State's":* M. Gladwell, "The Order of Things," *New Yorker,* Feb. 14, 2011.

18   *In 2012, the school's middle-of-the-pack:* "Best Law School Rankings," *U.S. News & World Report,* 2012.

18   *"The law school's reputation score":* A. Bellafiore, "Penn State's Dickinson School of Law Sees Drop in Rankings," *Penn State Collegian,* Mar. 15, 2012.

19   *"The Association of American Law Schools":* L. Edwards, "The Rankings Czar," *ABA Journal,* Apr. 2008, 41.

19   *That's good news . . . almost 2.0 in 2011:* Law School Admission Council, "LSAC—Data— LSAC Volume Summary," www.lsac.org/LSACResources/Data/LSAC-volume-summary .asp (accessed Sept. 2, 2012).

19   *They're not unique . . . test scores:* A. Mackey, K. Whitaker, and S. Bunge, "Experience-Dependent Plasticity in White Matter Microstructure: Reasoning Training Alters Structural Connectivity," *Frontiers in Neuroanatomy* 6, no. 32 (Aug. 22, 2012).

19   *University of Illinois College of Law:* An earlier version of the author's present analysis of the University of Illinois College of Law LSAT/GPA scandal first appeared in his blog post,

"The Other Big-10 Scandal," *The Belly of the Beast,* www.thebellyofthebeast.wordpress.com, reproduced on *Am Law Daily,* Nov. 18, 2011; Jones Day and Duff & Phelps, "Investigative Report: University of Illinois College of Law Class Profile Reporting," Nov. 7, 2011, www .uillinois.edu/our/news/2011/Law/Nov7.UofI.FinalReport.pdf (accessed Sept. 2, 2012), 34.

20   *"Had we been able to report":* Jones Day and Duff & Phelps, "Investigative Report," 56.

20   *"with a GPA profile worse":* Ibid., 53–54.

20   *"in the hiring sights":* Ibid., 57.

20   *"sustained pattern . . . class of 2014":* Ibid., 8.

21   *"Lawless Calculator":* Ibid., 35–36.

21   *"I told Paul [Pless] to push":* Ibid., 67.

21   *"is goal-oriented and intense":* Ibid., 9–10, fn. 3.

21   *"I haven't let a Dean down yet":* Ibid., 67.

22   *The University of Illinois College of Law dropped:* K. Hopkins, "In 2013 Best Law School Rankings Top Schools Switch Spots," *U.S. News & World Report,* Mar. 13, 2012.

22   *As a penalty to the institution:* J. Cohen, "University of Illinois Law School Censured, Fined," *Chicago Tribune,* July 25, 2012.

22   *Villanova Law School endured:* N. Koppel, "ABA Censures Villanova for 'Reprehensible' Conduct," *Wall Street Journal,* Aug. 16, 2011.

22   *"reprehensible and damaging":* Letter from H. Askew to P. Donohue and J. Golanda, Aug. 12, 2011, www.law.villanova.edu/About%20VLS/ABA%20Public%20Censure.aspx (accessed Sept. 2, 2012).

22   *The correct numbers dropped Villanova's ranking:* J. Blumenthal, "After Scandal, Villanova Falls in U.S. News Rankings," *Philadelphia Business Journal,* Mar. 24, 2011; K. Hopkins, "In 2013 Best Law School Rankings Top Schools Switch Spots," *U.S. News & World Report,* Mar. 13, 2012.

22   *For example, during David Van Zandt's final years as dean:* L. Gordon, "Transfers Bolster Elite Schools," *ABA Journal,* Dec. 2008.

23   *Northwestern accepted even more . . . the thirties:* Law School Admission Council, "Official Guide to ABA-Approved Law Schools, 2012," https://officialguide.lsac.org/release/Official Guide_Default.aspx, and archives 2006–2011, www.lsac.org/LSACResources/Publications/ official-guide-archives.asp (accessed Sept. 6, 2012).

23   *According to schools' individual ABA reports:* Ibid.

23   *"If the* U.S. News *incentive":* L. Gordon, "Transfers Bolster Elite Schools," *ABA Journal,* Dec. 2008.

23   *"Chrysler and General Motors don't agree":* Ibid.

24   *For example, the number of JDs that Northwestern awarded:* Law School Admission Council, "Official ABA Data," www.lsac.org/LSACResources/Publications/2011OG/aba2163.pdf (accessed Sept. 2, 2012).

24   *In 2011, the* New York Times *profiled:* D. Segal, "Law Students Lost the Grant Game as Schools Win," *New York Times,* Apr. 30, 2011.

25   *In 2010, validity studies investigating:* Law School Admission Council, "LSAT Scores as Predictors of Law School Performance," www.lsac.org/jd/pdfs/LSAT-Score-Predictors-of -Performance.pdf (accessed Sept. 2, 2012).

25   *"strange and unintended consequences":* Segal, "Law Students Lost the Grant Game."

25   *From 2005 to 2010, the number:* "Memorandum from Section on Legal Education and Admissions to the Bar, American Bar Association to Senator Charles Grassley" (Attachment 4), July 20, 2011, www.grassley.senate.gov/about/upload/ABA-response.pdf (accessed June 29, 2012).

25   *But non-need-based scholarship awards increased:* Ibid.

26   *"Enron-type accounting":* Segal, "Is Law School a Losing Game?"

26   *In 2012, employment rates for the class of 2011;* K. Sloan, "A Dismal Job Market for Law Grads Got Even Worse for Class of 2011," *National Law Journal,* June 7, 2012.

26   *Only 55 percent of 2011 graduates:* K. Sloan, "ABA: Only 55 Percent of Last Year's Grads Found Full-Time Legal Jobs," *National Law Journal,* June 18, 2012.

26   *Another study estimates:* P. Campos, "Served," *New Republic,* Apr. 25, 2011.

26   *At $20 an hour:* Segal, "Is Law School a Losing Game?"

26   *Georgetown wasn't the first or last school:* A. Wellen, "The $8.78 Million Maneuver," *New York Times,* July 31, 2005; E. Mystal, "Employment Statistics Shenanigans Open Thread: Which Schools Are Juking Their Stats?" *Above the Law,* May 16, 2011, http://abovethelaw.com/2011/05/employment-statistics-shenanigans-open-thread-which-schools-are-juking-their-stats (accessed Sept. 2, 2012).

27   *Recently, ABA-mandated disclosure requirements:* "ABA Section of Legal Education and Admissions to the Bar Update on Job Placement Data," www.abanow.org/2011/10/aba-section-of-legal-education-and-admissions-to-the-bar-update-on-job-placement-data (accessed Sept. 2, 2012).

27   *Three schools . . . hired more than 15 percent:* K. Sloan, "Data Trove Reveals Scope of Law Schools' Hiring of Their Own Graduates," *National Law Journal,* Apr. 16, 2012.

27   *In turn, that experience can lead:* Ibid.

27   *Duke University School of Law achieved:* K. Hill, "The Secret to 100% Employed at Graduation: Duke's Bridge to Practice," *Above the Law,* June 14, 2010, http://abovethelaw.com/2010/06/the-secret-to-100-employed-at-graduation-dukes-bridge-to-practice (accessed Sept. 1, 2012).

27   *The definitive test of law schools' motives:* Sloan, "Data Trove Reveals Scope."

28   *Its per-student expenditure:* Wellen, "The $8.78 Million Maneuver"; L. Edwards, "The Rankings Czar," *ABA Journal,* Apr. 2008, 41–42.

28   *In 2011, 85 percent:* S. Favate, "Law Students, How Much Debt Do You Want?" *Wall Street Journal Law Blog,* Mar. 23, 2012, http://blogs.wsj.com/law/2012/03/23/law-students-how-much-debt-do-you-want (accessed Nov. 2, 2012).

28   *At fifty schools:* "Best Law Schools," *U.S. News & World Report,* Mar. 2012.

28   *"The answer may be hard":* N. Hines, "Ten Major Changes in Legal Education over the Past Twenty-Five Years," *AALS Newsletter,* Aug. 2005.

29   *"Until such a change is made":* Ibid.

29   *"over the next fifteen years":* University of Iowa College of Law, "Law School History," www.law.uiowa.edu/about/milestones.php (accessed Sept. 2, 2012).

29   *In a March 28, 2008, email:* D. Lat, "The U.S. News Rankings: Law Schools React," *Above the Law,* Mar. 28, 2008, http://abovethelaw.com/2008/03/the-u-s-news-rankings-law-schools-lose-their-st-react (accessed Sept. 2, 2012).

30   *Whatever else came . . . twenty-seventh in 2011:* "Top 2012 Law School Rankings," last updated Mar. 2012, www.top-law-schools.com/rankings.html (accessed Sept. 2, 2012).

30   *In the rankings released in March 2012:* "Best Law Schools," *U.S. News & World Report,* Mar. 2012.

30   *It included this line: "When you obtain employment":* C. Crain, "Important Things to Do During Your Final Semesters at the University of Iowa College of Law," www.law.uiowa.edu/documents/L3_to_do_list.pdf (accessed Sept. 2, 2012).

31   *Here's what its "Best Career Prospects" lists looked like: The Best 170 Law Schools* (Framingham, MA: Princeton Review, 2008); *The Best 174 Law Schools* (Framingham, MA: Princeton Review, 2009); *The Best 172 Law Schools* (Framingham, MA: Princeton Review, 2010).

31   *In 2012, the list was: The Best 167 Law Schools* (Framingham, MA: Princeton Review, 2011).

32   *The 2013 list was: The Best 168 Law Schools* (Framingham, MA: Princeton Review, 2012).

32   *"Based on school reported data":* Princeton Review, "User's Guide to Our Law School Rankings," 2012, www.princetonreview.com/users-guide-law-rankings.aspx (accessed May 31, 2012).

33   *"Best Law Professors" category:* E. Mystal, "The Princeton Review Law School Rankings Are Out. Find a Category to Make Your Law School Look Awesome," *Above the Law,* Oct. 12, 2010, http://abovethelaw.com/2010/10/the-princeton-review-law-school-rankings-are-out-find-a-category-to-make-your-school-look-awesome (accessed May 31, 2012).

33   *In 2010, Cooley's overall ranking:* T. Brennan and D. LeDuc, "Judging the Law Schools," 12th ed. 2010, www.cooley.edu/rankings/_docs/Judging_12th_Ed_2010.pdf (accessed May 31, 2012).

33–34   *(After newly mandated . . . requiring bar passage):* J. Palazzolo, "Law Grads Face Brutal Job Market," *Wall Street Journal,* June 25, 2012; ABA Section of Legal Education and Admissions to the Bar, "Employment Summary Report."

34 *"accurate and transparent information":* E. Mystal, "Senator Boxer Keeps Pressure on the ABA," *Above the Law,* May 23, 2011, http://abovethelaw.com/2011/05/senator-boxer-keeps-pressure-on-the-aba (accessed May 31, 2012).

34 *"If more detailed information":* R. Morse, "U.S. News May Change Its Law School Ranking Methodology," *Morse Code: Inside the College Rankings,* June 16, 2011, www.usnews.com/education/blogs/college-rankings-blog/2011/06/16/us-news-may-change-its-law-school-ranking-methodology (accessed May 31, 2012).

35 *"Bob Morse could wake up":* Ibid.

35 *In July 2011, the ABA announced:* American Bar Association, "ABA Section of Legal Education and Admissions to the Bar Will Collect Additional Employment Information from Law Schools in its Annual Questionnaire," July 27, 2011, www.abanow.org/wordpress/wp-content/files_flutter/1311794682lawschool_employent_info_072711.pdf (accessed May 31, 2012).

35 *Two months later, the committee reported:* K. Sloan, "ABA Stalls on Honing Law Schools' Job Placements Reports," *National Law Journal,* Sept. 26, 2011.

35 *"expediting the collection and reporting":* American Bar Association, "ABA Section of Legal Education and Admissions to the Bar Update on Job Placement Data," www.abanow.org/2011/10/aba-section-of-legal-education-and-admissions-to-the-bar-update-on-job-placement-data (accessed May 31, 2012).

35 *Then in March 2012, the ABA's Council . . . rejected:* K. Sloan, "ABA Backs Off Making Law Schools Report Graduates' Salaries," *National Law Journal,* Mar. 19, 2012.

36 *Law school representatives, especially deans:* American Bar Association website, www.americanbar.org/groups/legal_education/about_us/leadership.html (accessed May 30, 2012).

36 *"There should be no doubt":* Sloan, "ABA Backs Off."

36 *"The Council specifically declined":* American Bar Association, "Reforms to Reporting of Law Graduate Employment Data Proposed By ABA's Section on Legal Education and Admissions to the Bar," press release, Mar. 20, 2012, www.americanbar.org/content/dam/aba/administrative/legal_education_and_admissions_to_the_bar/council_reports_and_resolutions/2012_proposed_standard_509.authcheckdam.pdf (accessed May 30, 2012).

36 *Overall . . . only 55 percent:* Palazzolo, "Law Grads Face Brutal Job Market."

37 *"do not characteristically go to work":* Ibid.

37 *"We consider this a problem":* Ibid.

37 *"You can't measure the value":* Ibid.

37 *Thomas Jefferson School of Law placed last:* "General Statistics Reports—July 2011 California Bar Examination," http://admissions.calbar.ca.gov/LinkClick.aspx?fileticket=PL6VLVgQEIM%3d&tabid=2269&mid=3159 (accessed Sept. 2, 2012).

37 *The school did better:* "General Statistics Reports—Feb. 2012 California Bar Examination," http://admissions.calbar.ca.gov/Portals/4/documents/Statistics/FEBRUARY2012STATS.pdf (accessed Sept. 2, 2012).

37 *"It's inconceivable to me":* D. Ingram, "ABA Head Has Little Sympathy for Jobless Lawyers," *Reuters,* Jan. 4, 2012.

39 *On May 26, 2011, a graduate:* Law School Transparency, http://lawschooltransparency.com/lawsuits/Alaburda_v_TJSL-Complaint.pdf (accessed May 21, 2012).

39 *In August 2011, unemployed alumni filed:* Lee, "Law Grads Sue over Tuition," *Wall Street Journal,* Aug. 11, 2011.

39 *The same lawyers . . . in early 2012:* S. Zaretsky, "Twelve More Law Schools Slapped with Class Action Lawsuits over Employment Data," *Above the Law,* Feb. 1, 2012, http://abovethelaw.com/2012/02/twelve-more-law-schools-slapped-with-class-action-lawsuits-over-employment-data (accessed May 31, 2012).

39 *The plaintiffs' claims against each school were similar:* K. Sloan, "Another 15 Law Schools Targeted over Jobs Data," *New York Law Journal,* Oct. 5, 2011.

39 *The plaintiffs' attorneys promised:* K. Mangan, "12 More Law Schools Face Lawsuits over Job-Placement Claims," *Chronicle of Higher Education,* Feb. 12, 2012.

39 *The court's core ruling:* P. Lattman, "9 Graduates Lose Case Against New York Law School," *New York Times,* Mar. 22, 2012.

39 *"There is no question that this dearth":* Alexandra Gomez-Jimenez, et al. v. New York Law School, Case No. 652226/11, Mar. 21, 2012, Decision and Order, 32–33, available at http://

dealbook.nytimes.com/2012/03/22/9-graduates-lose-case-against-new-york-law-school (accessed June 4, 2012).

40   *"Those schools would probably go out of business": Chicago Tonight*, WTTW, Feb. 7, 2012, http://chicagotonight.wttw.com/comment/4290 (accessed May 31, 2012).

41   *$75,700 (public) versus $125,000 (private):* D. Weiss, "Average Debt of Private Law School Grads Is $125K; It's Highest at These Five Schools," *ABA Journal,* Mar. 28, 2012.

41   *Recently it opened a new campus:* A. Wittrock, "Cooley Law School Expands into Florida, Welcomes First Class of Students," *M Live,* May 7, 2012, www.mlive.com/lansing-news/index.ssf/2012/05/cooley_law_school_expands_into.html (accessed June 5, 2012).

41   *"more than enough private law schools":* M. Leichter, "A Tale of Two (California) Law Schools," *Am Law Daily,* Sept. 7, 2012.

CHAPTER 3: INADEQUATE RESPONSES

43   *"deliberately changed their grading systems":* C. Rampell, "In Law Schools, Grades Go Up, Just Like That," *New York Times,* June 22, 2010.

44   *Evidently the goal was to make:* Ibid.

45   *In addition, ABA accreditation standards:* See B. Tamanaha, *Failing Law Schools* (Chicago: University of Chicago Press, 2012), 28–36.

45   *The six hundred . . . publish ten thousand articles a year:* D. Segal, "What They Don't Teach Law Students: Lawyering," *New York Times,* Nov. 19, 2011.

45   *Between 2001 and 2011 . . . two thousand opinions:* B. Newton, "Law Review Scholarship in the Eyes of the Twenty-First Century Supreme Court Justices: An Empirical Analysis," *Drexel Law Review* 4 (2012): 399.

45   *The problem is that 40 percent:* K. Sloan, "Legal Scholarship Carries a High Price Tag," *National Law Journal,* Apr. 20, 2011; T. Smith, "A Voice Crying in the Wilderness, and Then Just Crying," *The Right Coast,* July 13, 2005, http://therightcoast.blogspot.com/2005/07/voice-crying-in-wilderness-and-then.html (accessed May 20, 2012).

45   *"There is evidence that law review articles":* Segal, "What They Don't Teach Law Students."

45   *"Pick up a copy of any law review":* D. Weiss, "Law Prof Responds After Chief Justice Roberts Disses Legal Scholarship," *ABA Journal,* July 7, 2011.

46   *Adjuncts provide another benefit:* Segal, "What They Don't Teach Law Students."

46   *In fact, the trend toward interdisciplinary education:* Northwestern University School of Law, "Faculty Research & Achievement," www.law.northwestern.edu/faculty (accessed July 7, 2012).

46   *"can be fatal, because the academy":* Segal, "What They Don't Teach Law Students."

46   *When she left government in 1999:* C. Parsons, "U. of C. Law Faculty Didn't Back Kagan," *Chicago Tribune,* May 23, 2010.

47   *"Her papers were well-done, but":* Ibid.

47   *A prolific writer and commentator:* Richard A. Epstein, curriculum vitae, University of Chicago Law School, www.law.uchicago.edu/node/518/cv (accessed June 19, 2012).

47   *For example, Stanford Law School:* "Stanford Law School Advances New Model for Legal Education," *SLS News,* Feb. 13, 2012, http://blogs.law.stanford.edu/newsfeed/2012/02/13/stanford-law-school-advances-new-model-for-legal-education (accessed May 20, 2012).

47   *"case-based simulations":* P. Lee, "Law Schools Get Practical," *Wall Street Journal,* July 11, 2011.

47   *As dean, Elena Kagan:* S. Turow, "Afterword," *One L* (New York: Penguin, 2010), 276–279.

47   *Indiana University Maurer School of Law:* Lee, "Law Schools Get Practical."

48   *"It could enhance the reputation":* Ibid.

48   *"There's no employer out there":* K. Sloan, "What Is Law School For, Anyway?" *National Law Journal,* Jan. 16, 2012.

49   *Because almost all states require graduation:* Tamanaha, *Failing Law Schools,* 20–27.

49   *"Almost everyone who participated":* Northwestern University School of Law, "Plan 2008: Preparing Great Leaders for the Changing World," 2008, 17, www.law.northwestern.edu/difference/documents/NorthwesternLawPlan2008.pdf (accessed Sept. 2, 2012).

50   *"the opportunity to participate":* Northwestern University School of Law website, www.law.northwestern.edu/academics/ajd (accessed May 20, 2012).

50   *In his keynote address:* D. Van Zandt, "The Evolution of J.D. Programs—Is *Non*-Traditional Becoming *More* Traditional? Keynote Address Transcript," *Southwestern Law Review* 38, no. 4 (Spring 2009).

50   *In 2011, Northwestern sent 149 new graduates:* L. Jones, "Hiring More Deeply into Top Schools," *National Law Journal*, Apr. 14, 2008; K. Sloan, "It's Tough Out There," *National Law Journal*, Feb. 27, 2012.

50   *But the school's total number:* Law School Admission Council, "Official Guide to ABA -Approved Law Schools, 2012," https://officialguide.lsac.org/release/OfficialGuide_Default .aspx, and archives 2006–2011, www.lsac.org/LSACResources/Publications/official-guide -archives.asp (accessed June 29, 2012).

50   *In October 2015, Van Zandt's successor as dean:* "Northwestern Law Suspends Accelerated JD Program," News Release, Oct. 2, 2015, http://www.law.northwestern.edu/about/news /newsdisplay.cfm?ID=761.

51   *According to a recent survey, almost 40 percent:* K. Sloan, "Survey Suggests Prospective Law Students Still Have Stars in Their Eyes," *National Law Journal*, June 19, 2012.

52   *A relatively new company, JD Match:* JD Match, www.jdmatch.com (accessed May 20, 2012).

52   *Created in 1971 . . . NALP's original aim:* National Association for Law Placement, "Full Text of NALP Principles and Standards," www.nalp.org/fulltextofnalpprinciplesandstandards (accessed May 20, 2012).

53   *During the Great Recession, that happened:* E. Mystal, "Incoming Associates, Some of You Aren't Going to Be Working at Arent Fox," *Above the Law*, Sept. 24, 2009, http:// abovethelaw.com/2009/09/incoming-associates-some-of-you-arent-going-to-be-working -at-arent-fox; H. Russ, "Wildman Harrold Rescinds Incoming Associate Offers," Oct. 2, 2009, http://ip.law360.com/articles/126046; K. Hill, "Nationwide Start Date Roundup: More Firms Join the List," *Above the* Law, Apr. 29, 2009, http://abovethelaw.com/ 2009/04/nationwide-start-date-round-up-more-firms-join-the-list; National Association for Law Placement, "Entry-Level Recruiting Volumes Plunge, Some Start Dates Deferred," press release, Mar. 2, 2010, www.nalp.org/2009perspectivesonfallrecruiting (accessed May 20, 2012).

53   *In fact . . . professor William Henderson is concerned:* W. Henderson and R. Zahorsky, "The Law School Bubble: How Long Will It Last if Law Grads Can't Pay Bills?" *ABA Journal*, Jan. 1, 2012.

53   *IBR plans allow graduates:* "Federal Student Aid, US Department of Education, https:// studentaid.ed.gov/sa/repay-loans/understand/plans/income-driven. Borrowers prior to July 1, 2014 have a twenty-five-year repayment period.

53   *Although the debt forgiveness option . . . there's evidence:* K. Weise, "Private Student Loans Are Becoming More Competitive," *Bloomberg Business Week*, May 23, 2012.

54   *But notwithstanding . . . reduce entering class size:* J. Palazzolo and C. Phipps, "Law Schools Apply the Brakes," *Wall Street Journal*, June 11, 2012.

Chapter 4: Attorney Dissatisfaction

57   *In 1986, Professor G. Andrew Benjamin found:* K. Sloan, "How to Learn the Law Without Losing Your Mind," *National Law Journal*, Sept. 17, 2012.

57   *Professors Lawrence Krieger and Ken Sheldon:* Ibid.

57   *Yet somehow, a recent and wide-ranging survey reported:* Law School Survey of Student Engagement, "Navigating Law School: Paths in Legal Education—2011 Annual Survey Results," http://lssse.iub.edu/pdf/2011/2011_LSSSE_Annual_Survey_Results.pdf (accessed Sept. 7, 2012).

57   *"negative inner work lives":* T. Amabile and S. Kramer, "Do Happy People Work Harder?" *New York Times*, Sept. 3, 2011.

58   *Gallup-Healthways estimates:* Ibid.

58   *Well-being also affects:* L. Landro, "The Simple Idea That Is Transforming Health Care," *Wall Street Journal*, Apr. 16, 2012.

58   *For example, a 2007 ABA survey:* S. Ward, "The Pulse of the Legal Profession," *ABA Journal*, Oct. 1, 2007.

59   *An example is Francis Wolfe Jr.:* C. Sadovi, "Gentleman Lawyer to Retire: Second Career Devoted to Aiding Defendants," *Chicago Tribune,* Oct. 20, 2006.

59   *"From the time I was in law school":* Ibid.

59   *A comprehensive longitudinal study:* NALP Foundation for Law Career Research and Education and the American Bar Foundation, *After the JD: First Results of a National Study of Legal Careers,* 2004, www.americanbarfoundation.org/uploads/cms/documents/ajd.pdf (accessed Sept. 6, 2012); NALP Foundation for Law Career Research and Education and the American Bar Foundation, *After the JD II,* 2009.

60   *In fact, lawyers from elite schools:* R. Dinovitzer and B. Garth, "Lawyer Satisfaction in the Process of Structuring Legal Careers," *Law and Society Review* 1, no. 1 (2007).

60   *"I make a difference":* C. Kilgannon, "The Terrier of Traffic Court," *New York Times,* Feb. 5, 2012.

60   *A recent Valentine's Day issue:* "Why I Love Being a Lawyer," *ABA Journal,* Feb. 2011.

61   *This oft-repeated statistic comes from:* W. Eaton, J. Anthony, W. Mandel, and R. Garrison, "Occupations and the Prevalence of Major Depressive Disorder," *Journal of Occupational Medicine,* Nov. 1990, 1079–1087.

62   *Even so, subsequent surveys seem to confirm:* See, e.g., G. Benjamin, E. Darling, and B. Sales, "The Prevalence of Depression, Alcohol Abuse, and Cocaine Abuse Among United States Lawyers," *Journal of Law and Psychiatry* 32 (1990): 233–246; L. Johnson, "Stress Management," *Utah State Bar Journal,* Jan./Feb. 2003; M. Dolan, "Miserable with the Legal Life," *Los Angeles Times,* June 27, 1995; N. McCarthy, "Pessimism for the Future: Given a Second Chance, Half of the State's Attorneys Would Not Become Lawyers," *California State Bar Journal,* Nov. 1994; M. McBrien, "Fax Poll: Unhappy Lawyers Cite Hard Work, Fee Rewards," *Michigan Lawyers Weekly,* Dec. 26, 1994; M. J. Sweeney, "The Devastation of Depression," www.alabar.org/alap/articles/devastation_of_depression.pdf (accessed May 20, 2012); E. Ward, "Do You Need a Friend?" North Carolina Lawyer Assistance Program, www.nclap.org/article.asp?articleid=46 (accessed May 20, 2012).

62   *The 2007 ABA survey mentioned above:* Ward, "The Pulse of the Legal Profession."

62   *Another recent ABA survey:* T. Latham, "The Depressed Lawyer," originally published in *Therapy Matters* on May 2, 2011, www.psychologytoday.com/blog/therapy-matters/2011 05/the-depressed-lawyer (accessed May 20, 2012).

63   *"biased toward the positive side":* J. Heinz et al., *Urban Lawyers: The New Social Structure of the Bar* (Chicago: University of Chicago Press, 2005), 266.

63   *A 1989 study reported:* J. Organ, "What Do We Know About the Satisfaction/Dissatisfaction of Lawyers? A Meta-Analysis of Research on Lawyer Satisfaction and Well-Being," *University of St. Thomas Law Journal* 8, no. 2 (2011).

63   *Fewer than half:* Ward, "The Pulse of the Legal Profession."

64   *Attorneys do, however, maintain:* T. Smith, "Job Satisfaction in the United States," NORC/University of Chicago, Apr. 17, 2007, 3, 5, http://www-news.uchicago.edu/releases/07/pdf/070417.jobs.pdf (accessed May 20, 2012).

64   *Proponents of this "lawyer personality" theory:* S. Daicoff, *Lawyer, Know Thyself: A Psychological Analysis of Personality Strengths and Weaknesses* (Washington, DC: American Psychological Association, 2004).

64   *This has led to the "comprehensive law movement":* S. Daicoff, *Comprehensive Law Practice: Law as a Healing Profession* (Durham, NC: Carolina Academic Press, 2011).

65   *"associates most likely to fit in":* J. Foster, L. Richard, L. Roherer, and M. Sirkin, "Understanding Lawyers: The Personality Traits of Successful Practitioners," Hildebrandt Baker Robbins, 2010, 6.

65   *Psychologist Martin E. P. Seligman:* M. Seligman, *Authentic Happiness—Using the New Positive Psychology to Realize Your Potential for Lasting Fulfillment* (New York: Free Press, 2002).

65   *"a trait that makes you good at your profession":* Ibid., 178.

65   *"low decision latitude":* Ibid., 179.

66   *"For better or for worse":* Ibid., 181–182.

CHAPTER 5: THE TRANSFORMATION OF BIG LAW FIRMS

68　*"The large corporate firm continues to exercise":* A. Kronman, *The Lost Lawyer: Failing Ideals of the Legal Profession* (Cambridge, MA: Harvard University Press, 1992), 273–274.

68　*But in 1993, Kronman lamented:* Ibid.

69　*Johnson joined the firm immediately:* "Elmer W. Johnson: 1932–2008," *Chicago Tribune*, Feb. 22, 2008.

69　*"My historical perspective indicates":* "Interview: The (Im)moral Corporation—a Conversation with Elmer Johnson," *Civic Arts Review* 7, no. 2 (Spring-Summer 1994).

69　*This is evident from surveys showing:* W. Henderson and D. Zaring, "Young Associates in Trouble," *Michigan Law Review* 105, no. 6 (Apr. 2007): 1097, 1103.

69　*By 2012, DLA Piper had:* DLA Piper website, www.dlapiper.com/global/about/facts (accessed May 20, 2012).

69　*Twenty-one other firms had:* "The National Law Journal's Annual Survey of the Nation's Largest Law Firms," *National Law Journal*, Mar. 26, 2012.

70　*Such behavior begins to explain:* "The Associates Survey," *American Lawyer*, Sept. 2011; A. Erfati, "Associate Survey: Want to Leave? Big Law's OK with That," *Wall Street Journal Law Blog*, Aug. 1, 2007, http://blogs.wsj.com/law/2007/08/01/amlaws-associate-survey-want-to -leave-big-laws-ok-with-that; E. Mystal, "2009 Associate Survey," *Above the Law*, July 31, 2009, http://abovethelaw.com/2009/07/2009-associate-survey (accessed June 29, 2012). As previously noted, in 2012 overall associate satisfaction experienced its first uptick in years, but why that occurred and whether it will endure are open questions.

71　*In 1975, the Court hastened:* Goldfarb v. Virginia State Bar, 421 U.S. 773 (1975).

71　*"Flom Takes Over":* K. Eisler, *Shark Tank: Greed, Politics, and the Collapse of Finley Kumble, One of America's Largest Law Firms* (New York: St. Martin's Press, 1990), 116.

72　*"Lawyers, seeing what their colleagues":* Ibid., 121.

72　*"Every year, firm managers could compare":* A. Frankel, "2006 Am Law 100 Firms Feel Growing Pains," *American Lawyer*, May 2006.

72　*And so while in 1986 the overall average:* "Catching Up with the Class of 1985," *American Lawyer*, May 2010; *American Lawyer*, May 2012.

73　*"in the top echelon of the profession":* A. Press, "Erase the Am Law 100?" *American Lawyer*, May 2012.

73　*"Information turned loose":* Ibid.

73　*"The idea was simple":* A. Sachdev, "Mayer Move a Legal Stunner," *Chicago Tribune*, Mar. 12, 2007.

73　*"No one is forcing them":* "How Law Firms Reacted to the First Am Law 100—Interview with Steve Brill," *American Lawyer*, Apr. 27, 2012.

74　*"an audience of chairmen":* V. O'Connell, "Law Firms' Profits Called Inflated," *Wall Street Journal*, Aug. 22, 2011.

74　*Many of those discrepancies:* A. Press, "Citi and the Am Law 100," *American Lawyer*, Oct. 2011.

74　*"the possibility for mischief":* Ibid.

75　*In April 2012, the* American Lawyer *publicly announced:* J. Triedman, "Dewey & LeBoeuf's 2010, 2011 Profits, Revenues Revised," *Am Law Daily*, Apr. 3, 2012.

75　*"which we assume is the case":* Ibid.

75　*"Larger firms almost always spend more":* W. Bower, "Mining the Surveys: Diseconomies of Scale?" Altman Weil, Inc., 2003, www.altmanweil.com/dir_docs/resource/f44c154c-d8c6 -468d-a862-41474fe25634_document.pdf (accessed May 24, 2012).

76　*Another consultant estimates that the optimal size:* E. Wesemann, "What Is the Optimum Size for a Law Firm?" Mar. 12, 2011, Legal Research Group LLC, http://edwesemann.com/ articles/profitability/2011/03/16/what-is-the-optimum-size-for-a-law-firm (accessed May 24, 2012).

76　*"Unlike many other industries":* "A Conversation with a Strategist—Harvard Law School," Fall 2006, www.law.harvard.edu/news/ettinger.php (accessed May 24, 2012).

76　*"The firm hoped to boost":* A. Sachdev, "Profits Trump Legal Custom," *Chicago Tribune*, May 29, 2008.

76   *"We have to take the steps":* N. Koppel, "Sonnenschein Cuts Lawyers and Staff," *Wall Street Journal*, May 29, 2008.

76   *Spoiler alert: American Lawyer,* May 2009, 148.

76   *By 2011, it had become larger: American Lawyer,* May 2012, 156.

77   *The higher the leverage:* In 2009, the *American Lawyer* redefined leverage as the ratio of all attorneys (minus equity partners) to equity partners. That had the effect of lowering the nominal leverage ratio for all firms, but the economic concept and its implications remain unchanged.

77   *Before the onset of the Great Recession: 2010 Client Advisory,* Hildebrandt Baker Robbins/Citi Private Bank, http://amlawdaily.typepad.com/files/2010_client_advisory.pdf (accessed May 21, 2012).

77   *Although many firms froze rates: 2012 Client Advisory,* Hildebrandt Baker Robbins/Citi Private Bank, https://peermonitor.thomsonreuters.com/ThomsonPeer/docs/2012_Client_Advisory.pdf (accessed May 21, 2012).

77   *In 2012, rates were moving up:* J. Smith, "Biggest Lawyers Grab Fee Bounty," *Wall Street Journal*, Apr. 16, 2012.

77   *The average base salary:* V. Li, "Under Pressure," *American Lawyer*, Sept. 2011.

77   *Meanwhile, those firms charge clients:* S. Randazzo, "When It Comes to Billing, Latest Report Shows the Rich Keep Getting Richer," *American Lawyer*, Apr. 16, 2012; "Legal Billing Rates Continue to Rise Through Recession and Recovery According to CEB and TyMetrix Legal Analytics' 2012 Real Rate Report," TyMetrix press release, Apr. 16, 2012, www.tymetrix.com/press-releases/136/showArticle (accessed July 10, 2012).

77   *(In 2011, actual average billable hours . . . were 2,037.):* Li, "Under Pressure."

77   *But things become even more lucrative:* D. Lat, "Cravath Enters Bonus Wars—and Beats S&C," *Above the Law,* Jan. 31, 2011, http://abovethelaw.com/2011/01/associate-bonus-watch-cravath-enters-the-bonus-wars-and-beats-the-sc-scale; Find Legal, www.infirmation.com/shared/search/payscale-compare.tcl?city=New+York (accessed May 21, 2012).

78   *Productivity is the "relative measure": Business Dictionary,* www.businessdictionary.com/definition/productivity.html (accessed May 21, 2012).

78   *Scientific research has repeatedly demonstrated:* S. Robinson, "Why We Have to Go Back to a 40-Hour Work Week to Keep Our Sanity," Alternet.org, Mar. 13, 2012, www.alternet.org/visions/154518/why_we_have_to_go_back_to_a_40-hour_work_week_to_keep_our_sanity?page=entire (accessed May 21, 2012).

78   *That's why . . . the US Department of Transportation relies:* US Department of Transportation, Federal Motor Carrier Safety Administration, "Hours of Service Regulations," www.fmcsa.dot.gov/rules-regulations/topics/hos/index.htm (accessed May 21, 2012).

79   *In 1958, an ABA pamphlet:* American Bar Association, Special Committee on the Economics of Law Practice, *The 1958 Lawyer and his 1938 Dollar* (St. Paul, MN, 1958).

79   *It recommended that lawyers strive:* N. Kuckes, "The Hours: The Short, Unhappy History of How Lawyers Bill Their Clients," *Legal Affairs,* Sept./Oct. 2002.

79   *Today, most large firms expressly:* "A Look at Associate Hours and at Law Firm Pro Bono Programs," *NALP Bulletin,* Apr. 2010.

79   *That's the range appearing most often: 2012 NALP Directory,* www.nalpdirectory.com (accessed Sept. 4, 2012).

79   *Yale Law School's brochure:* Yale Law School, "The Truth About the Billable Hour," www.law.yale.edu/documents/pdf/CDO_Public/cdo-billable_hour.pdf (accessed May 21, 2012).

79   *That's lawyer-speak for fraud:* S. Turow, "The Billable Hour Must Die," *ABA Journal,* Aug. 1, 2007.

79   *Webster Hubbell:* R. Zitrin and C. Langford, *The Moral Compass of the American Lawyer: Truth, Justice, Power, and Greed* (New York: Ballantine Books, 1999), 82.

80   *Another partner in a prominent Chicago firm:* Ibid.

80   *Still another lawyer was caught:* A. Jones, "The Perfect Crime?" *Wall Street Journal,* Aug. 30, 2006.

80   *"The high point of law firm productivity": 2010 Client Advisory,* Hildebrandt Baker Robbins/Citi Private Bank.

80   *"The negative growth in productivity":* Ibid.

81   *According to the NALP Foundation:* NALP Foundation, "Toward Effective Management of Associate Mobility," 2005, 16.

81   *For every ten associates added:* NALP Foundation, "Update on Associate Attrition," 2008, 12.

81   *As recently as January 2008:* A. Williams, "The Falling Down Professions," *New York Times,* Jan. 6, 2008.

81   *Milwaukee-based Quarles & Brady:* L. Belkin, "Who's Cuddly Now? Law Firms," *New York Times,* Jan. 24, 2008.

82   *"assuming satisfactory performance":* NALP *Directory of Legal Employers,* online version, www.nalpdirectory.com/employer_profile?FormID=984&QuestionTabID=39&Search CondJSON=%257B%2522SearchEmployerName%2522%253A%2522Quarles%20%2526% 20Brady%2522%257D (accessed Sept. 3, 2012).

82   *The special bonuses have shrunk, too:* S. Harper, "Bonus Time—And Another Unfortunate Comment Award," *Am Law Daily,* Dec. 2, 2011.

82   *In a survey of twenty-five hundred associates:* NALP Foundation, "Update on Associate Attrition," 2012, 28.

82   *A single metric tells the tale:* "Catching Up with the Class of 1985," *American Lawyer,* May 2010.

82   *For example, Chicago-based Kirkland & Ellis:* Ibid.; *American Lawyer,* May 2012.

82   *Compared to the forty-four firms:* W. Henderson, "An Empirical Study of Single-Tier Versus Two-Tier Partnerships in the Am Law 200," 84 *North Carolina Law Review* 84 (2006): 1691, 1695.

82   *During the decade from 1999 to 2009:* K. Donovan, "Big Firms' Revenues and Profits Rise in American Lawyer Survey," *New York Times,* Apr. 11, 2011.

83   *But as the number of non-equity partners grew:* A. Press and J. O'Connor, "Lessons of the Am Law 100," *American Lawyer,* May 2009.

83   *The creation of a large cadre:* E. Reeser and P. McKenna, "Crazy Like a Fox," *American Lawyer,* Feb. 2012.

83   *"take on non-billable leadership":* Ibid.

83   *"retain some whiz-bang lawyers":* Ibid.

84   *In their book* Freakonomics*:* S. Dubner and S. Levitt, *Freakonomics: A Rogue Economist Explores the Hidden Side of Everything* (New York: William Morrow, 2006).

84   *For example, in its 2012 article:* K. Sloan, "It's Tough Out There," *National Law Journal,* Feb. 27, 2012.

84   *In 2007, the top twenty law schools:* K. Sloan, "Elite Firms Seem to Have Lost Their Appetites," *National Law Journal,* Feb. 27, 2012.

84   *But recent data on associates at big firms:* "Associates Promoted to Partner," *National Law Journal,* Feb. 27, 2012.

84   *That sounds like a lot, except . . . those big firms:* L. Jones, "Largest Law Firms Hire from Elite Schools," *National Law Journal,* Jan. 10, 2007.

84   *For the following law schools:* "Associates Promoted to Partner."

86   *The good news for the survivors: American Lawyer,* May 2012, 96.

87   *"Profits-per-partner [is] the key metric":* A. Press, "Lessons of the Am Law 100," *American Lawyer,* May 2008, 131.

87   *"We have objectives":* A. Sachdev, "Mayer Brown Cuts Partners," *Chicago Tribune,* Mar. 3, 2007.

87   *With 268 lawyers and 76 equity partners:* "America's Highest Grossing Law Firms in 1995," *American Lawyer,* July/Aug. 1996.

87   *At that point, the firm was two years into the reign:* N. Raymond, "Former Leader of Cadwalader Quietly Retires," *New York Law Journal,* Sept. 21, 2010.

88   *"Are we going to have difficulty":* A. Lin, "Does the Future Belong to Cadwalader?" *New York Law Journal,* Feb. 6, 2007.

88   *"There's a big imbalance":* Ibid.

89   *Still, a firm spokesperson expressed confidence:* A. Lin, "Cadwalader Laying Off 35 in Wake of Slumping Markets," *New York Law Journal,* Jan. 11, 2008.

89   *A month later, a new chair:* Raymond, "Former Leader of Cadwalader Quietly Retires."

89   *Meanwhile, ninety-six lawyers received:* A. Sorkin, "Cadwalader to Lay Off 96 Lawyers," *New York Times,* July 31, 2008.

89   *A week earlier, seven:* "Cadwalader London Hit by Seven-Partner Walkout," *Lawyer,* Jan. 14, 2009.

89   *After resolving a threatened lawsuit:* M. Taylor, "Cadwalader U.K. to Cut Jobs After Walkout," *Lawyer,* Feb. 12, 2009.

89   *A few days after losing:* J. Berris, "Cadwalader Loses Another NY Partner," *Lawyer,* Jan. 22, 2009.

89   *Cadwalader survived: American Lawyer,* May 2011, 139, 152.

89   *Profits declined slightly: American Lawyer,* May 2012, 140.

89   *After January 2009, the firm received:* B. Baxter, "Tallying Up the TARP-Related Legal Fees Racked Up by Am Law Firms," *Am Law Daily,* Apr. 18, 2012.

89–90   *"There's no question we had to make":* Raymond, "Former Leader of Cadwalader Quietly Retires."

90   *But that facile conclusion masks . . . 464 in 2011: American Lawyer,* May 2012, 140.

90   *Cadwalader had 76 equity partners: American Lawyer,* May 2007, 200.

90   *Five years later . . . Cadwalader had 21: American Lawyer,* May 2012, 168.

90   *Cadwalader placed 102nd:* "Ranking Midlevel Satisfaction," *American Lawyer,* Sept. 2011.

90   *It dropped to 125th:* "The Best Places to Work," *American Lawyer,* Sept. 2012.

90   *"The call on law firms":* M. Levs, "Call to Action: Sara Lee's General Counsel: Making Diversity a Priority," *Diversity & the Bar,* Jan.-Feb. 2005, www.mcca.com/index.cfm?fuseaction=page.viewpage&pageid=803 (accessed Aug. 27, 2012) (comments from Aon's general counsel, Cameron Findlay).

90   *In 1963, 4 percent of law students:* American Bar Association, "Enrollment and Degrees Awarded," www.americanbar.org/content/dam/aba/migrated/legaled/statistics/charts/stats _6.authcheckdam.pdf; "Women in Law in the U.S.," *Catalyst,* Jan. 2012.

90–91   *On law school faculties, female representation:* N. Hines, "Ten Major Changes in Legal Education over the Past Twenty-Five Years," *AALS Newsletter,* Aug. 2005; AALS Statistical Report on Faculty, 2008–2009, www.aals.org/statistics/2009dlt/gender.html (accessed June 27, 2012).

91   *Minorities constituted 8 percent:* Hines, "Ten Major Changes."

91   *In 1952 . . . Sandra Day O'Connor graduated:* S. Ehrlich Martin and N. Jurik, *Doing Justice, Doing Gender* (Beverly Hills, CA: Sage, 2007), 110.

91   *Today women remain overrepresented:* Ibid., 118–119.

91   *More women than men are also solo practitioners:* Ibid., 121.

91   *But in most large firms, the percentage:* V. Chen, "At Big Firms, Equity Gender Gap Continues," *Am Law Daily,* July 23, 2012.

91   *Likewise, minorities have been less likely:* E. Chambliss, "Miles to Go: Progress of Minorities in the Legal Profession," summary of 2004 report, www.law.harvard.edu/programs/plp /pdf/Projects_MilesToGo.pdf (accessed June 27, 2012).

91   *They are grossly underrepresented:* Ibid.

91   *Less than 5 percent of equity partners:* J. Leipold and J. Collins, "The Demographics of Equity," *NALP Bulletin,* Nov. 2011.

91   *For example, Yale Law Women (YLW) now identifies:* "2012 Top Ten Family Friendly Firms" Yale Law Women, www.law.yale.edu/stuorgs/topten.htm (accessed June 27, 2012).

92   *"backpedaled," as executive director James Leipold put it:* V. Chen, "What Women Want: Law Firm Partnership Details," *American Lawyer,* Feb. 24, 2010.

92   *A prominent group . . . wrote a public letter:* L. Jones, "Legal Heavyweights Lean on NALP to Track Nonequity Partners," *National Law Journal,* Apr. 8, 2010.

93   *As already noted, the number of non-equity partners: American Lawyer,* May 2009, 186.

93   *In 2009 and 2010, the number: American Lawyer,* May 2011, 79; "Editor's Note," *National Law Journal,* Mar. 26, 2012; *American Lawyer,* May 2012, 96.

93   *Using responses to its annual diversity survey, the publication:* V. Chen, "Looking into the Equity Box: Women and Partnership Status," *American Lawyer,* Sept. 2010.

93   *Eventually NALP asked their member law firms:* Leipold and Collins, "The Demographics of Equity."

93   *A 2012 survey:* Chen, "At Big Firms, Equity Gender Gap Continues."

93   *Prior to the economic downturn . . . a few law firms began:* E. Rosen, "Finding a Way Back to the Law," *New York Times,* May 26, 2006.

94   *"The goal," said a female partner:* Ibid.

94   *"Back to Business Law project has been sunset":* American Bar Association, Business Law Section, http://apps.americanbar.org/dch/committee.cfm?com=CL999500 (accessed June 27, 2012).

95   *All of the women partners were white: 2012 NALP Directory,* www.nalpdirectory.com/employer_profile?FormID=699&QuestionTabID=34&SearchCondJSON=%7B%22Search OrgTypeID%22%3A%223%22%2C%22SearchEmployerName%22%3A%22Cadwalader%22%7D (accessed Sept. 3, 2012).

95   *"We believe that diversity":* "Microsoft Adopts 'Pay for Performance' to Enhance Legal Diversity," Microsoft News Center, July 21, 2008, https://www.microsoft.com/en-us/news/features/2008/jul08/07-21lcadiversity.aspx (accessed Aug. 27, 2012).

95–96   *"I didn't want a long detailed document":* Levs, "Call to Action."

96   *"As a global corporation, we benefit":* Ibid. (comments from Arnold Pinkston, then general counsel of Eli Lilly and Co.).

96   *"To position ourselves to receive":* Ibid. (comments from Gary F. Kennedy, then senior vice president and general counsel of American Airlines, Inc.).

96   *"We want our workforce to reflect":* Ibid. (comments from Brian M. Nurse, then senior legal counsel for PepsiCo Inc.).

97   *In 2012, Brill's successor, Aric Press, argued:* A. Press, "Erase the Am Law 100?" *American Lawyer,* May 2012, 186.

CHAPTER 6: SURGING INCOME INEQUALITY

99   *"first as tragedy, then as farce":* K. Marx, "The Eighteenth Brumaire of Louis Bonaparte," *Die Revolution* 1 (1852).

100   *In many firms today, that internal:* P. Pasternak, "Partner Compensation: The Downturn's New Touchy Subject," *Recorder,* Oct. 4, 2010.

100   *So far, rich lawyers . . . between 1979 and 2005:* J. Bakija, A. Cole, and B. Heim, "Jobs and Income Growth of Top Earners and the Causes of Changing Income Inequality: Evidence from U.S. Tax Return Data," Apr. 2012, http://web.williams.edu/Economics/wp/Bakija ColeHeimJobsIncomeGrowthTopEarners.pdf (accessed May 21, 2012).

100   *In 1986, the Am Law 100 partner average:* M. Goldhaber, "The Long Run," *American Lawyer,* Apr. 27, 2012.

100   *By one estimate, the top one-tenth of 1 percent:* E. Porter, "Wall Street Protesters Hit the Bull's Eye," *New York Times,* Oct. 29, 2011.

100   *Nobel laureate Joseph Stiglitz and . . . Jeffrey Winters:* J. Stiglitz, "Of the 1%, by the 1%, and for the 1%," *Vanity Fair,* May 2011; J. Winters, "Oligarchy: History of How the Super-Rich Defend Their Wealth," WBEZ radio interview, Oct. 28, 2011, www.wbez.org/episode-segments/2011-10-28/oligarchy-history-how-super-rich-defend-their-wealth-93577 (accessed May 21, 2012).

101   *"Houses cost less in Pittsburgh":* N. Koppel and V. O'Connell, "Pay Gap Widens at Big Firms as Partners Chase Star Attorneys," *Wall Street Journal,* Feb. 8, 2011.

101   *"A small number of elite firms":* Ibid.

101   *He just used different cities:* I. Plagianos with J. Triedman, "Mind the Gap," *American Lawyer,* May 2012.

102   *The best firms . . . have sometimes turned:* P. Lattman and M. De La Merced, "Cravath to Hire Antitrust Chief," *New York Times,* July 6, 2011.

102   *"A majority of big law firms":* Koppel and O'Connell, "Pay Gap Widens."

102   *Sometimes the behavior is fear-driven:* V. Li, "This Time It's Personal," *American Lawyer,* Feb. 2012.

102   *A firm that thinks it can assess:* E. Reeser, "Pricing Lateral Hires," *Daily Journal,* June 18–22, 2012.

102   *For example, Frank Burch, co-chair of DLA Piper:* Li, "This Time It's Personal."

103   *"Over the last few years":* E. Reeser and P. McKenna, "Crazy Like a Fox," *American Lawyer,* Feb. 2012, 46.

103   *In fact, four . . . most-hires lists:* Li, "This Time It's Personal."

103   *In 2011, Jamie Wareham:* Koppel and O'Connell, "Pay Gap Widens."

103   *In 2015, Wareham moved:* B. Baxter, "Fried Frank Hires DLA Piper's $5 Million Man," *American Lawyer*, Apr. 1, 2015, www.americanlawyer.com/id=1202722364194/Fried -Frank-Hires-DLA-Pipers-5-Million-Man.

104   *After receiving his undergraduate degree from Yale, Kumble:* K. Eisler, *Shark Tank: Greed, Politics, and the Collapse of Finley Kumble, One of America's Largest Law Firms* (New York: St. Martin's Press, 1990), 15–19.

105   *They renamed the firm for themselves:* S. Brill, "Bye, Bye, Finley Kumble," *American Lawyer*, Sept. 1987, updated in *American Lawyer*, Sept. 1994.

105   *"In Finley, Kumble, money may not have been everything":* S. Kumble and K. LaHart, *Conduct Unbecoming: The Rise and Ruin of Finley Kumble* (New York: Carroll & Graf, 1990), 126.

105   *But egos have always abounded:* Eisler, *Shark Tank*, 47, 53.

105   *When name partner Robert Persky was convicted in 1973:* Ibid., 46, 48–49.

105   *"We come up against older guys":* Ibid., 84.

106   *"When you're the biggest":* Ibid., 65.

106   *Such moves became a template . . . had seventy attorneys:* Ibid., 89, x.

106   *Among other prominent hires:* Kumble and LaHart, *Conduct Unbecoming*, 124; Eisler, *Shark Tank*, x–xi.

106   *In what must have been . . . one of the firm's clients:* Brill, "Bye, Bye, Finley Kumble."

107   *The firm's Florida presence grew:* Kumble and LaHart, *Conduct Unbecoming*, 260.

107   *Geographically dispersed . . . partner meetings:* Ibid., 212.

107   *"The amount of business a lawyer brought in":* Ibid., 126.

107   *The internal spread:* Ibid., 183, 216, 225.

107   *"a total meritocracy":* Brill, "Bye, Bye, Finley Kumble."

107   *By 1986, the firm's cash flow:* Kumble and LaHart, *Conduct Unbecoming*, 249–250.

107   *Officially he was still a Finley Kumble partner:* Brill, "Bye, Bye, Finley Kumble."

107   *One former partner said:* J. Kowalski comment to S. Harper, "Who Remembers Finley Kumble?" *The Belly of the Beast*, Oct. 14, 2010, http://thebellyofthebeast.wordpress.com/2010 /10/14/who-remembers-finley-kumble (accessed Sept. 7, 2012).

108   *In early 1987, partners learned:* Eisler, *Shark Tank*, 203.

108   *Money had been the glue . . . began to leave:* E. Shipp, "Finley, Kumble, Major Law Firm, Facing Revamping or Dissolution," *New York Times*, Nov. 11, 1987.

108   *"What brought most people in was money":* Kumble and LaHart, *Conduct Unbecoming*, 264.

108   *At the same time that Steven Brill was writing:* Eisler, *Shark Tank*, 211–212.

108   *"The firm is making adjustments":* Ibid., 212.

108   *"Torn by dissension and debt":* Ibid., 216–217.

109   *Steven Kumble later explained:* Kumble and LaHart, *Conduct Unbecoming*, 246–250.

109   *"Looking back on it now":* Ibid., 275–276.

109   *On February 24, 1988, the banks forced:* Ibid., 275.

109   *"From the outside, it appears":* M. Oliver, "Massive Restructuring May Splinter Nation's 4th-Largest Law Firm," *Los Angeles Times*, Nov. 12, 1987.

110   *He described the internal compensation spread:* Kumble and LaHart, *Conduct Unbecoming*, 216.

110   *"Ultimately," he wrote, "that disparity":* Ibid., 225.

110   *Likewise, he admitted, "There was far too much emphasis":* Ibid., 224.

110   *"Over time . . . 'making the numbers' got out of hand":* Ibid., 216.

110   *"lacked the social fabric":* Ibid., 265.

110   *"Finley, Kumble fell apart because":* Ibid., 279.

110   *In the 2011 annual survey of law firm chairs:* S. Harper, "Fed to Death," *American Lawyer*, Dec. 2011.

111   *"Lawyers are not exactly the shining stars":* K. Rutman, "The Boom Abates: While Not Quite a Bust, 1991 Has Suggested That Smaller Might Be Better," *National Law Journal*, Sept. 30, 1991.

111   *"In most firms, current management has never operated":* Ibid.

111   *"The real problem of the 1980s":* C. Klein, "More Lawyers Than Ever in 250 Largest Law Firms: But Some of 5.3% Growth Fueled by Mergers, Contract Lawyers," *National Law Journal*, Sept. 30, 1996.

112   *In 2006, for the first time in its 118-year history:* N. Koppel, "Heller Ehrman and the Fable of Icarus," *Wall Street Journal,* Jan. 26, 2009; N. Koppel, "Recession Batters Law Firms, Triggering Layoffs, Closings," *Wall Street Journal,* Jan. 26, 2009.

112   *"There has been a philosophical adjustment":* D. Combs, "Stop-Loss," *American Lawyer,* May 2008.

113   *"Now that they have made money":* Koppel, "Recession Batters Law Firms."

113   *"various issues, including client and practice conflicts":* Ibid.

114   *"We worked extraordinarily hard":* Ibid.

114   *"There were tensions":* Ibid.

115   *In September 2010, it merged with Denton, Wilde, Sapte:* D. Weiss, "New Global Firm— Denton—Would Combine Sonnenschein and Denton Wilde," *ABA Journal,* May 26, 2010.

115   *The combined firm became a Swiss* verein: E. Reeser, "Swiss Verein—The Cassoulet Pot of Global Law Firm Structures," *San Francisco Daily Journal,* Aug. 18, 2011.

115   *In 2011, the firm's SNR side:* S. Lind, "SNR Denton Set to Hike UK Partner Profits After Cost-Cutting Measures," *Legal Week,* Mar. 30, 2012.

115   *"All of this expansion is driven":* Ibid.

115   *The reported combined average partner profits: American Lawyer,* May 2012, 156.

115   *For 2010 . . . 26 percent:* "The Efficiency Analysis," *American Lawyer,* May 2011, 153.

115   *SNR Denton's 2011 profit:* "Efficiency Equation," *American Lawyer,* May 2012, 173.

115   *Meanwhile, its ranking:* "Ranking Midlevel Satisfaction," *American Lawyer,* May 2012.

115   *(In 2012, it improved to 88th out of 129 firms):* "The Best Places to Work," *American Lawyer,* Sept. 2012, 72.

115   *"quantum leap that we never could have achieved":* A. Becker, "Hogan Lovells Merger Makes Firm One of Largest in U.S.," *Washington Post,* May 3, 2010.

115   *Hogan Lovells's reported average equity partner profits: American Lawyer,* May 2008, May 2009, May 2010, May 2011, May 2012.

115   *During 2009 . . . 37 percent:* "The Efficiency Equation," *American Lawyer,* May 2010, 169.

115   *For 2011, Hogan Lovells's profit margin:* "Efficiency Equation," *American Lawyer,* May 2012, 172.

115   *The combined firm's ranking:* "Ranking Midlevel Satisfaction," *American Lawyer,* May 2012; "The Best Places to Work," *American Lawyer,* Sept. 2012, 72.

116   *Boasting that clients would "benefit":* W. Reed and R. Shuftan, "Edwards Wildman Launches as an International Law Firm with 650 Lawyers and 14 Offices," Oct. 1, 2011, Edwards Wildman website, www.edwardswildman.com/newsstand/detail.aspx?news=2606 (accessed Sept. 3, 2012); "Edwards, Angell, Palmer & Dodge to Merge with Wildman Harrold," Aug. 15, 2011, www.edwardswildman.com/newsstand/detail.aspx?news=2473 (accessed July 11, 2012).

116   *The combined firm's leverage ratio: American Lawyer,* May 2012, 156.

117   *When Indianapolis-based Baker & Daniels:* B. Baxter, "Faegre & Benson, Baker & Daniels Say Their Merger Is Officially On," *Am Law Daily,* Oct. 12, 2011.

117   *"That can create very unhappy people":* A. Jones and N. Koppel, "Sonnenschein, Denton Wilde to Merge," *Wall Street Journal,* May 27, 2010.

117   *That created a single firm of 826 attorneys: American Lawyer,* May 2007, 175.

117–118 *In 2007, it added Seattle firm Preston, Gates & Ellis:* A. Jones, "Introducing . . . K&L Gates!" *Wall Street Journal Law Blog,* Dec. 15, 2006.

118   *In January 2008 it added Hughes & Luce:* D. Lat, "Law Firm Merger Mania: K&L Gates + Hughes & Luce," *Above the Law,* Dec. 17, 2007, http://abovethelaw.com/2007/12/law-firm -merger-mania-kl-gates-hughes-luce (accessed May 22, 2012).

118   *Six months later it picked up:* D. Weiss, "K&L Gates, Kennedy Covington Approve Merger," *ABA Journal,* June 24, 2008.

118   *In March 2009, it added:* M. Neil, "It's Official: K&L Gates and Bell Boyd OK Merger; Firm to Have Nearly 2K Lawyers," *ABA Journal,* Jan. 30, 2009.

118   *By the end of 2010, the firm's attorney head count: American Lawyer,* May 2011, 135.

118   *"Let me be clear about a couple of things":* E. Mystal, "The Two Faces of K&L Gates," *Above the Law,* Jan. 14, 2011, http://abovethelaw.com/2011/01/the-two-faces-of-kl-gates (accessed May 22, 2012).

119   *Before it merged with the Preston Gates firm: American Lawyer,* May 2008, 196, 219.

119   *By 2011, partner profits averaged $890,000:* American Lawyer, May 2012, 156, 172.

119   *Meanwhile, K&L Gates ranked 105th:* "Ranking Midlevel Satisfaction," *American Lawyer*, May 2012.

119   *The firm dropped to 115th:* "The Best Places to Work," *American Lawyer*, Sept. 2012, 72.

119   *(Some observers . . . aren't really law firms):* Kalis, "The Am Law 100: The Grand Illusion," *American Lawyer*, May 2011.

119   *DLA Piper made news in late 2011:* An earlier version of the author's present commentary on DLA Piper's hiring of Tony Angel first appeared in his blog post, "The Ultimate Lateral Hire," *The Belly of the Beast,* www.thebellyofthebeast.wordpress.com, reproduced at *Am Law Daily,* Jan. 27, 2012.

119   *The whirlwind courtship:* T. Huddleston, "DLA Piper Partners Appoint Tony Angel," *Am Law Daily,* Nov. 7, 2011.

120   *"Tony will work with the senior leadership":* "DLA Piper Appoints Tony Angel as Global Co-Chairman," Nov. 7, 2011, DLA Piper website, www.dlapiper.com/dla-piper-appoints-tony-angel-as-global-co-chairman-11-07-2011 (accessed May 22, 2012).

120   *"It's hard to get a guy that talented":* V. Li, "DLA Poised to Hire Tony Angel as Global Co-Chairman," *Am Law Daily,* Oct. 27, 2011.

120   *By the time he left, it had a global presence:* Huddleston, "DLA Piper Partners Appoint Tony Angel."

120   *Although DLA Piper's 2010 average partner profits:* "The Global 100," *American Lawyer,* Oct. 2011.

120   *Presumably, one way would be:* "Measuring the Efficiency Factor," *American Lawyer,* May 2008, 219; "Efficiency Equation," *American Lawyer,* May 2012, 172.

120   *Conversely, by 2010 Linklaters's average profits:* American Lawyer, Oct. 2011, 166.

121   *"brave move" that "might very well pay off":* A. Rubenstein, "DLA Hire May Signal Law Firms' Shift to Outside Managers," *Law 360,* Oct. 27, 2011, www.law360.com/bankruptcy/articles/280694 (accessed May 22, 2012).

121   *In the* American Lawyer's *2011 Midlevel Associate Satisfaction Survey:* "Ranking Midlevel Satisfaction," *American Lawyer,* Sept. 2011.

121   *To its credit, DLA Piper improved:* "The Best Places to Work," *American Lawyer,* Sept. 2012, 71–72.

CHAPTER 7: CONTINUING DESTABILIZATION

123   *And so it was that the average number:* "Number of Associate Hours Worked Declines," *NALP Bulletin,* Feb. 2011.

124   *Throughout the darkest days . . . average partner profits:* A. Press and J. O'Connor, "Lessons of the Am Law 100," *American Lawyer,* May 2009, 107.

124   *The effort to preserve equity partner wealth:* M. Neil, "Bloody Thursday: 6 Major Law Firms Ax Attorneys," *ABA Journal,* Feb. 12, 2009.

125   *A day after its cuts, DLA Piper announced:* J. Jeffrey, "Brutal Week May Not Be the End of Law Firm Layoffs," *Legal Times,* Feb. 17, 2009.

125   *A year later, that average:* American Lawyer, May 2010, 154.

125   *It dropped to $1.135 million:* American Lawyer, May 2011, 140; *American Lawyer,* May 2012, 156.

125   *"Wilson Sonsini blames downturn":* Lawyer, Jan. 26, 2009.

125   *"MoFo [Morrison & Foerster] cuts 201 jobs":* Lawyer, Jan. 28, 2009.

125   *"McDermott lays off 149":* Lawyer, Feb. 3, 2009.

126   *"There will be no layoffs":* K. Hill, "What's Up at Latham? (Morale, Thanks to a No-Layoffs Promise)," Mar. 26, 2008, *Above the Law,* http://abovethelaw.com/2008/03/whats-up-at-latham-watkinsmorale-thanks-to-a-no-layoffs-promise (accessed May 23, 2012).

126   *A year later . . .* American Lawyer *reported:* R. Lloyd, "The AM LAW 100: Latham Profits Drop 21 Percent, Off 470K per Partner," *Am Law Daily,* Feb. 9, 2009.

126   *Three weeks after that:* M. Neil, "February Free Fall: Major Law Firms Lay Off Another 2,000 Plus Attorneys and Staff," *ABA Journal,* Feb. 26, 2009.

126   *Latham wasn't alone:* Z. Lowe, "Breaking: Orrick Lays Off 100 Associates, 200 Staff," *Am Law Daily,* Mar. 3, 2009; E. Mystal, "Profits per Partner Down at O'Melveny," *Above the Law,*

Feb. 13, 2009, http://abovethelaw.com/2009/02/profits-per-partner-down-at-omelveny; J. Rosenblatt, "Sidley Austin Cuts 89 Associates, 140 Staff in US," *Bloomberg News*, Mar. 12, 2009; E. Mystal, "Nationwide Layoff Watch: Sidley Austin Cuts 229 at Least," *Above the Law*, Mar. 12, 2009, http://abovethelaw.com/2009/03/nationwide-layoff-watch-sidley-austin-cuts-229-at-least (accessed May 23, 2012); *American Lawyer*, May 2009.

126   *Hughes, Hubbard & Reed . . . finish in 2010:* V. Li, "Under Pressure," *American Lawyer*, Sept. 2011; A. Kolz, "Turning Pro," *American Lawyer*, July-Aug. 2010; D. Combs, "Upheaval in the Ranks," *American Lawyer*, July-Aug. 2011; S. Beck, "Familiar Faces," *American Lawyer*, July-Aug. 2012.

127   *Two of those firms, O'Melveny and Orrick: American Lawyer*, Sept. 2010; *American Lawyer*, Sept. 2011.

127   *The class of 2010 fared even worse—68 percent:* "Class of 2010 Graduates Faced Worst Job Market Since Mid-1990s: Longstanding Employment Patterns Interrupted," NALP press release, June 1, 2011, www.nalp.org/uploads/PressReleases/11SelectedFindings.pdf (accessed May 23, 2012).

127   *For the class of 2011, the drop continued:* J. Palazzolo, "Law Grads Face Brutal Job Market," *Wall Street Journal*, June 24, 2012.

128   *But at the end of 2011, the NLJ 250 employed:* "The NLJ 250," *National Law Journal*, Mar. 26, 2012.

128   *Formed by merger in 1998, Thelen, Reid & Priest:* "Bi-Coastal US Merger to Go Ahead," *Lawyer*, Apr. 14, 1998.

128   *Eight years later the Thelen firm:* P. Lattman, "LB Wedding Announcement: Thelen Reid & Brown Raysman," *Wall Street Journal Law Blog*, Oct. 30, 2006.

128   *Its 2007 leverage ratio exceeded 6: American Lawyer*, May 2008, 199 .

129   *Observers noted that "Thelen became bogged down":* D. Weiss, "Thelen's Former Chair: 'No Firm Has to Fail,'" *ABA Journal*, Oct. 29, 2008.

129   *Those efforts failed and partners voted for dissolution:* E. Mystal, "Thelen Officially Dissolves," *Above the Law*, Oct. 28, 2008, http://abovethelaw.com/2008/10/thelen-officially-dissolves (accessed May 23, 2012).

129   *"The decision to dissolve the firm":* Ibid.

129   *In contrast, a former Thelen chair blamed:* Weiss, "Thelen's Former Chair: 'No Firm Has to Fail.'"

129   *As recently as May 19, 2008:* "Visionaries," *Legal Times*, May 19, 2008.

129   *By February 1, 2011, he was hoping:* E. Shanahan, "Howrey Partners Pressed to Act on Winston Offers," *Am Law Daily*, Feb. 3, 2011.

129   *When Ruyak became chair in January 2000: American Lawyer*, July 2000, 109.

129   *"To achieve that vision, Ruyak knew":* "Visionaries."

130   *Howrey's 2008 profits were $1.3 million: American Lawyer*, May 2007, 189; *American Lawyer*, May 2008, 199; *American Lawyer*, May 2009, 173.

130   *In November 2008 Ruyak brought in:* J. Triedman, "The Fall of Howrey," *American Lawyer*, June 2011, 53.

130   *As Ruyak continued . . . partners were surprised:* Ibid.

130   *In early spring, the firm began to push people out:* Ibid.

130   *Still, in November 2010, Ruyak . . . assured partners:* Ibid., 54.

130   *Meanwhile, Ruyak and Boland were secretly working:* Ibid.

130–131 *Asked about the wave . . . Boland insisted:* E. Shanahan, "Howrey Vice-Chairman Heads to Dewey & LeBoeuf," *Am Law Daily*, Jan. 18, 2011.

131   *Winston wanted only certain Howrey groups:* J. Triedman, "The Fall of Howrey," *American Lawyer*, June 2011, 55.

131   *In subsequent interviews, Ruyak's partial explanation:* "Behind the Numbers," *American Lawyer*, May 2010, 101.

131   *"Partners at major law firms":* V. O'Connell, "What Else Happened to Howrey? Here's More from CEO Ruyak," *Wall Street Journal*, March 10, 2011.

132   *Law firm management consultant Peter Zeughauser:* Triedman, "The Fall of Howrey," 51–52, 54.

132   *The firm was "getting back to its strengths":* J. Jeffrey, "Examining Bunsow's Departure from Howrey," *National Law Journal,* Jan. 19, 2011.

132   *What happened at Howrey "was in no small part":* Triedman, "The Fall of Howrey."

CHAPTER 8: DEWEY & LeBOEUF: A CASE STUDY

134   *Only five years earlier, the profession had experienced:* P. Lattman, "Introducing . . . Dewey & LeBoeuf," *Wall Street Journal Law Blog,* Aug. 27, 2007.

134   *At the time of the October 2007 merger: American Lawyer,* May 2008, 195.

134   *LeBoeuf, Lamb, Greene & MacRae was formed:* Ibid.

135   *But as the negotiations proceeded:* N. Koppel, "Dewey, Orrick Merger Is Off," *Wall Street Journal,* Jan. 4, 2007.

135   *Meanwhile, Steven H. Davis had become:* P. Lattman, "Assigning Blame in Dewey's Collapse," *New York Times,* May 13, 2012.

135   *reportedly promised LeBoeuf Lamb to pay:* Ibid.; J. Triedman, S. Randazzo, and B. Baxter, "House of Cards," *American Lawyer,* July-Aug. 2012.

135   *Those discussions began during a May 2007 breakfast:* Ibid.

135   *But Davis had previously consolidated power:* Lattman, "Assigning Blame."

135   *"If you voted against the transaction":* A. Longstreth and N. Raymond, "The Dewey Chroniclers: The Rise and Fall of a Legal Titan," *Thomson Reuters News and Insight,* May 11, 2012.

135   *On September 28, he assembled:* Triedman, Randazzo, and Baxter, "House of Cards."

135   *According to Martin Bienenstock:* J. Smith and A. Jones, "Behind the Scenes as Dewey Tries to Save What Remains," *Wall Street Journal,* May 13, 2012.

136   *Bienenstock reportedly got a long-term:* J. Freedman, "Incoming Dewey Chiefs Agree Profit Caps as Firm Renegotiates Guarantees," *Lawyer,* Apr. 2, 2012.

136   *Instead of a 25 percent increase:* Lattman, "Assigning Blame."

136   *"The firm dealt with not being able":* P. Lattman, "Dewey's Bienenstock Discusses Law Firm's Demise," *New York Times,* May 14, 2012.

136   *By early 2009 . . . the compensation:* J. Triedman, "Dewey & LeBoeuf Cuts Compensation of 66 Partners," *American Lawyer,* Mar. 13, 2009.

136   *Davis also thinned the ranks:* "Dewey & LeBoeuf Private Placement Memorandum," 2010, 31, www.scribd.com/doc/93143761/Dewey-Secured-Note (accessed May 25, 2012).

136   *Dewey pursued a "barbell" approach:* Lattman, "Dewey's Bienenstock Discusses Law Firm's Demise."

136   *Some partners were making $300,000:* J. Smith, A. Jones, and S. Eder, "Woes at Law Firm Deepen," *Wall Street Journal,* Apr. 28, 2012.

136   *In April 2010, the firm issued:* C. Kolker, "Dewey & LeBoeuf Issues Bonds to Refinance Debt, as Law Firms Seek Capital," *Bloomberg News,* Apr. 16, 2010.

136   *"to refinance existing debt":* "Dewey & LeBoeuf Private Placement Memorandum."

137   *For the next three years, the firm told the* American Lawyer *that: American Lawyer,* May 2009, 169; *American Lawyer,* May 2010, 153; *American Lawyer,* May 2011, 139.

137   *As Dewey & LeBoeuf won awards . . . the firm made:* D. Combs, "Upheaval in the Ranks," *American Lawyer,* July 2011, 53.

137   *It became one of the top-ten firms:* Triedman, Randazzo, and Baxter, "House of Cards."

137   *"Now, we're moving into a new part of the cycle":* V. Li, "This Time It's Personal," *American Lawyer,* Feb. 2012, 55.

137   *"You have to own this problem":* Longstreth and Raymond, "The Dewey Chronicles."

138   *Again Davis explained that Dewey couldn't pay:* Triedman, Randazzo, and Baxter, "House of Cards."

138   *Nevertheless, he said, the "press stories":* D. Lat, "Dewey Have Comment on Recent Developments? Yes—Firm is Cutting 5 to 6 Percent of Personnel," *Above the Law,* Mar. 2, 2012, http://abovethelaw.com/2012/03/dewey-have-comment-on-recent-developments-yes-firm-is-cutting-5-to-6-percent-of-personnel/2 (accessed May 25, 2012).

138   *While all of that was happening, senior partner Richard Shutran:* D. Lat, "Dewey Owe Too

Much to Certain Partners?" *Above the Law*, Mar. 7, 2012, http://abovethelaw.com/2012/03/dewey-owe-too-much-to-certain-partners (accessed May 26, 2012).

138 *Meanwhile, the firm was in the process of drawing $75 million:* C. Hunter and L. Jones, "Update—Dewey & LeBoeuf Lender Deadline Draws Near—Course," Reuters, Apr. 24, 2012.

138 *The hemorrhaging of talent continued:* P. Lattman, "Twelve More Partners Leave Dewey Law Firm," *New York Times*, Mar. 18, 2012; J. Smith and A. Jones, "More Partners Leave Dewey & LeBoeuf," *Wall Street Journal Law Blog*, Mar. 23, 2012; J. Smith, "Another Dewey & LeBoeuf Partner Exits; Houston Managing Partner Heads for Litigation Boutique," *Wall Street Journal Law Blog*, Mar. 24, 2012.

138 *Davis sought to assuage his troops:* Lattman, "Twelve More Partners Leave Dewey."

138 *"Our first debt payment is in April 2013":* J. Smith and A. Jones, "Dewey & LeBoeuf Loses Partners," *The Wall Street Journal*, March 16, 2012, http://online.wsj.com/article/SB10001424052702303863404577285141452321850.html

139 *In late March, Dewey hired . . . Michael S. Sitrick:* L. Burton, "Dewey Hires Paris Hilton's PR Man to Fight Negative Press," *Lawyer*, Mar. 23, 2012.

139 *Shortly thereafter,* Fortune *magazine published:* D. McDonald, "Dewey & LeBoeuf: Partner Exodus Is No Big Deal," *Fortune*, Mar. 22, 2012.

139 *"The Wizard of Spin":* Michael S. Sitrick website, http://sitrick.com/about/michal-s-sitrick (accessed May 25, 2012).

139 *"If the direction we're taking the firm in":* McDonald, "Dewey & LeBoeuf: Partner Exodus Is No Big Deal."

139 *Less than a week later, Davis lost his chairship:* P. Lattman, "Dewey Overhauls Leadership amid Financial Difficulties," *New York Times*, Mar. 27, 2012.

139 *To allay concerns over the continuing departures:* L. Jones, "A Few Key Players May Determine Dewey's Fate," *Thomson Reuters News & Insight*, Apr. 11, 2012.

140 *the departures would "not have a negative impact on the firm":* S. Randazzo, "As Six More Partners Depart, Dewey Insists It's Getting Smaller by Design," *Am Law Daily*, Apr. 4, 2012.

140 *The furor intensified:* J. Triedman, "Dewey & LeBoeuf's 2010, 2011 Profits, Revenues Revised," *Am Law Daily*, Apr. 3, 2012.

140 *Dewey's general counsel responded:* Ibid.

140 *"They're just not comparable numbers":* J. Smith and A. Jones, "Dewey Partners Get Pep Talk," *Wall Street Journal*, Mar. 21, 2012.

140 *One prominent Dewey & LeBoeuf partner, John Altorelli:* S. Randazzo, "Dewey Defector Speaks, Opens Up About Partner Pay, Firm Leadership, and What May Come Next," *Am Law Daily*, Apr. 6, 2012.

141 *"Updated allocations provide a more equitable basis":* D. Lat, "Dewey Know How to Do the Taxes?" *Above the Law*, Apr. 17, 2012, http://abovethelaw.com/2012/04/dewey-know-how-to-do-the-taxes, accessed May 25, 2012.

142 *An April 21, 2012, article:* P. Lattman and M. J. de la Merced, "A Prominent Bankruptcy Lawyer Now Ministers to His Firm," *New York Times*, Apr. 21, 2012.

142 *The internal top-to-bottom partner income gap:* P. Lattman, "Assigning Blame in Dewey's Collapse," *New York Times*, May 13, 2012.

142 *But as Dewey unraveled, Bienenstock:* Freedman, "Incoming Dewey Chiefs Agree Profit Caps as Firm Renegotiates Guarantees."

142 *The* Times *also quoted Dewey's wizard of spin:* Lattman and de la Merced, "A Prominent Bankruptcy Lawyer Now Ministers to His Firm."

143 *Things got worse with reports:* L. Sandler, S. Pearson, and T. Kary, "Dewey Said to Be Subject of Probe as Deadline Nears," *Bloomberg News*, Apr. 27, 2012.

143 *"a group of Dewey partners presented evidence":* P. Lattman, "New York Prosecutors Examining Former Dewey Chairman," *New York Times*, Apr. 27, 2012.

143 *Dewey's banks were now controlling the end game:* J. Smith, "Dewey & LeBoeuf Faces Debt Deadline," *Wall Street Journal*, Apr. 23, 2012.

143 *At the same time, the federal Pension Benefit Guaranty Corporation:* J. Smith, "U.S. to Take Over Dewey Pensions," *Wall Street Journal*, May 11, 2012.

143 *There's no federal backstop for their pensions:* T. Bernard, "As Dewey Collapses, Partners and Retirees Face Big Financial Losses," *New York Times*, May 12, 2012.

143 *Then reports surfaced:* P. Lattman, "A Dewey Bond Offering Made No Mention of Partner Guarantees Omission of Partner Guarantees," *New York Times,* May 11, 2012.

144 *"no plans to file bankruptcy":* P. Lattman, "Dewey & LeBoeuf Said to Encourage Partners to Leave," *New York Times,* Apr. 30, 2012.

144 *The Greenberg Traurig firm had engaged in discussions:* J. Triedman, S. Randazzo, and B. Baxter, "House of Cards," *American Lawyer,* July 1, 2012.

144 *"All partners, including EC [Executive Committee]":* D. Lat, "Dewey Have a Shot of Surviving? Internal Memo Urges Partners to Seek 'Alternative Opportunities,'" *Above the Law,* May 2, 2012, http://abovethelaw.com/2012/05/dewey-have-any-shot-of-surviving-internal-memo -urges-partners-to-seek-alternative-opportunities/2 (accessed May 25, 2012).

144 *"The value for the stars has gone up":* P. Lattman, "Dewey's Jeffrey Kessler Heading to Winston & Strawn," *New York Times,* May 9, 2012.

145 *A day after Kessler and Shutran departed:* N. Raymond, "Top Bankruptcy Lawyer to Leave Dewey," Reuters, May 11, 2012.

145 *When Dewey & LeBoeuf's top management needed someone:* Smith and Jones, "Behind the Scenes."

145 *"The technique of using guarantees":* Ibid.

146 *"Here was a business with 2,000 people":* S. Kumble and K. LaHart, *Conduct Unbecoming: The Rise and Ruin of Finley Kumble* (New York: Carroll & Graf, 1990), 275–276.

146 *On Memorial Day, May 28, 2012:* P. Lattman, "Dewey & LeBoeuf Files for Bankruptcy," *New York Times,* May 29, 2012.

146 *It listed cash assets of $13 million:* J. Smith and A. Jones, "Storied Law Firm Dewey Files Chapter 11," *Wall Street Journal,* May 29, 2012.

146 *"Dewey's collapse has been attributed":* C. Winston and R. Crandall, "The Law Firm Business Model Is Dying," *Wall Street Journal,* May 29, 2012.

146 *In the July 2012 issue:* Triedman, Randazzo, and Baxter, "House of Cards."

147 *The firm persuaded his estate otherwise:* A. Jones and J. Smith, "Greenberg Traurig Explores Dewey & LeBoeuf Deal," *Wall Street Journal,* Apr. 15, 2012.

147 *For each Dewey partner, it was 36 percent:* "Defendants' Memorandum of Law in Opposition to Plaintiff's Motion for Summary Judgment," Aug. 17, 2012, *Citibank, N.A. v. Steven Otillar and Laura J. Otillar,* Case No. 12-cv-5092 (LLS).

147 *The bankruptcy trustee for Heller Ehrman chased:* J. Palank, "Debts of Defunct Law Firms Haunt Partners in Next Job," *Wall Street Journal,* Nov. 7, 2011.

147 *Coincidentally, on May 24, 2012: Development Specialists, Inc. v. Akin Gump et al.,* Case No. 11-CV-05994-CM (S.D.N.Y.), memorandum and order, May 24, 2012.

148 *The New York ruling followed a well-developed line: Jewel v. Boxer,* 156 Cal. App. 3d 171, 203 Cal. Rptr. 13 (Ct. App. 1984).

148 *On September 4, 2012, another judge in the same court: Geron v. Robinson & Cole,* Case No. 11 Civ. 8967 (S.D.N.Y.), memorandum and order, Sept. 4, 2012.

148 *"massive disruption":* C. Simmons, "Ripples from Dewey Collapse Swamp Lawyer Job Market," *New York Law Journal,* May 15, 2012.

148 *Likewise, new graduates who thought:* S. Randazzo, "Incoming Dewey Associates in Limbo as Firm Weighs Restructuring Options," *Am Law Daily,* Apr. 20, 2012.

148 *Second-year students who had accepted:* D. Lat and E. Mystal, "We Don't Have Any Summer Associates, Dewey?" *Above the Law,* Apr. 27, 2012, http://abovethelaw.com/2012/04/ we-dont-have-any-summer-associates-dewey-and-additional-info-about-a-possible-criminal -probe (accessed May 25, 2012).

149 *"I know these facts do not necessarily make":* D. Lat, "A Paralegal's Lament," *Above the Law,* Apr. 24, 2012, http://abovethelaw.com/2012/04/dewey-leboeuf-a-paralegals-lament (accessed May 25, 2012).

149 *As the Howrey firm was failing in January 2011, Dewey hired . . . Henry Bunsow: Henry Bunsow v. Steven H. Davis, Jeffrey L. Kessler, Joel Sanders, Stephen DiCarmine, James Woods, and Does 1 through 200 Inclusive,* San Francisco County Superior Court, Case No. CFC-12-521540 (complaint filed June 12, 2012).

149 *In the early 1990s, Bunsow had been a partner:* A. Frankel, "Is Dewey Partner Henry Bunsow the Angel of Death?" *Thomson Reuters News & Insight,* Apr. 26, 2012.

149 *After Dewey collapsed, Bunsow sued: Henry Bunsow v. Steven H. Davis et al.*

150 *"We worked extraordinarily hard":* N. Koppel, "Recession Batters Law Firms, Triggering Layoffs, Closings," *Wall Street Journal,* Jan. 26, 2009.

150 *"I don't have any regrets":* S. Randazzo, "Winston & Strawn Hires Ex-Howrey Chairman Ruyak," *Am Law Daily,* Sept. 12, 2011.

150 *Three months later he told another interviewer:* M. Kashino, "A Tale of Two Law Firms," *Washingtonian,* Dec. 2011.

150 *"to navigate the firm through challenging":* D. Lat, "Dewey Have More Partner Departures to Report? Sadly, Yes," *Above the Law,* Apr. 30, 2012.

150 *Morton A. Pierce served as Dewey Ballantine's chair:* A. Longstreth and N. Raymond, "The Dewey Chronicles: The Rise and Fall of a Legal Titan," Reuters, May 11, 2012.

150–151 *At age sixty-three, he reportedly negotiated a new one:* A. Jones and J. Smith, "As Dewey Turmoil Deepens, Top M&A Lawyer Defects," *Wall Street Journal,* May 3, 2012.

151 *"Morton Pierce is a Vice Chair":* Dewey & LeBoeuf website, www.deweyleboeuf.com/en/People/P/MortonAPierce (accessed Apr. 16, 2012).

151 *As the firm's road became rockier:* L. Jones, "A Few Key Players May Determine Dewey's Fate," *Thomson Reuters News & Insight,* Apr. 11, 2012.

151 *"I think the executive committee did the best job":* Jones and Smith, "As Dewey Turmoil Deepens."

151 *"Although looking at the Dewey & LeBoeuf merger":* Ibid.

151 *"I am sorry about what happened":* P. Lattman and K. Roose, "At Dewey & LeBoeuf, Notable Departures Continue," *New York Times,* May 3, 2012.

151 *In his interview, Pierce didn't mention:* P. Lattman, "Ex-Vice Chairman at Dewey Is Said to Claim That He Is Owed $61 Million," *New York Times,* May 7, 2012.

151 *He blamed Davis . . . the economy:* Smith and Jones, "Behind the Scenes."

CHAPTER 9: LAW SCHOOLS

156 *"failed academic who has done almost no scholarly work":* D. Weiss, "Law Prof Blogging on Law School Scam Is No Longer Anonymous," *ABA Journal,* Aug. 22, 2011.

157 *Another academic voice rose to condemn:* B. Tamanaha, *Failing Law Schools* (Chicago: University of Chicago Press, 2012), 186.

157 *Two professors at Emory University School of Law:* M. Cloud and G. Shepherd, "Law Deans in Jail," Social Science Research Network, http://papers.ssrn.com/sol3/papers.cfm?abstract_id=1990746 (accessed June 27, 2012).

157 *Predictably, another law professor at Emory:* F. Vandall, "Law Deans in Jail—Not," Social Science Research Network, http://papers.ssrn.com/sol3/papers.cfm?abstract_id=2029143 (accessed June 27, 2012).

157 *Another impractical suggestion:* J. McGinnis and R. Mangas, "'First Thing We Do, Let's Kill All the Law Schools,'" *Wall Street Journal,* Jan. 17, 2012.

158 *As previously noted . . . Hines would eliminate:* N. William Hines, "Ten Major Changes in Legal Education over the Past 25 Years," AALS, Aug. 2005, www.aals.org/services_newsletter_presAug05.php (accessed June 27, 2012).

158 *Professor Tamanaha suggests making private student loans:* Tamanaha, *Failing Law Schools,* 180.

158 *But because such loans account for:* W. Henderson and R. Zahorsky, "The Law School Bubble: How Long Will It Last if Law Grads Can't Pay Bills?" *ABA Journal,* Jan. 1, 2012.

159 *"In the coming years, a lot of people":* T. Lewin, "Burden of College Loans on Graduates Grows," *New York Times,* Apr. 11, 2011.

160 *Instead, he believes that the profession would evolve:* Tamanaha, *Failing Law Schools,* 172, 174.

161 *"an opportunity for a semester-long":* D. Van Zandt, "Client Ready Law Graduates," *Litigation* 36, no. 1 (Fall 2009): 20.

161 *For example, the Legal Services Corporation (LSC) endured:* T. Ruger, "More Legal Aid Lawyers on the Chopping Block, LSC Predicts," *National Law Journal,* Aug. 15, 2012.

162 *Even so, in 2007 CUNY School of Law:* "Community Legal Research Network," CUNY School of Law, www.law.cuny.edu/clinics/JusticeInitiatives/Community.html (accessed June 27, 2012).

162 *With the help of the Missouri Bar Association:* "Report of the Boston Bar Association Task Force on the Future of the Profession," Oct. 2011, www.bostonbar.org/docs/default-document-library/future-of-prof-task-force.pdf (accessed June 27, 2012).

162   *"The critics of legal education are right":* M. Smith, "Prestigious Law School Reduces Admissions, Marks New Trend," *USA Today,* May 1, 2012.

163   *George Washington University's former dean:* K. Sloan, "George Washington Joins Ranks of Law Schools That Are Scaling Back," *National Law Journal,* May 14, 2012.

163   *Albany Law School . . . 2011 incoming classes:* Ibid.

163   *Northwestern University Law School's new dean, Daniel Rodriguez:* L. Yue, "Northwestern, Loyola Law Schools Eye Cutting Class Sizes," *Crain's Chicago Business,* June 2, 2012.

163   *"I'm totally understanding of what":* Sloan, "George Washington Joins Ranks."

163   *The largest law school in the country:* K. Sloan, "Cooley's Florida Campus More Popular Than Forecast," *National Law Journal,* May 8, 2012.

163   *Cooley's associate dean, James Robb:* J. Palazzolo and C. Phipps, "Law Schools Apply the Brakes," *Wall Street Journal,* June 11, 2012.

163   *Nine months after graduation, only 38 percent:* "The Job Market for Law Graduates," *Wall Street Journal,* June 25, 2012.

163   *In 2009, two Vanderbilt University law students:* K. Sloan, "Law Students Push Schools for Better Employment Numbers," *National Law Journal,* Apr. 19, 2010.

164   *In April 2012, the Law School Transparency website:* "Law School Transparency," www .lawschooltransparency.com/clearinghouse (accessed June 27, 2012).

164   *Some already do, including:* "Recent Graduate Employment Data," University of Chicago Law School website, www.law.uchicago.edu/prospective/employmentdata (accessed Sept. 4, 2012).

164   *Stanford Law School reports:* "Facts & Statistics," Stanford Law School website, www.law .stanford.edu/careers/prospective/statistics/employment-salaries (accessed Sept. 4, 2012).

164   *But law schools could help reduce:* Some of the author's proposals in this section first appeared in "Great Expectations Meet Painful Realities (Part II)," *Circuit Rider—The Journal of the Seventh Circuit Bar Association,* Dec. 2011, 26–32.

165   *Finding instructors . . . service to society:* K. Rosman, "The Ultimate Power Hobby—Bankers, Lawyers, Executives Jockey to Teach a University Class, Play Professor," *Wall Street Journal,* Sept. 30, 2010.

166   *"Law professors now write novels":* W. Henderson and D. Zaring, "Young Associates in Trouble," *Michigan Law Review* 105, no. 6 (Apr. 2007): 1106.

CHAPTER 10: BIG LAW FIRMS

169–170   *"These developments are not the result of narcissism":* B. Burk and D. McGowan, "Schumpeter, Coase and the Future of the (Law) Firm," presented at the Georgetown Law Center for the Study of the Legal Profession conference, "Law Firm Evolution: Brave New World or Business as Usual?" Mar. 2010, www.law.georgetown.edu/LegalProfession/documents/Burk McGowan.pdf (accessed June 27, 2012).

170   *Even so, analogizing to economist Joseph Schumpeter's:* J. Schumpeter, *Capitalism, Socialism and Democracy* (New York: Harper & Row, 1942).

171   *Periodically over the past twenty years:* N. Koppel and A. Jones, "'Billable Hour' Under Attack," *Wall Street Journal,* Aug. 24, 2009.

171   *An October 2010 survey:* T. Huddleston, "Shifting Away from Hours . . . Eventually," *Am Law Daily,* Oct. 20, 2010.

171   *Another survey found:* "ALM Legal Intelligence Survey Finds Alternative Fee Arrangements Accounted for Just 16% of 2010 Revenues at Large Law Firms in U.S.," *Am Law Daily,* Apr. 4, 2011.

171   *"The results suggest that the billable hour":* D. Snow, "Survey Sees Slow Adoption of Alternative Fee Arrangements," *Law Technology News,* July 12, 2012.

173   *On a macroeconomic scale:* An earlier version of the author's suggested Working Culture Index first appeared in his blog post, "The Misery Index," *The Belly of the Beast,* www.thebellyofthe beast.wordpress.com, reproduced at *Am Law Daily,* Apr. 18, 2011.

174   *"No other company would treat":* J. Navarre, "How General Counsel Evaluates and Hires Law Firms," In-House Counsel Panel, ABA Section of Litigation Joint Committees' CLE Seminar, Jan. 19–21, 2012, www.americanbar.org/content/dam/aba/administrative/litigation/ 2012_jointcle_materials/2_4_HOW.authcheckdam.pdf (accessed Aug. 27, 2012).

174   *"We are looking at retention issues":* Ibid.

174   *And still another notes: Walmart Legal News* 1, no. 2 (Nov. 2009): 1, cited in C. Whelan & N. Ziv, "Privatizing Professionalism: Client Control of Lawyers' Ethics," University of Oxford Legal Research Papers Series, http://ssrn.com/abstract=1995819 (accessed June 27, 2012).

175   *Susan Hackett:* S. Hackett, "First Person: Worst Practices in Law Firm Diversity," *Law Practice Management*, Oct. 2003.

175   *"What's good for minority and women hires":* Ibid.

175   *"We look for our law firms":* Navarre, "How General Counsel Evaluates and Hires Law Firms."

175   *Many corporations already require:* Whelan and Ziv, "Privatizing Professionalism."

175   *A recent example came: Perdue v. Kenny A,* 559 U.S. __, 130 S. Ct. 1662 (2010).

177   *"The underlying principle is":* V. O'Connell, "Big Law's $1,000-Plus an Hour Club," *Wall Street Journal*, Feb. 23, 2011.

177   *"If you had cancer":* N. Schwartz and J. Creswell, "Who Knew Bankruptcy Paid So Well?" *New York Times*, May 1, 2010.

177   *That comment was as ironic:* J. Palank, "Law Firm Lehman's Tab May Reach $430 Million," *Wall Street Journal*, July 5, 2012.

177   *$400 million in compensation . . . billed $1,000 an hour:* "Application of Weil, Gotshal & Manges LLP, as Attorneys for the Debtors, for Final Allowance of Compensation for Professional Services Performed and Reimbursement of Actual and Necessary Expenses Incurred from September 15, 2008 Through March 5, 2012" (filed July 2, 2012) and "Tenth Interim Fee Application" (filed May 21, 2012), *In re Lehman Brothers Holdings Inc. et al.,* Chapter 11, Case No. 08-13555 (S.D.N.Y.).

177   *In 2011, Weil Gotshal's average:* S. Graham, "The Am Law 100, The Early Numbers: Weil's Profits Jump 8 Percent," *Am Law Daily*, Feb. 3, 2012.

178   *The top large firms charged more than $500:* S. Randazzo, "When It Comes to Billing, Latest Rate Report Shows the Rich Keep Getting Richer," *Am Law Daily*, Apr. 16, 2012.

178   *As previously noted, more than forty of Miller's partners:* Palank, "Law Firm Lehman's Tab."

178   *When the Justice Department's US trustee:* J. Palank, "The Daily Docket: Justice Department Presses Attorneys to Justify Their Fees," *Wall Street Journal*, June 4, 2012.

178–179 *Among the US trustee's concerns:* D. Ingram, "U.S. Bankruptcy Lawyers Resist Scrutiny over Fees," *Reuters*, June 4, 2012.

179   *"Disclosure of confidential rate information":* J. Palank, "$1,000/Hour Bankruptcies: Attorneys Justify Their Fees," *Wall Street Journal*, June 3, 2012.

179   *"Big law firms, which can throw":* Ingram, "U.S. Bankruptcy Lawyers Resist Scrutiny."

179   *At the time, Togut's firm had nineteen lawyers:* Togut, Segal & Segal, website, www.togutlawfirm.com/Attorneys (accessed June 10, 2012).

180   *Between 1985 and 2010, the average leverage ratio:* "Catching Up with the Class of 1985," *American Lawyer*, May 10, 2010.

180   *Notable examples:* "Efficiency Equation," *American Lawyer*, May 2012, 172; "Familiar Faces," *American Lawyer*, July/Aug. 2012, 55; "Turning Pro," *American Lawyer*, July/Aug. 2010, 61–65; "Upheaval in the Ranks," *American Lawyer*, July/Aug. 2011, 53.

181   *"A firm may look like a corporation":* C. Rampell, "For Law Students, Dewey & LeBoeuf Internships Evaporate," *New York Times*, May 2, 2012.

182   *In 1962, 11 percent:* A. Liptak, "U.S. Suits Multiply, But Fewer Ever Get to Trial, Study Says," *New York Times*, Dec. 14, 2003.

182   *Occasionally there are local aberrations:* J. Rooney, "Local Federal Court Sees Spike in Number of Jury Trials," *Chicago Law Bulletin*, Apr. 28, 2012.

182   *But the general trend has been downward:* See, e.g., J. Anderson, "Where Have You Gone, Spot Mozingo? A Federal Judge's Lament over the Demise of the Federal Jury Trial," *Federal Courts Law Review* 4, no. 1 (2010); "Report of the Special Committee to Study the Decline in Jury Trials," Florida Bar Association, Dec. 2011, www.floridabar.org/TFB/TFB Resources.nsf/Attachments/2CC9BF48C4496442852579950050E988/$FILE/final%20 report%20jury%20special.pdf?OpenElement (accessed June 27, 2012); B. Gee, "As Jury Cases Decline, So Does Art of Trial Lawyers," *Tennessean*, Feb. 5, 2011.

182   *In 2011, fourteen Am Law 200 firms: American Lawyer*, July/Aug. 2012, 73.

183   *Like senior associates, non-equity partners:* E. Reeser and P. McKenna, "Crazy Like a Fox," *American Lawyer,* Feb. 2012.

185   *"My view is that if someone says":* A. Longstreth, "Firms Hunting for Stars Re-Examine Partner Compensation," *American Lawyer,* May 7, 2007.

185   *"I don't know the answer to that":* Ibid.

186   *At Chicago-based Sidley Austin:* K. Donovan, "Big Firm Settles Age Discrimination Suit," *New York Times,* Oct. 6, 2007.

186   *"apostolic succession":* Ibid.

186   *They are one reason that, in 2007:* J. Palazzo, "Law Firm Nears Deal in Age Suit," *Wall Street Journal,* Mar. 7, 2012.

187   *"This is the time of year":* S. Randazzo, "Trove of Unsealed Court Documents Capture Kelley Drye Partner's Push to Get Paid After Age 70," *Am Law Daily,* Apr. 3, 2012.

187   *Kelley Drye's average equity partner profits: American Lawyer,* July 2000, 109.

187   *D'Ablemont got $574,000:* J. Palazzo, "Kelley Drye Settles with EEOC over Age-Bias Case," *Wall Street Journal,* Apr. 11, 2012; Consent Decree, *Equal Employment Opportunity Commission v. Kelley, Drye & Warren,* Civil Action No. 10-CV-0655.

188   *In 2007, the New York State Bar Association:* J. Creswell, "Law Firms Are Urged Not to Force Retirements," *New York Times,* Jan. 19, 2007.

188   *The ABA House of Delegates voted:* M. Neil, "Big Law Firms End Mandatory Retirement," *ABA Journal,* Nov. 7, 2007.

188   *"Our partners concluded":* Ibid.

189   *In April 2012 it dismissed:* S. Lind, "U.K. Supreme Court Rejects Key Challenge to Law Firm Retirement Policies," *Lawyer,* Apr. 26, 2012.

189   *Until America's big-firm leaders become wiser:* N. Schwartz, "Easing Out the Gray-Haired. Or Not," *New York Times,* May 27, 2011.

189   *"In my experience, it is much harder":* Ibid.

190   *There may be a way out of this conundrum:* A. Tugend, "Fears, and Opportunities, on the Road to Retirement," *New York Times,* June 3, 2011.

190   *"The point is not to have distinct phases":* Ibid.

190   *"The idea is to produce people":* A. Press, "Happily Ever After," *American Lawyer,* Apr. 2012.

191   *Indiana University Maurer School of Law professor:* W. Henderson, "More Complex Than Greed," *American Lawyer,* May 29, 2012.

191   *"a textbook example of an outfit":* A. Press, "Don't Look Back," *American Lawyer,* July/Aug. 2012.

191   *Axiom founder Mark Harris was an associate:* N. Sarkisian, "Who Says Being a Lawyer Has to Suck?" *San Francisco Magazine,* Jan. 2007.

191   *"new kind of law firm with no partners":* Ibid.

192   *Axiom is attracting some of the nation's:* Ibid.

192   *"[Axiom's] projects are notable":* Press, "Don't Look Back."

192   *"Retain profits and use those funds":* W. Henderson, "Rise and Fall," *American Lawyer,* June 2012.

192   *"for better or worse":* Henderson, "More Complex Than Greed."

192   *As a temporary measure:* A. Press, "A Partner Protection Plan," *American Lawyer,* June 2012.

193   *"a strong identity, loyal clients":* D. Combs, "A Firm of Equals," *American Lawyer,* July 2008.

194   *"We have not changed anything":* S. Beck, "Familiar Faces," *American Lawyer,* July/Aug. 2012.

194   *"We try to hire the very best available":* Combs, "A Firm of Equals."

194   *Longtime client Warren Buffett agrees:* Ibid.

CHAPTER 11: PROSPECTIVE LAWYERS

198   *The article's description of Levy:* R. Schmitt, "A Death in the Office," *ABA Journal,* Nov. 1, 2009.

198   *A month after Levy's tragic end, two more:* D. Weiss, "Disappointments Preceded Suicides by Lawyers at Three Major Law Firms," *ABA Journal,* May 11, 2009.

198   *Then in January 2010:* B. Baxter, "Suicide Victim a Barker & Hostetler Partner," *Am Law Daily,* Jan. 22, 2010.

198   *On July 15, 2010, a Chicago subway:* B. Baxter, "Reed Smith Partner's Death Deemed a Suicide," *American Lawyer,* July 22, 2010.

199   *It had grown to 140 attorneys:* "Reed Smith, Sachnoff & Weaver Merger Wins Partner Approval," Nov. 30, 2006, http://m.reedsmith.com/reed-smith-sachnoff—weaver-merger-wins-partner -approval-combined-firms-name-chicago-managing-partner-executive-committee-members -11-30-2006 (accessed June 27, 2012).

199   *Dolin had become head:* A. Sachdev, "Stewart Dolin, 1952–2010," *Chicago Tribune,* July 18, 2010.

199   *For example, when a sixty-four-year-old:* D. Malan, "Real Estate Lawyer's Suicide a Sign of Desperate Times for Some," *Connecticut Law Tribune,* Dec. 1, 2009.

200   *One of the most tragic:* S. Randazzo, "Autopsy Can't Say What Caused Skadden Associate's Death, but Puts Some Rumors to Rest," *Am Law Daily,* Nov. 15, 2011.

200   *Skadden ranked 69th . . . and 7th:* "Ranking Midlevel Satisfaction," *American Lawyer,* Sept. 2011; D. Combs, "Upheaval in the Ranks," *American Lawyer,* July/Aug. 2011; "The A-List," *American Lawyer,* July–Aug. 2012; "The Best Places to Work," *American Lawyer,* Sept. 2012; P. Lattman, "Assigning Blame in Dewey's Collapse," *New York Times,* May 13, 2012.

EPILOGUE

203   *When MacLeish left private practice:* J. Stefancic and R. Delgado, *How Lawyers Lose Their Way: A Profession Fails Its Creative Minds* (Durham, NC: Duke University Press, 2005), 15.

204   *"some of the incongruities of the life":* C. Halpern, "Escape from Arnold & Porter," *ABA Journal,* Feb. 2008.

204   *"I looked around at the senior partners":* Ibid.

205   *But in 2008, it was nineteenth:* "100 Best Companies to Work For," *CNN Money,* http://money.cnn.com/magazines/fortune/bestcompanies/2011/full_list (accessed June 24, 2012).

205   *Meanwhile, the firm's average partner profits:* *American Lawyer,* May 2009, 170; *American Lawyer,* May 2012, 155.

205   *"The law is a jealous mistress":* J. Story, "A Discourse Pronounced upon the Inauguration of the Author as Dane Professor of Law in Harvard University, August 25, 1829," reprinted in W. Story (ed.), *The Miscellaneous Writings of Joseph Story* (Boston: Little, Brown, 1852).

206   *"reward success and efficiency":* Bartlit, Beck, Herman, Palenchar & Scott website, www .bartlit-beck.com (accessed June 27, 2012).

206   *He suggested Martin E. P. Seligman's* Flourish: M. Seligman, *Flourish: A Visionary New Understanding of Happiness and Well-Being* (New York: Free Press, 2011).

206   *"explains how happiness comes from achievements":* S. Ward, "Lawyers Pick 30 Books Every Lawyer Should Read," *ABA Journal,* Aug. 2011.

207   *Along with many colleagues, he regretted:* N. Nohria, "It's Time to Make Management a True Profession," *Harvard Business Review,* Oct. 2008.

207   *"I believe that management education":* D. Middleton, "Harvard Business School Names New Dean," *Wall Street Journal,* May 4, 2010.

207   *James Ellis:* D. Middleton, "B-Schools Try Makeover," *Wall Street Journal,* May 6, 2010.

207   *Since then, students at some top schools:* L. Wayne, "A Promise to Be Ethical in an Era of Immorality," *New York Times,* May 29, 2009.

AFTERWORD

209   *Since 2006 alone, law student debt has surged:* "ABA Task Force Report on the Financing of Legal Education," June 17, 2015, 40–42, www.americanbar.org/content/dam/aba/admini strative/legal_education_and_admissions_to_the_bar/reports/2015_june_report_of_the_aba _task_force_on_the_financing_of_legal_education.authcheckdam.pdf.

209   *Perversely, as law school tuition has increased:* M. Leichter, "At Last, a Rational Explanation for Why Law School Tuition Keeps Rising," *American Lawyer,* Mar. 1, 2012, http://amlawdaily .typepad.com/amlawdaily/2012/03/at-last-a-rational-explanation-for-why-law-school -tuition-keeps-rising.html.

211   *Back in 2004, schools saw a record number:* Law School Admission Council, "End of Year Summary." ABA (Applicants, Applications & Admissions), LSAT Credential Assembly Service," www.lsac.org/lsacresources/data/lsac-volume-summary.

211   *As business schools gained in popularity:* "Digest of Education Statistics," National Center for Education Statistics, Institute of Education Sciences, Table 301—Degrees in business conferred by degree-granting institution, by level of degree and sex of student; Selected years, 1955–56 through 2007–08, https://nces.ed.gov/programs/digest/d09/tables/dt09_301.asp.

211   *By 2010, the number of law school applicants:* Law School Admission Council, "End of Year Summary."

211   *In 2010, first-year law school enrollment:* "Enrollment and Degrees Awarded," ABA Section on Legal Education and Admissions to the Bar, www.americanbar.org/content/dam/aba/administrative/legal_education_and_admissions_to_the_bar/statistics/enrollment_degrees_awarded.authcheckdam.pdf.

211   *Nine months after graduation, only about half:* The ABA defines "long-term" as a job expected to last at least one year; "2012 Law Graduate Employment Data," ABA Section of Legal Education and Admissions to the Bar, www.americanbar.org/content/dam/aba/administrative/legal_education_and_admissions_to_the_bar/reports/law_grad_employment_data.authcheckdam.pdf.

211   *By the fall of 2014, the total number:* Law School Admission Council, "End of Year Summary."

211   *Professor Theodore Seto of Loyola University School of Law:* T. Seto, "JD Job Prospects as Predicted by JD Degrees Per Capita," Tax Prof Blog, June 5, 2013, http://taxprof.typepad.com/taxprof_blog/2013/06/seto-.html.

211   *In fact, ten months after graduation:* "Employment Statistics," Loyola Law School–Los Angeles, www.lls.edu/resources/careerdevelopment/forcurrentstudents/employmentstatistics.

212   *For the class entering in the fall of 2014:* Law School Admission Council, "End of Year Summary."

212   *Today, anyone who wants to attend law school:* N. Kitroeff, "More Law Schools Drop the LSAT for Top Applicants," *Bloomberg Business,* May 19, 2015, www.bloomberg.com/news/articles/2015–05–19/more-law-schools-drop-the-lsat-for-top-applicants.

212   *He found that low-end law schools:* A. Taylor, "Diversity as a Law School Survival Strategy," *St. Louis University Law Journal* 59, no. 2 (Winter 2015): 321–385.

212   *Schools with the lowest median LSAT scores:* K. Sloan, "Law School Diversity Improves—But Only at the Bottom," *National Law Journal,* Feb. 10, 2015, www.nationallawjournal.com/id=1202717561690/Law-School-Diversity-ImprovesmdashBut-Only-at-the-Bottom?slreturn=20150229152311.

212   *For example, the schools in the lowest quintile:* M. Leichter, "Law School Diversity Improves at Schools with Worst Job Outcomes," *American Lawyer,* Apr. 3, 2015, www.americanlawyer.com/top-stories/id=1202722574012/Law-School-Diversity-Improves-at-Schools-With-Worst-Job-Outcomes?mcode=1202615731542&curindex=4.

212   *Those schools also have the worst graduate:* Ibid.

213   *The change emboldened Professor Seto and others:* "Occupational Separations Methodology," US Department of Labor, Bureau of Labor Statistics, www.bls.gov/emp/ep_separations.htm.

213   *In 2008, it anticipated an increase:* T. A. Lacey, "Occupational Employment Projections to 2018," *Monthly Labor Review,* Nov. 2009, 86, www.bls.gov/opub/mlr/2009/11/art5full.pdf.

213   *In 2012, it reduced that projection to 74,800:* "Lawyers," *Occupational Outlook Handbook,* US Department of Labor, Bureau of Labor Statistics, 2013 edition, www.bls.gov/ooh/legal/lawyers.htm.

213   *Taking into account retirements, deaths, and other attrition:* "Employment Projections," US Department of Labor, Bureau of Labor Statistics, 2013 edition, www.bls.gov/emp/ep_table_102.htm.

213   *The technical and analytical flaws:* See, e.g., M. Leichter, "2016 Grads Shouldn't Take Comfort in New Jobs Projection Approach," *American Lawyer,* Dec. 10, 2014, www.americanlawyer.com/columnists/id=1202678622429/2016-Grads-Shouldnt-Take-Comfort-in-New-Jobs-Projection-Approach?mcode=1202617685250&curindex=15&slreturn=20150302133842.

214   *At the end of December 2014, employment:* "Data Retrieval: Employment, Hours and Earnings

(CES)," US Department of Labor, Bureau of Labor Statistics, www.bls.gov/webapps/legacy /cesbtab1.htm.

214   *Professor Seto, whose 2014 prediction of a lawyer:* "Seto: New BLS Data Project More Lawyer Jobs than Grads in 2016," Tax Prof Blog, Nov. 19, 2014, http://taxprof.typepad.com /taxprof_blog/2014/11/seto-new-bls-data.html.

214   *Another law professor in denial, René Reich-Graefe:* "Employment," Western New England University School of Law, www1.law.wne.edu/careerservices/index.cfm?selection=doc.4946.

214   *He wrote that "recent law school graduates:* R. Reich-Graefe, "Keep Calm and Carry On," *Georgetown Journal of Legal Ethics* 27 (2014): 55, http://papers.ssrn.com/sol3/papers.cfm ?abstract_id=2404603.

214   *For his school alone that would have:* "Which Law School Graduates Have the Most Debt?" *U.S. News & World Report,* 2015, http://grad-schools.usnews.rankingsandreviews.com/best -graduate-schools/top-law-schools/grad-debt-rankings/page+3.

215   *from admissions officers:* See, e.g., S. Freedman, "#1 Intro—Enroll Today!" *Faculty Lounge,* Apr. 10, 2014, www.thefacultylounge.org/2014/04/1-intro-enroll-today.html.

215   *to prominent deans:* E. Chemerinsky and C. Menkel-Meadow, "Don't Skimp on Legal Training," *New York Times,* Apr. 14, 2014, www.nytimes.com/2014/04/15/opinion/dont-skimp -on-legal-training.html?_r=0; L. Mitchell, "Law School Is Worth the Money," *New York Times,* Nov. 28, 2012, www.nytimes.com/2012/11/29/opinion/law-school-is-worth-the -money.html?_r=1.

215   *For example, in March 2015, the president and dean:* D. LeDuc, "Lawyer Employment Jumps by 40,000 in 2014—Now Is the Time to Fulfill Your Dream of Becoming a Lawyer," Western Michigan University–Cooley Law School, Mar. 16, 2015, www.cooley.edu/commentary /lawyer_employment_jumps.html.

215   *The dream remained elusive for most 2014 graduates:* "Employment Summary for 2014 Graduates," www.cooley.edu/publicinformation/_docs/WMU_TMCLS_Placement_Sum mary_2014.pdf.

215   *Average student debt for his school's September 2013 graduates:* D. LeDuc, "Law Student Loans," Western Michigan University–Cooley Law School, Feb. 6, 2014, www.cooley.edu/commen tary/law_school_student_loans.html.

215   *The same analytical flaw—ignoring the different:* M. Simkovic and F. McIntyre, "The Economic Value of a Law Degree," *Journal of Legal Studies* 43, no. 2 (June 2014): 249–289.

215   *But even the authors of the study acknowledge:* M. Simkovic and F. McIntyre, "The Economic Value of a Law Degree," Mar. 21, 2014, version at http://papers.ssrn.com/sol3/papers.cfm ?abstract_id=2379146.

216   *But in 2013, only 24 of 201 ABA-accredited schools:* S. Harper, "Bankruptcy and Bad Behavior—The Real Moral Hazard: Law Schools Exploiting Market Dysfunction," *American Bankruptcy Institute Law Review* 23, no. 1 (Winter 2015), 347, 353–354.

217   *Using their data and methodology, the incremental:* M. Simkovic, "The Economic Value of a Law Degree—Week 1 Summary," *Brian Leiter's Law School Reports,* July 21, 2013, http:// leiterlawschool.typepad.com/leiter/2013/07/the-economic-value-of-law-degree-week-1-sum mary.html.

217   *For 2013 graduates, one group would have included:* S. Harper, "Bankruptcy and Bad Behavior—The Real Moral Hazard: Law Schools Exploiting Market Dysfunction," *American Bankruptcy Institute Law Review* 23, no. 1 (Winter 2015), 354–356.

217   *Among those institutions, 34 schools placed fewer:* Ibid., 356–357.

217   *and 13 placed less than one-third:* Ibid.

217   *But only 36 percent of their 2014 graduates:* "Employment Summary Report—Individual School Summary Reports," ABA Section of Legal Education and Admissions to the Bar," http://em ploymentsummary.abaquestionnaire.org.

218   *Meanwhile, Infilaw burdened their students:* "Which Law School Graduates Have the Most Debt?" *U.S. News & World Report;* "Employment and ABA Required Disclosures," Arizona Summit Law School, www.azsummitlaw.edu/gainful-employment-and-aba-required-dis closures.

218   *Consider this list of the student debt leaders:* "Which Law School Graduates Have the Most Debt?" *U. S. News & World Report;* "Employment and ABA Required Disclosures," Arizona

Summit Law School; "Employment Summary Report," ABA Section of Legal Education and Admission to the Bar. "FT-LT-JD" means a full-time position requiring a law degree and lasting at least one year. It excludes all "JD-Advantage," "professional," "nonprofessional," "law school–funded," part-time, and short-term positions.

219   *Examples of schools at the low end of employment outcomes:* "Which Law School Graduates Have the Most Debt?" *U.S. News & World Report*; "Employment Summary Report," ABA Section of Legal Education and Admission to the Bar.

219   *Compare those results to schools that have* lower *average student debt:* "Which Law School Graduates Have the Most Debt?" *U.S. News & World Report*; "Employment Summary Report," ABA Section of Legal Education and Admission to the Bar.

219   *My recent article for the* American Bankruptcy Institute Law Review: Harper, "Bankruptcy and Bad Behavior."

220   *In California, class of 2014 law graduates:* "Which Law School Graduates Have the Most Debt?" *U.S. News & World Report.*

220   *In Boston, the 2014 graduates of Suffolk University:* Ibid.

220   *Average student debt at graduation was $166,622:* Ibid.

220   *Compared to the fall of 2008:* "ABA Section of Legal Education Reports 2014 Law School Enrollment Data," ABA, Dec. 16, 2014, www.americanbar.org/news/abanews/aba-news-archives/2014/12/aba_section_of_legal.html; "Enrollment and Degrees Awarded," ABA Section on Legal Education and Admissions to the Bar, 1963–2012, www.americanbar.org/content/dam/aba/administrative/legal_education_and_admissions_to_the_bar/statistics/enrollment_degrees_awarded.authcheckdam.pdf; Law School Admissions Council, "End-of-Year Summary."

221   *During that period, not a single ABA-accredited:* Two Minnesota schools merged in 2015: Hamline and William Mitchell.

221   *In July 2013, Professor Deborah Merritt:* D. Merritt to K. Syverud, ABA Council Chairperson, July 17, 2013, Re: Proposed Change to Employment Status Determination Date and EQ Submission Deadline, www.americanbar.org/content/dam/aba/administrative/legal_education_and_admissions_to_the_bar/council_reports_and_resolutions/comments/2013_deborah_merritt_on_employment_determination.authcheckdam.pdf.

221   *The new ten-month rule didn't help:* "Statistics—Employment," ABA Section of Legal Education and Admissions to the Bar, www.americanbar.org/groups/legal_education/resources/statistics.html; as above, the stated FTLT JD-required rates exclude law school funded positions.

221   *However, the absolute number of graduates employed:* M. Leichter, "Class of 2014 Employment Report (Updated)," Apr. 24, 2015, The Law School Tuition Bubble, https://lawschooltuitionbubble.wordpress.com/2015/04/24/class-of-2014-employment-report-leaked-edition.

221   *At 58 of 203 ABA-accredited schools:* Ibid.

222   *Its chairman, former ABA president Dennis W. Archer:* S. Harper, "A Troublesome Task Force," May 7, 2014, http://thelawyerbubble.com/2014/05/07/a-troublesome-task-force.

222   *Even with the new ten-month rule:* "Employment Summary Report," ABA Section of Legal Education and Admission to the Bar.

222   *It found that 25 percent of law schools:* "ABA Task Force Report on the Financing of Legal Education," June 17, 2015, 7, 22, www.americanbar.org/content/dam/aba/administrative/legal_education_and_admissions_to_the_bar/reports/2015_june_report_of_the_aba_task_force_on_the_financing_of_legal_education.authcheckdam.pdf.

222   *But the Task Force decided that any attempt:* Ibid.

222   *Instead of meaningful solutions, the Task Force:* Ibid.

223   *In the summer of 2013, President Obama entered:* P. Lattman, "Obama Says Law School Should Be Two, Not Three, Years," *New York Times*, Aug. 23, 2013, http://dealbook.nytimes.com/2013/08/23/obama-says-law-school-should-be-two-years-not-three/?_r=0.

223   *As that happens, no one should be surprised:* J. Gershman, "Decline in Bar Exam Scores Sparks War of Words," *Wall Street Journal*, Nov. 10, 2014, http://blogs.wsj.com/law/2014/11/10/decline-in-bar-exam-scores-sparks-war-of-words.

224   *That option is appealing until reality rears:* S. Harper, "Unhappy Attorneys and the Expectations-Reality Gap," *Litigation* (ABA) 41, no. 2 (Winter 2015).

224   *Even during the Great Recession, rates:* A. Press, "Big Law's Reality Check," *American Lawyer,*
      Nov. 2014, 45, www.americanlawyer.com/id=1202674273215/Special-Report-Big-Laws
      -Reality-Check?mcode=1202674273215.

225   *In 2004, 24 percent of all partners:* Ibid.

225   *They seem indifferent to scholarly studies proving:* W. Henderson and C. Zorn, "'Of Partners &
      Peacocks': Is Reliance on Lateral Hiring Destabilizing Firms?" *American Lawyer,* Feb. 2014,
      53–55 ("The data is telling us that for most law firms there is no statistically significant rela-
      tionship between lateral partner hiring and higher profits.").

225   *Ed Newberry, co-global managing partner:* D. Parnell, "Ed Newberry of Squire Patton Boggs:
      'Law Firms That Change Will Survive and Thrive,'" *Forbes,* Aug. 20, 2014, www
      .forbes.com/sites/davidparnell/2014/08/20/ed-newberry-law-firms-that-change-will-survive
      -and-thrive.

225   *In a 2013 survey, managing partners:* Hildebrandt Consulting/Citi Private Bank, "Client
      Advisory—2013," http://hildebrandtconsult.com/uploads/Citi_Hildebrandt_2013_Client_Ad
      visory.pdf.

225   *In 2014, the percentage dropped to 57:* Hildebrandt Consulting/Citi Private Bank, "Client Ad-
      visory—2014," www.privatebank.citibank.com/pdf/CitiHildebrandt2014ClientAdvisory.pdf.

225   *In 2015, it dropped again:* Hildebrandt Consulting/Citi Private Bank, "Client Advisory—
      2015, www.privatebank.citibank.com/pdf/CitiHildebrandt2015ClientAdvisory.pdf.

226   *But in the immediate aftermath of that merger:* B. Baxter, "Squire Patton Boggs Health Care
      Leaders Defect, Plus More Lateral Moves," *American Lawyer,* Feb. 8, 2015, www.american
      lawyer.com/law-firm-profiles-result/id=1202717358248/Squire-Patton-Boggs-Health-Care
      -Leaders-Defect-Plus-More-Lateral-Moves; C. Ho, "Former Longtime Patton Boggs Man-
      aging Partner Stuart Pape to Leave Firm," *Washington Post,* Feb. 4, 2015, www.washington
      post.com/business/former-longtime-patton-boggs-managing-partner-stuart-pape-to-leave
      -firm/2015/02/04/0d37d550-acb7-11e4-abe8-e1ef60ca26de_story.html; K. Polantz, "Squire
      Patton Boggs Shows Stable Revenue Per Lawyer After Merger," Mar. 25, 2015, www
      .nationallawjournal.com/id=1202721637806/Squire-Patton-Boggs-Shows-Stable-Revenue
      -Per-Lawyer-After-Merger?slreturn=20150329163436.

226   *Over the next fifteen years, he orchestrated ten mergers:* A. Nanda and M. Brewerton, "Bingham
      McCutchen: Combinational Mathematics," Harvard Law School—The Case Studies, Sept.
      30, 2011.

226   *In 2009, it absorbed two-hundred-lawyer McKee Nelson:* Ibid.

226   *After all, as a 2011 Harvard Law School case study:* Ibid.

226   *Looking to the future, Zimmerman said:* Ibid., 20.

227   *After Bingham's 2002 merger with the three-hundred-lawyer:* Ibid., 11, 13, 14.

227   *He boasted that his mergers and lateral hires:* Ibid., 15.

227   *When Bingham began to unravel in 2013:* "Partner Pay Spreads by Firm," *American Lawyer,*
      July 3, 2014, www.americanlawyer.com/id=1202661733760/Partner-Pay-Spreads-Firm
      -By-Firm.

227   *To retain important McKee Nelson partners, Bingham:* C. Sullivan, "Bingham Lawyers Who
      Grew Through Mergers Face Undoing by Merger," *Reuters,* Oct. 3, 2014, www.reuters.com
      /article/2014/10/03/us-lawfirms-m-a-bingham-insight-idUSKCN0HS09F20141003.

227   *As the firm stumbled in 2014, former partners:* B. Baxter, "At Bingham, Big Guarantees
      Raise More Questions," *American Lawyer,* July 29, 2014, www.americanlawyer.com
      /id=1202665178239/At-Bingham-Big-Guarantees-Raise-More-Questions?slreturn=2014
      1025111834.

227   *In early 2014, the firm revealed that 2013 revenues:* "The Am Law 100 at a Glance," *American
      Lawyer,* May 2015, 127.

227   *Browne publicly urged his fellow partners:* D. Fernandes, "Once-Booming Boston Law Firm
      Struggles to Survive," *Boston Globe,* Oct. 22, 2014, www.bostonglobe.com/business
      /2014/10/21/future-uncertain-for-one-city-largest-law-firms/OghtwclNVe1PoDnuAu
      PfEM/story.html.

227   *Rather than merge, the firm undertook:* B. Baxter and G. Passarella, "Morgan Lewis Votes to
      Admit 227 Bingham Partners," *American Lawyer,* Nov. 14, 2014, www.americanlawyer

.com/id=1202676489097/Morgan-Lewis-Votes-to-Admit-227-Bingham-Partners?mcode
=1202615717726.

227   *Eventually, Morgan Lewis agreed to take on:* B. Baxter, "Morgan Lewis Finalizes Bingham Mc-
Cutchen Deal," *American Lawyer,* Nov. 24, 2014, www.americanlawyer.com/home/id
=1202677252929/Morgan-Lewis-Finalizes-Bingham-McCutchen-Deal?mcode=12026170
75486&curindex=0.

228   *Otherwise, the remnants of Bingham McCutchen:* "Four Firms Move Up," *American Lawyer,*
May 2013.

228   *A partnership cobbled together through a series:* "The Am Law 100 at a Glance," *American
Lawyer,* May 2014.

228   *As far back as 2003, law firm management consultant Altman Weil:* W. Bower, "Mining the Surveys: DISeconomies of Scale?" Altman Weil, 2003, www.altmanweil.com/dir_docs
/resource/f44c154c-d8c6–468d-a862–41474fe25634_document.pdf.

229   *Then-chairman Alan Levin candidly admitted:* B. Baxter, "Locke Lord, Edwards Wildman
Leaders Discuss Proposed Union," *American Lawyer,* Sep. 10, 2014, www.american
lawyer.com/id=1202669652924/Locke-Lord-Edwards-Wildman-Leaders-Discuss
-Proposed-Union#ixzz3JL3oIHWG.

229   *The report concludes that "growth for growth's sake:* "2014 The Report on the Legal Profession,"
Georgetown Law Center (Center for the Study of the Legal Profession) and Thomson
Reuters Peer Monitor, 14, https://peermonitor.thomsonreuters.com/wp-content/uploads
/2014/01/2014_PM_GT_Report.pdf.

229   *The varied financial performance of firms:* "The 2015 Am Law 100: Rich and Richer,"
American Lawyer, May 2015, www.americanlawyer.com/home/id=1202489912232/The-2015
-Am-Law-100-Rich-and-Richer?mcode=1202615705844&curindex=0.

230   *Kent Zimmermann, a law firm management consultant:* G. Passarella, "Morgan Lewis Merger
with Bingham a 'Strategic Change,'" *Legal Intelligencer,* Sep. 23, 2014, www.thelegalintelli
gencer.com/id=1202670898612/Morgan-Lewis-Merger-With-Bingham-a-Strategic
-Change?slreturn=20141017103629.

230   *Similarly, when a Bingham-Morgan merger:* Ibid.

231   *In late 2013, IBM general counsel Robert Weber:* J. Smith, "Big Law Merges Fuel Skepticism,"
Wall Street Journal, Nov. 10, 2013.

231   *Cravath's average partner profits for 2013 and 2014:* J. Triedman, "The Early Numbers: Elite
New York Firms Once Again Break from the Pack," *American Lawyer,* Mar. 13, 2015,
www.americanlawyer.com/id=1202720572685/The-Am-Law-100-the-Early-Numbers
-Elite-New-York-Firms-Once-Again-Break-From-the-Pack.

231   *In January 2015, Dentons combined with:* J. Triedman, "Dentons, Dacheng Seal the Deal for
a Union, *American Lawyer,* Jan. 27, 2015, www.americanlawyer.com/top-stories/id=120
2716267881/Dentons-Dacheng-Seal-the-Deal-for-a-Union?mcode=1202615731
542&curindex=2.

232   *In responding to anticipated questions:* J. Triedman, "Dentons and China's Dacheng Poised for
Historic Union," *American Lawyer,* Jan. 22, 2015, www.americanlawyer.com/id=1202
715772786/Dentons-and-Chinas-Dacheng-Poised-for-Historic-Union.

232   *According to the* American Lawyer, *average revenue:* J. Triedman, "Dentons, Dacheng Seal the
Deal for a Union."

232   *Dentons's 2013 revenue per lawyer was $505,000:* "Dentons Law Firm Profile," *American
Lawyer,* www.americanlawyer.com/law-firm-profiles-result?firmname=Dentons&slreturn
=20150101171038.

232   *Remarkably, only three months after completing:* S. Randazzo, "Law Firm Dentons Extends
Reach with Yet Another Merger," *Wall Street Journal,* Apr. 9, 2015, http://blogs.wsj
.com/law/2015/04/08/dentons-mckenna-long-to-merge.

232   *The two firms had discussed merging:* B. Baxter, "Dentons, McKenna Deal Officially Dead,"
American Lawyer, Nov. 26, 2013, www.americanlawyer.com/id=1202629787375/Dentons
-McKenna-Deal-Officially-Dead.

232   *Because the prevailing big law firm model:* M. P. McQueen, "Lateral Hiring Stays Strong, But
Firms Curb Pay Pledges," *American Lawyer,* Jan. 29, 2015, www.americanlawyer.com
/id=1202715673289/Lateral-Hiring-Stays-Strong-but-Firms-Curb-Pay-Pledges.

232   *As one of the group's leaders explained:* K. Polantz, "Covington Picks Up Heart of McKenna's Government Contracts Group," *Legal Times,* May 1, 2015, www.nationallawjournal.com /legaltimes/id=1202725169744/Covington-Picks-Up-Heart-of-McKennas-Government-Contracts-Group?kw=Covington%20Picks%20Up%20Heart%20of%20McKenna%27s %20Government%20Contracts%20Group&et=editorial&bu=National%20Law%20Journal &cn=20150501&src=EMC-Email&pt=Legal%20Times%20Afternoon%20Update&slreturn =20150402115002.

233   *But lest anyone doubt the self-interest:* B. Baxter, "Dentons, McKenna Long Reach Merger Deal," *American Lawyer,* Apr. 8, 2015, www.americanlawyer.com/id=1202723001290 /Dentons-McKenna-Long-Reach-Merger-Deal?slreturn=20150318123252.

233   *"There is no logical end.":* S. Randazzo, "At Dentons, Strategy Is to Go Big," *Wall Street Journal,* Apr. 13, 2015, www.wsj.com/articles/at-global-law-firm-dentons-strategy-is-to-go-big -1428877996.

233   *Dentons's global chairman Joseph Andrew echoed:* Randazzo, "Law Firm Dentons Extends Reach with Yet Another Merger."

233   *The median in 2014 for all partners:* "Partner Pay Spreads: Minding the Gap," *American Lawyer,* July 2, 2015, www.americanlawyer.com/id=1202731244097/Partner-Pay-Spreads -Minding-the-Gap?kw=Partner%20Pay%20Spreads%3A%20Minding%20the%20Gap&et =editorial&bu=The%20American%20Lawyer&cn=20150706&src=EMC-Email&pt =Am%20Law%20Daily&slreturn=20150606113056.

234   *Eighty-five percent of CLO respondents:* "Chief Legal Office Survey," Altman Weil, 2014, www.altmanweil.com/CLO2014.

234   *In another recent survey, big law leaders:* "Law Firms in Transition—2013—An Altman Weil Flash Survey," Altman Weil, 2013, www.altmanweil.com/LFiT2013.

234   *According to an Altman Weil survey, 40 percent:* Ibid.

234   *Likewise, a 2013* American Lawyer *annual survey:* "Firm Leaders Survey: Slow Growth on Tap for 2014, *The American Lawyer Law Firm Leaders Survey,* Dec. 2013, www.altman weil.com/LFiT2013.

235   *African Americans and Hispanics compose 26 percent:* J. Smith, "Microsoft Wades into Law Firms' Diversity Debate," *Wall Street Journal,* Dec. 10, 2013, http://blogs.wsj.com /law/2013/12/10/microsoft-wades-into-law-firms-diversity-debate.

235   *Fewer than 2 percent of big law firm partners:* D. Rhode, "Law Is the Least Diverse Profession in the Nation, and Lawyers Aren't Doing Enough to Change That," *Washington Post,* May 27, 2015, www.washingtonpost.com/posteverything/wp/2015/05/27/law-is-the-least -diverse-profession-in-the-nation-and-lawyers-arent-doing-enough-to-change-that.

235   National Survey on Retention and Promotion of Women in Law Firms," National Association of Women Lawyers, Feb. 12, 2014, www.nawl.org/p/bl/et/blogid=10&blogaid=56; Rhode, "Law Is the Least Diverse Profession in the Nation, and Lawyers Aren't Doing Enough to Change That." S. Ward, "Women at Big Firms Make Up 70 Percent of Staff Attorneys, 15 Percent of Equity Partners," *ABA Journal,* Oct. 23, 2012, www.abajournal.com/news/article/women_at_big_firms_make_up_70_percent_of_staff _attorneys_15_percent.

235   *Mary Snapp, deputy general counsel of Microsoft:* Smith, "Microsoft Wades into Law Firms' Diversity Debate."

235   *Richard Susskind, wrote: "Most law firm:* R. Susskind, *Tomorrow's Lawyers: An Introduction to Your Future* (Oxford: Oxford University Press, 2013), 61.

236   *Brad Hildebrandt, founder of Hildebrandt Consulting:* B. Hildebrandt, "What the Critics of Lateral Hiring Get Wrong," *American Lawyer,* Apr. 2, 2014, www.americanlawyer.com /id=1202649440768/What-Critics-of-Lateral-Hiring-Get-Wrong.

236   *Erwin Chemerinsky, who appears regularly:* "Four New Faces Join List of Most Influential People in Legal Education," *National Jurist,* Nov. 10, 2014, www.nationaljurist.com/ content/4-new-faces-join-list-most-influential-people-legal-education.

236   *And with the economy improving and law-school enrollments:* Chemerinsky and Menkel -Meadow, "Don't Skimp on Legal Training."

236   *But the 2012 data on which Dean Chemerinsky relies:* "2015 Employment Questionnaire (for

2014 Graduates)—Definitions and Instructions," ABA Section of Legal Education and Admissions to the Bar, http://employmentsummary.abaquestionnaire.org.

236　*Moreover, Chemerinsky's 2012 data include only:* "Employment Rate Falls Again, But Law Firm Jobs Are Up," *NALP Bulletin,* Aug. 2013, www.nalp.org/0813research.

236　*Nine months after graduation, only 57 percent:* "2013 Law Graduate Employment Data, Section of Legal Education and Admissions to the Bar," www.americanbar.org/content/dam/aba/administrative/legal_education_and_admissions_to_the_bar/statistics/2013_law_graduate_employment_data.authcheckdam.pdf.

237　*Ten months after graduation, 63 percent:* "Employment Summary Report," ABA Section of Legal Education and Admission to the Bar.

237　*In Professor Epstein's review of* The Lawyer Bubble: R. Epstein, "The Rule of Lawyers," *Wall Street Journal,* May 5, 2013, http://online.wsj.com/articles/SB10001424127887323494504578342612775060362.

238　*More than two hundred years ago, Thomas Paine wrote:* T. Paine, *Common Sense* (New York: Fall River Press, 1995), Author's Introduction.

238　*The Thomson Reuters Peer Monitor "Mid-Size Law Firm Report":* Thomson Reuters Peer Monitor, "Mid-Size Law Firm Report," Mar. 31, 2014, 2.

238　*An analysis of 2 million invoices:* "Firms with 201–500 Attorneys Increasingly Winning Market Share," *Business Wire,* Oct. 22, 2013, www.businesswire.com/news/home/20131022005406/en/Research-Law-Firms-201–500-Attorneys-Increasingly-Winning#.VGpWJCgRgTs.

239　*In the 1963 landmark case of* Gideon v. Wainwright: 372 U.S. 335, 345 (1963).

239　*As two commentators recently observed:* S. Bright and S. Sanneh, "Fifty Years of Defiance and Resistance After *Gideon v. Wainwright,*" *Yale Law Journal* 22, no. 8 (June 2013), www.yalelawjournal.org/essay/fifty-years-of-defiance-and-resistance-after-gideon-v-wainwright.

239　*The National Center for Access to Justice:* "The Justice Index: Project of the National Center for Access to Justice," Cardozo Law School, www.justiceindex.org/findings/self-represented-litigants.

239　*Measured in constant 2013 dollars, funding:* "Funding History," Legal Services Corporation, www.lsc.gov/congress/funding/funding-history.

240　*In the past ten years alone, LSC's funding:* S. Beck, "Big Law and Legal Aid," *American Lawyer,* July 2015, 39, www.americanlawyer.com/id=1202730102717?keywords=Susan+Beck&publication=TAL+2008.

240　*The National Center for Access to Justice estimates:* Ibid., 40.

240　*Texas is lowest: 0.43 per 10,000:* "The Justice Index: Project of the National Center for Access to Justice," Cardozo Law School.

INDEX

Steven J. Harper is an adjunct professor at Northwestern University's Law School and Weinberg College of Arts & Sciences. A former litigation partner at Kirkland & Ellis LLP and a fellow of the American College of Trial Lawyers, he has appeared in numerous compilations of the best lawyers in America. A graduate of Harvard Law School and Northwestern, he lives in Wilmette, Illinois.